Advance Praise for
Interpersonal Arguing

"I would argue (pun intended) that Dale Hample's *Interpersonal Arguing* is an outstanding book that discusses an evolutionary view of arguing and the prudent necessity for framing arguments. He presents empirical studies as well as situational examples. The appendix of instruments is worthwhile. I particularly was enthralled with the chapters on serial arguing and arguing as a personality trait (think of the current president's tweets in which conflict is taken personally). The discussion of argument frames is enticing in an age in which some people think that arguments that are not based on scientific research are equally credible (e.g., climate change deniers, believers in conversion therapy). Indeed, as stated in the book: 'The belief that everyone is entitled to an opinion does not logically imply that all opinions have the same merit, which is an unfortunate impression that some people have (Kuhn, 1991).' This is a great book with massive applications to everyday relationships, persuasion/marketing appeals, negotiations, campaign consultants, and understanding intergroup conflict."

—*James Honeycutt, Professor, Communication Studies,*
Louisiana State University

"Anyone who studies arguing among dyads or in interpersonal relationships needs to have this book for their personal library. Dale Hample's book clearly explains how argument is developed by two people and how it affects the relationship between them. He writes in a conversational tone accessible to those with a wide variety of prior knowledge of the area. This book should be useful to those in argumentation, conflict, and other related areas such as persuasion, intercultural, and relational communication."

—*Amy Janan Johnson, Professor, Department of Communication,*
University of Oklahoma

Interpersonal Arguing

This book is part of the Peter Lang Media and Communication list.
Every volume is peer reviewed and meets
the highest quality standards for content and production.

PETER LANG
New York • Bern • Berlin
Brussels • Vienna • Oxford • Warsaw

Dale Hample

Interpersonal Arguing

PETER LANG
New York • Bern • Berlin
Brussels • Vienna • Oxford • Warsaw

Library of Congress Cataloging-in-Publication Data
Names: Hample, Dale, author.
Title: Interpersonal arguing / Dale Hample.
Description: New York: Peter Lang, 2018.
Includes bibliographical references and index.
Identifiers: LCCN 2017036923 | ISBN 978-1-4331-4890-3 (hardback: alk. paper)
ISBN 978-1-4331-3438-8 (paperback: alk. paper) | ISBN 978-1-4331-4894-1 (ebook pdf)
ISBN 978-1-4331-4895-8 (epub) | ISBN 978-1-4331-4896-5 (mobi)
Subjects: LCSH: Interpersonal conflict.
Classification: LCC BF637.I48 H365 2018 | DDC 158.2—dc23
LC record available at https://lccn.loc.gov/2017036923
DOI 10.3726/b12877

Bibliographic information published by **Die Deutsche Nationalbibliothek**.
Die Deutsche Nationalbibliothek lists this publication in the "Deutsche Nationalbibliografie"; detailed bibliographic data are available on the Internet at http://dnb.d-nb.de/.

© 2018 Peter Lang Publishing, Inc., New York
29 Broadway, 18th floor, New York, NY 10006
www.peterlang.com

All rights reserved.
Reprint or reproduction, even partially, in all forms such as microfilm, xerography, microfiche, microcard, and offset strictly prohibited.

Dedication
To all the students and colleagues who have collaborated with me on my research projects, or who have invited me to collaborate on theirs.

Contents

Acknowledgements	xi
List of Tables	xiii
List of Figures	xv
Chapter One: A Conceptual Inventory	1
Argument Structure	3
An Argument, Generally	3
Syllogisms	4
Argument Schemes	8
Toulmin Model	11
The Enthymeme	14
Interactive Arguments	15
The Momentary Exchange of Reasons	15
Conversational Arguments in a Critical Discussion	19
Summary: Structure	21
The Situation-Goals-Plans-Action Model	21
Situations	22
Goals	24
Plans	25
Action	25

Summary: SGPA	26
Arguing as a Fundamental Human Process	26
Summary	31
Chapter Two: Argument Frames	**35**
The Three Sets of Frames	36
First-Order Frames: Pursuing Own Goals	37
Second-Order Frames: Respecting the Other Arguer	45
The Third Frame: Reflective Understandings of Arguing	51
Summary: The Idea of Argument Frames	53
Empirical Results	54
Undergraduates and Older Adults	54
Men and Women	56
Associations Among the Frames Measures	58
Frames and Other Features of Personality	61
Conclusions: Empirical Work to Date	66
General Conclusions	67
Chapter Three: Argument Situations	**71**
Interpersonal Situations	72
Argument Topics	75
Deciding Whether or Not to Argue	81
Features of Situations Involving Arguing	90
Reasonably Apparent Features	91
Primary Goals	93
Subjective Situational Features	94
Secondary Goals	98
Conclusions	99
Chapter Four: Serial Arguments	**103**
The Nature of Serial Arguments	104
The Original Study	105
Serial Argument Topics	110
Consequences of Serial Arguments	113
Situational Effects and Intrapersonal Dynamics	115
Data	116
Situation	118
Goals, Tactics, and Outcomes	122
Statistical Details	123
Back to the Main Story	125
Section Summary	134
Conclusions	135

Chapter Five: The Rationality Engine	141
Group Thinking	143
Evolutionary Reasons for Optimism	144
Contemporary Evidence	148
Debiasing Arguments	149
Cognition	151
Motivation	155
Design	157
Understanding Debiasing	159
How Good Conversation Improves Argumentation	161
Fallacies	164
Convergent Arguments	168
Analogies	171
Conclusions	174
Chapter Six: Relational Dialogues	179
Walton's Theory of Dialogue Types	181
Cionea's Theory of Dialogues in Relationships	188
Investigating Argument Dialogues in Relationships	192
Operationalizing the Dialogue Types	192
Connecting Dialogue Preferences With Other Argumentation Measures	194
General Preferences for Dialogue Types	194
Argumentativeness and Verbal Aggressiveness	196
Argument Frames	198
Correlations Among the Dialogue Types	199
Summary	201
Couples and Their Dialogues	202
Summary	206
Chapter Seven: Arguing and Culture	211
Culture	212
Mapping the Globe: Initial Considerations	216
Mean Differences: Nations High and Low	219
Argument Motivation	220
Argument Frames	222
Personalizing Conflict	224
Sex Differences	227
Dynamics of Arguing Motivations	232
The Opposites Theory	233
The Basis for the Opposites Theory	235

Trying to Understand the Presence or Absence of Opposites	237
Hofstede Values	237
World Values Survey	240
How Strong a Conclusion Should Be Drawn?	241
Comparing Dynamics in Detail	242
Argument Motivations	242
Argument Frames	243
Personalizing Conflict	245
Conclusions	247
Chapter Eight: The Processes of Interpersonal Arguing	253
Multiple Simultaneous Processes	254
Observable Arguments	257
Individual Arguments	265
Shared Arguing	273
Conclusions	281
Appendix: Instrumentation	287
Argument Frames	288
Costs and Benefits of Arguing	291
Taking Conflict Personally	294
Scoring Directions	295
Dialogue Types	297
Argument Stakes	300
Index	303

Acknowledgements

I am grateful to Sue Kline, Ioana Cionea, Amy Johnson, and Jim Honeycutt for reading all or parts of this book in manuscript, and giving me valuable feedback. I am even more grateful to the dozens of students, colleagues, and collaborators who have done research with me over the decades. That research formed the basis of nearly every chapter of the book. In fact, putting so many things together was one of my main motivations in doing this project. Thanks to all of you.

Tables

Table 2.1:	Comparisons of U.S. Adults and Undergraduates on Frames Measures	55
Table 2.2:	Comparisons of Male and Female Scores on Frames Measures	57
Table 2.3:	Correlations Among the Frames Measures	59
Table 2.4:	Correlations Between the Frames Measures and Other Personality Instruments	61
Table 4.1:	Means of Serial Argument Measures by Relationship Type	119
Table 4.2:	Means of Serial Argument Measures by Topic Type	120
Table 4.3:	Means of Serial Argument Measures by Respondent Sex and Role	121
Table 4.4:	Significant Unstandardized Predictors of Latent Variables	125
Table 4.5:	Correlations Within Panels of Latent Variables	131
Table 5.1:	Crosstabulation of Fallacy Type and Response to Fallacy, Both Frequencies and Column Percentages	167
Table 6.1:	Mean Intentions to Use Argument Dialogue Types	195
Table 6.2:	Correlations Among Dialogue Types, Argumentativeness, and Verbal Aggressiveness	197
Table 6.3:	Correlations Among Dialogues and Argument Frames	198
Table 6.4:	Correlations Among the Dialogue Types	200
Table 6.5:	Correlations of Dialogue Preferences From One Partner to the Other.	203

Table 6.6: Correlations Between Dialogue Preferences and Relational Quality	205
Table 7.1: Characteristics of the World Argumentation Studies	220
Table 7.2: National Means for Argumentativeness and Verbal Aggressiveness	221
Table 7.3: National Means for Argument Frames	223
Table 7.4: National Means for Taking Conflict Personally	225
Table 7.5: Sex Differences by Nation, Indicating Which Sex Had Higher Scores	228
Table 7.6: Correlations Among Argumentativeness and Verbal Aggressiveness Subscales, by Nation	234
Table 7.7: Correlations Among Argument Frames Measures for France and India	243
Table 7.8: Correlations Among Taking Conflict Personally Measures for France and India	245

Figures

Figure 4.1: Trapp and Hoff's Model of Serial Arguing — 106
Figure 4.2: Conceptual Representation of the Intrapersonal Dynamics of Serial Arguing Processes — 123
Figure 4.3: Effects of Approach and Avoid on Endogenous Variables — 127
Figure 4.4: Effects of Goals on Tactics: Distributive, Integrative, I Demand, Other Demands — 128–129
Figure 4.5: Effects of Tactics on Outcomes: Perceived Resolvability, Civility, and Satisfaction/Climate — 132–133
Figure 5.1: Convergent Argument (from Hample, 2011a) — 169
Figure 5.2: Coding of Genuine Participants' Responses to Examples, Weak Causal Arguments, and Analogies by Ordinal Position in the Conversations (from Hample, 2016) — 173
Figure 7.1: Scatterplot and Regression Line for Power Distance and Percentage of Sex Differences — 231
Figure 7.2: Scatterplot and Regression Line for Equality and Percentage of Sex Differences — 231
Figure 8.1: A Sketch of Three Simultaneous Lines of Experience — 254
Figure 8.2: Scholarship Oriented to the Observable Processes in Arguing — 257
Figure 8.3: Scholarship Oriented to the Individual Processes in Arguing — 266
Figure 8.4: Scholarship Oriented to the Shared Processes in Arguing — 275

CHAPTER ONE

A Conceptual Inventory

This book is about interpersonal arguing. By "arguing" I mean an exchange of reasons, and not particularly an explosive emotional detonation. In ordinary talk, we tend to mean the second thing and not the first: "Why are you so upset?" "I had an argument with my neighbor this morning." Obviously the person is unhappy about some sort of nasty experience, not about offering and testing reasons. We will be focusing on exchanges of reasons as the main meaning of argument, and will consider nasty emotional experiences only as special cases of arguments that have gone wrong.

It might be easier just to avoid the word "argument" completely for what this book is about, but that would be unfortunate. The term, in one language or another, has been important for about two and a half millennia and some of the great Western minds have written about it: Aristotle, Cicero, Boethius, Augustine, Francis Bacon, Adam Smith, Schopenhauer, Nietzsche, Descartes, and hundreds of others. Also, the modern scholarship I will be discussing uses "argument" to say what it is about. Like a related term, "rhetoric," the best usage has been colloquially outvoted by a worse usage, but I think that is no reason to concede. Instead, I think the right course is to try to improve the situation and help people to get a better, sharper grasp of the ideas.

The vast majority of writing about argumentation has treated an argument as a textual thing, first historically as a syllogism, then as an enthymeme, and then as an argument scheme. We will discuss those terms later, but for now it is enough to note that all these theories consider an argument to be something on paper, sometimes even as a thing that has to be translated into formal propositions before it can be properly analyzed. In contrast, this book considers arguments in the context of interpersonal communication. The argument is said, producing something that can be transcribed as a text, but it also exists in both people's minds. One person has a thought, speaks a version of the thought, and yet another version of the thought is registered by the other person. Since texts don't act or think or feel, what is really important in this book is what the people have in their minds. We will usually regard the spoken or written argument as an artifact of what the first person thought and felt, and a stimulus to what the second person thinks and feels. We want to understand the people, and that means that we have to situate arguing in their experiences, not on a bit of person-independent paper.

Arguments are not negligible things in our lives. We reason with one another frequently, customarily, and quietly. We offer facts in support of a choice to have eggs or toast for breakfast, we announce our reasons for wanting more intimacy in a romantic relationship, we give excuses for not having put gasoline in the car, we object to the irrelevance of past practice for what we need to do now, we say why we reject someone else's reasoning. This is a normal part of human communication.

It is also quite an important part. Arguments are our primary way of making meaning, of expressing our own meanings and of proposing meanings for other people (Hample, 2009). The basic structure of an argument—I will give more detail soon—is that you begin with some uncontroversial idea and then show how that notion implies something else, something that was less obviously agreeable in the first place. For instance: "If we participate in a process, we endorse it and assert its legitimacy. Voting in gerrymandered districts is a waste of time because the district has been defined so that only one party can win. That's dishonest and an insult to the idea of democracy. Consequently it is our civic duty not to vote, so that we don't endorse the insult." This might not be a wonderful argument (actually I think people should vote), but you can see how it proceeds from a fairly uncontroversial thought (participation is endorsement) to a controversial ending (don't vote). In other words, using a taken-for-granted starting point, the arguer is trying to create a new thought or meaning (that not voting is a civic responsibility) for the other person. In our everyday lives, we receive and create meanings about movies, sports, childcare, finances, and everything else we talk about, and we often do it by means of arguing. Meanings can also be created without arguments—for instance, a dramatic unreasoning emotional display by a child can convey that she really wants some candy—but arguing seems to be the main way that adults handle thoughts socially.

To a considerable degree, we conduct our interpersonal relationships by managing meanings for one another. Besides all the things that we are aware of negotiating (Who should go to the grocery? Who gets to keep the TV remote control?), we also conduct the relationship by means of the identities we project for ourselves, for the other person, and for the relationship itself (Watzlawick, Beavin, & Jackson, 1967). Once in a while, this last sort of thing is explicit ("I think we should be exclusive now") but most of the time it is only implied. If one person says, "I love you," this projects quite a few identity definitions: the speaker is committed to the other person, the other person is lovable, and the relationship has profound value. Statements like that one can be endorsed, ignored, or contradicted ("If you really loved me, you'd be on time for our dates"). All the meanings in this paragraph (grocery responsibilities, TV remote obligations, exclusive relationships, emotionally committed people, desirable people, and deeply valued relationships) are negotiated in some sense. Even if some meaning seems only to be unilaterally asserted, it isn't a mutual meaning (e.g., a deeply valued relationship) unless and until the assertion is accepted and endorsed by the other person. Obvious statements don't get much elaboration, but if there is any tinge of uncertainty people naturally explain themselves. That is, they offer reasons. Much of relational negotiation is thereby done by means of interpersonal arguing.

These are some of the most basic ideas in the book. They are going to be elaborated in a lot of detail. For that, we need to have some shared concepts and vocabulary. The rest of this chapter is intended to explain some essential ideas so that we will have a common basis for exploring interpersonal arguing in depth.

Argument Structure

An obvious starting point is to describe what an argument is. There are two sorts of structures that we need to understand. The first is argument generally, in isolation from interaction dynamics. The second is what an argumentative exchange looks like. That second thing shows arguing's simple interactive nature.

An Argument, Generally

An argument, whether it appears in an interaction, a newspaper editorial, or a scholarly article, has two main components. One is its point, what we will call its claim or conclusion. The other is the reason that is offered in support of the claim. To insure that readers have some basic acquaintance with various theoretical traditions, I will first cover syllogisms and argument schemes, partly for their own merit and partly to contrast them to other views that I will prefer. Then I will settle on a standard description, the Toulmin model, which is more general and more congenial to the research I am going to cover.

Syllogisms. Formal logic, beginning with Aristotle, has focused on syllogisms. These are simplified systems of propositions. A proposition is a formalized sentence, constructed with exacting precision and having very few allowable forms of expression. The idea of a syllogism is that if we can specify the propositions and assume that they are true, we can determine whether the conclusion also has to be true. This is so when the syllogism has a valid form. Validity (in the sense of formal logical validity) is the key normative standard for the evaluation of a syllogism. Valid logical forms are "truth-preserving" in their movement from premises to conclusion. Syllogisms implement deduction, which is an art of forms rather than material truth. Deduction is often contrasted with induction, which interrogates empirical observations to create generalizations.

There are several kinds of syllogisms. I will review the most basic varieties. Even though we will relax the formal properties of syllogisms in most of this book, the reasoning principles that deduction exposes are correct and are the best models of pure abstract thought.

First is the categorical syllogism. Here, the propositions describe the categories of things. Membership in the categories is described as always true ("all") or false ("no" or "none") or as sometimes true ("some"), and the connections between the categories are always "is." These adjectives and connective are the only allowable ones. If an arguer wanted to say "occasionally," "on Tuesdays," or "when the mood strikes me," these phrases would have to be translated as "some" in order to rewrite the materials into propositional form. Connections such as "causes," "gave birth to," "ordains," or other possible connections have to be made into "is" somehow to work in this kind of syllogism. Categorical syllogisms have three terms—A, B, and C—and the adjectives I have mentioned. The most familiar example is

> All men (A) are mortal (B)
> Socrates (C) is a man (A)
> So Socrates (C) is mortal (B)

This is simple transitive word algebra: A is B, C is A, so C is B. The Greeks seem to have believed that their language was a sort of encyclopedia of knowledge, so that if they could put words into a new legitimate order they would have discovered a new fact.

Categorical syllogisms have a number of different forms, created by modifying A, B, and C with "all," "none," or "some." For example, No A is B, All C is A, so No C is B. The Greeks, Romans, and medieval logicians explored dozens of possible forms and determined which were valid and which were invalid. Here is an invalid example:

> Some dogs are affectionate animals
> Some affectionate animals are herbivores
> So all dogs are herbivores

Notice that the invalidity is due to form: Some A are B, Some B are C, so all A are C. The premises are both true even though the form is invalid. The conclusion is false, but that is an accident. Sometimes an invalid syllogism can land on a true conclusion by happenstance.

> Some dogs are affectionate
> Some affectionate animals eat meat
> So all dogs eat meat

This example is also invalid but the conclusion happens to be true. Notice that finding a fault in an argument's form doesn't automatically permit rejection of the conclusion. Syllogism evaluation works the other way around and is more limited: if the premises are true and the form is valid, then the conclusion will also be true. If you find a structural flaw in an argument, all you can really conclude is that *those* reasons don't prove the conclusion and we need some other way to evaluate its accuracy.

As the centuries went on, logicians discovered syllogisms of other sorts so that categorical syllogisms are not the only kinds anymore. Where categorical syllogisms manipulated nouns and adjectives (A, B, and C), the new kinds of syllogisms dealt with whole propositions at a time. This was a major advance because it meant that anything that could be expressed clearly could be used in a formally specifiable way. The propositions are normally labeled p and q, and this is where the expression "mind your p's and q's" comes from. Although p and q can contain just about any meanings, they can only be connected with a few terms, such as "if," "then," "or," and "not." Two especially important syllogism types of this sort are the hypothetical and disjunctive syllogisms.

The hypothetical (or conditional) syllogism is very important in evaluating scientific and other claims that have to do with causality. The syllogism itself only has an "if-then" structure, but this lends itself nicely to thinking about causation once the forms have been applied to some real phenomena. There are only four forms of hypothetical syllogisms, so I will list them all.

If p then q	If p then q	If p then q	If p then q
p	q	Not p	Not q
So q	So p	So not q	So not p
Valid	Invalid	Invalid	Valid

Each form begins with the same initial premise (if you wanted to say "p isn't true" or "q is wrong" you would just put the negative inside the proposition and call it p or q). Each of the four forms has a different second premise, as the table shows. The first and fourth forms are valid. The second form is invalid and the error is called affirming the consequent (q being the consequent, or the thing that follows from p in the first premise). The third form is also invalid and is called denying the antecedent (p being the antecedent, the thing that comes before q).

Being able to contain just about any clear thought as a proposition allows some flexible reasoning that can be evaluated as to its validity. For example,

If you have a good diet (p) then you will be healthy (q)
You are healthy (q)
So you have a good diet (p).

This syllogism has invalid form, even though it is possible that most of its premises, including the conclusion, are true. Here is some valid reasoning:

If you have a good diet (p) then you will be healthy (q)
You are not healthy (not q)
So you do not have a good diet (not p)

This example is valid. It isn't necessarily true, but that is because the first premise isn't necessarily true, either.

The application of hypothetical syllogisms to causal reasoning is this. If p actually does cause q and no other factors are involved in their relationship, then it will be true that "if p then q." Inconveniently, however, "if p then q" can also be true without a causal relationship between p and q. For instance, "if someone is a widow, then she used to be married" is true, but widowhood certainly doesn't cause a history of marriage, at least in any scientific sense of "cause." Even worse, if it is true that q causes p and nothing else causes p, then it will also be true that "if p then q." But the causality is actually reversed, because we stipulated that q causes p. Many circumstances including chance can result in p and q co-occurring.

P causing q is only one of them. This may be the source of people mistaking correlation for causality.

Consequently, scientists have to be very careful in their use of this sort of reasoning. Prior to the middle of the 20th century, they seemed to be using this sort of syllogism to justify their conclusions:

> If the hypothesis is true (p) then the data will look like this (q)
> The data look like this (q)
> So the hypothesis is true (p)

You can now see that this is the second form in the table and it is invalid. Popper (1959) figured out a better way to reason through to good scientific claims:

> If the hypothesis is true (p) then the data will look like this (q)
> The data do not look like this (not q)
> So the hypothesis is not true (not p)

This is the fourth form and it is valid. But it makes thinking scientifically a lot harder. Instead of trying to verify the truth of hypotheses (as in the invalid example), scientists have to try to falsify their hypotheses (the valid syllogism). Hypotheses are never directly proved—they only survive falsification efforts. The more times a hypothesis survives a good test, the more confidence the scientific community has in it. This is what gives rise to all the double and triple negatives in learning scientific inference: "we failed to disconfirm the null hypothesis," for example.

The final sort of syllogism I will review is the disjunctive syllogism. This also deals with propositions but instead of saying that one proposition follows from another ("if p then q") this syllogism posits that the propositions are alternatives ("p or q"). The simple word "or" turns out to be ambiguous in this context and logicians have had to work out different logics for the exclusive or (p or q, and only one of them can be true, and one of them must be true) and the nonexclusive or (p or q, but both of them can be true at once, and at least one of them must be true). As always, only a few words can be used along with the propositions, mainly not and or.

There are only a few forms of this sort of syllogism, too. On the assumptions that p and q cannot both be true at once and that one of them must be true, here are the valid forms:

p or q	p or q	p or q	p or q
p	q	Not p	Not q
Not q	Not p	q	p

You can work out the invalid forms easily enough. For example, if p is true, then it would be invalid to conclude that q is also true.

Disjunctive syllogisms are useful when choices need to be made or when one alternative has to be chosen in preference to others. Here is an example:

We must either raise taxes (p) or cut Federal spending (q)
I think we should raise taxes (p)
So I do not think we should cut Federal spending (not q)

The disjunctive syllogism is simple enough in this summary. A dichotomy is stipulated in the first premise, a choice is made or rejected in the second premise, and the other possibility is either rejected or retained in the conclusion. Analysis of this sort of argument often leads to a focus on whether p and q are really the only available choices (are they a false dichotomy?) and whether "or" is exclusive or nonexclusive (can we have both of them, or do we really have to choose?).

The obvious strength of the logical approach to argument is the validity judgment it produces. This is a clear normative standard and it is so straightforward that it can even be made automatically, perhaps by a computer or maybe looked up in a table. The weakness of the logical approach is that the only thing it does is to generate those validity judgments, and it does this by formalizing things. An actual argument taken from a conversation has to be converted into propositions (sometimes expressing things that were unsaid but possibly assumed), the small handful of allowable terms has to be applied, the form has to be labeled, and then the analyst still cannot say anything about whether or not the conclusion is true.

These difficulties have been noticed for nearly as long as we have had logic. But in the middle of the 20th century, somewhat similar critiques of formal logic were made by two very influential books: *The Uses of Argument* by Toulmin (1958) and *The New Rhetoric* (Perelman & Olbrechts-Tyteca, 1969) written in French in 1958 and translated into English in 1969. These analyses fell on fertile soil and stimulated several academic movements. One of those was informal logic.

Argument Schemes. Informal logic began as a pedagogical movement (Blair, 2011). Philosophers who taught formal logic (including the syllogisms just reviewed) became frustrated that their students didn't seem to be applying logic to their lives out of class. Learning logic was supposed to make students smarter, but it seemed as though they treated it as just another set of intricate hurdles that stood in between them and graduation. So the informal logicians worked hard to bring examples of real arguments into class, and then hit on a much more radical idea: instead of teaching syllogisms (valid argument forms) they would teach fallacies (bad arguments). The idea was that students might be able to see fallacies in the world more easily than they saw syllogisms.

Fallacies are of two types, formal and material. Formal fallacies are failures of syllogistic form. Each of the invalid syllogism forms mentioned above has its own name, for example. This is just another way of teaching syllogisms, and it was not the point of informal logic. Material (or informal) fallacies have to do with the substance in the argument (its material), not its form. So if you buy a particular car exactly and only because your neighbor has one, your reasoning problem isn't that you have used a wrong form—it is that you have used a silly premise ("I should do what my neighbor does") as part of the materials you are reasoning with.

There are many material fallacies. Here are some that you may remember being taught: bandwagon ("do it because everyone else does it"), glittering generality ("liberals are all kind and nurturing"), black or white ("you are with me or against me"), ad hominem ("he's dumb, so his conclusion must be wrong"), post hoc ergo proper hoc (Latin for "after this, therefore because of this"), and others. The informal logicians would choose a list of the worst or most common material fallacies, and that would be the course.

As the years went by, informal logic became a genuine branch of philosophy and scholars began taking the material fallacies more seriously than in centuries past. Problems soon began to crop up. Perhaps the most vexing one was that fallacies sometimes turned out not to be bad arguments at all.

Here is a basic example. Normally the arguer's character has nothing to do with the quality of his or her conclusion. The argument (the reasoning) is supposed to be the only thing that bears on whether or not to accept the claim. Rejecting someone's argument because you disapprove of the arguer is the ad hominem fallacy ("against the person"). But in a court of law, finding out whether the witness is a criminal or an habitual liar is obviously a smart thing to do, and produces a good argument rather than a fallacy.

This sort of thing began turning up more and more often as the scholars thought deeply about fallacies. Accepting a conclusion because everyone else does is supposed to be the bandwagon fallacy, but if you want to go to college with your friends it is good to discover where they are applying and apply there yourself. If a street gang threatens you unless you agree to do what they say, this is the ad baculum fallacy ("from the stick"), but if a group of thugs were really holding a weapon on you it would be an excellent idea to give them your wallet. After a few years, exceptions had been found for nearly every fallacy, and no one had any confidence that so-called fallacies were always bad arguments.

So the informal logicians improved our understanding of argument structure by coming up with the idea of argument schemes. A scheme is a structure, but it is not quite so rigidly formalized as the syllogisms are. Each fallacy is an argument scheme, but so are other arguments, arguments that had never been suspected of being universally awful. Schemes include argument by example, argument from definition, argument from analogy, causal arguments, and many more. Along with specifying the schemes, however, the informal logicians went a step further. They attacked the problem of "sometimes a fallacy, sometimes a good idea" by listing the critical questions for each scheme. Once you identify an argument's scheme—Is it an analogy? An example?—then you ask the critical questions to evaluate it. If the answers to the critical questions are acceptable, then you have a good argument; otherwise you have a bad one. In this way "argument scheme" has replaced "fallacy" in our thinking.

Here is an example, taken from the standard work that lists argument schemes and their critical questions (Walton, Reed, & Macagno, 2008, p. 336). It shows how to think through an ad hominem argument scheme. First it describes the scheme and then it supplies the critical questions.

> *Character Attack Premise*: a is a person of bad character.
> *Conclusion*: a's argument α should not be accepted.
> Critical Questions
> CQ1: How well supported by evidence is the allegation made in the character attack premise?
> CQ2: Is the issue of character relevant in the type of dialogue in which the argument was used?
> CQ3: Is the conclusion of the argument that α should be (absolutely) rejected, even if other evidence to support α has been presented, or is the conclusion merely (the relative claim) that α should be assigned a reduced weight of credibility as a supporter of α, relative to the total body of evidence available?

Notice that the argument scheme itself (the character attack premise and the conclusion) doesn't place many restrictions of how the argument is phrased. It only has to include these two meanings somehow. The more important contribution is the list of critical questions. Here we see the key considerations in deciding whether the scheme was properly applied (a good argument) or was inappropriate (what used to be called a fallacy). Is the character allegation true? Is it a pertinent consideration in this sort of argument (e.g., about the credibility of an eye-witness)? And even if it is sound, how much difference does it make (should we reject the conclusion or just not count this argument as very strong support for it)?

Every argument scheme has its own list of critical questions. The critical questions generally reduce to three considerations, although they have to be expressed differently for each scheme. In informal logic, these three ideas are the bases for argument evaluation. First is *acceptability*: Is each premise acceptable (true, probable, obvious, supportable)? Second is *relevance*: Does each premise bear on whether or not to accept the conclusion? In other words, there has to be a connection between premise and conclusion such that the premise does at least some of the work of proving the claim. And finally, *sufficiency*: Are all the premises, collected together, enough to prove that the claim is so? Is there any way for those premises to be right and the conclusion to be wrong? ARS—acceptability, relevance, and sufficiency—replace the older ideas of truth and validity. They give us less clear-cut judgments, but that is actually an advantage. Instead of having to say only black and white things about an argument (false, valid) we can say that an argument is weak or strong, helpful or irrelevant, supportive or inconclusive, and we can allow these things to be matters of degree (Johnson, 2000).

A difficulty with informal logic as it stands today is that it is dominated more by lists than by theories. The number of argument schemes is limited only by scholars' imaginations and willingness to make tiny distinctions, and a similar thing can be said about the number of critical questions for each scheme. If I have an argument that I can immediately recognize as one of the common schemes (analogy, for example), I turn to informal logic for analytical help. But if I had a large corpus of argumentative discourse and wanted to describe it, I would not begin by applying anyone's list of argument schemes because I have no assurance that any of the lists satisfy the basic scientific standards of being mutually exclusive (nothing can be classified in two or more categories) and mutually inclusive (nothing is left out). There are several lists of schemes that seem more generalizable (van Eemeren & Grootendorst, 1992; Perelman & Olbrechts-Tyteca, 1969), but those lists are so short that they don't give the sort of detailed critical questions that the longer lists do (e.g., Walton et al., 2008). Consequently I prefer a simpler way to describe argument's structure, one that actually pre-dates informal logic.

Toulmin Model. That is the Toulmin (1958) model, proposed at the dawn of informal logic and modern argumentation studies. Toulmin, trained in traditional logic and analytic philosophy, had several of the objections to formal logic we have already noticed. He did not feel it was particularly appropriate for the understanding of how people *use* arguments (hence the title of his book), so he developed a different way to understand how arguments work.

His model has six components. The first of these is the claim (C) or conclusion, what we have called the point of the argument. He developed his model in terms of how the argument recipient reacted to the arguer's proposals, which was an innovation of its own. If the recipient immediately accepts the claim, nothing more is required. Without a reason, we might call this (a naked claim) an assertion or a primitive argument or something along those lines. But if the recipient asked,

"Why do you think so?" Toulmin felt that the obvious answer involved providing data (D) or evidence for the claim. Data is factlike material that the arguer feels is relevant to the conclusion. Saying that the evidence is "factlike" is obviously looser than saying it is true, but it therefore avoids the many delicate issues involved in figuring out what "true" means. In modern terms, Toulmin was merely saying that the evidence for a claim has to be acceptable (the first element in the ARS standards). If the evidence isn't immediately acceptable, the arguer needs to back up and establish the acceptability of the evidence with a subordinate argument that supports the legitimacy of the data with other support. However, if the evidence is immediately acceptable and also seems like appropriate support for C, the argument will stop there. On the other hand, the recipient might ask, "What does that have to do with C?" To answer this hesitation, the arguer needs to provide the third argument element, the warrant (W). The warrant is an inference link or a license. It explicitly connects the data to the claim. It explains why if the evidence is so, the conclusion is so as well.

These three elements—C, D, and W—are the core of the argument. To begin an example, suppose an arguer says, "The United Nations is really just a tool for power assertion by Western nations (C)." If the receiver doesn't immediately agree, the arguer might then supply some evidence: "The United Nations' budget is dominated by dues from the U.S. and other Western nations (D)." Upon being tasked to explain the relevance of this bit of information, the arguer could then assert a warrant: "Money talks. If the U.N. doesn't do what the West wants, the money will be withdrawn and the U.N. will be impotent (W)." The combination of D and W is a pretty full provision of a reason for the conclusion. D, W, and C can all be critiqued, of course, but with D, W, and C provided, we have a fairly complete expression of an argument.

Toulmin, however, supplied three more elements of a fully elaborated argument. The next is backing (B), which supports the warrant. The idea of backing is that the warrant itself might be somewhat controversial. Instead of making it the claim of another subordinate argument, Toulmin made a space in the main argument to offer reasons in support of the warrant. The reasons, naturally enough, need to be factlike materials that are linked to the warrant. The backing will be as elaborate as the interlocutor needs. Here, the backing might be, "In November 2013, the U.S. suspended its dues to UNESCO (a UN agency) because it objected to UNESCO recognizing the Palestinian Territories as a nation. This jeopardized UNESCO's ability to operate (B)." If the argument's recipient thought this was sufficient to support the warrant ("Money talks," etc.), then this would be the only backing provided. Otherwise, the arguer might continue in an effort to sustain the warrant.

Suppose the interlocutor thinks that the warrant has been reasonably supported. Even if it is generally acceptable at this point, one might still be able to think of conditions in which it might not hold. This brings us to the next component of an argument, the reservation (R) or rebuttal. In contrast to the other parts of an argument, this one can be supplied by the argument's recipient. The interlocutor might offer something like this to specify conditions under which the generally acceptable warrant ("Money talks," etc.) would not apply: "Unless the UN or UNESCO has the courage to stand up against the West (R)," or "Unless the UN or UNESCO can develop another funding stream (R)." While Toulmin was clear that none of the elements of an argument have to have any particular wording or form, the idea of "unless" is essential to the reservation. The reservation has to be evaluated by the arguers, but Toulmin did not discuss this process. The rebuttals need to be scrutinized for their acceptability, their connection to the warrant they are being applied against, and their overall relevance to the argument's conclusion.

Finally we come to the last element in the Toulmin model, the qualifier (Q). This is very important in discussing ordinary arguing. The qualifier is a modal term that attaches to the conclusion, to indicate how strongly the conclusion holds given the rest of the argument. Examples of qualifiers include "probably," "maybe," "rarely," "almost certainly," "whenever money is tight," "when it's my turn to cook," and so forth. This important insight is that the conclusion needs to be expressed as strongly (but no more strongly) than its support justifies. The qualifier should reflect the strength of the D-W-C connections, the support for the warrant (B), and the possibility of exceptions to it (R). So if we selected "certainly" as our qualifier for the claim (so that we have "The United Nations is *certainly* just a tool...") this might actually be a weaker overall argument than one that concluded that "The United Nations is *sometimes* just a tool..." Arguments often aim at claims that are not black or white, true or false. Sometimes the best available conclusion is that "maybe" something is so. If that is the best available claim, then an argument supporting it will be a stronger one than an argument that over-claims or under-claims what has been established.

The Toulmin model is simple enough that it permits analysis of any argument in use. It doesn't generate the tight judgments of truth or validity that formal logic aims at, but it also doesn't bog us down in classification details like informal logic does. And it provides us with some clear lessons about arguing: (1) The elements of an argument are not propositions, they are meanings. D, W, C, and the rest are functions of discourse, not forms of it. (2) Arguments vary in their degrees of strength, and consequently conclusions should be expressed with varying levels of force. A pointed set of reasons should lead to a nearly unqualified conclusion but an uncertain set of reasons justifies a carefully nuanced statement of what has been proved. Matching the force of a conclusion to the force of its justification is a key aspect of good arguing. And (3) arguments are used by people, and it is the interaction of the people that determines what is momentarily acceptable, what can be omitted, and what must be proved.

The Enthymeme. This brings us to one of the most fundamental ideas in argumentation, or communication generally. That is the enthymeme. Many writers over the centuries have defined an enthymeme as a syllogism with a missing premise, but this obscures the key point. Enthymemes are not deficient or incomplete syllogisms. An enthymeme is an argument whose parts are supplied partly by the arguer and partly by the listener (Bitzer, 1959). The key lesson is that an argument is a joint production. The arguer presents some of the material and, by understanding it, the hearer provides the rest. This is a natural feature of comprehension. We don't require the other person to say everything that could be said about some matter. We only require that he or she say enough for us to fill in the rest (Aristotle, *Rhetoric*, I.2, 1357a).

For example, suppose an arguer said, "Franklin Roosevelt was America's finest President because he established the social net to catch people who can't provide for themselves." Possibly this makes perfect sense to you. But notice that the link between the conclusion ("finest President") and the data ("established the social net") isn't present in the argument as stated. The warrant is something like, "Creating a support network for retirement income and health care is the best thing an American President has ever done." You needed to understand something like that, just to make the argument coherent and comprehensible. Now that I have specified a warrant, you might be uncomfortable with its phrasing and might want to modify it at bit, or to qualify the conclusion (maybe "*one of* (Q) America's finest Presidents").

This illustrates several key ideas. Listeners are full participants in arguments, and supply part of what appears to be the other person's argument. There is value in fully specifying an argument, even one that left things out but seems to make sense when it is completely acceptable and understood. These considerations, particularly the first one, are the reason I regard the enthymeme as a fundamental concept in the understanding of argumentation and communication.

So we have explored several ways of describing the structure of an argument. The best detailed methods were those of formal and informal logic, but both have the deficiency of regarding an argument as essentially the textual product of one person. Toulmin obviously contemplated the possibility of argumentative interaction between two people, and the idea of an enthymeme insists upon it. This book is about interpersonal arguing. One way to study that topic would be to imagine that one person produces an argument, the other person produces an opposing chunk of reason, the first person gives new evidence and inference links, and so forth. That possibility has actually been debated within the argumentation community. But it is unsatisfying because people don't talk that way, any more than they express themselves in syllogisms. What has been reviewed about argument structure is fundamental but incomplete. To fill out the structural description of argument, we need to consider how people argue together in conversation.

Interactive Arguments

We are still on the introductory topic of argument structure, but we pass now from "an argument, generally" to what arguments look like when people do them face-to-face. This is related to the classic distinction made by O'Keefe (1977). He said that the word "argument" has two meanings in ordinary use. One is the idea of a fully expressed reason-conclusion system. He called this argument$_1$ (oralized as "argument one"). An argument$_1$ is something people *make*. Prototypically, an argument$_1$ is made by one person, as when someone writes an argumentative essay or gives a speech. However, essays and other sorts of arguments$_1$ can be co-authored. The other meaning of "argument" is called argument$_2$. An argument$_2$ is something that people *have*. So when two people are trying to work out how they should spend their weekend, if they are offering and evaluating reasons, they are having an argument$_2$.

Many scholars loosely express O'Keefe's distinction as being between argument as product or process, but this isn't quite right. An interactive argument$_2$ generates a joint conversational *product* that can be transcribed and a newspaper editorial (an argument$_1$) might go through a *process* of reconsideration and revision as it emerges. Most of the time, it is true, an argument$_1$ is the product of one person and an argument$_2$ emerges from the process of interpersonal interaction, but it is more precise to focus on the distinction between making and having an argument. When we begin to consider interpersonal arguing, we are very much in the context of argument$_2$, having arguments. It is worth remembering, however, that we are still treating arguments as exchanges of reasons and not as emotional flares.

Here I want to discuss two sorts of structures for interpersonal argumentation. One is the immediate argument in the moment, and the other is a larger structure that has places in it for the exchange of reasons.

The Momentary Exchange of Reasons. Quite a few conversation analysts have had a run at specifying what an interpersonal argument looks like, and there is value in all their work (Coulter, 1990; Jackson & Jacobs, 1980; Kopperschmidt, 1985; Schiffrin, 1985). However, I favor the approach of Muntigl and Turnbull (1998) for its simplicity and wide applicability. What we are looking for is a description of arguing that displays the kernel of the process, always understanding that the kernel is going to be enlarged, shrunk, chained, and repeated in actual conversations.

Muntigl and Turnbull (1998) describe conversational arguing as having a three-turn sequence at its core. Their analysis begins with the claim and regards the reasons as subordinate to it. That is sensible because we have said that an argument's conclusion is its point. Toulmin taught us that the reasons (the data and warrant) will only be produced if they are called for, and Muntigl and Turnbull include that idea, permitting interpersonal arguments to be enthymematic. Without the reasons, we would only have an exchange of claims. We might learn something by examining that sort of exchange, but in our terms it would only be a primitive argument and not really recognizable as what we are studying here.

The three turns are these:

T1: Person A makes a claim
T2: Person B disputes the claim
T3: Person A disagrees with person B by either supporting T1 or disputing T2

Each of the turns can be accomplished with a huge variety of actual expressions. Claims can be made forcefully or only implied; disagreement can be simple or elaborated; support for something said earlier can be constructive or defensive. The three turns are functions that need to be fulfilled somehow by what is said (or gestured, but I will generally assume that things are said).

As in Toulmin's analysis, the sequence will be as developed as the participants require. In fact, if the original claim is acceptable T2 won't occur and we won't be able to detect that an argument was ever present. If T2 seems like a better idea than T1, T3 won't be generated. It is only when there is some dubious challenge (expressed or anticipated) that anyone supplies a reason. Once we have a claim and a reason, we know that we have an argument. And notice that it is wrong to say that we are looking at Person A's argument in this sequence. It depends just as much on Person B for its existence. And both A and B will be supplying the content and meanings that we understand to be conclusions and reasons.

Here is an example. Two people are talking about a classic movie that they have just watched together.

1 (T1) A: I really liked this movie. I think *The Sting* is one of the most entertaining films ever.
2 (T2) B: I don't know. I have trouble getting behind characters when they're committing crimes.
3 (T3) A: Yeah, but Newman and Redford are astonishingly good looking. And you don't seem to mind all the destruction in your comic book movies.

This fictional example matches Muntigl and Turnbull's structural description pretty closely. Notice that B can express doubt about the claim in T1 in a variety of ways. Here B actually provides a reason for his or her hesitation. This is not technically necessary. B could just have said, "I don't know," and left it at that. Person A could have replied to that, but wouldn't have been able to be as interesting or pointed as in T3. By giving a reason in T2, B fleshed out his or her thinking and enlarged the topical scope of the exchange. As a consequence, by the end of T2 we can see two potential argument topics on the floor: one is about entertainment and the other is about whether we should approve of charming criminals. This gives A several choices about what to do in T3. Person A ends up doing two things, asserting some detail about what was entertaining (the two attractive actors) and aggressively pointing out a biographical inconsistency in what B has said (the point about destruction in comic book movies that B likes). Actually A didn't really need to pursue either point. Person A could just have said, "Hey, I'm entitled to feel any way I want." That would have reinstantiated the claim in T1, but would have avoided much in way of a reason. We would be entitled to critique A for not having given a real reason when B's comment called one out (see Kuhn, 1991, for how often this happens).

As it is, we can still critique A for having quietly made "crime" equivalent to "destruction" in T3. Perhaps Person B could have made that point in a fourth turn by saying, "Destruction isn't necessarily criminal. Sometimes the Hulk has to pound open a wall to get to the bad guy." This would have converted A's T3 into another T1 (this time about destruction and crime), and the argument could have gone on from there. This illustrates a virtue of Muntigl and Turnbull's analysis. The three-turn argument kernel can replicate itself over and over again, moving from one conversational topic to another related one. And of course the argument can stop whenever the two people get tired of arguing, perhaps because one of them realizes that the other one is right.

The three-turn sequence can also shrink. Suppose A had anticipated B's objection, and says this to start things off: "I really liked this movie. I think *The Sting* is one of the most entertaining films ever, partly because Newman and Redford are astonishingly good looking." Here we see part of T3 included in the first remark, possibly because A foresaw B's hesitation and tried to pre-empt it with an answer. Person A begins with a fairly elaborated reason (for a conversation, at least), and in that turn we can see a T1, an anticipation of T2, and a T3 compressed into one turn at talk.

Just as the content of the interpersonal argument is a joint production, so is the course of the episode. Person B could have agreed in the original T2, and that would have been the end of the exchange. Interpersonal arguments are not crudely co-authored, with one person responsible for certain parts of it and the other person responsible for the rest. Even in the compressed example in the last paragraph, we might say that B's doubt about T1 was present in A's anticipations. Sometimes, too, one person will make a point and the other person will express some undeveloped part of it. For instance,

1. (T1) A: Baseball is the best sport because its strategy is so intricate.
2. (T2) B: Yes, there's nothing like watching the defense react to the possibility of a bunt, even if there isn't one.
3. (T3) A: Nice point. That's the kind of thing I meant.

Who made the point about bunt defense involving intricate strategy? Person A was the one who first expressed the whole idea of strategy, and he or she might actually have had bunt defense in mind. But the point was made explicit by B, who probably would never have said such a thing if A hadn't made the first remark. It seems most sensible to attribute the content to the conversation, not to its individual participants. Interpersonal arguments emerge *between* the participants.

But that was an easy example of emergent meanings because the exchange involved agreement, even though it also contained reasons. The T2 didn't even turn out to be a dispute about T1 because A endorsed T2 and absorbed it into T1. Here's another version of the same conversation, but with disagreement this time:

1. (T1) A: Baseball is the best sport because its strategy is so intricate.
2. (T2) B: Yes, there's nothing like watching the defense react to the possibility of a bunt, even if there isn't one.
3. (T3) A: No, no. You know I don't mean bunts. I mean things like pitch selection and working the count. Bunting isn't strategy after you're about 10 years old.

Now we can see that T2 was actually a disagreement, an effort to lead A into B's particular appreciation for baseball. (It is worth noticing that it was A's T3 that made T2 into a disagreement. It is exactly the same remark that we counted as an agreement a moment ago.) Maybe they have had this argument about bunting before, and B knew that T2 would get a rise out of A. Maybe if we could hear B's tone, we would know that T2 was sarcastic in the first place. This example is perhaps more obviously an interpersonal argument that the earlier baseball exchange. Even so, we can still see that the two participants have generated a little theory of baseball strategy between them. They both have a point of view about bunting (a different point of view, as it turns out), they both apparently have an appreciation for strategy, both think no comment is required about the equivalence between "best sport" and "intricate strategy," and they both see strategy as being relevant to baseball.

We could divide up the bunting remarks if we wanted, but the rest of the reasoning is a joint thing, one that was born in the conversational space between the two people. Even if we decided to label this exchange as "a disagreement about bunting," both people contributed essentially to the disagreement. Interpersonal arguments are emergent between the two arguers. This is why the understanding of interpersonal arguing means that we have to appreciate the interaction and not just the positioning of data, warrant, and claim in the exchange. From this point on in the book, it should be natural to discuss two arguers, not an arguer and a recipient.

At any rate, the Muntigl and Turnbull system gives us a simple structural analysis of conversational argument. We can elaborate the system when we observe an actual exchange of reasons by noticing that someone doubted a warrant, someone used the argument scheme of example, someone had trouble addressing a critical question, and so forth. The structural elements that we examined earlier find their natural homes within the three-turn sequence of assertion, doubt, and defense.

Conversational Arguments in a Critical Discussion. Interpersonal arguments always take place in a context of some sort. Aakhus (2003, 2007) has explored how various task settings can be designed to facilitate or hinder good argumentation. In any context, the two arguers have a particular relationship and a unique joint history, they are in a specific place at an exact time, they are doing a particular thing together, they have both ordinary and arbitrary constraints on what they can say, and so forth. Which of these features is important in the moment depends on how the arguers experience things, and we will spend a lot of space in this book exploring that issue.

Here, however, let us consider a particular task that people do by means of arguing. It is not the only thing that people try to accomplish with arguments, but it may be the basic one, the task that provides the model for all the other uses of interpersonal argument. That task is the critical discussion.

The critical discussion has been analyzed normatively by van Eemeren and Grootendorst (1983, 2004). Their normative standards generate an ideal for this sort of interaction. A critical discussion is one in which two parties propose and test a position on some issue. They do so with certain attitudes and commitments. They seek the truth and do not pursue personal agendas. They operate only by reason, and control their impulses to be evasive, or charming, or domineering. van Eemeren and Grootendorst have worked out what is dialectically required for two arguers to reach agreement on the merits of some issue.

Among the key contributions made by these scholars is the specification of the four stages in a critical discussion. Within those stages, we can clearly see where the arguing fits. These are theoretical stages, by the way. Very little work has been done to learn how explicit these stages are in actual conversation or how often people actually follow the normatively necessary pattern. That isn't the point of a normative theory, such as van Eemeren and Grootendorst's. If descriptive research shows that people don't follow the pattern, the standards encourage us in the judgment that the people have messed up, not that the normative theory is wrong.

The first stage is called *confrontation*. This isn't a personalized confrontation like a nasty conflict would be. Instead, this is the point at which the two people realize that they have a disagreement, that their views confront one another. Should they decide to resolve their differences, they move to the second stage, *opening*. In these moments, they determine where they stand on background matters, they assign sides (who proposes a point of view and who resists it), and they agree on how to proceed (for example, who needs to give evidence and who can merely express doubt). Much of the material in this stage is generally left unspoken, in my experience. Stage three is the one of special importance to us, because it is the *argumentation* stage. This is the phase in which the arguers' reasons are expressed, tested, revised, elaborated on, questioned, and critiqued. The last stage is called *concluding*. In principle, what happens in the final phase is that the original point of view is withdrawn or agreed to.

Aside from giving us a vantage from which to analyze and critique actual arguing practice, one contribution of this theory is to emphasize that arguing is not really an independent thing, an autochthonous event that comes from nothing and affects nothing else. An argument is part of a larger conversation (even if a lot of the preceding and following material is understood and left implicit, sort of an interactional enthymeme). Arguing is also part of an ongoing relationship most of the time, so that it takes its place within the relational lives shared by the two parties.

Within the argumentation stage, we would expect to see the other things that we have been discussing: evidence, warrants, argument schemes, three-turn sequences, and so forth. The argumentation stage is likely to be the longest of the four in practice, because it is then that the standpoints get constructed, explored, refuted, and defended.

This analysis of critical discussions is a transportable theory. We can apply it to many settings—a family argument, a case at law, a parliamentary debate, a scholarly dispute in journals. The theory requires that a disagreement be recognized, that the character of the discussion be agreed upon, that the arguments be made, and that a conclusion be drawn on the merits. It is hard to imagine how anyone could hope to argue productively if any of these elements were omitted or mistimed. The normative character of the theory is essential to its value. By seeing how people go through their discussions imperfectly, we can get insight into how arguments derail and why some of them explode into nasty emotional displays.

Summary: Structure

An essential starting point for this book is to say what an argument is, and I have done so by detailing its structure. Several different structural descriptions have been given. These include formal logic and its syllogisms, informal logic's argument schemes, the Toulmin model, the enthymeme, the three-turn sequence, and the stages of a critical discussion. Each of these has something to teach us. The general descriptions use ideas such as premises, conclusions, evidence, and warrants and thereby give us our most precise understanding of what a reason is. The interpersonal descriptions show us how reasons appear in conversation, and emphasize the emergent character of an interpersonal argument.

The Situation-Goals-Plans-Action Model

Even though this book is about *interpersonal* arguing, it remains the case that every contribution in a conversation is made by an individual person. What is said during an exchange is restricted by various rules of interaction. For example, if you are in the midst of a conversation, your remarks are supposed to be relevant to what has gone before. This may involve global relevance (staying on the general topic) or local relevance (picking up some part of the immediately prior utterance and remarking about it) or both (McLaughlin, 1984). Conversation, even fierce disagreement, must be cooperative in some respects or the exchange will simply be incoherent. Speakers must therefore act in respect to Grice's (1975) maxims, either obeying them or using them as exploitable resources to say things implicitly. The maxims are quality (be truthful), quantity (say exactly as much as is required), relation (be relevant), and manner (be clear). But these restrictions (and others that could be listed) leave a great deal of freedom for the individual. The things people can say in a given conversation are almost innumerable. Among those things, of course, are arguments.

In a conversational moment a person must generate a contribution that respects the various constraints that have just been mentioned as well as others (such as politeness and cultural norms) that will be discussed at length in this book. But the constraints do not do a very complete job of dictating what a person says. They eliminate possibilities, but they do not affirmatively generate much content. Most of our conversational actions are not as automatic as just respecting constraints. A person, acting out of his or her particular uniqueness, will generate remarks that exhibit some aspect of identity, pursue individual goals, avoid foreseeable obstacles, draw on idiosyncratic knowledge, and adapt to the other person. We need an individualistic theory that explains how this happens. A useful general theory of message production is the goals-plans-action model initiated by Dillard (1990a, 1990b, 2004; Dillard, Segrin, & Harden, 1989). Here I call it the SGPA model (situation-goals-plans-actions) because I want to give more attention to the situation than others have done. Otherwise I am remaining consistent with Dillard's formulations in most details.

A simple summary of the SGPA is this. A person comes into contact with a social situation that seems to invite him or her to say something. The invitation activates the person's social goals (e.g., to persuade, to ask a favor, to make a new friend) and one of those goals rises to the fore. This goal is in contact with the person's long-term memory, which includes words, phrases, recollections of past social disasters, rules of how to behave, and many more things. In concert with those cognitive stores, the goal activates or helps construct a message that might be uttered. Before it is, normally the person tests that message against other goals (such as how to be polite, how to preserve your resources, how to avoid humiliation) and the message is revised (that is, planned) before it is made public. Once the person has settled on an acceptable plan, the plan is performed, and this public performance is the "action" in the model's title. The model applies to all kinds of messages, but very often messages involve arguments and argumentative moves in conversation.

Situations

Now we need to complicate this simple summary. Let us begin with the situation. The GPA researchers have had very little to say about situations, except to indicate that they contain goals and are actually defined by their unique constellations of goals (Dillard & Solomon, 2000). The idea is that the sorts of circumstances that call out messages are *social* situations that are recognized as involving certain desired, allowable, and forbidden goals. So if you meet a friend on the sidewalk and realize that you have some unfinished business together, these factors might immediately call up the impulses to mention the unfinished task, give assurances about your intentions, and avoid blaming the other person for the incompleteness. These last three are goals, of course, but notice that the situation also involved "friend" and "sidewalk," and these things are not goals at all. They are part of the context of your spontaneous meeting. In a different context (e.g., during a pastoral prayer at church) suddenly noticing your friend would not stimulate the same goals I just listed, at least not to the point of message production. And if the other person were a superior rather than a friend, you would approach the interaction differently, perhaps emphasizing your intentions more forcibly and even taking some responsibility for the task being undone. Furthermore, if you were in a hurry, you might not pause to talk to either a friend or a boss. Your message might only consist of a smile and a head nod.

An interpersonal argument, by definition, will only take place in an interpersonal situation. When we begin to think about what gives structure and meaning to an interaction, we immediately realize that many things *other than goals* are important: the nature of the other person (friend, boss, romantic partner, detested neighbor), your identity needs relative to that person (being seen as sociable, reliable, loving, firm), the relationship you want to project between the two of you (friendly, professional, intimate, uninvolved), your current circumstances (at leisure or harried), the resources you presently have available (feeling depressed or happy, being flush with cash or unable to repay a debt, being cautious or adventuresome), and many other considerations. These elements have influence over what goals you form, but they are not goals themselves.

Those are general considerations that apply to any sort of interaction. We need to go further to try to understand what calls out arguing, and Chapter 3 will concentrate on that. For now, an obvious candidate factor would be awareness or suspicion of a disagreement, but even here we need to notice that people do not pursue every difference of opinion. Sometimes we just let things go. So in addition to the possibility of having diverging views (the confrontation stage in a critical discussion), we need to pay attention to the stakes involved in the disagreement (Hample, Dai, & Zhan, 2016). If a romantic partner suddenly announces the desire to have children, few people would let that pass without some mutual reasoning. But expressing a wish to have green beans for lunch instead of corn probably doesn't rise to the level that impels a person to resolve the issue or even discuss it. Later, we will see that the topics of disagreements (whether they are about personal matters or public ones) have a strong influence on the possible stakes of an argument, and help us predict when people will or will not engage in arguing. Other argument-relevant factors in the situation involve the other person. Does he or she argue pleasantly? Is the other person open-minded? Considerate? Domineering? We also need to consider the first person's own self-confidence: What are the chances of winning an argument? How much does the person actually know about the topic? And finally, we will need to examine the propriety of arguing. Is this the right time, place, and person with whom to work things out? Later chapters will provide data on all these points. For now, it is enough to notice that situational elements other than goals are likely to be pertinent to interpersonal arguing.

Goals

Next, let us consider the goals in more detail. In one of the nicest theoretical moments in the development of the GPA, Dillard distinguished between primary and secondary goals. The primary goal frames or defines the situation. It is the first flash of what a person wants to do—to persuade, to give solace, to ask a favor, to pass the time. The original GPA research was aimed at understanding persuasion so the early papers all talk about influence being the primary goal, but the theory is more general than that. The goal that gives definition and structure to the person's intentions might be to seek entertainment, to make a new friend, to jockey for a new assignment at work, or any other social goal that a person can have. Secondary goals are those that modify the primary goal. They can reinforce it, but they might also counter it in some respects. For example, the desire to be thought of as pleasant might cause a person to rephrase the first aggressive or unfeeling thing that comes to mind. Or the desire to avoid exploitation might make a person less ready to offer help. The distinction between primary and secondary goals is not one of force. Schrader and Dillard (1998) found that sometimes the secondary goals actually have more motivational energy than the primary goal. This would be the case when a secondary goal (e.g., avoid being exploited) overwhelms the primary goal (e.g., give assistance) so that the message is not produced at all, or produced half-heartedly, or expressed so ambiguously that no offer of help is really detectable. The distinction between primary and secondary is which goal *defines* the situation and gives it a mental label for the participant. That is the primary goal. Dillard said that people only have one set of goals and that the situation makes one of them primary in the moment, temporarily leaving the others in secondary roles (or even making them irrelevant to that conversational instant). He also gave a list of possible goals, but I will not particularly respect his list as being complete. Anything that can motivate social behavior can motivate a message.

Many messages, though not all of them, involve arguing. It is obvious that a person trying to persuade another will probably give some reasons for what is wanted. But other primary goals may involve offering and discussing reasons as well. If a friend needed comfort, it would be natural to give reasons as to why things will seem better in the morning or why a particular course of action might solve the immediate problem. If one were asking for date, it might be appropriate to give a reason for going out together, such as pleasant company, a good meal, or an entertaining movie. Declining to repay a loan is typically accompanied by an excuse or justification, which would be a reason why the money isn't forthcoming. A babysitter introducing him- or herself to a small child might give reasons for the toddler to look forward to the evening. Sometimes we manage our goals with a grunt and a nod, but reason giving is natural, especially when we are trying to explain ourselves, saying how or why we are pursuing that objective. And none of this even addresses the complication of giving reasons to disguise a goal, as when you trick a friend into going to a surprise party. Theorists should probably assume that most goals and messages involve reason giving, and to analyze the occasional absence of reasons as interesting in itself.

Plans

Planning is intricately involved with goals. Once motivated to speak or argue, a person assembles an inventory of things that might be said and ways to say them. Some people just say the first thing that comes to mind (Hample, Richards, & Skubisz, 2013; Swann & Rentfrow, 2001), but most people give at least micro-momentary consideration to the possible consequences of saying something. These people edit what they say (Hample & Dallinger, 1987), and we know something about the editorial standards they use, that is to say, the primary and secondary goals they bring to bear. They may suppress or revise a possible message because it wouldn't be effective, because it is just the wrong sort of thing to say, because it would be false or irrelevant, or because it would have social repercussions of some sort. Planning draws on long-term memory to recall past episodes in which similar messages have been tried, and those lessons are applied to the immediate moment (Meyer, 1997). Candidate messages are held up against all a person's activated goals, primary and secondary, and consequences are estimated. If the anticipated harms are too great, the message will be revised or abandoned. Sometimes a person cannot think of anything good to say. Then the person will either be quiet or have to say something regrettable (but less regrettable than silence). Planning can be quick or can be an elaborate cycle of revision (imagine diplomats crafting an official note of displeasure).

Action

Once the planning is complete—that is, something survives the editorial process—then we finally see the public product. That message may or may not include argumentative moves, but it often will. It will almost certainly contain some other features, such as facework, conventional politeness, and so forth. These other elements modify the argument, sometimes in a fundamental way. "I need to borrow

$100 right now to get my car out of police storage," means something a little different from "I'm terribly embarrassed about this, but I need to borrow $100 right now to get my car out of police storage." On the face of it, both examples contain the same request and reason, but the second one is couched more politely, shows more modesty, and is more adapted to the listener. These change the meaning of the argument from being a near-demand to being a plea for help. So we will need to pay attention to editing that goes beyond just selecting evidence, qualifiers, and warrants for a conclusion.

Summary: SGPA

In sum, our base SGPA model of argument production is this. A situation is perceived and registered with particular meanings, thereby inviting an argument. The defining argumentative objective is the primary goal. That goal, along with the first flash of what might be said, is brought into contact with situation-relevant secondary goals, and all the goals are used to test, refine, and judge the message. When a message is finally regarded as tolerable, it is performed and made public. All of this sounds as though I am describing a careful, conscious process here, but I am not. The whole process may happen in an instant—actually, it has to occur in an instant to match the pacing of a conversation—and very commonly no part of it will be conscious at all. The fact that we are not normally aware of any of these processes makes researching them a little more difficult, but as the book progresses you will see how much we have discovered about all of this.

Arguing as a Fundamental Human Process

I have often mentioned how common arguments are in our lives. I have said that they create and modify meanings, they often dominate our messages, they are emergent productions in important conversations, they have the capacity to bring people together, and they are essential in pursuing our social goals. Most of these claims are simple observations that you can probably confirm just by paying focused attention to how much joint and public reasoning is going on around you for a day or two. Here I want to review some recent theorizing that explains why all this is so—why arguing is so foundational to human social life. The explanation is rooted in our understandings of how humans evolved.

Humans are not the only animals with language. The vocabularies of many species have been decoded (Bradbury & Vehrencamp, 1998; Bright, 1984). These languages are not as sophisticated as human ones, of course. Most of the vocabulary consists of utterances like, "This is my branch, stay away," "I see a snake," and "There is good pollen in this direction." Particularly advanced species are able to deceive using calls or other signals (Searcy & Nowicki, 2005). Animals can certainly figure things out, but to my knowledge, we have no evidence that they give reasons to one another or test one another's evidence and warrants. Humans can.

Contemporary human capabilities are no accident. Our abilities to run, throw, digest, mate, see, hear, make vocal noise, and so forth have been guided by evolutionary processes. Quirky abilities or actions that promoted survival (and therefore reproduction) were favored by evolution, and so the biological structure that permitted or required the originally quirky thing would be selected for and increasingly represented in the genetic pool. Some of the biological structure has to do with our skeletons and muscles, but the brain is biological, too. We cannot think anything that our brains cannot register.

As we work through this analysis, an important thing to keep in mind is that modern civilization is an eye blink in our species' history. Human evolution took place long ago, most markedly in the Pleistocene Period, which began about 2.5 million years ago and ended around 10,000 BCE. European early modern humans came on the stage about 45,000 years ago but anatomically modern humans were present in Africa perhaps as early as 200,000 years ago. Primates that evolved into modern humans as well as those that eventually became chimpanzees and gorillas were present even earlier. Evolutionary changes were in response to what is called the EEA, the environment of evolutionary adaptedness. For humans, that is the Pleistocene. To get much idea what must have been happening to our species, we need to study those earliest days, with small tribal groups, simple tools, dangerous hunts, nomadic migrations, and hopeful foraging expeditions. One of several useful introductions to all of this is Rossano (2003). Buss (1995) nicely explains the scientific logic used in testing hypotheses about evolution, even though you might suppose we are millions of years late in collecting data.

If this is the first time you have thought about this in connection with arguing, it would be natural for you to suppose that the key evolutionary product for argumentation must have been logical thought. After all, as we have seen, formal logic produces reliable conclusions when it is based on secure premises. Coming to accurate conclusions would seem to promote survival and reproduction. There are some immediate problems with this thought, however. Most obviously, logic actually has to be taught in classes, and even bright students exposed to good instruction get problems wrong on exams. Eyesight, in contrast, doesn't have to be taught.

A more delicate problem is that logic applies to any sort of thinking, but some of our reasoning appears to be domain-specific. A clear demonstration of this is Cosmides and Tooby's (1992) work on cheater detection. In the EEA, being cheated could be a serious survival problem. A person could lose all his food or her chance at mating if someone else deceived him or her. Consequently humans developed special reasoning habits to detect cheaters, and these processes do not follow the dictates of formal logic.

The demonstration has to do with Wason's selection task, commonly used in cognitive psychology. The task involves four cards. Variations of the test have been used. Here is a version Cosmides and Tooby (p. 182) used.

> Part of your new clerical job at the local high school is to make sure that student documents have been processed correctly. Your job is to make sure the documents conform to the following alphanumeric rule: "If a person has a 'D' rating, then his documents must be marked code '3.'" You suspect the secretary you replaced did not categorize the students' documents correctly. The cards below have information about the documents of four people who are enrolled at this high school. Each card represents one person. One side of a card tells a person's letter rating and the other side of the card tells that person's number code. Indicate only those card(s) you definitely need to turn over to see if the documents of any of these people violate this rule.

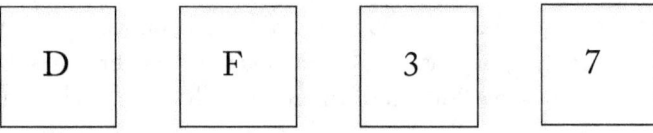

This problem involves a hypothetical syllogism whose first premise is "If a person has a 'D' rating (p) then the documents must be marked code '3' (q)." The only way for this rule to be violated is if there is a D on one side and something besides a 3 on the other. The solution is to turn over two cards: the D (to see if it has a 3 on the back) and the 7 (to see if the other side is a D). Turning over the F card is uninformative because even if there is a 3 on the back, the rule hasn't been violated. Turning over the 3 card isn't informative because even if there isn't a D on the back, the rule hasn't been violated either. The correct choice is turning over the p and the not-q cards. Only about a quarter of people get this right immediately when the problem is expressed abstractly. It is common to turn over only the D card, or to turn over the D and the 3 cards. Evolution obviously hasn't helped us much with this problem, so the ability to do the Wason task certainly has not been selected for.

The other part of the Cosmides and Tooby research invited people to detect cheating, and the project becomes especially interesting for us at this point. The cheater detection problem came in two versions. The idea is that someone has offered to take some immediate benefit from you and repay you later. For example, in the Pleistocene Era, the offer might have been "Give me your meat now and I'll bring you some of mine later." Cheating involves taking the benefit and not paying off the cost. Respondents were told to enforce one of these rules: "If you take the benefit, then you pay the cost," or "If you pay the cost, then you take the benefit." Both rules have the logical form "if p then q," although the contents of p and q have been switched in the second version. Participants in the study needed to decide what card(s) to turn over to see if the rule they had been given had been obeyed. They were told each card said whether the possible cheater had taken the benefit on one side, and whether he or she had paid the cost on the other. Here are their cards:

| Benefit accepted | Benefit not accepted | Cost paid | Cost not paid |

As before, the logically correct choice is to turn over the p and the not-q cards. For the first version of the rule (if benefit, then cost), the rule's proper test is to turn over the first and fourth cards. For the second version of the rule (if cost, then benefit), the correct choices are the third and second cards. But notice that if you are really worried about being cheated, your concern should focus on the first and fourth cards. These two are the only ones that that could prove whether you have been cheated. For the first rule (if benefit, then cost), this is also the logically correct solution. For the second rule (if cost, then benefit), it is not. Regardless of which rule people were told to check on, they overwhelmingly turned over the first and fourth cards. They were looking for cheaters, not validity.

Cheater detection is therefore a domain-specific kind of reasoning (the domain being "catch cheaters"). Logic is domain-general, but apparently it is only in play when no relevant particular domain has been primed. Possibly we have other reasoning systems for food sharing, personal danger, mating, hunt organization, and other fundamental survival issues in the EEA. We have already noticed, for instance, that ad hominem is often a reasoning fallacy. Generally speaking, we should follow advice based on its soundness, not based on who gave it. However, Richards (2012; Richards & Hample, 2016) has argued that several variables that affect persuasiveness (e.g., the source's sex, racial similarity, facial attractiveness, vocal pitch, and athletic ability) are traceable to evolution-encouraged cues as to who would be a good hunter and who would be trustworthy regarding the division of a hunt's proceeds.

The relevance of all this to argumentation was highlighted by Mercier and Sperber (2011), who gave an evolutionary account of human reasoning (also see Mercier, 2016; Mercier & Sperber, 2017; Santibáñez Yáñez, 2012). They took on and disputed the usual explanation of reasoning—that it evolved so humans could discover the truth and refine the accuracy of their world understandings. We have already seen some grounds to doubt this. Early humans used their thinking to pursue food, safety, and mates, not syllogistic validity. Mercier and Sperber said instead that reasoning evolved to supply the materials for arguing. And the essential purpose of arguing, they said, was persuasion, not truth seeking.

They offered several sorts of evidence in support of their views. We have already noticed one bit of this—that people do not solve abstract logical problems especially well. When those same problems are expressed concretely in a familiar domain, people do better but still not perfectly (as we just saw with the cheater detection problem).

A particularly illuminating set of research results has to do with the confirmation bias (Nickerson, 1998). This well-documented phenomenon is that people will tend to judge an argument as correct if it arrives at a conclusion they favor and will ignore reasoning flaws that they would notice if the conclusion had been one they disagree with. They are also quite willing to offer bad arguments in support of something they want or agree with. Mercier and Sperber say that this is entirely explicable if we understand arguing's purpose to be persuasion, rather than truth seeking. Instead of starting out with acceptable premises and finding out what conclusion they support, people apparently start with the conclusion and rationalize it with anything that seems at all relevant. We say and hear arguments out of the same confirmation bias. Arguing is for persuasion, not for philosophy.

Early humans were social. They banded together and rarely tried to survive alone. They cooperated in hunts. They needed to share food because hunts take time and are not always successful. They raised their children together, and the women had to trust the men to come back from the hunts with food. The species needed for humans to mate, and reasonable genetic diversity had to be present. Small groups had to defend themselves against dangerous predators and other humans. Being social meant that people needed to coordinate with one another. If cooperation on one course of action was not immediate, they needed to bring one another into line. Persuasion was a reliable way to do this. Beatings, for example, are only effective as long as the threat is present, but persuasion holds out the possibility of the listener genuinely coming to believe that the proposed action is a good one that should be followed voluntarily (see Kelman, 1958). Successful persuasion of another person would produce cooperation without the need for continual vigilance.

The centrality of argument to the possibility of human civilization is not a new idea. Two millennia ago, Cicero (*de Inventione*, I. ii. 2) expressed a similar thought:

For there was a time when men wandered at large in the fields like animals and lived on wild fare; they did nothing by the guidance of reason, but relied chiefly on physical strength; there was as yet no ordered system of religious worship nor of social duties; no one had seen legitimate marriage nor had anyone looked upon children whom he knew to be his own; nor had they learned the advantages of an equitable code of law. And so through their ignorance and error blind and unreasoning passion satisfied itself by misuse of bodily strength, which is a very dangerous servant.

At this juncture a man—great and wise I am sure—became aware of the power latent in man and the wide field offered by his mind for great achievements if one could develop this power and improve it by instruction. Men were scattered in the fields and hidden in sylvan retreats when he assembled and gathered them in accordance with a plan; he introduced them to every useful and honourable occupation, though they cried out against it at first because of its novelty, and then when through reason and eloquence they had listened with greater attention, he transformed them from wild savages into a kind and gentle folk.

We would now say that Cicero's mythic story was not accurate in detail. But his general idea—that communication and reasoning brought humans to a more elevated level of civilization—seems to have a kernel of truth to it. "Reason and eloquence"—what Mercier and Sperber would more quietly call argumentation and persuasion—are essential to coordination, cooperation, and the possibility of social life. That is why arguing is a fundamental human process.

Summary

The purpose of this first chapter has been to settle on some common vocabulary and concepts. We have reviewed several different but useful ways of describing an argument—a syllogism, an argument scheme, a Toulmin model, an enthymeme, a three-turn sequence, and a critical discussion. In all of these descriptions, we can see people moving from an accepted basis to a conclusion that was not originally obvious. In this way, we generate meanings. The meanings may be about substance ("Income taxes are too high") but they will also be about identities ("I am a thoughtful person") and relationships ("We can work this out together").

We have also examined a productive way to understand how people produce arguments, the SGPA. People come into contact with a situation that stimulates a primary goal, the goal suggests a message, the message is tested against many goals, it is revised or replaced if necessary, and finally a private thought becomes a public argument. Each of the elements of the SGPA deserves scrutiny, and we will explore each of them in the book.

And finally we have seen that arguing is a basic feature of human life. It is not something that happens occasionally, nor is it restricted to one or two sorts of interaction. It certainly does not inherently involve uncontrolled emotional displays. We experience our essential sociality in great part through the experience of producing and receiving arguments. A better understanding of what is going on when we exchange reasons should lead to insight about our lives.

References

Aakhus, M. (2003). Neither naïve nor critical reconstruction: Dispute mediators, impasse, and the design of argumentation. *Argumentation, 17*, 265–290.
Aakhus, M. (2007). Communication as design. *Communication Monographs, 74*, 112–117.
Aristotle. (1984). *Rhetoric*. (W. R. Roberts, Trans.). In J. Barnes (Ed.), *The complete works of Aristotle* (2 Vols). Princeton, NJ: Princeton University Press.
Bitzer, L. F. (1959). Aristotle's enthymeme revisited. *Quarterly Journal of Speech, 45*, 399–408.
Blair, J. A. (2011). Informal logic and its early historical development. *Studies in Logic, 4*, 1–16.
Bradbury, J. W., & Vehrencamp, S. L. (1998). *Principles of animal communication*. Sunderland, MA: Sinauer Associates.
Bright, M. (1984). *Animal language*. Ithaca, NY: Cornell University Press.
Buss, D. M. (1995). Evolutionary psychology: A new paradigm. *Psychological Inquiry, 6*, 1–30.
Cicero, M. T. (1960). *De Inventione*. (H. M. Hubbell, Trans.). Cambridge, MA: Loeb Classical Library.
Cosmides, L., & Tooby, J. (1992). Cognitive adaptations for social exchange. In J. H. Barkow, L. Cosmides, & J. Tooby (Eds.), *The adapted mind: Evolutionary psychology and the generation of culture* (pp. 163–228). New York, NY: Oxford University Press.
Coulter, J. (1990). Elementary properties of argument sequences. In G. Psathas (Ed.), *Interaction competence* (pp. 181–203). Lanham, MD: University Press of America.
Dillard, J. P. (1990a). A goal-driven model of interpersonal influence. In J. P. Dillard (Ed.), *Seeking compliance: The production of interpersonal influence messages* (pp. 41–56). Scottsdale, AZ: Gorsuch Scarisbrick.
Dillard, J. P. (1990b). The nature and substance of goals in tactical communication. In M. J. Cody & M. J. McLaughlin (Eds.), *The psychology of tactical communication* (pp. 70–91). Philadelphia, PA: Multilingual Matters.
Dillard, J. P. (2004). The goals-plans-action model of interpersonal influence. In J. S. Seiter & R. H. Gass (Eds.), *Perspective on persuasion, social influence, and compliance gaining* (pp. 185–206). Boston, MA: Allyn & Bacon.
Dillard, J. P., Segrin, C., & Harden, J. M. (1989). Primary and secondary goals in the production of interpersonal influence messages. *Communication Monographs, 56*, 19–38.
Dillard, J. P., & Solomon, D. H. (2000). Conceptualizing context in message-production research. *Communication Theory, 10*, 167–175.

van Eemeren, F. H., & Grootendorst, R. (1983). *Speech acts in argumentative discussions.* Dordrecht: Foris.
van Eemeren, F. H., & Grootendorst, R. (1992). *Argumentation, communication, and fallacies: A pragma-dialectical approach.* Hillsdale, NJ: Lawrence Erlbaum Associates.
van Eemeren, F. H., & Grootendorst, R. (2004). *A systematic theory of argumentation: The pragma-dialectical approach.* Cambridge: Cambridge University Press.
Grice, H. P. (1975). Logic and conversation. In P. Cole & J. L. Morgan (Eds.), *Syntax and semantics, vol. 3: Speech acts* (pp. 41–58). New York, NY: Academic Press.
Hample, D. (2009). Argument: Its origin, function, and structure. In D. S. Gouran (Ed.), *The functions of argument and social context* (pp. 1–10). Alta, UT: National Communication Association.
Hample, D., Dai, Y., & Zhan, M. (2016). Argument stakes: Preliminary conceptualizations and empirical descriptions. *Argumentation and Advocacy, 52*, 199–213.
Hample, D., & Dallinger, J. M. (1987). Cognitive editing of argument strategies. *Human Communication Research, 14*, 123–144.
Hample, D., Richards, A. S., & Skubisz, C. (2013). Blurting. *Communication Monographs, 80*, 503–532.
Jackson, S., & Jacobs, S. (1980). Structure of conversational argument: Pragmatic bases for the enthymeme. *Quarterly Journal of Speech, 66*, 251–265.
Johnson, R. H. (2000). *Manifest rationality: A pragmatic theory of argument.* Mahwah, NJ: Lawrence Erlbaum.
Kelman, H. C. (1958). Compliance, identification, and internalization: Three processes of attitude change. *Journal of Conflict Resolution, 2*, 51–60.
Kopperschmidt, J. (1985). An analysis of argumentation. In T. A. van Dijk (Ed.), *Handbook of discourse analysis, vol. 2* (pp. 159–168). London: Academic Press.
Kuhn, D. (1991). *The skills of argument.* Cambridge: Cambridge University Press.
McLaughlin, M. L. (1984). *Conversation: How talk is organized.* Beverly Hills, CA: Sage.
Mercier, H. (2016). The argumentative theory: Predictions and empirical evidence. *Trends in Cognitive Sciences, 20*, 689–700.
Mercier, H., & Sperber, D. (2011). Why do humans reason? Arguments for an argumentation theory. *Behavioral and Brain Sciences, 34*, 57–111.
Mercier, H., & Sperber, D. (2017). *The enigma of reason.* Cambridge, MA: Harvard University Press.
Meyer, J. R. (1997). Cognitive influences on the ability to address interaction goals. In J. O. Greene (Ed.), *Message production: Advances in communication theory* (pp. 71–90). Mahwah, NJ: Lawrence Erlbaum Associates.
Muntigl, P., & Turnbull, W. (1998). Conversational structure and facework in arguing. *Journal of Pragmatics, 29*, 225–256.
Nickerson, R. S. (1998). Confirmation bias: A ubiquitous phenomenon in many guises. *Review of General Psychology, 2*, 175–220.
O'Keefe, D. J. (1977). Two concepts of argument. *Journal of the American Forensic Association, 13*, 121–128.

Perelman, Ch., & Olbrechts-Tyteca, L. (1969). *The new rhetoric: A treatise on argumentation.* J. Wilkinson & P. Weaver (Trans.). Notre Dame, IN: University of Notre Dame Press.

Popper, K. (1959). *The logic of scientific discovery.* New York, NY: Routledge.

Richards, A. S. (2012, November). *Survival of the persuasible: An evolutionary approach to interpersonal influence based on nonverbal source characteristics.* Paper presented at the annual conference of the National Communication Association, Orlando, FL.

Richards, A. S., & Hample, D. (2016). Facial similarity mitigates the persuasive effects of source bias: An evolutionary explanation for kinship and susceptibility to influence. *Communication Monographs, 83,* 1–24.

Rossano, M. J. (2003). *Evolutionary psychology: The science of human behavior and evolution.* Hoboken, NJ: John Wiley & Sons.

Santibáñez Yáñez, C. (2012). Mercier and Sperber's argumentative theory of reasoning: From the psychology of reasoning to argumentation studies. *Informal Logic, 32,* 132–159.

Schiffrin, D. (1985). Everyday argument: The organization of diversity in talk. In T. A. van Dijk (Ed.), *Handbook of discourse analysis, vol. 3* (pp. 35–46). London: Academic Press.

Schrader, D. C., & Dillard, J. P. (1998). Goal structures and interpersonal influence. *Communication Studies, 49,* 276–293.

Searcy, W. A., & Nowicki, S. (2005). *The evolution of animal communication.* Princeton, NJ: Princeton University Press.

Swann, W. B. Jr., & Rentfrow, P. J. (2001). Blirtatiousness: Cognitive, behavioral, and physiological consequences of rapid responding. *Journal of Personality and Social Psychology, 81,* 1160–1175.

Toulmin, S. (1958). *The uses of argument.* Cambridge: Cambridge University Press.

Walton, D., Reed, C., & Macagno, F. (2008). *Argumentation schemes.* Cambridge: Cambridge University Press.

Watzlawick, P., Beavin, J. H., & Jackson, D. D. (1967). *Pragmatics of human communication.* New York, NY: Norton.

CHAPTER TWO

Argument Frames

Sometimes an interpersonal argument takes us by surprise and we only realize what is happening once it is under way. Other times we can see that an argument or disagreement is just about to happen. Sometimes we are the instigator: we might decide to "have it out" well in advance of the interaction, or perhaps we simply take a conversational opportunity to make a point. But whether we plan the episode or just find ourselves enmeshed in it, we have some experiential awareness: we know we are in an argument. We might privately think of it as a discussion, a conflict, a fight, or something else, but these are just common ways of labeling arguments. There is a disagreement, one or the other of us is providing reasons of some sort, and we realize it.

What do we actually think is going on? That is the topic of this chapter. Small children don't have very much reflective awareness of their communication activities. They just do the next thing and express their impulses. But as we grow older, we naturally begin to notice that there are different sorts of conversations—joking, encouraging, comforting, explaining, and disagreeing, for example. Recognizing a "sort" of communication episode is a big step toward abstracting it and being reflective about it. People mature in this respect at different rates and some adults have more sophisticated understandings about a particular kind of interaction than others do. Arguing seems to be something that different people have quite distinguishable levels of understanding about.

The argument frames project (Hample, 2003, 2005a, 2005b) was begun to answer the question, "What do people think they are doing when they are arguing?" The idea was to capture people's understandings and expectations about the process of arguing face to face.

A frame refers to an interpretive context. A picture frame directs your attention to what is inside the frame because it defines the boundaries of what to look at and gives a special standing to whatever is inside. The difference between a child's framed elementary school drawing and something that is just scrawled onto the living room wall when no one was watching is that the first one is officially "art" and the second one isn't. In an analogous way, a conceptual frame (for arguing or anything else) tells us what to look for, what is seeable. Frames for arguing tell us what arguments are for, what they do, how they feel, and what they are like. The frames are subjectively experienced, of course, but many of them are common enough that generalizations about various groups of people can be drawn. This chapter will be restricted to the basic ideas of frames, with data drawn from U.S. undergraduates and somewhat older adults. In Chapter 7, I will examine how people from other nations use these same frames.

The Three Sets of Frames

Even at the start of the work, it was understood that people think many things about arguing, and that not everyone would have the same ideas. In fact, they might not even have the same categories of ideas about what the experience of arguing entailed. Based on some early theorizing many candidate constructs were conceived, and then I moved immediately to trying to capture those concepts with self-report scales. Some of the early candidates were abandoned because I could not operationalize them properly, and probably had not conceptualized them precisely enough. There is no reason to suppose that the current list of frames is complete, but the list that is presented in this chapter has been the topic of some informative research. The actual self-report instrument is in the Appendix of the book.

Later in the chapter, I will report various average scores on the frames scales. If you are interested in seeing how your views compare with those of other people, I suggest you respond to the Appendix items now, before you read how the scores are interpreted. If you read the chapter first, you may get some ideas about what the "right" answers are, and that might unconsciously influence your responses.

The frames are conceptualized as falling into three general sets. These groups are in order of sophistication. No research on children has been done to date, but it seems likely that the frames are probably also in order of developmental acquisition. The basic ordering is that the first set of frames only concerns self, the second set takes the other person into consideration, and the third set summarizes abstract reflections about arguing considered as a sort of interpersonal interaction.

First-Order Frames: Pursuing Own Goals

The first set of frames concerns personal motivations for arguing. These are the reasons a person argues ("reasons" in the general sense of motives or impulses, not in the sense of evidence for something). If a friend or romantic partner gave you reasons—made an argument—why you should pick up a pizza on the way home and you asked him or her, "Why are you saying that?" the answer would probably be, "To get some pizza." If we included all the answers of that sort, we would have a very long list indeed. So it was obvious that some abstraction and categorization had to be done on our part. Based on my theoretical thinking as well as my efforts to measure things properly, I ended up with four first-order frames: utility, identity display, dominance assertion, and play. In responding to the relevant instruments, people simultaneously indicate what they do themselves and what they notice when other people argue.

Utility is a member of the first group of frames. By utility I mean that a person argues for a practical reason: to get something, to avoid some disagreeable possibility, to obtain some personal benefit. So under this heading we would include arguments intended to get pizza, to dodge having to attend a family picnic, or to borrow someone's laptop. If you look to the Appendix, you will see that people who have high scores on utility respond very positively to items like, "When I argue with someone it is to get what I want," and "Arguing is meant to resolve issues."

Most argumentation theory presumes that arguing is done for practical (utilitarian) reasons. Arguing is generally theorized as a means of persuasion or as a way of finding out the truth to settle some matter. As you will see momentarily, these are not actually the only reasons that people argue. However, utility is probably the motive that gives interpersonal arguing its most basic nature. The arguer finds some agreeable starting point and reasons from there, until the other person comes to some new conclusion about the topic. The idea is to lead the other person to some thought that the initiating arguer had in the first place, a thought that would lead to some benefit for the person who began the argument. As we saw in Chapter 1, Mercier and Sperber (2011, 2017; Mercier, 2016) said that the social need for this sort of activity is what led early humans to develop reasoning skills in the first place.

This means that utility arguing gives definition and direction to the argumentative process. When people argue for other reasons, they still use the forms and tactics of arguments designed for personal benefit. So when we look at particular argumentative exchanges we sometimes see something confusing.

One possible confusion occurs when a utility argument is being used on the surface, but the point of the argument is actually something else. For instance, one spouse might berate the other for being inconsiderate, giving all sorts of evidence and reporting many instances of failure. The apparent utilitarian aim would be to persuade the target that he or she had failed to do errands or help around the house. But the real point of the argument might be to express that the first spouse feels neglected or disrespected. Coser (1956) distinguished between realistic and unrealistic conflicts to make this point. A realistic conflict is one that is actually about what it appears to be. An unrealistic conflict is when the surface conflict and its topic are being used to cover or submerge some underlying issue that the arguer doesn't want to make explicit, or perhaps cannot quite articulate. This is a reminder that every message conveys both content ("pick up around the house") and relational ("respect me more") meaning, as we also saw in Chapter 1 (Watzlawick, Beavin, & Jackson, 1967). When the argument is being used as a vehicle for something other than its substantive reasoning, the relational meanings are probably the real point of what is happening. In that case, it would be an analytical mistake to identify the evidence, warrant, and other content elements and assume that we had thereby analyzed the real argument.

The second possible confusion appears when some other motive appears on the surface, but the real point is some hidden reasoning that aims at a utilitarian objective. For instance, someone might make a joke, but it could be quite a pointed one intended to make a strong argument about some issue (Alberts & Drzewiecka, 2008). A famous example of this is comedian Dick Gregory (1932–2017). Prior to the Civil Rights Movement in the U.S., he was a reasonably popular stand-up comedian. But he became an important civil rights spokesperson and often used his comedy to convey his arguments and also worked humor into his more formal speeches. For example, here is one of his jokes: "For a black man, there's no difference between the North and the South. In the South, they don't mind how close I get, as long as I don't get too big. In the North, they don't mind how big I get, as long as I don't get too close" (http://scomedy.com/quotes/Dick-Gregory). There are certainly arguments here, and they are clearly utilitarian because he wanted people to recognize injustice and set themselves to repair it. But reconstructing this joke to identify the argument's evidence, warrant, and even conclusion would be very challenging. Nonetheless, if we were to have asked Gregory why he made this joke, he would probably have indicated that his main impulses were utility and play, and he would likely have agreed that he was using humor argumentatively.

So even if we understand that utility arguments are probably the base kind, that doesn't mean that they will necessarily be obvious. They may be submerged, as in Dick Gregory's humor, or they can submerge something else, as in the unhappy spouse's complaints. Just as a crescent wrench can be used as a paperweight and not to loosen nuts, the form of a utility argument can be enlisted for other purposes than to obtain benefit for self.

The second of the first-order frames (the self-oriented ones) is argument to display identity. The idea here is that someone makes an argument that may not be controversial at all, but that illustrates some valued element of own identity. For example, a conservative politician addressing a rally of conservative supporters might spend time detailing all the conservative positions he or she had taken. Whether an elected official should be voting conservatively was not an issue for that audience, and presumably they were already aware of the politician's relevant credentials or they would not have attended the rally. But reviewing commitments and giving reasons for them displayed and reinforced the politician's identity. There was no real persuasive aim here because everyone was already in agreement.

A colleague and I did a focused study on arguing to display identity (Hample & Irions, 2015). Among other things, we explained to respondents what an identity display argument was and asked them to describe episodes of that type in which they had argued to exhibit some prized feature of self. Here are some of their answers:

- I was trying to rationalize to my friends why I was going on a community service spring break trip instead of going with them to Panama City. They were not angry nor was it a controversy that I was not going with them but I still felt the need to defend myself and show why I was making the decision. I said that this was my last chance to go on this type of trip before I graduate and it is more important for me in the long run because I am very involved in community service and want to go into a field of nonprofit when I graduate. The other person just said ok and that I didn't need to justify it to them if that is what I want to do and if so then do it. But I still felt judged for the decision I was making.
- In a conversation that was describing my political affiliation and how I identify, I was explaining the reasons why I was conservative, and discussing topics about abortion. I told the other person that I would not get an abortion because my mom doesn't believe in it and I lean to the right. The other person was not hostile and I could tell was trying to be understanding.

☐ In telling my friends I was going home next week for Yom Kippur, they asked me why since I am not religious. I told them it was important to my family to be there, and that my family felt my presence was needed at services twice a year (Rosh Hashanah and Yom Kippur). My friends told me it was weird and that I'd be missing class. I agreed with them. But I reinforced that it was important to my family, so I could not say no.

These are a reasonable sampling of what we found. You can see that people were definitely giving reasons, and that the arguments were supposed to reflect well on the arguer. The first person showed a commitment to community service, the second expressed her conservatism, and the third displayed that family wishes were valued more than personal convenience. These were all elements of own identity that the arguers obviously valued.

Controversy is necessary to bring out a utility argument, but it is not required for an identity display. In the second example, the respondent noted that the other person wasn't hostile, indicating that there was no disagreement in the episode. But in the first example, the person said, "I still felt judged for the decision I was making," and this proposes that the arguer felt that there was some opposition to overcome. And in the third example, "My friends told me it was weird," so again there might have been some persuasion to do. We asked our respondents to say whether they felt there was any controversy involved in the situation in which they had done an identity display argument. They could say "clearly no," "maybe," or "clearly yes." 42% chose "clearly no," 30% "maybe," and 28% "clearly yes."

Those percentages do not suggest any special pattern, any particular theoretical connection, between controversy and identity display arguments, except that controversy is possible but not necessary. A person can initiate an argument for the sole purpose of displaying identity, as in our fictional conservative politician example, or in the case of arguing as part of your answer to an essay question to show how smart you are. Or an opportunity to hold out some valued feature of self might occur in a conversational lull. Or something about self might actually be at issue (is it "weird" to miss class for a religious holiday you don't seem to value?), and the need to defend self is a natural part of the conversation's substantive development. Controversy and disagreement are entirely optional in the case of arguing to display identity, and this underscores a key difference between arguments undertaken for this reason as opposed to utilitarian aims.

A third member of this first self of frames is arguing to assert dominance. Here, the idea is that an arguer more or less "picks a fight" just to show that he or she is in charge, and is entitled to declare what is the correct conclusion. For example, the manager in a fast food restaurant might give reasons why the floor has to be mopped, and stop after every reason to insist that the employee agree. Or perhaps you have had the feeling that a teacher made arguments for or against some social policy just to show that his or her learning and commitments were superior to those of the students.

Arguing is an act of assertiveness. A standard precondition of making an argument, particularly a utilitarian one, is that you think you are right and the other person requires correction. Even if you are polite about what you say, the underlying fact that you think you are superior on this matter cannot be erased because it is true and the other person knows you think so. Therefore dominance is inherently part of the relational level of meaning for many arguments, especially the practical ones. Consequently it is natural, even perceptive, to notice that an arguer is asserting dominance. This recognition may stimulate psychological reactance (Brehm, 1966), which is the tendency to push back when you feel pressured. When people feel that the point of an argument is for the other person to assert dominance over them, the result might be grudging acceptance, resentment, or excessive disagreement, depending on whether the other person really is dominant (e.g., a boss for a job you want to keep) or not (e.g., an annoying acquaintance). Notice that people can mistake the impulse that led to an argument: the initiator may be intending it as utilitarian and even helpful, but the other person might regard it as nothing but a naked power play. Many of us spent a few years of our adolescence assuming that everything our parents said was to assert dominance, but in retrospect they were probably actually trying to guide us constructively.

On the other hand, sometimes people really do initiate an argument just to show that they are entitled to settle it unilaterally. The Appendix reports the items that people agree to when they score high on the dominance frame: for instance, "When I'm in an argument, winning is more important to me than being kind," and "Regardless of what an argument is supposed to be about, it is very often really about who has power over whom." These items display not only the awareness that arguments can be used in this way, but also the report that the respondent carries this awareness into his or her own arguing. How many people keep arguing after they suddenly realize that they are wrong? They are unwilling to admit the truth, because that would place them in an inferior position, at least in the moment.

The difficulty for the argument target is to figure out what motive is predominant: is it to teach you how to manage your finances, or to show off that your parents have money and you don't? If you think back about your adolescent years or a tumultuous romantic relationship, you may realize that this is not always an easy discrimination to make. And it can be even harder to figure out in the middle of an exchange that the other person has in fact realized that you are right, but is now carrying on out of nothing but pride. Pointing this out is not often helpful, by the way. It is just a way of projecting your own superiority.

Asserting dominance is, of course, a sort of identity display. One argues in order to indicate that he or she has a superior job, a better boyfriend, a more reliable car, or more knowledge, and any of these can be a valued element of identity. The reason that these two purposes for arguing are distinguished is that people often react pleasantly to an uncontroversial identity display, but resentfully to dominance assertion. The connection of dominance assertion to the presence of controversy has not been investigated yet, but we might well suppose that some dominance displays involve initiating or pursuing a false controversy that is simply used as a pretext for asserting superiority.

The last of the first-order frames is play. Some readers will find this very odd. I have discovered in teaching that many of my students are astonished that other students enjoy arguing and seek out opportunities for it. The idea is that some people regard arguing as a sort of entertainment. They are not seeking to win the argument, merely to experience it. In fact, sometimes they prefer that the argument never be resolved (Yankees or Red Sox?) so that they can re-engage it in the future. People who score high on this measure (see the Appendix) answer affirmatively to items like these: "Arguing is sometimes just a way of passing the time between two friends," and "Sometimes I say something outrageous, just to have the entertainment of defending it." Interscholastic debating is an activity that attracts people who regard arguing as fun.

Several of us did a focused study on playful arguing, to investigate exactly how playful it really is (Hample, Han, & Payne, 2010). We wondered if it were genuinely enjoyable and recreational, or whether it was like teasing (e.g., Keltner, Young, Heerey, Oemig, & Monarch, 1998), with an uncertain balance of pleasant fun and nasty aggression.

As in the identity study, we asked respondents to share examples of when they had argued playfully. Here are some of their reports:

- It began with a simple, non-significant disagreement over an issue. It continued by the other person pressing on for fun, even though both of us knew that there really was no valid reason for doing so. It ended in a reconciliation, with both of us laughing off the issue.
- I just wanted to tease her, as a friend. She got to laughing about it and decided to join in. We just stopped coming up with funny things to say to each other.

These two descriptions are encouraging. The two partners appeared to be enjoying the interactions, and both of them seemed to understand that the arguing wasn't serious. But here are some other descriptions:

- I decided I wanted to get my friend angry, so I started making fun of him about a certain issue. He got defensive and started making fun of me. I started laughing and just told him I was just messing around.
- I was at work and one of my co-workers made a comment to another one of my co-workers who happens to be in the ROTC program. The comment was something like, "I hate living in this country." The ROTC member first ignored the comment, but you could tell he was deeply offended. My other co-worker would not back down and kept making comments knowing it would get a rise out of the ROTC member. The ROTC member calmly said, "Then why don't you move to another country?" and walked away.

These examples are not encouraging at all. Readers should remember that they were both supplied when we explained what playful arguing is, and asked for an example from the respondent's own experience. So people believed that these arguments were done for fun. But in the first example, the other person became defensive and the respondent just laughed at his or her reaction. In the second example, we can pretty clearly see that the ROTC member did not find any enjoyment in the episode. How could these be labeled "playful?"

The answer is that the respondent thought so, and our reporters were apparently not very perceptive about the other person or perhaps didn't consider that the other person's views were relevant to whether or not the episode was entertaining. Remember that these first-order frames are self-oriented. I will have more to say about this in a moment, but the point here is that *the initiator* was enjoying himself or herself. In the same way, teasers may not understand that they are hurting the other person's feelings, or sexual harassers may not realize that the object of their affections feels threatened by the harasser's position. We may be dealing with what Watzlawick et al. (1967) called impermeability: the failure to register and adapt to the other person's reactions.

So you can see why we wanted to investigate the relationship between playful arguing and aggression. We asked respondents to fill out a great number of self-report instruments, many of which measured one sort of aggressive impulse or another. We found that the respondent's playfulness was correlated with high scores on these instruments: the antisocial subscale of the verbal aggressiveness measure (Infante & Wigley, 1986), psychological reactance (Dowd, Milne, & Wise, 1991), the approach scale of the argumentativeness instrument (Infante & Rancer, 1982), the dominance assertion frame (discussed above), positive valence for conflicts (Hample & Dallinger, 1995), and masculinity (Bem, 1974). In contrast, a high score on the play frame was associated with low scores on these measures: the prosocial subscale of verbal aggressiveness, the avoidance subscale of argumentativeness, the cooperative frame (discussed below), femininity, and the civility frame (discussed below). The profile of the playful arguer, in other words, is that of the aggressor. He or she is acting forcefully and dominantly, not cooperatively or politely.

It is interesting that the playful arguers themselves produced these scores. In other words, it was not the researchers who observed that the playful arguers were being aggressive. The same people who reported that they argue for fun also said that they were aggressive, uncooperative, and impolite. This is self-perceptiveness, to some degree. What they seemed to be lacking was the awareness that the other person was not mirroring their views of the interaction. Like some teasers, people can argue for fun without realizing that the entertainment is not being shared.

Does this mean that all playful arguing is a sham, a cover for interpersonal aggression? Not necessarily. What I think it means is that arguing can only be fun if *both* parties want to argue for entertainment. The essential thing that we found is that playful arguers often seemed to be unconscious of the harm they were doing. Or perhaps they did perceive it, but enjoyed themselves so much that they did not care very much. In either case, arguing playfully is not a very socially advanced activity unless it is clear that the other person is arguing playfully, too. Then it can be genuinely fun for both parties.

Stoltz (2017) has recently distinguished two kinds of playful arguing. These are substantive (like an interscholastic debate) and superficial (like arguing light-heartedly about which sports team is better). This distinction, and people's differing reactions to the two kinds of social interaction, may eventually provide clues that help us understand how and whether two people will both orient themselves to the possible entertainment value of arguing, or will find themselves out of sync and annoyed.

These, then, are the first-order frames: utility, identity display, dominance assertion, and play. They have some things in common, most fundamentally that they are all experienced from the point of view of only one person, the initiator. In this, they are like the primary goals of the SGPA model from Chapter 1. Obviously, two people are going to be involved in any interpersonal argument, but arguers may or may not see the other participant as a genuine person. By this I mean that as far as these frames are concerned, the other person is just a foil, a means to get what the initiator wants. Benefits are extracted from the other person, one's identity is displayed to a more or less passive listener, dominance is projected onto a lesser person, and the other is used as a playing partner. If these are the only reasons that a person has for arguing, we can see that arguing will be a very self-oriented activity for him or her. The other person has to be there, has to listen, and must respond as wanted, but does not really have to be taken into account or adapted to. These are matters that arise only when we consider the second-order frames.

Second-Order Frames: Respecting the Other Arguer

As we move conceptually to the second-order frames, we begin to encounter the possibility of seeing the other arguer as a genuine person, possessed of legitimate beliefs, attitudes, values, and goals. Successful persuaders (those making utility arguments, for instance) will of course have adapted to the other person's beliefs and attitudes, but may have done so only for the purpose of manipulation, not out of respect. A car salesperson will notice the color of the clothes you are wearing and use this information to choose what color of car to show you, but not because the salesperson actually approves of your fashion sense. What is being measured with these second-order frames is the degree to which the arguer sees the other person as deserving of respect, as having wishes whose importance is on a par with the initiator's. The philosopher Henry Johnstone, Jr. (1982) wrote about the idea of "bilaterality" in ideal arguments. In contrast to unilateral arguments in which the arguer only respects his or her own thoughts and commitments, in bilateral arguing both people give equal weight to both arguers' needs and thoughts, and are truly open to the possibility that the other person might be right. People approach bilaterality (or not) in some degree, and that is the general impulse that the second-order frames try to capture.

The second-order frames are blurting, cooperation, and civility. People with low scores on blurting and high scores for cooperation and civility are those who participate most fully in the second-order project of genuinely respecting the other person in an argument. These frames are theorized to be more advanced than the first set because these require not only a commitment to self but also a commitment to the other person.

The second-order frames are not alternatives to the first-order ones. Arguers still need motivations to argue, and they will still want to accomplish practical aims, show themselves off, or play. Even sophisticated people still like it if someone else picks up the pizza. The question is how they go about it—unilaterally, forcefully, and closed-mindedly, or with respect for the other person. Enacting other-respecting behaviors like being polite is only part of what is going on here. The idea is that surface consideration follows from inner conviction, not just obedience to social conventions.

Blurting is the first of the second-order frames. People who blurt just say what is on their minds without adapting what they say to make it more suitable for the other person. Editors are the opposite of blurters. Editors have a thought but then immediately estimate how it will be received and then reshape their message before they say it (Hample, 2005a; Hample & Dallinger, 1987; Meyer, 1997). The Appendix has the items that blurters agree with: for example, "Sometimes when I think of a really good point to make, I just can't stop myself from making it, even if I should," and "In an argument, if I think it, I will say it." Blurting is not necessarily due to some sort of cognitive or developmental deficit (although little children can be entertaining to listen to in this regard). Blurters often believe that it is dishonest to think one thing and say another, and that they should get social approval because other people "always know where they stand with me." They just have a different understanding of how social interaction ought to proceed. B. O'Keefe (1988) would say that they have an "expressive" message design logic.

Three of us set out to study blurters explicitly (Hample, Richards, & Skubisz, 2013). One of the first things we established in that study was that in fact blurters (people with high scores on the blurting frame instrument in the Appendix) edited fewer of their messages than other people did. It was the editors who were trying to connect suitably with the other arguers, of course. The blurters were resisting participation in second-order understandings of an argument episode.

However, being a blurter is not a yes-or-no sort of thing. Everyone is spontaneous sometimes, and everyone at least occasionally gives careful consideration to how to say something. Consequently, we asked people to give us two examples out of their own experience: one in which they blurted, and one in which they almost blurted but stopped themselves.

Here are some examples of when respondents said they blurted:

- I was in a fight with my best friend. We rarely fight. We were fighting because of another person, not because one of us did something wrong. I was in my dorm room and we were not fighting in person, but rather through texting, because we are both not confrontational. I criticized her mentality and called her immature. I said that we could no longer be friends and asked for money back that I had lent her.
- I was with my grandparents leaving our church for my little brother's first communion when I realized my car had been stolen. I was clearly frustrated and annoyed at the situation. I screamed out "God Dammit, my car got stolen from a church??" Meanwhile, my grandparents looked at me in shock and close to 50 people walking out of the church heard me as well.
- (I was) arguing with my sister when I was 12 and she was 13. I screamed, "I hate you" during an argument.

By the fact that these were reported to us as blurts, we can be confident that we are seeing things that people wish they had not said. The remarks were hurtful, or embarrassing, or inappropriate. They did not show respect for the other person or conventional conversational behavior. We asked a follow-up question, inquiring why the episode was being labeled as a blurt. The main answers were that it was offensive (39%), that there were or could have been negative consequences (20%), that the speaker regretted saying it (17%), that it was actually not true (12%), and that it was embarrassing to the speaker (6%).

We may be able to see some of these same self-recognitions when we examine the examples of episodes when people were tempted to blurt, but pulled back and either edited or stayed silent at the last moment. Here are a few of those reports:

- My girlfriend was discussing something that her friends had done, and I don't particularly like her friends or how they act. I thought that her friends were acting like whores but chose not to say that.
- In my apartment of six girls, we have an agreement that if you use a dish or utensil or cup, you have to wash it yourself. However, more than often half of the girls do not carry their weight and do not do what they are supposed to, and the other three of us are left cleaning all of their stuff in addition to our own. It had gotten to the point where we got so fed up of them not cleaning up after themselves that we just refused to wash their things, and there just became a massive pile of dishes piling up in our kitchen sink. I wanted to tell them off and say that I was sick and tired of living in their filth and that it is very disrespectful of them to not carry their weight like the rest of us do. I didn't do anything. We decided to make a sign asking to "please do your dishes" and hang it up over the sink. It worked for about a week and then everything went back to the way it used to be before the sign.
- I was serving a table of 5 people. The bill came out to 80 dollars and they decided to tip me a dollar. When in reality the service I was providing wasn't great but wasn't bad by any means. (I thought) that these people are cheap and have no respect for people. Maybe they were racist towards me. I said, "Thanks, have a good night."

Our respondents didn't say why they declined to express their thoughts (we didn't ask them to), but we can pretty clearly see that they realized that their first impulse was hurtful or inappropriate or might have started a nasty interaction. In the first example, our respondent just said nothing, but in the other instances they made a sign ("please do your dishes") or said something innocuous ("Have a good night") and did not express their true feelings. In our study, we examined what people said or did instead of their first thought. More than half (54%) said nothing, and 46% did some sort of editing and then spoke. Of those who edited, 86% said that they made a kinder, gentler remark, and 14% changed the conversation to a somewhat related topic. So when gripped by a nasty impulse, if people didn't blurt it out, most just swallowed their thought and tried not to give a hint of what they were actually thinking. Only about 40% (46% times 86%) actually edited themselves to produce a more socially satisfactory remark. When we compared people's ratings of the situations in which they blurted or didn't blurt, one standout result was that there were much higher potential relational consequences in the non-blurting episodes. This suggests that people were more likely to blurt when they didn't care very much about the social stakes.

We were very interested in learning what sort of people blurt the most, so we asked everyone to fill out a number of other instruments. A first group of interesting results concerned the other frames. Blurters (compared to people with lower scores on the blurting instrument) tended to have higher scores on the first-order frames. I will give frame-to-frame correlations later in the chapter, but for now it is enough to notice that blurters were more insistent about arguing for utility, identity display, play, and especially for dominance assertion. They also had lower scores on cooperation, civility, and professional contrast, the frames that we will examine next.

The other thing we did was to ask people to fill out measures of other communication or personality traits. Blurting had positive correlations with the antisocial subscale of verbal aggressiveness (Infante & Wigley, 1986), indirect interpersonal aggression (e.g., gossiping behind someone's back; Beatty, Valencic, Rudd & Dobos, 1999), psychological reactance (Dowd et al., 1991; Hong & Faedda, 1996), sensation seeking (Kalichman & Rompa, 1995), masculinity (Bem, 1974), spontaneity (Swann & Rentfrow, 2001), impulsiveness (Stanford et al., 2009), and the psychoticism, extraversion, and neuroticism scales that form the Big Three inventory of personality supertraits (Eysenck, Eysenck, & Barrett, 1985). So blurters tend to be more aggressive and impulsive than other people. They are that way in their lives and particularly in their arguing. They do and say what they want, and do not take other people into account in shaping their actions and expressions. But it is worth remembering that this is a matter of degree, and that everyone blurts sometimes and edits sometimes as well.

People can adapt to others competitively or cooperatively, and this brings us to the next second-order frame, cooperation. Competitors notice the other's goals, but try to overwhelm those wishes with their own or use the other person's motivations manipulatively, in a sort of argumentative judo. Cooperation involves taking up the other's motivations and trying to help the other accomplish his or her aims at the same time that the initiator pursues his or her own. As the Appendix indicates, cooperators agree with items such as "A genuine agreement from the other person is more satisfying to me than a forced agreement" and "The other person's needs are really an important consideration to me when I'm trying to settle a disagreement with him or her." The idea is that in an argument, a cooperator tries to meet the other's needs not only on the disputed topic but also on the matters that give rise to it.

Cooperation is unlikely without being perceptive about what the other person thinks and wants. But being perceptive is only the first requirement. The next step, the one that determines whether an arguer is being cooperative or competitive, involves how that information informs one's argument. Taking a win/lose approach to a disagreement ("whatever I win has to be a loss for you") is competitive. The cooperative orientation is win/win ("we need to find a way for both of us to come out ahead, or at least no worse off than we started"). Competitors demand; cooperators discuss. As long as reasons are given, both demanding and discussing are arguments. But the cooperative reasons have a different character because they integrate the other person's position with one's own.

So cooperation is outward looking, whereas competition is solely rooted in oneself. Impulses that do not respect the other person—the aggressiveness we have seen connected to blurting and play, for instance—are not consistent with a cooperative frame. Later in the chapter we will see that cooperation is not empirically consistent with play or blurting, or with aggressively oriented personality traits either. Many people immediately identify arguing with verbal fighting, and this leads them away from any understanding that disagreements can be conducted without needing to sacrifice one person's values for those of the other. Cooperation is a more advanced frame than competition.

The last of the second-order frames is civility. Here the issue is how people expect arguments to be conducted. Some naturally suppose that an argument will be emotional, irrational, loud, and closed-minded. Others see, expect, and perhaps insist upon the opposite possibilities. The Appendix indicates that there are ten items to the civility scale, and they differ in their directionality. Agreement with some shows that the respondent expects civility and agreement with the others reflects the expectation of nastiness when people exchange reasons in disagreement. When people have high scores for civility, they agree that arguments involve cooperation by the parties, positive relational outcomes when the arguments are over, successful problem-solving, and a genuine exchange of views by both parties. Civility-expecting arguers disagree with the following descriptions of arguing: loud and negative voices, closed-mindedness by the parties, irrational emotional displays, negative relational outcomes, hostility, and physical violence. People who do not expect civility have the opposite reactions to those items, of course.

The point about physical violence is a particularly important one. Arguments are verbal and only have an inherent physical character insofar as the body is involved in making words and gestures. Argumentation scholars often suggest that arguing is an alternative to violence (e.g., Perelman & Olbrechts-Tyteca, 1969), and nearly everyone's parents encouraged them to "use your words" when engaged in a disagreement.

However, everyone does not share this understanding. One theory of domestic violence is, to simplify, that people hit because they cannot argue well (Infante, Chandler, & Rudd, 1989). They think they are right, but they cannot quite say why, or cannot explain themselves in an effective way. So instead of preventing violence, arguing becomes a step toward it for these people.

When I first encountered evidence for this, I was quite surprised. I was doing a study with some graduate students in which we were trying to describe the steps involved in conflictive conversations (Hample, Dean, Johnson, Kopp, & Ngoitz, 1997). Using an open-ended instrument, we asked people to write down what they would do or say during an argument, step by step. Our most general results were not especially remarkable: the first step was initiation (realizing there was a disagreement), the second was development (criticizing, becoming defensive), the third was maintenance of the dispute (feelings of anger, listening), and the last was completion (calm, compromise). The surprise came when I saw that physical violence was often included as an element of maintenance. Fully 5% of our respondents indicated that throwing objects could be a part of an interpersonal argument, 5% included threats (including physical threats), 9% mentioned swearing, 27% mentioned anger, and 42% included physical violence in their descriptions. I hasten to explain that we weren't asking people how every argument proceeds. We were just asking what *could* happen in argument considered generally. So the results do not mean that 42% of our respondents experienced physical violence in all their arguments. But the results do mean that 42% of our respondents have a "slot" in their argument schema for violence, so that they know right where it will occur if it happens. For them, violence belongs in a full description of interpersonal arguing.

As I said, I was surprised by this. I had been educated to believe as Perelman and Olbrechts-Tyteca and so many others did, that arguing is a productive and peaceful way to work through our disagreements. In fact, I remember that when I first saw descriptions of kicking and hitting in respondents' protocols, I honestly thought that they were not being responsible about doing the survey. But as the data piled up, I had to take it seriously.

So I participated in three studies with Pamela Benoit to explore this finding (Benoit & Hample, 1998; Hample & Benoit, 1999; Hample et al., 1999). We were interested in the connection between the perceived explicitness and perceived destructiveness of arguments. That is, the more obvious it was that an argument was going on (i.e., that it was explicitly an argument), would people also think that it was more destructive? In a word, yes. Arguments can be explicit ("I disagree with that") or implicit (one person makes a claim, and the other grimaces and goes to another room), and of course this is a matter of degree. Whether we had people self-report their own arguments or had them respond to arguments we described to them, the more obviously an interaction was an argument, the more destructive people thought it was. In fact, the correlations between explicitness and destructiveness ranged from $r = .50$ to as high as $r = .80$, depending on the study conditions. The destructiveness measures included reference to both relational damage and physical violence.

So saying that you expect arguments to be conducted in a civil manner is not a small thing. Quite a few people expect the opposite, and the clearer the argumentative nature of the episode is, the more worried people become. Every close relationship involves disagreement of some sort because people are not identical in what they want, or in what position they are in relative to something anyone would want. By the latter, I mean for example that we both might want fruit pie, but I want you to bake it and you want me to do the cooking. To be able to work through these mundane disagreements without relational breakage, physical harm, or emotional flooding is obviously an important adult accomplishment. People vary in the degree to which they expect this to happen, and that is what the civility instrument measures. Civility requires respect for the other person.

These, then, are the second-order frames: blurting, cooperation, and civility. Scores on these scales indicate the degree to which people's understandings of interpersonal arguments accommodate the other person. To blurt without concern for how the other person will take it, to force your point of view while ignoring the other's, and to conduct yourself in an uncivilized way—these are all self-centered arrogances. Everyone puts self first fairly often, but some people are notable for their concern for others. When you expect editing, cooperation, and civility from yourself and others, you are well into second-order framing for arguments.

The Third Frame: Reflective Understandings of Arguing

The first-order frames dealt with self's motives and the second-order frames described how (and whether) the initiator takes the other person into account. The third-order frame (it only has one scale) considers how people conceive the general idea of arguing. This requires that the person has abstracted the activity and can label it (or recognize it) as an "argument." This abstract idea can have a number of interpretations, and some of these are more sophisticated than others.

The scale, called professional contrast, actually originated in an examination of some leading differences between how ordinary people often understand arguing, contrasted with how argumentation scholars understand it (Hample, 2003). I have already mentioned one clear difference, the one dealing with whether arguing is an alternative to violence or an invitation to it. There are others as well, and the items for the scale (see the Appendix) attempt to express them. The contrasts are presented as bipolar items, and respondents indicate which pole they find most accurate, and to what degree. Here is the set of contrasts:

> competition v. cooperation
> aggression v. assertiveness
> uncontrolled emotionality v. reason giving
> violence v. pacifism
> dominance v. issue resolution
> personally punishing v. personally satisfying
> relationally damaging v. relationally developmental

I have arranged the items so that the argumentation scholars' general view is on the right, and the less sophisticated understanding is on the left.

Readers may immediately have the reaction that this is an elitist measure, valorizing professors' theories over the common sense of ordinary actors. That may be so, but I don't apologize for it. The centuries of study and the library shelves full of researchers' best thinking should be respected until disproved. The belief that everyone is entitled to an opinion does not logically imply that all opinions have the same merit, which is an unfortunate impression that some people have (Kuhn, 1991). Some opinions should be weightier, and I straightforwardly propose that the views of argumentation scholars about arguing genuinely have more value than the opinions of other people.

At any rate, the items above are the professional contrast scale. It is scored so that people with high scores are the ones who most agree with the professional judgments. By examining the items, you will see that the scholars believe that arguing should be essentially cooperative and assertive but not aggressive, that it should feature reasoning rather than emotional explosions, that it is an alternative to violence and a route to issue resolution, and that it ought to be personally satisfying and constructive within personal relationships.

This does not mean that the professionals think that all arguments meet these standards, of course. We are quite aware that there are awful arguments that explode and make things worse, sometimes much worse. In fact, we often study these possibilities and try to account for them. The pragma-dialecticians say that these arguments are "derailed," which I have always thought was a nice term for it (van Eemeren & Grootendorst, 2004). The assumption behind describing a bad argument as derailed is that the argument was on a good course to begin with, or could have been, and something (perhaps an inappropriate conversational move) threw it off the tracks. I am encouraged by the optimism of thinking that the natural course of an argument is to be on the tracks, and hope that readers can arrange or rearrange their lives so that the assumption makes sense to you, if it doesn't already.

Inspection of the items should make you suspect that the professional contrast scores are correlated with those from the second-order instruments, and this is so. For example, one of the professional contrast items mentions cooperation, which is one of the second-order scales, and civility is implied by the items about emotionality and issue resolution. Professional contrast scores therefore tend to be positively associated with the civility and cooperation scales, and negatively with blurting scores. Professional contrast scores do not have any special connections with several of the first-order frames, because one can argue for utility, for instance, from either a sophisticated or unsophisticated point of view about arguing. Dominance displays, however, do not match what professionals think is an appropriate use for arguing.

Summary: The Idea of Argument Frames

Together, the various frames instruments were intended to give a sketch of people's main views about the activity of arguing. The originating question was, "What do ordinary arguers think they are doing when they argue?" Some other instruments have also been designed to approach this question (Johnson, 2002; Rancer, Kosberg, & Baukus, 1992), and they have also produced worthwhile results.

The frames instruments deal with people's motives, understandings, and expectations about arguing. Several leading motives are included: utility, identity display, dominance assertion, and play. These may not be the only things that stimulate someone to argue, but they seem to describe a good range of impulses. The ways in which people argue—primarily theorized as they way they connect with the other people—are characterized as blurting (versus adaptive editing), cooperating (versus competing), and being civil (versus nasty). All these first- and second-order scales reflect not only what the respondent does and thinks, but also the things that he or she expects of other people. The last frame, measured with the professional contrast scale, was developed to summarize ordinary people's own theories about arguing. They may understand it as inherently productive or destructive, and those understandings will of course guide people as they participate, once they have realized that they are in an argument.

Empirical Results

A number of studies dealing with argument frames have been conducted, and there is enough data now to draw some fairly firm conclusions. In this chapter, I will restrict myself to the data gathered in the United States. The data from other nations is summarized in Chapter 7, which discusses argument and culture.

Most of the data came from undergraduates at the University of Maryland, which is a large selective public university in the U.S. I also gathered data from adults in the U.S., partly to see whether people have the same scores at different ages and partly to compare with adult samples from other nations.

In this portion of the chapter, I will share several sets of results. First, we will examine whether undergraduates and somewhat older adults have similar scores. Then we will contrast men and women on the instruments. Next, we will see what the empirical associations among the frames instruments are. Finally, we will review some of the correlations between the frames instruments and several personality instruments that have already been mentioned in this chapter.

Undergraduates and Older Adults

The undergraduate data was all collected at the University of Maryland. Students completed the instruments online in exchange for some minor extra credit in their courses. In some studies, the students were Communication majors and tended to be juniors and seniors. In other studies, respondents were mainly students taking some general education courses, and they tended to be freshmen and sophomores. The older adult data was gathered using mTurk, a commercial data-gathering tool operated by Amazon (see Sheehan & Pittman, 2016). Participants are paid for completing surveys. Each of the adults received $0.50 for completing the survey, which was also provided online. The average age for the undergraduates was 21, and the older adults averaged 36 years of age.

Let us see whether the adults and undergraduates had different scores. College students are now called "emerging adults," a phrase that indicates that they are approaching stable adult values in their traits and orientations. Although there is controversy about this claim's details, a general guide to the relationship between personality and age is that personality traits are fairly enduring after age 30 (Costa & McCrae, 1988) and were substantially affected by heredity in the first place

(Polderman, et al., 2015). Table 2.1 shows comparisons between the older adult and undergraduate samples, and reports whether the observed differences were statistically significant.

Table 2.1: Comparisons of U.S. Adults and Undergraduates on Frames Measures

	Adults	Undergraduates	t	r^2
Utility	5.16	5.43	2.68**	.01
Identity Display	6.17	6.60	3.86***	.02
Dominance Assertion	4.18	4.55	2.68**	.01
Play	3.92	4.52	3.69***	.01
Blurting	5.17	5.20	0.24 ns (p = .81)	
Cooperation	6.99	6.89	0.92 ns (p = .36)	
Civility	6.04	6.32	2.66**	.01
Professional Contrast	6.69	6.50	1.26 ns (p = .21)	

Note. All means are on a 1 to 10 scale, meaning that 5.5 is the theoretical middle score. All t tests are two-tailed, with corrections for unequal variances. Sample sizes were 256 for the adult sample and 880 for the undergraduate sample.
** p < .01; *** p < .001.

All of the first-order frame scores were different between the two groups, with the undergraduates having higher scores for each of the reasons for arguing. Very little variance (the r^2 values) was explained by the fact that respondents were in different age groups. However, on a 10 point scale, several of the mean differences were about half a scale point. This indicates that the differences were not dramatic, but they were clearly present. The undergraduates were more sensitive to, or inclined to argue to pursue, utility, identity display, dominance assertion, and play. These results are quite consistent with the fact that undergraduates also had higher scores on argument approach (5.68 versus 5.27, t = 3.07, p < .01, r^2 = .01) and the antisocial part of the verbal aggressiveness measure (4.42 versus 3.77, t = 4.86, p < .001, r^2 = .03). Older adults, in short, were less interested in arguing for any reason than were the undergraduates. Arguing seemed to be a more central part of undergraduates' lives than those of older adults. Perhaps with advancing adulthood more things are settled (hardly any 35 year olds change their majors, for instance), or at least the unsettled things do not seem as though they have to be addressed with disagreement, compared to emerging adulthood.

The second-order frames seemed to be already in place by college age. The table shows that the two groups did not differ significantly on either blurting or cooperation. Interestingly, the undergraduates had higher civility scores. For the younger sample, then, argument episodes were thought to be more pleasant than the older adults estimated. This was connected with willingness to argue. For both samples combined, the correlation between civility and argument approach was positive ($r = .17$), and the association between civility and the prosocial subscale of verbal aggressiveness was even higher ($r = .26$; both correlations were statistically significant). These associations can be understood equally well in two ways: as one's expectations that arguments are civil increases, so does one's interest in arguing; or as the civility expectation fades, so does the inclination to argue. Either way, arguing impulses went hand in hand with the estimate that the interactions will go well.

The third-order measure, professional contrast, also showed no difference between the two groups of people. These means were among the highest in the table, indicating that people's degree of similarity to professional viewpoints was noticeably higher than most of the first-order impulses for arguing, for instance. In fact, the table shows that people's highest scores tended to be on the measures that reflect the most sophistication about arguing: professional contrast, cooperation, and civility. Among the first-order measures, people were most attracted to arguing for identity display, which is the least confrontive of the reasons for arguing.

So the results indicate that undergraduates are probably readier to argue than older adults. Particularly marked were the differences in the play scores (which might indicate that adults have figured out that play is often a cover for aggression), and the identity display scores (which might reflect the less stable social environments of college students, in which fewer people have many years of history with the respondent's projected identity). The measures of socially advanced behaviors and understandings generally showed that the undergraduates already had the levels of sophistication that the older adults showed.

Men and Women

Sex is an important social category and is one of the first things we notice when meeting a new person. Girls and boys have different childhood experiences and people have different standards and expectations for the two sexes. For instance, hardly anyone ever says, "Girls will be girls," to excuse bad behavior. Arguing is assertive behavior, which is more strongly associated with masculinity than femininity in Western cultures. So it is a natural question to wonder whether males and females view the activity differently. Table 2.2 contrasts men and women from the two samples.

Table 2.2: Comparisons of Male and Female Scores on Frames Measures

	Males	Females	t	r^2
		Older Adults		
Utility	5.54	4.83	3.94***	.06
Identity Display	6.55	5.85	3.50***	.05
Dominance Assertion	4.55	3.86	2.80**	.03
Play	4.74	3.20	5.56***	.11
Blurting	5.31	5.05	1.15 ns (p = .25)	
Cooperate	6.91	7.05	0.72 ns (p = .47)	
Civility	6.14	5.96	0.96 ns (p = .35)	
Professional Contrast	6.73	6.65	0.30 ns (p = .77)	
		Undergraduates		
Utility	5.60	5.36	3.04**	.01
Identity Display	6.78	6.53	2.59**	.01
Dominance Assertion	4.96	4.37	4.61***	.02
Play	5.48	4.11	9.38***	.09
Blurting	5.25	5.19	0.64 ns (p = .52)	
Cooperation	6.63	6.99	3.78***	.02
Civility	6.28	6.34	0.70 ns (p = .49)	
Professional Contrast	6.46	6.52	0.50 ns (p = .62)	

Note. All means are on a 1–10 scale. All t tests are two-tailed, with corrections for unequal group variances when necessary. Sample sizes: for the older adults, 119 males and 137 females; for the undergraduates, 260 males and 619 females.
** p < .01; *** p < .001.

First consider the older adults. There we see that the men were higher on all the first-order frames than the women. Particularly marked was the difference in their willingness to argue playfully, with 11% of the variance in play scores accounted for by the fact of sex. On the 10 point scale, the men were a point and a half higher than the women. Men were also more oriented to utility arguing, with 6% of the variance due to sex. Here the difference was about three-quarters of a point on the scale. All in all, the men seemed more willing to argue for any of the first-order reasons in the frames battery. Consistent with that interpretation, men had higher scores on argument approach (5.89 versus 4.74, t = 4.75, p < .001, r^2 = .08) and the antisocial subscale of verbal aggressiveness (4.24 versus 3.36, t = 3.63, p < .001, r^2 = .05). However, men and women had essentially the same scores on the second- and third-order frames. This indicates that both sexes had about the same social expectations about interpersonal arguing, and essentially the same level of sophistication.

A similar pattern appears when we examine the undergraduate results. The men had higher scores on all the first-order measures. The play score was again the most discriminating, with men scoring about a point and a half higher again. The other first-order differences also appeared, but with less explained variance than in the older adult sample. As in the other sample, the undergraduate men had higher scores on argument approach (5.93 versus 5.58, $t = 3.23$, $p < .001$, $r^2 = .01$) and antisocial impulses (4.95 versus 4.20, $t = 6.97$, $p < .001$, $r^2 = .05$). The only other important difference between the two main samples is that for the undergraduates, women had higher scores on the cooperation instrument. Women's scores were also marginally higher in the older adult sample, but there the sexes had moved together so closely that the difference was not statistically significant.

So there was a consistent pattern of sex differences, whether we examined emerging or older adults. Men were more argumentative and produced higher scores on the self-oriented motives for arguing. However, men and women had essentially the same levels of other-orientation and reflective awareness about arguing. The one difference we noticed in that regard in the undergraduate sample dissipated in the older sample, and it was the men whose scores seemed to be improving to match the women's. Readers should notice that many of the effect sizes (the r^2 measures) were small. This means that a typical man and a typical women will mostly have comparable scores, even on the measures that show statistically significant differences. Distinctions in arguing for play or utility might be the only ones easily observable in a small social circle.

Associations Among the Frames Measures

Although the discussion to this point has certainly implied various associations among the frames measures, let us now examine that matter empirically. Table 2.3 contains correlations among them, separately for each of our samples. The question here is how the various impulses and expectations are related to one another. Since the older adult and undergraduate samples showed essentially the same patterns of intercorrelation (see Table 2.3), there is no real need to distinguish them in this discussion.

I will begin by considering the first-order frames. These, as we have seen, are all essentially self-oriented motives for arguing. People argue to get things for themselves, to show off special personal features, to assert superiority over the other person, or to play. Each of these is something that a person might want, and the other arguer does not need to be anything more than a vehicle to carry the initiator to greater satisfaction. Given that understanding, it is perhaps no surprise that all four of these measures were positively correlated. In the only real distinction between the two samples, this internal consistency was higher among the older adults than the undergraduates. The first-order frames reflect wanting, and the ethos of wanting crosses over the boundaries of the various things that are sought.

Table 2.3: Correlations Among the Frames Measures

	1	2	3	4	5	6	7
			Older Adults				
1. Utility							
2. Identity	.56***						
3. Dominance	.58***	.45***					
4. Play	.45***	.59***	.52***				
5. Blurting	.37***	.16*	.42***	.19**			
6. Cooperate	.17**	.29***	−.16*	−.07	−.08		
7. Civility	.09	.22***	−.26***	.14*	−.29***	.35***	
8. Contrast	−.04	.05	−.28***	−.04	−.18**	.27***	.43***
			Undergraduates				
1. Utility							
2. Identity	.38***						
3. Dominance	.42***	.24***					
4. Play	.32***	.44***	.41***				
5. Blurting	.35***	.15***	.42***	.22***			
6. Cooperate	.09*	.26***	−.23***	−.11***	−.09**		
7. Civility	−.05	.12***	−.33***	.04	−.32***	.29***	
8. Contrast	.03	.12***	−.22***	.03	−.13***	.24***	.50***

Note. Sample sizes were 256 for the older adult sample, and between 857 and 880 for the undergraduates. All significance tests were two-tailed.
* $p < .05$; ** $p < .01$; *** $p < .001$.

The first-order frames had several connections to the second-order ones. Blurting is really a sort of transitional measure, indicating whether a person passes from the first-order impulses to the social constructiveness of the second order. People who blurt a lot are still self-oriented, and therefore we see substantial positive correlations between blurting and the first-order frames. Cooperation and civility had weaker and less consistent relationships to the first-order frames. Several of the correlations were not significant in spite of the substantial sample sizes, and others were significant but negative. Dominance and play were associated with lower appreciations for the possibilities that arguments might be cooperative and civil. This was most marked for dominance assertion, which was connected to significantly lower expectations about cooperation and civility in both samples.

The first-order frames, with the exception of dominance, tended not to have much connection to the professional contrast scores. As I remarked before, people argue a lot regardless of their level of argumentative sophistication. Arguing for utilitarian reasons had no relationship with professional contrast, perhaps because arguing is simply how everyone does a lot of their social business. Identity display was associated with somewhat more argumentative sophistication for the undergraduates but not for the older adults. The clearest results had to do with dominance, which was clearly contraindicated by those people with the most perceptive insights about arguing. Somewhat surprisingly, play was not negatively associated with sophistication (as dominance assertion was). Perhaps the more sophisticated among us are able to choose play partners more perceptively, so that their playful episodes are actually that, instead of being a cover for aggression.

The second-order frames also had sensible connections with one another. Blurting tended to have negative relationships to cooperation and civility. Blurters, of course, still occupy essentially self-oriented positions with regard to arguing, and it is the low blurters (i.e., the editors) who are more adaptive, and therefore more cooperative and civil. So the negative correlations with blurting were expectable. Cooperation and civility were positively and substantially correlated with one another in both samples. Cooperative impulses should lead to greater civility, and the data were consistent with that idea.

The second-order frames also had theoretically consistent associations with professional contrast. Blurting, as we would expect, was negatively correlated to the sophistication measure. Cooperation and civility were positively correlated to professional contrast in both samples.

The associations in Table 2.3 describe patterns of arguing orientations. People who are self-oriented (i.e., have high scores for the first-order frames and blurting) are a fairly discrete group, and do not really participate in the higher order frames. Dominance and play are impulses that signal that an arguer is not being particularly reflective about arguing, and probably not very cooperative or civil, either. On the other hand, people who see arguments as more cooperative and civil are also those who have fuller and more nuanced understandings of what arguing is for, what it is really about, and how to engage in it constructively.

Frames and Other Features of Personality

Argument frames are certainly not self-contained. These understandings and motives come out of whole people, who have many other personality traits. No doubt many of those traits are irrelevant to arguing, but some of them seem as though they should be. Describing someone's personality is to say many things about him or her, things that have implications for great swaths of the person's life. So if we can identify connections between argument frames and some of these more general measures, we will have enlarged our understandings of who argues in what way, and for what reasons. Table 2.4 reports correlations between the frames measures and several important personality instruments. Notice that some of these measures were common across several studies, while others were only collected in a single investigation. For that reason, I have combined the undergraduate and older adult samples for the calculations in the table. The studies that contributed data to this table are Hample and Anagondahalli (2015), Hample et al. (2010), Hample and Irions (2015), and Hample et al. (2013).

Table 2.4: Correlations Between the Frames Measures and Other Personality Instruments

	Utility	Ident	Dom	Play	Blurt	Coop	Civil	Contrast
				Arguing Motivations				
Approach	.30***	.39***	.27***	.41***	.11***	.00	.17***	.05
Avoid	−.01	−.08**	.01	−.22***	.12***	.17***	−.22***	−.06*
Antisocial	.34***	.29***	.51***	.38***	.40***	−.28***	−.21***	−.22***
Prosocial	−.03	−.01	−.26***	−.14***	−.19***	.53***	.26***	.23***
				Aggressiveness				
Indirect Agg	.22***	.23***	.41***	.28***	.29***	−.23***	−.19**	−.28***
Reactance	.33***	.36***	.42***	.45***	.39***	−.20***	−.01	−.10
				Taking Conflict Personally				
Direct	.10**	.05	.10**	−.17***	.25***	.14***	−.19***	−.09*
Stress	.04	−.05	.07*	.24***	.15***	−.11***	−.17***	−.12***
Persecution	.26***	.09**	.31***	.02	.36***	.01	−.33***	−.21***
PosRel	.35***	.40***	.16***	.36***	.08*	.25***	.30***	.18***

Table 2.4: Continued

	Utility	Ident	Dom	Play	Blurt	Coop	Civil	Contrast
NegRel	−.02	−.06	.02	−.18***	.14***	.17***	−.20***	−.04
Valence	.27***	.33***	.30***	.61***	.05	−.19***	.11***	.02
				Big Three				
Psychoticism	.12***	−.03	.20***	.29***	.20***	−.32***	−.11**	−.09**
Extraversion	.09**	.05	−.02	−.07	.06	.05	.10**	.11***
Neuroticism	.07*	.07*	.14***	.05	.21***	−.05	−.17***	−.16***
Lying	−.22***	−.14***	−.23***	−.18***	−.28***	.12**	.12**	.13***
				Gender Orientations				
Masculine	.14***	.26***	.09**	.24***	.11***	.04	.14***	.07
Feminine	−.03	.09**	−.16***	−.11***	−.04	.33***	.10**	.08*
Empathy								
Perspective	−.10	−.07	−.35***	−.03	−.35***	.36***	.20***	.22***
Concern	−.17**	−.04	−.24***	−.28***	−.17**	.24***	.05	.04
				Cultural Orientations				
PowerDist	.07	.09	.27***	.11	.09	−.18*	−.24***	−.24***
Individualsm	.11	.10	−.07	.02	−.09	.03	−.02	.13
Collectivism	−.08	.02	.01	−.11	−.06	.25***	−.05	−.10
				Other Measures				
CommAppr	−.01	−.05	.12	−.21**	.21**	.02	−.18*	−.21**
Sen-Seeking	.20***	.08	.14*	.17**	.22***	−.04	.03	−.02
Self-Monitor	.14*	.10	.10	.14*	.08	−.06	−.04	−.04

Note. Sample sizes were highly variable, ranging from 188 to 1113. All significance tests were two-tailed.
* $p < .05$; ** $p < .01$; *** $p < .001$.

Table 2.4 is daunting and I do not wish to bog down this discussion by remarking on every correlation. Instead I will focus on those results that most help us to understand how argument framing is situated within broader personality profiles.

First consider the associations between the frames and argument motivations, in particular those assessed with the argumentativeness (Infante & Rancer, 1982) and verbal aggressiveness (Infante & Wigley, 1986) scales. The first-order frames and blurting were all positively associated with the tendencies to approach arguments and to be antisocially aggressive. These were substantial and consistent correlations, and point us to the conclusion that the first-order frames have a key role in motivating people to engage in either arguments or nasty disagreements. On the other hand, cooperation was strongly connected with argument avoidance and prosocial intentions, suggesting that this frame is connected to more passive and other-centered motives. The expectation that arguments will be civil, however, was predicted by the motive to engage in arguments and to behave prosocially; it was negatively associated with argument avoidance and antisocial impulses. Civility therefore appears to be a more mature understanding than mere cooperation, because those who saw arguments as civil were quite willing to engage in them. Professional contrast had a correlational profile similar to that for civility. The most argument-sophisticated people disdained argument avoidance and hostility in favor of prosocial intentions.

These same patterns appeared when some other measures of aggressiveness were tested. These were indirect interpersonal aggressiveness (Beatty et al., 1999) and psychological reactance (Dowd et al., 1991). Aggression was positively associated with blurting and the first order frames, and negatively correlated with the second- and third-order frames. Consistently, the Big Three supertrait of psychoticism (Eysenck et al., 1985), which is the tendency to be hostile or emotionally flat, had a pattern comparable to the aggression measures.

In the results reviewed to this point, we can see evident associations between the frames and various sorts of aggressive or assertive impulses. The more aggression, the higher the scores on the first-order frames and blurting, and the lower the scores on the more advanced frames measures.

Emotional and cognitive reactions to interpersonal conflict are assessed with the taking conflict personally battery of measures (Hample & Dallinger, 1995). Those instruments that indicate negative feelings and expectations about conflict (direct personalization, stress reactions, persecution feelings, and negative relational consequences) often had positive associations with the first-order frames and blurting, although there were some exceptions. This is perhaps not immediately sensible, since one might suppose that people who had negative emotional reactions to conflict would want to avoid it, but we see that utility and dominance motives were particularly strong for people who took conflict personally. Perhaps their unfavorable feelings about conflict were connected with the sense that others argue in order to exploit them (utility) or subordinate them (dominance), and so possibly they feel that those are the ways to behave. Not surprisingly, people high in personalization of conflict had lower civility scores and they tended not to have sophisticated understandings of the nature of arguing. Elsewhere I have expressed the idea that personalization of conflict is not just some odd misperception about how to manage disagreement; instead, it is a summary of one's life experiences with interpersonal clashes (Hample, 1999). For personalizers, conflict is genuinely not a civil sort of interaction, and their lives have not led them to experiences that would justify optimistic projections about the possibilities for civil disagreements. The people who were not personalizers (low scores on the instruments mentioned earlier, but also high estimates of positive relational effects and valence) had higher scores on almost all the frames. They were more interested in arguing for any of the first-order reasons, and described arguments as civil, understanding them in a perceptive way.

These findings are a bit complex, but they give some additional insights into how the frames relate to people's emotional lives. Conflict personalizers were very sensitive to the use of arguing for utility and dominance, and generally saw arguments as unhappy personal experiences. People who were more positive about engaging in interpersonal conflict were highly motivated to argue for any of the reasons, including some very high scores for play, and tended to regard arguments as cooperative and civil, and to have generally productive interpersonal potential.

Earlier in the chapter, we took note of several sex differences, and here we can examine gender effects. Gender is not synonymous with sex. Sex is biological, and gender is psychological. If you have known a woman with masculine traits or a man who was a little feminine, you have personal experience with the difference. (Sexual orientation is yet a third thing, but I have no data to offer on that point.) Table 2.4 shows the associations between the frames measures and the standard instrument for assessing gender orientations (Bem, 1974). Earlier (Table 2.2) we saw that men had higher scores on the first-order frames, but that men and women had few differences on the second- or third-order instruments. For the first-order frames and blurting, we see a parallel pattern for masculinity and femininity. Masculinity was associated with higher scores on the first-order frames and blurting, whereas femininity tended to have negative correlations. However, Table 2.4 also shows that people with feminine orientations (nurturing, for example) saw arguments as more cooperative and civil, and were somewhat more likely to have better scores on professional contrast. In this set of frames, masculinity only had one significant correlation, the one with civility.

So the gender results were consistent with the sex results insofar as the first-order frames and blurting were concerned. Masculine people (of either sex) were more motivated to argue for any of the reasons we have been studying, and were also more prone to blurt. But the feminine people were the ones who had the most advanced and optimistic understandings of the nature of arguing. This last result had no parallel in our analysis of men versus women.

I have been emphasizing the difference between the self-orientation of the first-order frames and the other-orientation of the higher order measures. The idea of empathy is that a person can understand and indirectly participate in other people's experiences. Two of the empathy measures in Davis (1983) were used to assess perspective-taking and concern for others. Results in Table 2.4 indicate that higher empathy was connected to less use of arguments for dominance assertion, a reduction in the view that arguments can be playful, and less blurting. Empathy was also positively correlated with cooperative orientations to arguing. The ability to take the other's perspective was associated with a more advanced understanding of arguing, along with a higher estimate of its civility. So empathetic people were less motivated to argue, they more rarely blurted, and they had a more constructive impression about arguing's social potential.

Chapter 7 examines various arguing orientations (including frames) in other nations. As background to that chapter, Table 2.4 reports some information about the connections between frames and some common instruments used in cross-cultural research. It is important to remember that all the Table 2.4 results came from U.S. residents, but there is natural variability on these culture-relevant measures in every nation. Self-construals (Singelis, 1994) refer to a person's orientation to individualism (independence, or promoting own goals) and collectivism (interdependence, or promoting group or family goals ahead of one's own). Table 2.4 reveals that these measures were not especially related to the argument frames, except that collectivists saw arguing as more cooperative. Their arguments with in-group members probably are quite other-centric, so this result makes sense. The absence of any connections between individualism and the first-order frames is a bit puzzling. Power distance (Hofstede, 2001) refers to the degree to which people accept that power is unequally distributed in a society. Young people who characteristically call their elders by a first name probably have low power distance, and those who address a superior formally even after years of friendly collaboration probably have high power distance. Table 2.4 shows that those who are comfortable with higher power distance were also quite sensitive to the possibility of arguments being used for dominance assertion, saw arguments as less cooperative and civil, and had less sophistication about the nature of interpersonal arguing.

This set of results for power distance obliquely raises the question of the degree to which the argument frames theory really only characterizes Western nations (because they valorize equality and often disapprove of status differences, whereas other cultures have the opposite suppositions). Perhaps what I have been saying is the preferred set of answers to the professional contrast items is only really preferred in the West. This general question of the degree to which our argumentation theories are U.S.-only is in fact one of the main motivations for doing the cross-national work reported in Chapter 7.

This covers nearly all the measures in Table 2.4. Exceptions are the results for communication apprehension (McCroskey, 1978), which had modest connections to playful arguing, blurting, civility, and professional contrast; sensation-seeking (Kalichman & Rompa, 1995), which had consistent positive correlations to most of the first-order frames and blurting; and self-monitoring (Snyder, 1974), which had little to do with people's responses on the frames instruments. Readers with pointed research interests may wish to explore other results than the ones I have highlighted, and in some cases the null results might be as interesting to explain as the highly significant ones.

Exploring all these personality traits leads to a crude sketch of how people's framing for arguments emerges from their broader social orientations. Aggressiveness was clearly an important platform for high scores on the first-order frames and blurting, and it interfered with the possibility of seeing the pleasant, socially constructive affordances of interpersonal arguing. Taking conflicts personally was also an impediment to seeing the positive contributions arguing can make to one's life, and this set of results was paralleled by those for the supertrait of neuroticism (anxiety). Expecting positive relational consequences from conflict, however, led to thinking that arguing is cooperative, civil, and productive. A masculine outlook on life was associated with more insistent arguing from any motive, but feminine and empathetic people saw arguing's cooperative, civil, and constructive possibilities more clearly.

So as I said at the beginning of this subsection, argument frames are not an isolated part of a person's mental equipment. Understanding a person's framing predilections can give hints as to what kind of person he or she is, and the reverse is true as well.

Conclusions: Empirical Work to Date

The overall set of empirical results has been fairly consistent with the ideas that have informed the argument frames project. The first-order frames were most insistently connected with various self-oriented impulses, such as aggression. The more advanced frames found their correlates among those personality features we see as more socially sensitive, such as empathy.

But the work to date has all been about self-reports and has not involved any efforts to connect arguing frames with actual arguing behavior. Do people with higher scores on the first-order frames actually say nastier things? Are they more domineering? Are they less considerate of the other person's needs? The self-report data summarized here supports the hypotheses that all those answers should be "yes," but behavioral studies certainly need to be done before those conclusions are secure.

General Conclusions

When people argue, what do they think is going on? What do they see, and what do they miss? How do they think they should conduct themselves, and what do they anticipate from others? These are the issues that motivated the argument frames research and they are important questions because arguing is not a minor part of anyone's life. We disagree all the time with people we have feelings for or connections to (Gilbert, 2014), and the disagreements need to be managed somehow. Using reasons is not the only way to do it. Some people blunder through with expressive blurts and others just try to bulldoze their way with forceful insistence. But exchanging reasons has productive possibilities. It can lead to personal insight, constructive development of relationships, and of course, getting pizza.

These argument frames are not simply a matter of knowing what you are doing when you argue. Bullies and closed-minded people probably know exactly what they are doing, for instance. But I have to wonder if they realize that there is another way. Being open, participating bilaterally, and conducting oneself in a civil way are all routes not only to better arguments, but probably also to a more satisfying life. As we mature we should begin to see that the social world offers us an opportunity to notice that we should watch what we say, that arguments can be cooperative, and that we can interact politely and constructively. Taking clearer note of these possibilities advances us in the sophistication of our understandings of arguing. These perceptions also help us to identify others who are less constructive, and perhaps to lead them or perhaps to adapt to them in some other way.

References

Alberts, J. K., & Drzewiecka, J. A. (2008). Understanding the communication and relational dynamics of humor. In M. T. Motley (Ed.), *Studies in applied interpersonal communication* (pp. 229–244). Los Angeles, CA: Sage.
Beatty, M. J., Valencic, K. M., Rudd, J. E., & Dobos, J. A. (1999). A 'dark side' of communication avoidance: Indirect interpersonal aggressiveness. *Communication Research Reports, 16*, 103–109.
Bem, S. L. (1974). The measurement of psychological androgeny. *Journal of Consulting and Clinical Psychology, 42*, 155–162.

Benoit, P. J., & Hample, D. (1998). The meaning of two cultural categories: Avoiding interpersonal arguments or cutting them short. In J. F. Klumpp (Ed.), *Argument in a time of change: Definitions, frameworks, and critiques* (pp. 97–102). Annandale, VA: National Communication Association.

Brehm, J. W. (1966). *A theory of psychological reactance.* New York, NY: Academic Press.

Coser, L. A. (1956). *The functions of social conflict.* New York, NY: Free Press.

Costa, P. T., & McCrae, R. R. (1988). Personality in adulthood: A six-year longitudinal study of self-reports and spouse ratings on the NEO Personality Inventory. *Journal of Personality and Social Psychology, 54,* 853.

Davis, M. H. (1983). Measuring individual differences in empathy: Evidence for a multidimensional approach. *Journal of Personality and Social Psychology, 44,* 113–126.

Dowd, E. T., Milne, C. R., & Wise, S. L. (1991). The Therapeutic Reactance Scale: A measure of psychological reactance. *Journal of Counseling & Development, 69,* 541–545.

van Eemeren, F. H., & Grootendorst, R. (2004). *A systematic theory of argumentation: The pragma-dialectical approach.* Cambridge: Cambridge University Press.

Eysenck, S. B. G., Eysenck, H. J. & Barrett, P. (1985). A revised version of the psychoticism scale. *Personality and Individual Difference, 6,* 21–29.

Gilbert, M. A. (2014). *Arguing with people.* Peterborough, ON: Broadview Press.

Hample, D. (1999). The life space of personalized conflicts. *Communication Yearbook, 22,* 171–208.

Hample, D. (2003). Arguing skill. In J. O. Greene & B. R. Burleson (Eds.), *Handbook of communication and social interaction skills* (pp. 439–478). Mahwah, NJ: Erlbaum.

Hample, D. (2005a). *Arguing: Exchanging reasons face to face.* Mahwah, NJ: Lawrence Erlbaum Associates [Taylor & Francis].

Hample, D. (2005b). Argument frames: An initial investigation into operationalizations. In C. A. Willard (Ed.), *Critical problems in argumentation* (pp. 568–576). Washington, DC: National Communication Association.

Hample, D., & Anagondahalli, D. (2015). Understandings of arguing in India and the United States: Argument frames, personalization of conflict, argumentativeness, and verbal aggressiveness. *Journal of Intercultural Communication Research, 44,* 1–26.

Hample, D., & Benoit, P. J. (1999). Must arguments be explicit and violent: A study of naive social actors' understandings. In F. H. van Eemeren, R. Grootendorst, J. A. Blair, & C. A. Willard (Eds.), *Proceedings of the fourth international conference of the International Society for the Study of Argumentation* (pp. 306–310). Amsterdam: SICSAT.

Hample, D., Benoit, P. J., Houston, J., Purifoy, G., VanHyfte, V., & Wardell, C. (1999). Naive theories of argument: Avoiding interpersonal arguments or cutting them short. *Argumentation and Advocacy, 35,* 130–139.

Hample, D., & Dallinger, J. M. (1987). Cognitive editing of argument strategies. *Human Communication Research, 14,* 123–144.

Hample, D., & Dallinger, J. M. (1995). A Lewinian perspective on taking conflict personally: Revision, refinement, and validation of the instrument. *Communication Quarterly, 43,* 297–319.

Hample, D., Dean, C., Johnson, A., Kopp, L., & Ngoitz, A. (1997, May). *Conflict as a MOP in conversational behavior.* Paper presented to the annual meeting of the International Communication Association, Montreal, Canada.

Hample, D., Han, B., & Payne, D. (2010). The aggressiveness of playful arguments. *Argumentation, 24,* 405–421.

Hample, D., & Irions, A. (2015). Arguing to display identity. *Argumentation, 29,* 389–416.

Hample, D., Richards, A. S., & Skubisz, C. (2013). Blurting. *Communication Monographs, 80,* 503–532.

Hofstede, G. (2001). *Culture's consequences: Comparing values, behaviors, institutions, and organizations across nations* (2nd ed.). Thousand Oaks, CA: Sage.

Hong, S.-M., & Faedda, S. (1996). Refinement of the Hong psychological reactance scale. *Educational and Psychological Measurement, 56,* 173–182.

Infante, D. A., Chandler, T. A., & Rudd, J. E. (1989). Test of an argumentative skill deficiency model of interspousal violence. *Communication Monographs, 56,* 163–177.

Infante, D. A., & Rancer, A. S. (1982). A conceptualization and measure of argumentativeness. *Journal of Personality Assessment, 46,* 72–80.

Infante, D. A., & Wigley, C. J. (1986). Verbal aggressiveness: An interpersonal model and measure. *Communication Monographs, 53,* 61–69.

Johnson, A. J. (2002). Beliefs about arguing: A comparison of public-issue and personal-issue arguments. *Communication Reports, 15,* 99–112.

Johnstone, H. W., Jr. (1982). Bilaterality in argument and communication. In J. R. Cox & C. A. Willard (Eds.), *Advances in argumentation theory and research* (pp. 95–102). Carbondale, IL: Southern Illinois University Press.

Kalichman, S. C., & Rompa, D. (1995). Sexual sensation seeking and sexual compulsivity scales: Reliability, validity, and predicting HIV risk behavior. *Journal of Personality Assessment, 65,* 586–601.

Keltner, D., Young, R. C., Heerey, E. A., Oemig, C., & Monarch, N. D. (1998). Teasing in hierarchical and intimate relations. *Journal of Personality and Social Psychology, 75,* 1231–1247.

Kuhn, D. (1991). *The skills of argument.* Cambridge: Cambridge University Press.

McCroskey, J. C. (1978). Validity of the PRCA as an index of oral communication apprehension. *Communication Monographs, 45,* 192–203.

Mercier, H. (2016). The argumentative theory: Predictions and empirical evidence. *Trends in Cognitive Sciences, 20,* 689–700.

Mercier, H., & Sperber, D. (2011). Why do humans reason? Arguments for an argumentation theory. *Behavioral and Brain Sciences, 34,* 57–111.

Mercier, H., & Sperber, D. (2017). *The enigma of reason.* Cambridge, MA: Harvard University Press.

Meyer, J. R. (1997). Cognitive influences on the ability to address interaction goals. In J. O. Greene (Ed.), *Message production: Advances in communication theory* (pp. 71–90). Mahwah, NJ: Lawrence Erlbaum Associates.

O'Keefe, B. J. (1988). The logic of message design: Individual differences in reasoning about communication. *Communication Monographs, 55,* 80–103.

Perelman, Ch., & Olbrechts-Tyteca, L. (1969). *The new rhetoric: A treatise on argumentation.* (J. Wilkinson & P. Weaver, Trans.). Notre Dame, IN: University of Notre Dame Press.

Polderman, T. J. C., Benyamin, B., de Leeuw, C. A., Sullivan, P. F., van Bochoven, A., Visscher, P. M., & Posthuma, D. (2015). Meta-analysis of the heritability of human traits based on fifty years of twin studies. *Nature Genetics, 47,* 702–709.

Rancer, A. S., Kosberg, R. L., & Baukus, R. A. (1992). Beliefs about arguing as predictors of trait argumentativeness: Implications for training in argument and conflict management. *Communication Education, 41,* 375–387.

Sheehan, K. B., & Pittman, M. (2016). *Amazon's mechanical turk for academics: The HIT handbook for social science research.* Irvine, CA: Melvin & Leigh.

Singelis, T. M. (1994). The measurement of independent and interdependent self-construals. *Personality and Social Psychology Bulletin, 20,* 580–591.

Snyder, M. (1974). Self-monitoring of expressive behavior. *Journal of Personality and Social Psychology, 30,* 526–537.

Stanford, M. S., Mathias, C. W., Dougherty, D. M., Lake, S. L., Anderson, N. E., & Patton, J. H. (2009). Fifty years of the Barratt Impulsiveness Scale: An update and review. *Personality and Individual Differences, 47,* 385–395.

Stoltz, N. (2017, November). *The playful divide: A new look at arguing for fun.* Paper presented at the annual meeting of the National Communication Association, Dallas, TX.

Swann, W. B. Jr., & Rentfrow, P. J. (2001). Blirtatiousness: Cognitive, behavioral, and physiological consequences of rapid responding. *Journal of Personality and Social Psychology, 81,* 1160–1175.

Watzlawick, P., Beavin, J. H., & Jackson, D. D. (1967). *Pragmatics of human communication.* New York, NY: Norton.

CHAPTER THREE

Argument Situations

Like any other sort of communication, arguing is always situated. That means partly that it always takes place at a particular time, in an identifiable context, and with a specific person. More than that, though, it means that arguing is *responsive* to those elements of the social world. You argue in one way with a police officer, differently with your romantic partner, and in yet another way with an acquaintance. You argue with one attitude in a coffee shop, differently in a dangerous bar, and take still another tack when asking for a salary raise. You are part of the situation, too, so this means that how you feel, what you were just doing, what kind of person you are, and why you were motivated to argue also make a difference. Some people aren't very responsive to situational differences, and this can result in them saying inappropriate things. People with bad tempers or who cannot control their vocabulary are examples of arguers who aren't sensitive enough to where they are and whom they are with. Blurters, who are discussed in Chapter 2, are a noticeable group of people who aren't very situation-responsive (Hample, Richards, & Skubisz, 2013).

But most adults are responsive to situational features much of the time, and this chapter reviews what elements of an arguing situation make a difference, and what sorts of differences we presently know about. Before moving into those details, however, it might be best to clarify what is meant by "situation." This has been a common but ambiguous concept in theories of interpersonal communication (Argyle, Furnham, & Graham, 1981, ch. 1; Kelley et al., 2003, ch. 1).

Interpersonal Situations

Although many people have written useful things about situations, it is confusing to try to put it all together because different scholars meant different things. For instance, sometimes the only thing that was described was the physical circumstances: Are people at home or out in the world? Are they seated comfortably or uncomfortably? Are they watching TV together or having coffee at a small table? Sometimes "setting" is used to describe elements like this, but setting and situation are nearly synonyms, so the terminology is not helpful and is not consistently applied.

A more profound confusion comes from identifying situations with goals. For instance, many of us write easily about conflict situations, or comforting situations, or persuasive situations. I have already loosely used the phrase, arguing situation. This is a natural way to describe a communication episode, but unfortunately it equates a situation with its framing goal and ignores any other considerations. Once an episode begins, we have seen that people do frame it with their primary goal—to persuade, to make an initial acquaintance, to break bad news (this is part of the SGPA model; see Chapter 1). But a situation has more things in it than a framing goal or even a constellation of interaction goals. It probably has constraints on what you can say or how long you can talk, it has a physical setting, it might include obstacles to be overcome, it may be a continuation of a previous interaction, and most of all, it has two complex people in it and they may have an important relational history and different feelings about the exchange. An interpersonal situation, once it begins to develop, also has a "feel" to it. It may seem tense, or happy, or confusing, or boring, for instance. All these things affect how we communicate, and all of them need to be included in a full understanding of what a situation is. It is worth noticing that nearly all these things are also constructed by our communication behaviors, so that if an interaction is rude, or sensitive, or intemperate, or conflictive, for example, the two participants somehow produced that effect, even if they did not intend to.

I have written a paper aimed at clarifying the nature of situation and its connection to interaction goals (Hample, 2016). I tried to show how the ideas of primary and secondary goals fit into an understanding of other situational features that include but go beyond the ideas of physical circumstances and interaction goals. I suggested that four categories of things appear more or less in sequence during a face-to-face episode. These are the reasonably apparent features of the situation, the episode's primary goal, the subjective elements of the situation, and secondary goals.

Reasonably apparent features include things that an outsider can probably observe and that a participant is unlikely to make a mistake about. These include your own sex, the other person's sex, the conversational topic, the number of people present, the medium of communication (e.g., face-to-face, email, phone), the nature of the relationship between the interactants (e.g., friend, parent, coworker), the type of interaction (e.g., academic, job, social), and setting (e.g., home, walking around, classroom). These things are simple to notice and uncontroversial to define. We make mistakes about them occasionally, for instance realizing you are talking to a man and not a woman, but the realization is always jarring and that reaction itself conveys that we were supposed to be able to take our first thought (e.g., "I am talking to a woman") for granted. These are the quick impressions that guide us in the first instants of the episode. It is hard to say whether some of these might be more important than others, but readers should notice that topic is one of these elements. You know what you are talking about, or at least you initially take on a topical context for what you say. This will be especially important later in the chapter.

These reasonably apparent features give rise to the second element to appear, the primary goal (see Hample, 2016, for the empirical tests of the sequencing in the theory). As we saw in Chapter 1, this is the goal that gives definition to your intentions and messages. We do not have a secure list of goals because anything that can motivate human action can also motivate communication, and that is a long list of goals indeed. But some of the primary goals that are important in studying arguing include those studied in the argument frames project: utility, identity display, dominance assertion, and play (see Chapter 2). Others that I found in the interpersonal situations study include relational maintenance, fulfilling role obligations, managing own face, cathartic expression, and planning some future event. Taking on any of these contextualizing intentions shapes what you say and how you want to be understood. We adopt these primary goals because of some interplay between the relatively apparent features of the situation and our interior lives. For example, you might know that you have unfinished business with that person on that topic, and that this is an appropriate time to bring it up. We communicate in an effort to achieve something, and whatever that is becomes the scaffold for what we say or do.

Adopting a primary goal, says the theory, affects the character of one's engagement in the conversation, and so gives rise to the subjective features of the situation. These are the personally perceived and experienced facets of the interaction, and it is mainly the participants who have access to this information because much of it is private, and the public performances may disguise people's interior feelings. These subjective features are emergent in the conversation. That is, they are not mainly caused by one person (not even by the perceiver) but instead are due to the conjunction of the two people's actions, feelings, and thoughts. Subjective features of a conversation include its politeness, its rudeness, its argumentative nature (are reasons being offered?), its conflictive nature (do the people express disagreement?), the perceived presence of obstacles to accomplishing one's goals, the possibility of suppressed remarks, and both people's emotional reactions. The emotions that were most salient in people's descriptions of interpersonal communication situations were anger, anxiety, disappointment, happiness, sadness, surprise, guilt, fear, gratitude, and boredom (Hample, 2016). Together, all these elements give an approximate description of a conversation's "feel," or climate.

Experiencing an interaction these ways has the consequence of activating secondary goals. As we saw in Chapter 1, the idea is that these assert themselves in modifying (and perhaps even overwhelming) how one pursues the primary goal. For instance, worry about being exploited might cancel or modify how you answer an ex-partner's request for help, even after the episode has been framed as a supportive interaction. The very goals that can frame one episode can be secondary goals in another, so the same goals that can be primary can also be secondary in a different moment. The research literature often singles out politeness and identity goals as those that might shape how one seeks to persuade or comfort, but in principle we can bring an even larger constellation of goals to our interpersonal actions. The secondary goals that rise up during interaction are closely connected to the subjective features of the situation.

Our messages grow out of our experience of the situation, including all the elements mentioned in this part of the chapter. The basic sequence—reasonably apparent features, primary goal, subjective features, secondary goals—is certainly too simple. The research has not advanced to the point of being able to prove it, but it seems likely that we cycle back and forth within this sequence as the conversation moves along.

However, the main point of this section of the chapter has been to outline the sorts of things that ought to be included in a full description of an interpersonal episode. There are obvious things and subjective ones, conscious goals and unconscious ones, things said and things suppressed. Both people have perceptions and feelings about what is going on. Physical circumstances and goals are certainly elements of a situation, but so are obstacles, relational histories, and emotional reactions.

Arguing is common in human interaction, but not every interpersonal exchange necessarily involves offering, criticizing, or defending reasons. Still, interpersonal arguing obviously takes place within interpersonal situations, so having this preliminary description will help us to understand arguing.

Argument Topics

We have just noticed that one of the reasonably apparent elements of an interpersonal situation is the topic of the conversation. Argument topics are obviously important because they establish a domain of content, a mutual inventory of the things that one's reasons can be about. They have considerable control over the ideas in an argument, the meanings that can be in play. Just as with any social interaction, argument topics can range from banal and superficial (e.g., "should we watch NCIS tonight?") to profoundly involving (e.g., "did you sleep with him?"). Arguments and their reasons can flow from either sort of topic (e.g., "Mark Harmon is handsome;" "if I had, you would have heard it from me").

The type of relationship between the arguers is also a reasonably apparent feature of communication situations, and naturally many argument topics are tied to the sort of connection between the arguers. Married people can argue about child rearing, and coworkers can argue about job responsibilities. Many researchers have investigated what are the most common topics in various sorts of interpersonal relationships.

Let us consider married couples. Papp, Cummings, and Goeke-Morey (2009) asked 100 husbands and 100 wives to keep a conflict diary for 15 days. The researchers coded the diaries and generated a list of disagreement topics, as noted by husbands and wives, as follows: children (husbands 36%, wives 39%), chores (25%, 24%), communication (22%, 22%), leisure (20%, 20%), work (including jobs, 19%, 19%), money (18%, 19%), habits (16%, 17%), relatives (11%, 12%), commitment (8%, 9%), intimacy (including sex, 8%, 8%), friends (7%, 8%), and personality (6%, 9%). The details of the list depend on how things were coded (e.g., other researchers might have combined money and work), and on the age of the sample (they were in their late 30s, on average, and had been married for about 12 years), which of course has implications for whether child rearing, educational, and financial issues have been settled or not. The percentages of husbands and wives who reported each topic were fairly close. This doesn't mean that the topics were equally important to the men and women, but it does mean that they both knew what the disagreements were about, and were equally careful about keeping the diaries.

Notice, because this will become important momentarily, that all these topics were plausibly related to the character of the marriage, its negotiated definition.

Naturally, different topics appear when different kinds of relationships are involved in the study. For example, Laursen (1995) asked 319 high school sophomores and juniors (who lived at home with both parents and at least one sibling and also had both a boyfriend/girlfriend and a best friend) to list their previous day's disagreements on a questionnaire. The students reported an average of about 7.7 conflicts for that day. The most common topic was responsibilities (12%), followed by school (11%), autonomy (10%), difference of opinion (9%), friendship (9%), standards of behavior (8%), transportation (8%), money (7%), heterosexuality (such as romantic issues, 7%), criticism and teasing (6%), annoying behavior (6%), and use of telephone or television (6%). As before, the details depend on how the researchers coded things (and in 1995 computers and cell phones would have been minor issues), but we still see a very different pattern than for the married couples. As we would expect, the high school students were focused on the life space of a high school student, and many of the things that can make high school unpleasant simply evaporate as we grow older. Marriage generates other issues that are almost unknown to most high school students. But again, we can see that many of the disagreements could have been relationship-defining, although here several relationships were involved, not just marriage. More arguments took place with the students' mothers than with any other sort of person. Mothers were followed in frequency by close friends, boyfriend/girlfriend, siblings, father, mother and father, other peers, teachers, and finally employers or coaches.

This sort of literature review could continue indefinitely without coming to any firm conclusions. Honeycutt (2001; Honeycutt & Sheldon, 2017) has studied couples' arguments and has come up with a simple list of topics, including money, sex, communicative compatibility, and drugs. Prison inmates, Chinese students in their first week at a U.S. university, and divorce lawyers in court surely would produce still different lists of argument topics. These would be of interest if one were studying inmates, student sojourners, or attorneys, but they would not cumulate into anything very useful for the general study of interpersonal arguing. What we need is a theory of topics, one that cuts across different life circumstances.

Fortunately we have one, due to Amy Johnson (2002, 2009). She distinguished between personal and public topics for arguments. Personal topics are those that immediately concern the definition or conduct of the relationship between the arguers. The relationship could be marital, or friendship, or classmate, or any other kind of relationship. Examples of personal topics for a romantic couple living together might be, Whose responsibility is it to put gas in the car? Why aren't you more affectionate? Why do you spend so much time with your friends and leave me home alone? These probably vary in their importance to the relational definition, but all of them are matters that arise exactly and only because the two people are involved in an interpersonal relationship. The resolution (or lack of it) for arguments on these issues has implications for the nature of the relationship (do both people do each task, or are the tasks divided between them?), how the partners feel about one another ("how much do you love me?"), and how they situate their relationship within their social worlds ("how much do you value your friends, compared to me?").

Public topics, in contrast, are external to the relationship. Possible examples of arguments might concern whether civilians should be allowed to own handguns, whether the movie rating system is accurate, or when the baseball season starts. Notice that the arguers can still be in a very close (or superficial, for that matter) relationship with one another, and that one or both might have very firm convictions on the topic. The question is not how close the arguers are to one another. It is whether the argument topic either could be relationship-defining or whether it takes on its meanings from the fact that the arguers are in that sort of relationship. The same people probably argue about both kinds of topics with one another. Thus spouses could argue about both childcare choices and what is the best color for a stop sign.

The relational context, of course, determines whether a topic is personal or public. It makes a difference if you complain about a coworker's laziness to your spouse or to the coworker. The argument topic would be public in the first case, but "personal" in the second. The reason those topics are called personal in the literature is that nearly all the research has been done on undergraduates involved in romantic or close friendship relationships, making the key connection between the people personal and intimate rather than professional or therapeutic or something else. It might have been better to call these topics relational, to take account of more sorts of relationship. But I will stay consistent with the literature's terminology and continue to call them personal.

Several of us undertook a fairly comprehensive review of the empirical research dealing with personal and public arguments (Johnson, Hample, & Cionea, 2014). That paper contains many details not covered here, but also an over-riding conclusion: that personal argument issues were more involving. "Involving" can mean many things, but here it indicates that the personal topics were closer to a person's most private and valued considerations. People were more invested in these topics and they engaged them with more focus, compared to public issues. They were more careful about what they said because they understood that these arguments were consequential. Whenever you say something in an argument, you are committed to it and to your statement's assumptions (Chapter 6 will have much more to say about "commitment stores"). Making a commitment about the quality of German cuisine is quite a different thing than making one about whether the two of you should combine your money into a single checking account, and people understand this.

Notice that this greater involvement derives from the importance of the personal relationship that houses the argument. Most people value their close relationships very highly, and that is why we found so much evidence that people cared more about the personal issues than the public ones. We can imagine a few people for whom this might not be true. On the early seasons of the television show *The Big Bang Theory*, it seems likely that the character Sheldon Cooper might care more about an argument concerning quantum physics than about one of his friends' romantic entanglements. For him, something we would probably code as a public issue would be more involving than a personal topic. A surprising number of people are somewhat like Sheldon Cooper: the things they value most are video games, or getting another drink, or organizing a public protest, for instance. But they seem to be in the minority, and so what we have found about the personal/public distinction probably applies to most of us. Let us turn to some of the detailed findings.

The early work pointed clearly to the conclusion about involvement. In the first paper on this subject, Johnson (2002) surveyed undergraduates about their arguments. Most of them were with friends. She found that the public issue arguments were clearly more enjoyable and self-affirming, but the personal topics were more ego-involving and were rated as having more substantial pragmatic consequences for the arguer. These findings are consistent with the general idea that personal issues are more enmeshing. When stakes are low, people were more likely to enjoy arguing and to say things for the sake of self-expression. But when matters were personal, they were also more important and involving. A follow-up study (Johnson, 2009) explored what was going on in the two kinds of argument. Public arguments contained more information exchange work than personal ones, and the same was true of expressing one's views and passing the time. But personal issues produced higher scores for care in presenting one's identity and resolving behavioral incompatibilities. Because public topics are not relationship-defining, people have more freedom to argue casually without worrying much about consequences. But the personal matters are the ones that concern how people act toward one another and how they see one another. Having a friend think you are wrong about driving directions to Indianapolis is far less consequential than having a romantic partner think you are wrong about sexual equality. Most of these findings have been replicated in a study of serial arguments between undergraduates and their families (Johnson, Kelley, et al., 2014; serial arguments are recurring arguments on the same topic, and are the subject of Chapter 4).

From this empirical basis, quite a bit of additional work has been done to explore somewhat smaller questions. Some of this research is summarized elsewhere in this book. For instance, the scholarship on serial arguments (Chapter 4) showed that people have recurring arguments about both types of topic, but that personal topics were more strongly associated with stress and health problems. Furthermore, the personal issues were the ones that involved the most pointed impulses to express emotions, which might be dangerous, but these issues also generated the greatest use of integrative tactics, which is more encouraging. Personal topics were more emotional, but their importance seems to have led people to discipline themselves to argue more constructively.

Even though personal issues are more emotional and involving, this does not lead them to be more combustible. In spite of the higher levels of emotionality, several studies indicate that people are more careful, perceptive, and precise when they argue about personal topics as opposed to public ones. Hample, Sells, and Inclán Velázquez (2009) asked undergraduates to read descriptions of a public and a personal issue argument exchange. Each script ended with one of the fictional arguers expressing a fallacy. The fallacies made more difference for the personal topics. Those arguments were rated as being less appropriate, less effective, and less sound than essentially the same fallacies in the public issue vignettes. This offers evidence that people were more perceptive about personal arguments, and that they had higher standards for appropriateness and quality. Another study explored whether people also hold themselves to these higher standards when they are producing personal arguments, and found evidence that this was so (Warner & Hample, 2008). Given lists of things that could be said on either a public or a personal topic, people were more selective about what they were willing to say on the personal topic and showed more sensitivity to relational issues as a reason for suppressing possible remarks. So higher stakes imply more emotional involvement (Hample, Dai, & Zhan, 2016), but instead of resulting in interpersonal explosions this sort of topic leads to more care in deciding what to say and in evaluating what the other person says.

Since this book is about the connections between arguing and interpersonal life, one might suppose that the findings about personal topics are the most important. Bates and Samp (2011) reported that arguments on personal topics were harder to resolve than those about public matters. Personal-issue arguments certainly do deal with relationship-defining issues and some might even concern "deal breaker" sorts of matters, so it makes sense that they might not be simple to settle. However, we also argue about less weighty matters. We might enjoy spending a few minutes debating who is the most disgusting pop singer; we might learn some useful things by going back and forth about which political party is least responsive to basic values; and we might get a better idea of a friend's character by hearing him or her go on about foreign policy. These sorts of arguments also fill up our social lives.

I have concentrated on the contrasts between personal and public topics in this section because it is important and well-researched. However, two other topic types have received some attention. Several studies have examined workplace arguments (e.g., Hample, Paglieri, & Na, 2012). These investigations were motivated by the simple observation that people often argue at work. Results indicate that workplace arguments tend to fall between personal and public topics on most of the matters discussed in this section of the chapter.

Dai and Zhan (2016) have explored a more intriguing additional sort of argument topic, namely arguing about *other people's* personal topics. An example of this would be if one romantic couple were arguing about what a second couple should do about their problem. This is less involving than arguing about the same problem within one's own relationship and so might let the issue be more safely explored. In addition, working through the matter at one remove ("should my friend move in with her boyfriend?") might be a deniable sort of dry run for how that issue would play out in your own relationship. Dai and Zhan found that arguments on other people's personal topics were less ego-involving than arguing about one's own personal topics, and had other sensible relationships to results for personal and public topics. This idea is interesting in part because it suggests a way that romantic partners could test the waters on some relationship-defining issue without committing too early to a particular standpoint.

The general theoretical point I have been aiming at in this section (and it is general, indeed) is that the sort of thing we argue about affects how we conduct ourselves. Different relationships lend themselves to different realms of argumentative possibilities. Within each sort of relationship, how we argue and what we think about the activity is affected by whether the topic is relationship-defining or external to it. Many of these behaviors and reactions are important, and it is interesting to notice that they are clearly influenced by some of the obvious features of the situation (topic and relationship), rather than being solely affected by the emergent qualities of the episode. In fact, they probably contribute to subjective features such as politeness and emotional reactions. We will explore that last possibility later in the chapter.

Deciding Whether or Not to Argue

Just about any interpersonal encounter could provide a platform for arguing. Even a remark as mundane as "I'm happy to see you" might result in a refutation: "No you're not, you hypocrite." We are sometimes surprised to find ourselves in the middle of a disagreement. Some people seem to be ambushers, always on the lookout for a chance to prove that another person is wrong, or inferior, or thoughtless. Others often seem to blunder into conflicts, not understanding that they have given offense until too late. Putting those two sorts of people together would be ugly, although it would be interesting to observe—from a distance. Surprise arguments haven't really been studied to my knowledge, so it might be productive to review your own life in that regard and see what hypotheses you can generate. I think there are at least three distinct causal possibilities: one person is imperceptive about how his or her remarks will be taken ("Hey, I didn't mean it that way"), one person might be an ambusher, or somehow the combination of the two people creates a lot of special friction (e.g., at the end of a romantic relationship). Some hints as to how one might pursue the study of surprise arguments may be in the literature: the first sort of person might be a blurter (Hample et al., 2013), the second might be verbally aggressive (Infante & Wigley, 1986), and Baxter (1984) identified the tactic "cost escalation" in relationship termination reports.

At any rate, whenever you find yourself arguing you had a choice about it. The choice was probably not a conscious one, but your cognitive system assessed the situation and pushed you forward into verbal defense or aggression. You could have dodged, hedged, evaded, said something conciliatory, or just ignored the situation. You might have been provoked into arguing, or only invited. You didn't actually have to engage. But you argued. Why?

You may recall from Chapter 1 that in the pragma-dialectical theory, critical discussions are supposed to follow four stages (van Eemeren & Grootendorst, 1983, 2004). The first is confrontation (people realize they disagree), the second is opening (people decide to pursue the disagreement and how to do it), third is argumentation (positions are offered, criticized, and defended), and last is concluding (an agreement appears). All four stages are expectable in retrospect if a critical discussion actually took place, but people can abandon the process at any point. They can fail to register any disagreement, they can notice one but decide not to pursue it, they can decline to attack or defend, or they can refuse to agree on anything. The research in this section of the chapter deals with the transition from the first stage to the second. Given that a difference of opinion is noticed, what causes people to open an argument and what encourages them to walk away?

One answer is that your decision to argue was based on your estimate of what would happen if you did. A recent line of research condenses various possible perceptions and evaluations into a small set of costs and benefits. This work was begun by Paglieri (2009; also see Paglieri & Castelfranchi, 2010). He analyzed the worries people might reasonably have about getting into an argument, with a particular emphasis on the factors that could cause an argument to escalate into a nasty interpersonal experience. His list of factors was somewhat condensed and then used as a set of predictors in an empirical research program aimed at finding out why people do or don't engage in arguing.

The first study (Hample et al., 2012), presented the list of costs and benefits, and used them to predict the decision to engage in a possible argument. Here are the costs and benefits that we felt people might register and consider. The actual items used to measure them are in the Appendix.

General *costs* to arguing included concerns about the effort involved, the possible emotional exposure that elaboration of one's thoughts might entail, and the likelihood of relational damage due to the argument. Sample items included "If we argued, it would take a long time to settle anything," "If we argued, the argument would get very complex and bring in a lot of issues," and "If we argued, it would damage the relationship between my friend and me." This was intended as a fairly global measure, designed to capture any costs that the more specific scales omitted.

We had a similar motivation behind the formation of the general *benefits* subscale. Here, the global items had to do with feeling better about self, the issue, and the relationship due to having the argument. Sample items included "Having this argument would clear the air," "Having this argument would ultimately be beneficial to me," and "Having this argument would ultimately be beneficial to the relationship between my friend and me." The items gave respondents an opportunity to express benefits concerned with identity, relationship, and task, which were the general categories of communication goals proposed by Clark and Delia (1979).

Other instruments were more specific, and reflected Paglieri's ideas in more detail. *Resolvability* was expected to be important, with the supposition that people would be more likely to engage in arguments that held out hope of a successful solution. This instrumentation and idea were originally developed in the serial arguments research literature (see Chapter 4). Items included "I would think it would go on forever," "I would think that a productive solution could occur," and "I would think that it was just going to get worse and worse and never get better." We theorized that resolvability would make the possible benefits more likely but that hopelessness about the argument's fate would nearly guarantee that the costs would be incurred without any benefits to balance them.

We also measured *civility*, which was an instrument originally worked out by Pamela Benoit and also integrated into the serial arguments research as well as the argument frames work (see Chapters 2 and 4). The concept refers to the question of whether an argumentative interaction would be conducted constructively or explosively. Sample items included "The argument would involve loud and negative voices," "The argument would involve successful problem solving," and "The argument would involve physical violence." We thought that anticipated civility would facilitate arguing, and if a person expected the episode to be uncivil (hostile, nasty, threatening) this would discourage engagement.

The *other's reasonability* was thought to be similar in its facilitative or hindering effects on arguing intentions. Arguing with an unreasonable partner doesn't hold out much chance of finding the best conclusion on the merits of the case, but if both of you have open minds then genuine progress on the issue is much more likely. We used items such as these: "My friend would be stubborn if we argued," "My friend would change his/her mind if I gave better reasons and evidence if we argued," and "My friend would be mature about it if we argued." The decision to engage in an argument is also (always) a decision to engage with a particular person. Stubborn, over-sensitive, or insecure people are poor partners if you actually want to accomplish something with your mutual reasoning.

One measure that turned out to be quite important was *likelihood of winning*. These items asked for a self-assessment about the quality of one's reasons and evidence, and for a general estimate that the person would "win" the argument if it happened. Items included "If we argued, I think my friend would win," "If we argued, I think my arguments would be better than my friend's," and "If we argued, I think my friend would have to admit he/she was wrong." This scale presumed a distributive, win/loss attitude toward arguing. As we have seen this isn't the most advanced or productive view to take, but it is a common one.

The last subscale, *appropriateness* of arguing, was also important to our results. There is a time and place for arguing with a particular person on a topic, and arguing under different circumstances would be inappropriate. Some of the items were "It would be appropriate to argue about this topic—with this person, at this time, and in this place," "It would be inappropriate to argue about this topic with my friend," and "I was brought up not to argue about this sort of thing in circumstances like this." Even if an argument needs to happen, it doesn't necessarily have to take place in that particular moment.

For the most part, the items used to measure all these variables mainly refer to the probability that an outcome will occur (see Appendix). We took for granted that the "benefit" things would be positively valued by respondents and the "cost" items would be disliked. This assumption, which might well be open to question under particular circumstances (e.g., maybe someone wants a "good fight"), has been tested in Richards and Cionea (2015), who collected information on both the probability that some outcome would occur (e.g., that the other person would be reasonable) and the degree to which it was valued (positively or negatively). By multiplying these two figures together for each scale, they created a classic subjective expected utility model (e.g., Sillars, 1980) that predicted intentions by the product of probability and value for each variable. Their results showed a slight improvement in the model's predictive accuracy when the product terms were used, as compared to only using the probability measures. The improvement was small, however, and this means that the original assumptions about what people would value or dislike were pretty much on target. Consequently I will omit Richards and Cionea's complications to the model in my summary of results here.

You might also notice that all the scales are double-edged, and the direction of scoring indicates whether the items measure a cost or a benefit, a facilitator or an impediment. So the costs scale could be used indirectly to assess benefits, the appropriateness items also index inappropriateness, and so forth. You might also have noticed that all the items refer to "my friend." This is because we did the initial studies with materials that proposed that you might argue with a close friend. Other studies would require minor rewording to refer to a parent, a spouse, or whatever relational roles are under study.

All these variables were used to predict *intention to argue*, and those items are also in the Appendix. The studies we designed gave respondents little descriptions of situations and asked whether the participants would be interested in arguing or not. We intentionally wrote the situations so that arguments were invited, but not required. We did this to maximize the freedom of decision that our respondents would have. We also used several situations in each study. One dealt with a personal topic, one with a public topic, and one with a workplace topic. We added the last kind of topic because we felt that these issues were common, even in the lives of undergraduate respondents, and we were curious to see how they compared to the better-researched public and personal topics.

We used the same situations in several studies. Here they are:

- [Public topic:] You and a good friend are both very fond of music. Besides just listening to lots of music over the radio and on iPods, when you have a little extra money, both of you like to go to fairly expensive concerts. You really like different sorts of music, however, and always have. One day when you're just spending a little time together, your friend makes a remark about how good the sort of music s/he likes is, and says that the kind of music you like is awful.

- [Personal topic:] You and a good friend have just had a third person come into your lives because your friend has been dating him/her. The problem is that you and the third person really don't get along very well. You don't like him/her because you don't trust him/her to treat your friend well, and he/she doesn't seem to like you, either. You and the third person have made some effort to be pleasant to one another for the sake of your common friend, but your friend has begun to notice that you seem to be holding back a little. One day when you're just spending some time together, your friend makes a remark about how you don't seem very sincere about liking the third person, and that you really should make more of an effort.
- [Professional topic:] You and a good friend work together in an office. You have essentially the same job and your common boss gives the two of you similar work to do. Your boss pays attention to how you're doing on your current tasks, and when one of you has finished, your boss gives that person the next set of assignments. You think that the two of you work at about the same pace and do about the same quality of work. But your friend has apparently begun to feel that you're not quite doing as much as he/she does. One day at work when you're just spending a little time together without much to do, your friend makes a remark about how you don't seem to be doing your share and that he/she is a little resentful about having do extra work.

All three of these situations invited arguing but also allowed room for the respondent to avoid engagement, too. On the public topic, the respondent might defend his or her musical choice, or might just grunt and change the topic. On the personal issue, the respondent might explain why the third person isn't trustworthy, or might just give a hollow promise to try harder. The workplace topic might call out a reasoned defense of the respondent's conduct, or a counter-attack on the friend's laxity, or a little joke about just getting through the day. We designed these so that a reasonable person might argue or not. In fact, people were pretty variable in their intentions to engage.

The results showed that we made a good choice to include different sorts of topics. Though some predictors were fairly common, we found that the topic type (public, personal, workplace) made a difference in why people were willing to argue or not. Let me summarize what Hample et al. (2012) discovered.

For the public topics, people had more intention to engage in the argument when such an argument would be appropriate, when it was expected to be civil, and most importantly, when the respondent expected to win. Interestingly, intention to argue was higher when the other person was expected to be unreasonable.

This last result reminds us of the low stakes in many public issue arguments, and of the possibility of arguing for play (see Chapter 2). For this sort of argument, people wanted it to be civil, enacted in suitable circumstances, and to hold out the possibility of being able to prove that the respondent was right. Some stubbornness on the other person's part might actually make the interaction more engaging and interesting. Notice the things that didn't enter into the engagement intention: general costs, general benefits, and resolvability. For a pass-the-time argument about music (probably not the first one), there really weren't important costs and benefits, and resolving the dispute wasn't important at all.

Arguments about the personal topic generated a different pattern. For that issue, the engagement intention was most affected by a positive estimate that the respondent would win the argument, and was also increased by anticipation of possible general benefits and a sense that arguing was appropriate under those circumstances. The effects of winning and appropriateness were similar to those for the public topic, but here there also needed to be a feeling that the argument would be beneficial if it happened. Interestingly, resolvability was again unimportant. Perhaps respondents understood that this matter was unlikely to be settled in a single episode, but that it needed to be explored anyway. Costs also didn't enter into the intention. Important issues justify some effort and emotional exposure, so perhaps respondents felt the likelihood of resource or emotional expense could be neglected. Similarly, civility and other's reasonableness didn't predict intention. These, too, might be negligible considerations when an important relational issue is at stake.

Results for the workplace topic were different from those for the other two sorts of issue. Respondents were more likely to argue with their coworker when they felt the circumstances were appropriate, when there was a chance of resolving the matter, and most importantly, when the respondent felt that he or she would win. A curious result was that intentions to argue were higher when respondents felt there would be substantial costs to engaging. This may have been because a workplace argument will ordinarily only take place when there are substantial stakes. If the argument were cost-free—that is, if the arguing didn't require effort or risk—it might not be worth pursuing at all. Possibly, people take the attitude that work life is going to be filled with minor annoyances anyway, and these should just be ignored. Higher stakes imply more costs, and perhaps these are the only sorts of things that people are really willing to dispute about at work.

Besides reinforcing the importance of topic type, this initial study emphasized the general importance of appropriateness and, most strongly of all, the estimate that the arguer would prevail. The finding about appropriateness is encouraging, because it presumes that people are sensitive to these matters. Being able to see that an argument ought to be delayed or resituated in order to be more constructive is an advanced understanding. The importance of winning is somewhat less encouraging, because it participates in a distributive "I win/you lose" orientation to arguing. If both people have it, the result is likely to be combative, what is technically called eristic arguing (see Chapter 6). Serial argument research has shown that distributive tactics are associated with unfavorable outcomes, whereas integrative tactics lead to more relational satisfaction, civility, and estimated resolvability (see Chapter 4).

Soon after the first study was completed, Cionea, Hample, and Paglieri (2011) wondered whether these sorts of results would generalize to other populations, so they designed a similar study to be conducted in Romania. One thing that made Romania an interesting site for study is that the nation had only emerged from the Soviet bloc in the previous generation. In post-communist Romania the younger generation, who had spent little time under Soviet constraints, aggressively sought intellectual and expressive freedom, but the older generations had learned to be more circumspect. In this study, all the topics were what we would classify as public ones, but people were asked to respond in terms of either a friend or a romantic partner. Possible argument topics were taste in movies and preference for political candidates. Most of the respondents were university students.

Results had many similarities to the Hample et al. (2012) work with U.S. undergraduates. In Romania, intention to argue was increased by the estimate of appropriateness, the likelihood of winning, and the perception that the other person would be reasonable. The magnitude of the effects was less than in the U.S. study, but the general set of continuing factors was similar. Interestingly, it did not make a difference whether the argument (on the same topic) was with a friend or a romantic partner.

As I noted above, all the situational stimuli were written in such a way that argumentation was invited but not required. Hample and Irions (2014) decided to pursue this matter by rewriting the stimuli to produce two versions, one in which arguments were invited and one in which arguing was more or less demanded. We created the "demanding" conditions by adding verbally aggressive remarks to the end of the scenarios. For example, the public topic about music had this comment added: "Your friend says, 'That crap you listen to is just stupid,' and it's obvious that s/he is being very aggressive and wants a verbal fight." This manipulation created a clear demand, an indication that the other person insisted on engagement, so that avoidance could be interpreted as a failure of commitment or a concession of some sort. It was still possible to decide not to argue, but that choice was not as conveniently available as in the "invited" conditions.

Results showed that the demands generated more intention to argue, but only for the personal (new romantic partner) and workplace (slacking off) topics. For the public issue (music), intention to argue was about the same regardless of whether arguing was invited or demanded. This might well be due to the differing stakes in the possible arguments. Personal issues, as we have seen, are more involving than public ones. Workplace matters seem to be intermediate between them. So people may engage on the public topics for their own reasons—to have fun arguing, to pass the time, to share conversation with a friend. These opportunities can be taken up or passed, depending on one's mood. But for more consequential matters, a demand might signal an urgent necessity to participate.

This study also afforded the opportunity to check the original results in Hample et al. (2012) to see if they held with a replication sample from the same undergraduate population. Engagement in public topics was affected by the estimate that one would win and by the sense that circumstances made arguing appropriate. These results appeared in both the original paper and in the Romanian one, but those investigations also reported some effects for civility and other's reasonableness, which were missing here. On personal topics, people had the highest intentions to argue when they thought they would win, believed arguing would be appropriate, expected the other person to be unreasonable, and anticipated higher costs and benefits (and had been demanded to argue). Several of these findings—winning, appropriateness, and high benefits—appeared in the first study. The findings about costs and (relatedly) the other's unreasonableness were new here, but this may be a phenomenon similar to the one I speculated about earlier with regard to workplace arguing: people may only undertake relationally important arguments when the issue is daunting, and this could imply costs and stubbornness. Finally, the workplace topic generated higher arguing intentions when people expected to win, thought arguing would be appropriate, estimated a good chance of resolving things, and anticipated high costs. This is precisely the same list of factors produced by Hample, Paglieri, and Na.

This list of costs and benefits has also been applied to the organizational context, to see whether it would affect whether and how employees would dissent when they thought something was wrong at work (Zhan & Hample, 2016). Employees who do express themselves can address their remarks to superiors, to coworkers, or to external others (e.g., a spouse). All of the costs and benefits from this research program were involved in predicting which sort of person would hear the employees' remarks. Whether or not people would dissent directly to their superiors was particularly well predicted by these estimates of arguing's perceived costs and benefits.

Though this line of research is young, several things are coming clear. Appropriateness and optimism about winning contribute to the intention to engage across the board—regardless of topic type, whether the other person was a friend or romantic partner, whether the data were collected in the U.S. or Romania, or whether arguing was invited or demanded. The other predictors appeared in some topic/relationship/demand conditions but not others. An intriguing finding is that workplace and perhaps personal topics especially call out arguing when expected costs are high, not low. There seems to be something about important issues that includes the idea that arguing will take a lot of effort and involve noticeable risk. These might prove to be defining features of high-stakes topics. We found this sort of results for the workplace and personal topics, but not public issues.

Cionea, Richards, and Straub (2017) have recently reconsidered this idea that argument engagement decisions are due to cost/benefit calculations. They noticed that all the variables—prospect of winning, appropriateness, other's reasonability, and so forth—came from Paglieri's initial theoretical analysis. If Paglieri's thinking were incomplete or wrong, that would be a problem with the whole line of research. So they restarted everything by asking ordinary people what they took into account when deciding whether to engage or avoid. This is an inductive approach to the problem, in contrast to the deductive one inspired by Paglieri's theory. The researchers received almost 2,000 descriptions of engagement-relevant considerations, which were eventually condensed to about 90 items that were used to measure 15 factors (e.g., own motives, social context, other's preparedness, right to speak, etc.). They conducted a study that related these 15 scores with intention to engage. They also varied topic type (personal or public) and relationship type (friend or romantic), as well as sample (undergraduate or mTurk). Neither topic nor relationship type had much influence on the engagement decisions, which suggests that Cionea and colleagues may be looking at some fairly general factors.

On one hand, results from the new measurement system were grossly comparable to the prior work: costs and benefits did in fact predict intention to engage. In detail, however, Cionea and colleagues found different variables to be important than in the Paglieri-stimulated work. Perhaps this was to be expected because the variance in people's cost/benefit estimates was being parceled into 15 categories instead of half that number. Where their likelihood of success variable didn't predict engagement, their measure of one's own preparedness for the argument did, and one might suppose these two measures would tap the same general expectations. Their appropriateness factor didn't predict engagement either (as it had in the Paglieri work), but they had some other measures that might have been siphoning off some of the specific elements of appropriateness (e.g., social context).

So some further work will be needed to reconcile the Paglieri-stimulated results with those from the new inductively generated measurement program. It will be worthwhile to have such a merger. While that work is going on, however, we can still be reasonably confident that the anticipated costs and benefits of arguing are decisive in determining whether a person will argue or not. The Paglieri results have been replicated more often to this point, and if detailed guidance is needed it should probably come from those studies for the time being. The research community is merely pursuing some detailed investigation of how to describe "cost" and "benefit" most usefully.

Features of Situations Involving Arguing

At the beginning of the chapter I outlined an understanding of situations and goals that derives from a recent study (Hample, 2016). To review, the idea is that reasonably apparent features of the situation lead to primary goals, that those goals lead to subjective elements of the episode, and that those then result in development of secondary goals. Two of the subjective situational features in that study were whether the episode was argumentative and whether it was conflictive. These two things can certainly co-occur, but they are conceptually distinct. Whether the interaction was argumentative was measured by asking if reasons and evidence were exchanged, and "conflictive" was operationalized by asking if the conversants explicitly disagreed. A person can argue without disagreement being present, as when someone argues to display identity (see Chapter 2). And a person can engage in disagreement without doing any reasoning (as when someone just yells or repeats a position loudly). Being either argumentative or conflictive was regarded as a subjective, emergent situational feature because they were both thought to develop (or not) as the conversation progressed. Even if one person wanted to argue or do conflict, the other person probably had to be open to the possibility for it to happen, and that is why these two things are emergent.

Here, I want to pull out the data regarding arguing to highlight connections to all the other situational elements: the reasonably apparent features, the primary goals, the other subjective factors, and the secondary goals. Some of the results that follow were not reported in the original paper. The study involved several substantial data sets. Two were open-ended (with about 500 respondents) and involved coding people's descriptions of interactions they had experienced. The first of these asked people to report about recent interpersonal interactions and the second asked them to give information about memorable encounters. The recent interactions did not have to be important and the memorable ones did not have to be recent. Neither had to involve arguing or conflict. A third data set (about 1,500 respondents) was closed-ended, and respondents gave their own estimates of whether arguing and conflict would likely be involved. In that investigation, respondents were assigned to imagine they were in an academic, a relational, a workplace, or a daily activities situation that I described to them.

Let us begin by seeing whether there were any differences between recent (probably routine) interactions and memorable ones. The first result that deserves our attention is that arguing (exchanging reasons) was much more common in the memorable situations, 38% versus 25% ($p < .001$). The same was true for the presence of conflict (clear disagreement), 28% versus 15% ($p < .001$). An immediate implication is that people argue for reasons other than dealing with disagreement, because the frequency of arguing was higher than that for conflict in both sorts of situation. People spontaneously give reasons for what they think or do, and this does not need to be stimulated by the presence of any disagreement.

But the more interesting result was that memorable interactions involved more arguing than the routine conversations did. More or less by definition, memorable encounters are highly consequential and they can result in life changes and/or personal insights. Relational issues, for example, accounted for 23% of the memorable topics but only 8% of the recent ones. Many of the memorable interactions probably involved new meanings for participants—a reason to go to college, a realization that he or she needs to change attitudes toward the opposite sex, an abrupt understanding of financial realities, a change in the composition of one's nuclear family, and so forth. We saw in Chapter 1 that management of meanings is the key function of arguing. The more consequential interactions were also the ones most likely to be developed by means of arguments. In the closed-ended data set, the more involving an episode was, the more likely it was to contain arguments ($r = .29$), but there was far less connection between being involving and containing conflict ($r = .05, p = .06$).

Reasonably Apparent Features

So let us examine the relationships between arguing and the other elements of the situations. We will begin with the reasonably apparent features. These included own and other's sex, the episode's topic, the type of interaction (academic, social, etc.), the relationship between the interactants, the physical setting, the medium of communication, and the number of people present. Arguments are co-constructed and emergent in a conversation, but these situational features are simple facts, easily observable, and generally not negotiated by the conversants in the moment. Do any of them open or close an interactional space for arguing?

For the recent interactions, arguing was more common for discussions about material goods, relational issues, and finances ($p = .06$); with best friends, Greek brothers/sisters, or superiors (boss, teacher); and in the respondent's residence ($p = .08$). Arguing was equally likely for male and female respondents, for male and female co-interactants, for all the types of interaction (academic, job, social, and business/professional), for all the media of communication (face-to-face, phone, and internet), and regardless of the number of people present.

In the memorable episodes, arguing was more frequent on relational topics, for social interactions, and with present or former romantic partners. Arguing was equally likely in any physical setting, with either sex of respondent, with either sex of interlocutor, and with any number of people present. Finally, arguing was less common in face-to-face interactions (as opposed to phone or Internet).

In the closed-ended study in which respondents were assigned to topic conditions, arguing was most common for relational issues and for female respondents. It was equally likely with either sex of interlocutor or in any of the physical settings, and it was least frequent for the daily activities topic.

Several common results appeared when comparing the reasonably apparent features to the presence or absence of arguing in the recent and memorable situations studies. Relational topics were particularly likely to call out reasoning. Males and females (whether they were the study participants or the other person) showed no difference in whether or not they gave reasons. Arguing occurred most often in close relationships, but for the recent episodes these were friendship and for the memorable encounters they were romantic partners. Elements of setting and medium made no discernible difference to whether people argued or not. The closed-ended data collection reinforced the importance of relational topics for the natural appearance of arguments, and the near-irrelevance of people's sex to whether or not they argue.

These details lead to an interesting take-away point. The reasonably apparent features of a situation are more or less given. That is, they really aren't constructed in the moment, they are obvious rather than subtle or subjective, and they aren't emergent either. They are just there, and participants don't have any real control over them (except that they can choose not to participate in the conversation). These simple social realities have influence on whether or not people argue. Some social facts seem to call out or at least make a place for reasoning, and others seem to impede it. This book emphasizes the mutuality of arguing, the sense it which it emerges between the two people as a result of their shared efforts to make meanings and understand the world. But here we have noticed several things that are pretty much invulnerable to interpretive or intersubjective work but that still affect whether it is natural to give reasons in conversation.

Primary Goals

Primary goals are the framing ones, those that define what sort of situation a person is in. Emergence of a primary goal gives direction to one's thoughts and actions. The framing goal generates the first impulse as to what to say. That impulse may be edited later, based on secondary goals and the arguer's understanding of what kind of interaction is beginning to develop, but this is where our motivational energies begin.

Dillard (e.g., Dillard, Segrin, & Harden, 1989), who initiated this idea, developed a list of primary goals, but because of his research interests that list took for granted that persuasion was at the root of the interaction. We would like something more general because people argue for more reasons than to persuade (e.g., to express themselves, to show off, to pass the time, to play, and so forth). In the first two studies on situations (Hample, 2016), one of the things that we did was to code the open-ended descriptions for what goals we thought were present. Notice that this new list refers to interactions generally, and not specifically to those that are centered on persuading or arguing.

Here is the list we generated, along with the proportion of the time each goal was found to be the primary one. The results were a bit different for the recent and memorable episodes, and both were clearly different from the closed-ended survey. The most common defining goal in recent and memorable interactions was relational maintenance (56% in the recent interactions, and 45% in the memorable ones). This was followed in both data sets by "obtain benefit" (23% in recent interactions, and 36% in memorable ones). Third most common was "fulfill organizational role," which is almost never studied (12% for recent, and 7% for memorable episodes). The other goals we found were less common. These included "manage own face" (3% recent, 4% memorable), "cathartic emotional expression" (2% recent, 5% memorable), and "plan a future event" (4% recent, 3% memorable).

We found quite different results in the study in which we supplied the situation descriptions and asked people to imagine what they would say or do, rather than permitting people to remember their own interactions. In the closed-ended data set, cathartic expression was by far the most common primary goal (59%), followed by relational maintenance (17%), managing own face (10%), fulfilling role obligations (7%), obtaining a benefit (5%), and planning a future event (3%). The differences in the proportions from study to study are obviously due to the situation the respondent was thinking about, and whether the people recalled one themselves or we supplied one ready-made. But all these goals have the capacity to define a particular interaction.

Was arguing differentially associated with primary goals? That is, once an interaction was privately defined as being in pursuit of a particular objective, did that affect whether or not people would give reasons?

The data really do not give a clear pattern, but that is a finding in and of itself. Here are the details. For the recent encounters, the framing goal didn't affect whether or not people argued, because the incidence of arguing was pretty evenly distributed across the goal types. But in the memorable conversations the primary goal did make a difference as to whether or not people reported giving reasons. Arguing was most common in the relational maintenance and catharsis frames, and least common when the interaction was defined as being about role fulfillment or own face management. The closed-ended study also showed clear differences in arguing behavior depending on which goal the respondent chose to frame the interaction. The most arguing appeared for the cathartic expression and planning future events goals, and the least for relational maintenance and fulfilling role obligations (own face management and obtaining a benefit were in between).

So, as I said, this was not a clear pattern, except that cathartic expression was especially argumentative. Apparently people do not express themselves by just saying highly emotional things—they give *reasons* for how they feel and what they think. Many people in Western cultures have been taught that reason and emotion are opposites—that the more you do one, the less you do the other. This has never been true. You can do both at a high level simultaneously, or can do neither at all when you speak or think reflexively. Our feelings are usually not mysteries to ourselves—we can generally say why we are upset or happy, and that means that we can give reasons for our emotional states. Nor do we go through life pausing randomly to reason something out as though we were doing a geometric proof. We have motivations for what we think about and say, and those motivations mean that arguing originates in impulses and feelings. That is one way of explaining the importance of goals in the SGPA model of message production (see Chapter 1).

So we can say that any of the primary goals in these investigations make arguments welcome, but that none of them require reasons. This is not a disappointing finding at all. It means that arguing is not constrained by framing goals, and that any goal can be pursued by means of reasons if the person is so inclined.

Subjective Situational Features

To this point, we have examined reasonably apparent features of a situation, which are more or less under the world's control, and primary goals, which are privately determined by one person. But once the conversation gets underway, it can take on a course of its own. It is metaphorical to say that a conversation is alive, but the idea is useful. One comment can spark another, and suddenly neither person is talking about what he or she intended to say a moment ago. The conversation partly controls what happens, and it shares this responsibility with the two people. So as you participate in an interaction, the conversation itself becomes an object outside of you, one that you can perceive and react to. The same is true for the other person, of course. As things move along, you notice different things and you absorb them into your own expectations, prejudices, and prior understandings. The meanings that result are neither reasonably apparent nor necessarily shared by the other person. So they are subjective.

In the research projects we have been dealing with here, two of the subjective features were whether the conversation was *argumentative* or *conflictive*, as I have said. Other subjective elements included both *politeness* and *rudeness*. These were analyzed separately because an interaction can be polite at one moment and rude in another, or both all the time, or neither at any point. I also looked for evidence that people perceived *obstacles* to what they wanted to accomplish, and whether they reported *omissions*, things that they might have said but decided not to. In addition, I sought information about the participants' *emotions*, and asked what the respondent thought the other person's feelings were as well. I found evidence for the existence of the following emotions, and used the same list for self and other: sad, angry, anxious, disappointed, happy, dissatisfied, surprised, guilty, fearful, proud, grateful, hopeful, and bored.

Our immediate interest is to see whether arguing was associated with any of these other subjective experiences. Perhaps arguing is part of a group of impressions, so that if we have a particular sensation we are more or less likely to argue. Or maybe arguing is equally likely no matter what we think is going on. What subjective experiences are associated with conversational reasoning?

To begin, let us see whether arguing and conflict were related. For recent conversations they were, such that arguing was most likely in the presence of disagreement, and least likely when conflict was absent. The same was true for the memorable conversations that people recalled. But in the survey in which people were assigned to a situation description that I wrote, respondents reported no association at all between arguing and noticing disagreement. I am inclined to discount the last result in favor of the first ones on the grounds that people probably had a much better grasp of what happened in their actual conversations than in their imagined ones.

The civility of conversations can be approximated by seeing how the people managed themselves while talking. Politeness was not associated with arguing in the recent conversations, but rudeness was. Only a few of these conversations were recalled as having been rude, but when they were, arguing was more common.

Neither politeness nor rudeness was associated with arguing in memorable episodes. But in the survey, with its greater statistical power, arguing was noticeably associated with politeness ($r = .41$) and contraindicated by the presence of rudeness ($r = -.09$). Politeness and rudeness were negatively related, as we would expect ($r = -.58$). The survey results are probably more trustworthy here because they were based on gradations of things rather than just their presence or absence, and did not have any problem with small cell frequencies. The connection between politeness and arguing could mean several things: that people are more polite because they are being somewhat aggressive when they argue and have to compensate for that, that a polite climate makes a place for arguing, or that a well-mannered argument is noticed as being polite.

Obstacles might well be argumentative problems and an omission could be a solution to the difficulty. Chapter 2 mentioned blurters, and indicated that more capable arguers edit what they say. However, just about every adult blurts sometimes and edits sometimes. Omission is a kind of editing. Were omissions connected to other subjective experiences? In recent episodes, we found some connection ($p = .06$), such that arguing was most common in the presence of worries about offending the other person or escalating the argument (these were among the specific obstacles we coded for). Arguing was unconnected to omissions. For the data describing memorable conversations, giving reasons was securely associated with obstacles. Arguing was most common when participants were concerned about offending the other person or third parties, escalating the argument, or avoiding negative feelings for self. It appears that arguing was taken to be a way of protecting oneself from making things worse. For these same memorable conversations, arguing and omissions were associated, with people arguing more often when they said they had suppressed something else they were thinking. In the closed-ended survey, arguing was associated with both obstacles ($r = .18$) and omissions ($r = .17$). Obstacles and editing co-occurred at a high level, $r = .70$, suggesting why the two main results were so similar. So all three studies showed that obstacles were associated with more arguing activity.

In other words, conversational challenges were met with public reasoning. When people dealt with obstacles by editing what they were going to say, the memorable and closed-ended surveys indicated that arguing was also more likely. So the omissions resulted not in silence but in further argumentation. Perhaps people suppressed their first argument and gave their second one, or perhaps they simply fictionalized some rationalization for their conclusion when they were unwilling to say what they actually thought.

This brings us to emotions for self and other. Only a few emotions were coded often enough to justify statistical analysis for the recent and memorable conversations data. For recent interactions, arguing was more common when our respondent was angry. When the other person was reported as having been angry, arguing was more likely then as well. For the memorable conversations, arguing was also somewhat more common ($p = .09$) when the respondent was angry, and more likely to occur when the other person was angry, too. So in these recalled conversations, a consistent result was that arguing was associated with anger. Perhaps the reasoning created the anger, perhaps the anger stimulated the arguing, or perhaps both happened from moment to moment.

The survey had a much larger sample size and it measured the degrees of emotions rather than just their presence. This afforded more precise statistical estimates. Those results showed that arguing was more common when the respondents reported that they would have had these feelings: anger ($r = .11$), anxiety ($r = .18$), happiness ($r = .28$), and gratitude ($r = .35$). Arguing was less likely when participants felt sad ($r = -.13$), surprised ($r = -.05$), guilty ($r = -.13$), or bored ($r = -.24$). The respondents indicated more arguing activity when the other person would have been happy ($r = .19$) or grateful ($r = .24$), but less arguing when the other person was expected to have been angry ($r = -.06$), disappointed ($r = -.12$), sad ($r = -.09$), bored ($r = -.16$), or guilty ($r = -.08$).

The survey results agreed on the association between arguing and own anger, and added some additional detail that the two other studies were not really equipped to discover. The associations between arguing and positive emotions are interesting. Arguing was more common when the participant imagined self or other feeling happy or grateful for the conversational experience. Negative emotions aside from anger were also relevant. Guilt, boredom, and sadness on the part of either person reduced the argumentative energy of the conversation. So these more statistically sensitive results reveal the other side of arguing's coin. Arguing does happen more often in the presence of anger, but it is also associated with happiness. This reminds us that all arguing is not combative, and that it can also serve constructive social ends, such as clarifying relationships, displaying identity, and cementing agreements. Arguing can be associated with either frustration or satisfaction, depending on the developing qualities of the conversation.

In sum, interpersonal arguing is one of the emergent properties of an interaction. One person can decide to give reasons, but only two people can exchange or challenge them. Statements can often be interpreted as either assertions or reasons, so even if one person is happily reasoning along the other person might not even register that any efforts to manage meaning are happening. Arguing is part of the emerging character of a conversation and tends to be associated with disagreement, obstacles, and anger, but it seems to be done politely in ordinary circumstances and is often associated with positive feelings about the conversation.

Secondary Goals

The final part of our theorized sequence is secondary goals, which are thought to be formed in light of the subjective elements of a communication episode (Hample, 2016). People only have one set of goals, and in a particular circumstance one of them will probably become the primary goal that defines what kind of encounter is going on for that person. The other goals are still available, however, and their motivational energies might modify (or even overrule) the direction set by the framing goal. So for this research summary, the list of secondary goals is the same as the list of primary ones: relational maintenance, obtaining a benefit, promoting or defending own face, cathartic expression, fulfilling a role obligation, or planning a future event.

Goals indicate what is wanted, and arguing is a way to accomplish many things in the social world. Is arguing associated with any of the secondary goals in particular?

First let us examine the studies in which people reported actual conversations to us. In the recent conversations data set, arguing was more common when people were managing their own face needs or doing cathartic expression. The other goals—relational maintenance, fulfilling role requirements, obtaining benefits, and planning future events—made no difference to the frequency with which people argued. When respondents described memorable episodes to us, our coding gave these results: arguing was more common when people were managing their own face needs and were sensitive to relational maintenance needs. Obtaining benefits was also associated with arguing, but negatively: people argued less when pursuing this secondary goal. Perhaps they tried to obtain benefits by simply asking without giving a reason. Arguing was unrelated to cathartic expression, fulfilling role obligations, and planning future events. In both studies, people managed their face requirements—projecting a favorable image, defending one's character against attacks—by using arguments. This is reminiscent of the identity frame for arguing (Chapter 2). The other results were more scattered, perhaps because our coding only indicated whether something was present or absent and not the degree to which it appeared.

The survey did not have those problems. There, arguing was more common when any of the goals was in play: relational maintenance ($r = .25$), fulfilling role obligations ($r = .35$), managing own face ($r = .37$), cathartic expression ($r = .40$), obtaining benefits ($r = .23$), and planning future events ($r = .34$). This is the whole list of goals, so we can see that arguing was a natural impulse in (secondary) pursuit of any of them.

The studies of recalled conversations associated arguing most clearly with doing facework for self. A glance back at the primary goals part of this section will remind you that own face was rarely the framing goal for any of the conversations people recalled for us. The most common primary goal was relational maintenance. In the survey, it was cathartic expression. So what we have seen in this section, particularly in the survey results, is that when secondary goals came into play, arguing came with them. Once a person is pursuing multiple goals, things immediately become more complex than when only one objective is in sight (Caughlin, 2010). The evidence from this section of the chapter shows that arguing is a way of navigating that complexity. That should not be any surprise, since arguing is perhaps our most capable tool for dealing with subtle meanings and complex social moments.

Conclusions

The purpose of this chapter has been to summarize how arguing is situated within conversations. Quite a bit of the chapter dealt with starting points, things that happen in or before the first moment of interaction. These were reasonably apparent features, especially topics, and the cost and benefit estimates that people use to decide whether to argue or not. But we also saw how arguing moves through the conversational experience of developing a framing goal, getting a feel for the climate of the interaction, and making complicating choices of what secondary goals need to be in play to generate a satisfying episode. Arguing participated in all these meanings—What am I mainly doing here? What is my sense and feel for what is going on? What else do I need to do? In fact, arguing by yourself or with the other person may well be helping to shape those meanings. Reasoning gives local focus to an exchange and points people in the direction of what they need to talk about.

Some of the findings in the last part of the chapter were encouraging but not especially striking. Arguing is equally likely regardless of the participants' sex, it doesn't matter very much where the conversation takes place, and reasoning can be used in pursuit of any of the goals. The encouraging part of this is that it shows that arguing is a widely applicable tool, available to anyone in any setting, useful in nearly any social pursuit.

The need for more concentrated research on these issues is apparent when we compare the findings about public and personal topics to the more general findings about topics from the Hample (2016) data sets. In the latter, we mainly noticed that arguing was especially common on relational topics. But this doesn't go very far in saying why that is so, or how those arguments are shaped by their topical domain. In the personal/public research, we learned much more about topics, at least in regard to that one distinction. We saw, for instance, that personal arguments are more involving, that public ones are more enjoyable, and that personal issues are those with the highest stakes. These were deep differences, of the sort unavailable in the results of the more general studies summarized in the final section of the chapter. If we can learn so much more about argument topics by studying them in detail, perhaps we can learn far more about goals, climates, face needs, and other matters by focusing theory and research on them one at a time. Some recent work on the idea of "argument stakes" may prove fruitful in delineating more precise research questions (Hample et al., 2016).

This chapter should have made clear that arguing is a choice, a more or less intentional effort to do something. Some circumstances invite arguing—expecting to win, seeing it as appropriate in that time and place, and having the prospect of a civil encounter with an open-minded partner. Sometimes the presence of noticeable challenges is only a signal that the topic is important and needs to be resolved. We might argue in order to work through a relationship problem, to deal with identity issues for self or other, or to accomplish some specific task. Achieving any of these goals is a benefit, but arguing always involves costs as well. Thinking is effortful, expressing oneself politely can be a strain, and explaining what you think can expose parts of your inner life that you might want to keep private. This is true of the other person as well, and the two of you together will construct a conversation that might be pleasant or explosive (or boring). All these considerations are fleeting and the ratio of cost to benefit can change from instant to instant. If the conversation takes an ugly turn, the benefits you were pursuing may no longer seem worth seeking. If the conversation opens up into a welcoming place when you were uncertain about your reception a moment earlier, you might be more expansive in your reasoning and aims.

This is a long way around to get back to the first point in the chapter—that arguing is always situated. This isn't a simple observation, as it must have seemed at the start. Instead it is a summary of manifold complexities that never repeat themselves from one interaction to another, or even from one moment to the next. You are responsive to your social environment, and among the responses you make some are argumentative. You may pursue a claim, evade an engagement, or modify what you are doing in light of what is happening in that instant. The more perceptive you are about these matters, the better you will argue.

References

Argyle, M., Furnham, A., & Graham, J. A. (1981). *Social situations*. Cambridge: Cambridge University Press.

Bates, C. E., & Samp, J. A. (2011). Examining the effects of planning and empathic accuracy on communication in relational and nonrelational conflict interactions. *Communication Studies, 62*, 207–223.

Baxter, L. A (1984). Trajectories of relationship disengagement. *Journal of Social and Personal Relationships, 1*, 29–48.

Caughlin, J. P. (2010). A multiple goal theory of personal relationships: Conceptual integration and program overview. *Journal of Social and Personal Relationships, 27*, 824–848.

Cionea. I. A., Hample, D., & Paglieri, F. (2011). A test of the argument engagement model in Romania. In F. Zenker (Ed.), *Argumentation: Cognition and community: Proceedings of the 9th international conference of the Ontario Society for the Study of Argumentation.* Retrieved from http://scholar.uwindsor.ca/ossaarchive/OSSA9/papersandcommentaries/6/

Cionea, I. A., Richards, A. S., & Straub, S. K. (2017). Factors predicting the intent to engage in arguments in close relationships: A revised model. *Argumentation, 31*, 121–164.

Clark, R. A., & Delia, J. G. (1979). Topoi and rhetorical competence. *Quarterly Journal of Speech, 65*, 187–206.

Dai, Y., & Zhan, M. (2016, November). *Re-conceptualizing argument type: The utility of arguments about others' personal issues.* Paper presented at the annual meeting of the National Communication Association, Philadelphia, PA.

Dillard, J. P., Segrin, C., & Harden, J. M. (1989). Primary and secondary goals in the production of interpersonal influence messages. *Communication Monographs, 56*, 19–38.

van Eemeren, F. H., & Grootendorst, R. (1983). *Speech acts in argumentative discussions.* Dordrecht: Foris.

van Eemeren, F. H., & Grootendorst, R. (2004). *A systematic theory of argumentation: The pragma-dialectical approach.* Cambridge: Cambridge University Press.

Hample, D. (2016). A theory of interpersonal goals and situations. *Communication Research, 43*, 344–371.

Hample, D., Dai, Y., & Zhan, M. (2016). Argument stakes: Preliminary conceptualizations and empirical descriptions. *Argumentation and Advocacy, 52*, 199–213.

Hample, D., & Irions, A. L. (2014). Argument engagement under invitational versus demanding conditions. In C. H. Palczewski (Ed.), *Disturbing argument* (pp. 149–154). New York, NY: Taylor & Francis.

Hample, D., Paglieri, F., & Na, L. (2012). The costs and benefits of arguing: Predicting the decision whether to engage or not. In F. H. van Eemeren & B. Garssen (Eds.), *Topical themes in argumentation theory: Twenty exploratory studies* (pp. 307–322). New York NY: Springer.

Hample, D., Richards, A. S., & Skubisz, C. (2013). Blurting. *Communication Monographs, 80*, 503–532.

Hample, D., Sells, A., & Inclán Velázquez, A. L. (2009). The effects of topic type and personalization of conflict on assessments of fallacies. *Communication Reports, 22*, 74–88.

Honeycutt, J. M. (2001). Satisfaction with marital issues and topics scale (SMI). In J. Touliatos, B. F. Perlmutter, & M. A. Straus (Eds.), *Handbook of family measurement techniques* (Vol. 1, p. 92). Thousand Oaks, CA: Sage.

Honeycutt, J. M., & Sheldon, P. A. (2017). *Scripts and communication for relationships* (2nd ed.) New York, NY: Peter Lang.

Infante, D. A., & Wigley, C. J. (1986). Verbal aggressiveness: An interpersonal model and measure. *Communication Monographs, 53*, 61–69.

Johnson, A. J. (2002). Beliefs about arguing: A comparison of public-issue and personal-issue arguments. *Communication Reports, 15*, 99–112.

Johnson, A. J. (2009). A functional approach to interpersonal argument. Differences between public- and personal-issue arguments. *Communication Reports, 22*, 13–28.

Johnson, A. J., Hample, D., & Cionea, I. A. (2014). Understanding argumentation in interpersonal communication: The implications of distinguishing between public and personal topics. *Communication Yearbook, 38*, 145–173.

Johnson, A. J., Kelley, K. M., Liu, S.-J., Averbeck, J. M., King, S. D., & Bostwick, E. N. (2014). Family serial arguments: Beliefs about the argument and perceived stress from the argument. *Communication Reports, 27*, 116–128.

Kelley, H. H., Holmes, J. G., Kerr, N. L., Reis, H. T., Rusbult, C. E., & van Lange, P. A. M. (2003). *An atlas of interpersonal situations*. Cambridge: Cambridge University Press.

Laursen, B. (1995). Conflict and social interaction in adolescent relationships. *Journal of Research on Adolescence, 5*, 55–70.

Paglieri, F. (2009). Ruinous arguments: Escalation of disagreement and the dangers of arguing. In J. Ritola (Ed.), *Argument cultures: Proceedings of OSSA 2009*. http://scholar.uwindsor.ca/ossaarchive/OSSA8/papersandcommentaries/121/

Paglieri, F., & Castelfranchi, C. (2010). Why argue? Towards a cost-benefit analysis of argumentation. *Argument and Computation, 1*, 71–91.

Papp, L. M., Cummings, E. M., & Goeke-Morey, M. C. (2009). For richer, for poorer: Money as a topic of marital conflict in the home. *Family Relations, 58*, 91–103.

Richards, A. S., & Cionea, I. A. (2015). Extending the argument engagement model: Expected utility and interacting traits as predictors of the intention to argue with friends. *Journal of Argumentation in Context, 4*, 110–133.

Sillars, A. L. (1980). The stranger and the spouse as target persons for compliance-gaining strategies: A subjective expected utility model. *Human Communication Research, 6*, 265–279.

Warner, B., & Hample, D. (2008, May). *Argument engagement, argumentativeness, verbal aggressiveness, topic type, and argument realism: Their effects on editorial choices*. Paper presented at the annual meeting of the International Communication Association, Montreal, Quebec.

Zhan, M., & Hample, D. (2016). Predicting employee dissent expression in organizations: A cost and benefit approach. *Management Communication Quarterly, 30*, 441–471.

CHAPTER FOUR

Serial Arguments

This chapter is concerned with serial arguing, a phenomenon that has a lot of importance to the experience of an interpersonal relationship. What it feels like to be in a particular relationship—one's experience and satisfaction in it—probably has dozens of causes and many of them overlap. But some things seem to be threads in all relationships, and find their way into many relevant theories. These elements include politeness, desires to like and be liked, and power dynamics (Brown & Levinson, 1987; Dillard, Solomon, & Samp, 1996). Those threads imply certain sorts of tension for people during arguments, particularly a balance between being nice and being assertive. This tension really comes to the fore in an argument with a valued relational partner. An arguer wants to obtain agreement or defend his or her position, but probably not at the cost of damaging the relationship. Few people pursue a "scorched earth" policy in their interpersonal arguments, at least on purpose. Usually arguers balance the motive to win with the desire to enjoy the relationship (Gilbert, 2014). This is yet another tension inherent to arguing with valued others. These frictions and worries can appear in any interpersonal argument, but some arguments are particularly important to the relationship. Especially crucial are those arguments that occur over and over again and concern themselves with critical topics. These are called serial arguments.

The Nature of Serial Arguments

A serial argument is one that recurs within a relationship (Trapp, 1990; Trapp & Hoff, 1985). A serial argument is therefore a collection of related episodes, given continuity by a common topic. Each episode looks like a standard interpersonal argument—it usually involves a disagreement, reasons and evidence are probably given for at least one position, the three-turn sequence will be detectable, arguers generally aim at resolving the difference of opinion, and the interaction has an episode-bounding ending, explicit or understood.

But because the argument recurs we immediately know several additional things about it. First, it has a recognized context. People would not be able to say the argument is serial without having registered it as a continuation of an earlier part of their relational history. The participants probably remember the status of the argument's previous ending, what the other has said and made commitments to, and how each person has already responded to the other's concerns. And it has a context only because the participants found it worth remembering that it had happened before.

So second, a serial argument bears on an important issue. Many single-episode arguments are not important enough even to pursue to a conclusion in the moment, and certainly have too little weight to justify bringing back onto the table (Vuchinich, 1990). But serial arguments repeat themselves, often a dozen times or more according to our research. Obviously, at least one arguer must have believed that the argument was not satisfactorily resolved *but needed to be*. So even if a particular episode was bounded by an apparent agreement, if that conclusion was insincere or turned out to be too hurtful to maintain, the topic can be re-opened. Certainly if an earlier episode of argumentation on an important matter was terminated by some sort of avoidance, that topic is an obvious candidate for re-opening. Should one person consistently avoid engagement there may be a question as to whether or not that person recognizes the stakes involved in the argument, but even here one suspects that the avoider will eventually come to recognize that the recurrent topic has genuine importance, at least to the relational partner. Part of the evidence of the issue's weightiness is the mere fact of recurrence.

And finally (this is a consequence of the first two observations), a serial argument is quite likely to exhibit and influence the felt quality of the relationship. Arguing at all is chancy, and arguing on important matters is especially risky. Genuinely settling a key disagreement can be an important moment in the mutual definition of a relationship. A serial argument might produce a decision about how many children to have, whether to keep a job, when to enroll in college, how to deal with an addiction, or other consequential matters. A relationship might emerge with new strength or with fatal deficiencies once a serial argument is resolved. On the other hand, inability to agree on a serial argument's issue might well lead to frustration, anger, or loss of confidence in the relationship.

The Original Study

Trapp and Hoff (1985) were the first in the argumentation community to notice serial arguments. Their study was not actually designed to be about that phenomenon. They simply set out to explore the relational implications of having arguments with one's partner. They asked participants questions like, "What did this argument tell you about your relationship? Did this argument change your relationship?" But before asking those questions, they began simply by asking people to describe the argument, and it was in those answers that they made the serendipitous discovery that many of the relationally relevant arguments were serial. They conducted interviews with twelve couples, and their sample included a nice variety of relationship types: friends, siblings, a parent and child, dating partners, spouses, and friends who used to date. Trapp and Hoff found that eleven of the twelve couples spontaneously talked about serial arguments. Only one dyad reported an argument that seemed to have been resolved in a single episode.

One of the lost insights of this original paper is that Trapp and Hoff noticed that serial arguments are more than just face-to-face exchanges of reasons between the two arguers. They were arguments$_2$, of course, but they also took part of their character from their significance to the arguers' relational lives. The arguments spread to third parties, who would be consulted, recruited, or avoided. Some of the interactions between the principals would be arguments, but others would be "discussions" or less confrontive sorts of exchanges. Although some of the serial arguments were resolved in a matter of hours, Trapp and Hoff found that others lasted for months, during which time the participants thought privately but separately about the issue. Trapp and Hoff also noticed that the two partners sometimes disagreed on whether or not the argument was finished. One partner might think things were resolved and the other partner might not be so sure. In short, a serial argument was always contextualized within all the activities and feelings that constituted the relationship. It found its beginning, its perpetuation, its process, and its conclusion in the ethos of its generative relationship.

As they listened to their informants, Trapp and Hoff developed a model that captured what they were hearing. That model is in Figure 4.1. It includes four main categories of considerations: antecedent conditions, primary processes, secondary processes, and consequent conditions. In contrast to most of the later research on serial arguments, the Trapp and Hoff model clearly incorporates the reality that serial arguments are not simple linear events. Various things cycle forward and backward as the argument moves through relational time. Most of the other work I will later review lacks this obviously useful feature, because the later work tends to concentrate on a single episode of the serial argument. Trapp and Hoff, in contrast, locate the whole set of sequences within the relationship. That is why this is the first theoretical account we need to examine.

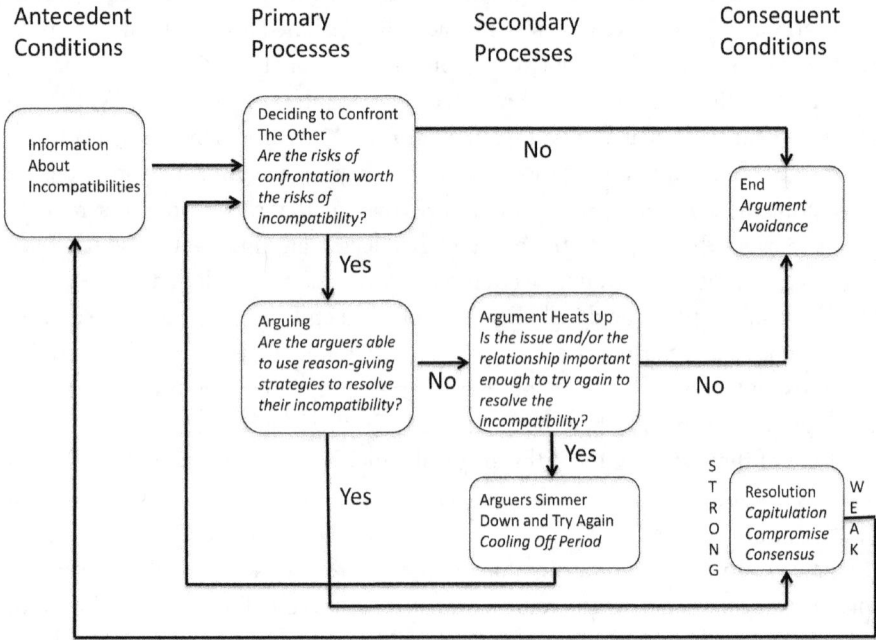

Figure 4.1: Trapp and Hoff's Model of Serial Arguing

Source: Trapp & Hoff (1985, p. 4)

The antecedent conditions are those that give rise to the serial argument. This stage of Trapp and Hoff's model corresponds roughly to the confrontation stage in the pragma-dialectical theory (van Eemeren & Grootendorst, 2004; see Chapter 1). The key antecedent element is the awareness of incompatibility. The first intimation of incompatibility might occur to just one member of the relationship, but eventually the awareness becomes mutual. The serial argument itself might be what brings the issue to light for the other partner, and this can be one of the functions that serial arguments accomplish. Trapp and Hoff (1985, p. 3) defined incompatibility broadly as "any situation when arguers have what they construe to be incompatible views of reality." "Reality" is itself a broad social term, including what we have earlier called content and relational meanings of messages (Watzlawick, Beavin, & Jackson, 1967). Disagreements about reality can be about content-based issues ("Do you have a good driving record?") or can concern themselves with the identities of the people and the nature of their relationship ("Can I trust you if I lend you my car?"). Trapp and Hoff observe that sometimes the incompatibility is noticed long before anyone argues about it, and this is another insight that has been lost to many writers. A difficulty can brew without comment for a time before it ever surfaces in interaction. Incompatibilities do not automatically lead to arguments, a thought that is also captured in pragma-dialectics' distinction between the confrontation and opening stages of a critical discussion.

Once participants consider that they might argue about the issue, we have arrived at what Trapp and Hoff called the primary processes. These are two related decisions about whether or not to proceed with an argument. Just for clarification, some alternatives to arguing might be to ignore the issue, to command the other person to do something, to leave at the first hint of the topic, to take unilateral action to remove the disagreement (e.g., by mowing the lawn yourself), or to give false assurances that things will soon change. Exchanging reasons about the matter is not the only course relational partners can pursue. Arguing is effortful, risky, and costly, and is not always undertaken whenever possible (Paglieri & Castelfranchi, 2010).

Trapp and Hoff distinguished two issues that define the primary processes. The first concerns the two costs they found to be central: the cost of continuing to leave the incompatibility unresolved, and the relational danger of arguing about it (similar costs were found in the argument engagement research summarized in Chapter 3). It is interesting that these matters were expressed to Trapp and Hoff as "risks." Participants might have looked forward to the *benefit* of resolving the incompatibility and the *benefit* of putting the relationship on a better footing. But they framed these matters as costs, as things to worry about. Trapp and Hoff mention that the decision to confront is not necessarily a quick one. A relational partner might stew about things for some time, and this connects to other findings about rumination and imagined interactions making things seem worse (e.g., Hample, Richards, & Na, 2012; Miller & Roloff, 2014; Wallenfelsz & Hample, 2010). Initiation of an argument might come simply, or it might be an explosion of no-longer-controllable feelings and projections. If the balance of risk and reward makes arguing seem a bad idea, the diagram in Figure 4.1 shows that people move to avoidance.

Otherwise, people move on to the second key question in this primary stage, Will both people argue constructively? Some people lack arguing skills (Infante, Chandler, & Rudd, 1989; Kuhn, 1991). They cannot (or do not try to) track another person's reasoning, they conflate the arguer with the argument, and they respond intemperately rather than thoughtfully. This may be due to some relatively permanent deficiency, or it may be due to this being the wrong moment for a constructive argument. Research indicates that people do make estimates of how the other person will react to argument initiation, and if the partner is expected to be closed-minded or nasty, this makes the initiation less likely (Hample, Paglieri, & Na, 2012, and the other argument engagement research mentioned in Chapter 3). Figure 4.1 shows that if honest exchanges of reasons do occur, the arguers proceed to resolution, what van Eemeren and Grootendorst (2004) might call the concluding stage, which we will discuss momentarily. But if reasoning cannot control the argument, escalation is likely, leading either to avoidance or a cooling off period, as Figure 4.1 illustrates.

This brings us to the third phase, the one Trapp and Hoff called the secondary processes. These consist of heating up and cooling down. They are called "secondary" because they are not actually necessary for the enactment of a serial argument. Notice in the diagram that they are only initiated if the partners decide to argue but conduct themselves badly. Argument escalation occurs due to bad behavior. In pragma-dialectics, this is felicitously labeled "derailing," and it is caused by nonrational moves in the discussion (van Eemeren & Grootendorst, 2004). Trapp and Hoff (1985, p. 7) said, "Arguments flare up as arguers feel more and more frustration with their inability to convince the other person to change their views on the issue. A typical occurrence in light of this frustration is that arguing switches from ideational disagreement to highly personal disagreement as arguers switch the locus of their attacks from the idea to the person." This change is precisely the difference between being argumentative and being verbally aggressive (Rancer & Avtgis, 2014). Constructive arguing centers on the issue, and changing one's focus to criticize the quality of the other person is nearly always destructive.

Once things have started to go badly, Figure 4.1 does not display any immediate hope of a good mutual conclusion. Instead, if the relationship or the issue's importance to it has little weight, people just move to avoidance. They see things are proceeding nastily, they assess the issue's potential damage to their life as minor, and they just quit arguing. If the stakes are higher, however, people make a different decision. They move instead to a cooling off period, and eventually cycle back to the beginning. Notice that in the moment, avoidance and cooling off probably look the same. It is only later, when the argument is rejoined or forgotten, that an observer can interpret what it meant when the people quit arguing. Even the participants may not be immediately certain. Figure 4.1 says little about timing. The argument might restart in a few minutes, or a few days, or not at all.

Finally, let us consider the consequent conditions in Figure 4.1. Avoidance has already been mentioned. The other possible condition is resolution, and here, too, Trapp and Hoff made some nice points that rarely appear in later research. They distinguished three sorts of resolution—capitulation, compromise, and consensus—and emphasized that each of these can have weak, strong, or intermediate force. Capitulation means that one arguer concedes, compromise means that they both give in a little to gain a little, and consensus means that they reach a joint decision that takes both people fully into account and satisfies each of them. Any of these will end the argument, or at least the episode, but the arguers can vary in their commitment to the ending. Capitulation, for instance, might occur because one partner realizes that s/he was quite thoroughly wrong, and this will be sincere and permanent. But it might occur just to end the exchange, without any genuine private concession. Compromise, too, can involve strong or weak commitment, and consensus can also be sincere or superficial. Figure 4.1 indicates that when the resolution involves weak commitment, matters cycle back to the first stage when people are privately aware of incompatibility. The argument might begin again, in spite of having been apparently concluded. A weak resolution does not end the serial argument. It only supplies a new moment in the argument's relational history and delineates a commitment one or both arguers are supposed to take responsibility for. The only way for the serial argument to end permanently is if the participants argue well and come to a resolution that is mutually felt, with both arguers being strongly committed to it. As far as this theory is concerned, it does not matter if the resolution involves capitulation, compromise, or consensus, but it matters a great deal whether the parties are truly committed to the argument's official resolution.

The Trapp and Hoff model has not completely controlled the research that followed. More recent work has tended to focus on some of the details implied by Trapp and Hoff's report. Goals have been specified in more detail, the sorts of arguing tactics have gotten close attention, and more outcomes than argument resolution have been examined. This detail work has been fruitful, but it has mainly considered one argument episode at a time, and often only one person at a time. Thus, the work tends to lose the clear relational siting that Trapp and Hoff provided. As we read about the more recent investigations, we will need to remind ourselves of the cyclical relationship-defined nature of the whole serial enterprise, because it will not always be evident in the research designs. In contrast to the variety of Trapp and Hoff's original sample, most of this later work has drawn its data from U.S. undergraduates, and the interpersonal relationships have mostly been friendships or romantic pairings. With only a few exceptions (e.g., Bevan, 2014; Bevan & Sparks, 2014; Worley & Samp, 2016), just one person in each relational dyad has been studied at a time. These limitations, too, we will need to correct as best we can as we read.

Nonetheless, a great deal more about serial arguing has been learned since Trapp and Hoff (1985) first reported about it. In particular, we have gained a lot of knowledge about serial argument topics, the relational consequences of serial arguing, and the intrapersonal dynamics of a serial argument episode.

Serial Argument Topics

Not every serial argument involves topics that have obvious consequentiality. Sometimes the issue may be minor and it is just the fact that it cannot be resolved that creates its relational importance, just as a tiny pebble in one's shoe can annoy out of proportion to its size.

Here are some examples of undergraduates' reports of their serial arguments, drawn from my own work. One can easily judge that some of these issues ought to have been dealt with simply, but that others seem to be deeper and more obviously complex. The relational contexts for these reports are generally friendship or romance.

- After a few months my girlfriend, [Name], and I got back together from our "break." I was having second thoughts about our relationship mostly because I didn't trust her. The main reason why I didn't trust her was because she told me she had only hooked up with a friend of hers from her school when me and her were on a break, but I had a strong feeling it went further than that. So, I confronted her about it, and she admitted to it and told me she didn't want to hurt me and just wanted me back, which is why she lied to me. I was very angry and upset. This issue was brought up many times because I felt like she had to regain my trust back and she wasn't doing much to do so.
- I was irritated that I always had to drive home to see him, when he is perfectly capable of getting in his own car and coming to see me.
- Whenever the bathroom needs to be cleaned, I tell my friend that he needs to clean it because he NEVER does it. He just yells back saying that I am crazy he does it all the time. Meanwhile, you cannot even walk in the bathroom because all of his clothes and items are all over the place. So I will argue with him and finally convince him that he needs to clean it, and he says he will, but immediately forgets because he's a space cadet. So this just leads to more arguing and me cleaning the bathroom.
- After a long night of drinking and my friend's aggressiveness that was on full display because he drank too much liquor, I approached him about the topic of him drinking liquor. I told him how he shouldn't be drinking it,

because he knows he gets overly aggressive and violent when he uses it. He responded with, "It's not that dude, shit happens though. Don't worry about it." I responded with "[Name], this isn't the first time. This has happened before and last night got way out of hand." He answered, "I know I know. Whatever, it's over with." He avoided the problem and me.
- I got mad because my [best friend] never plans anything and he always says it doesn't matter to him where we go.
- We both started to pray before dinner, and got into a fight because neither of us appreciated the other one praying in a different manner.
- The argument was about who was better at basketball. The first time, we were stating our strong points, such as I am a better shooter and ball handler. He said he would dominate me inside on rebounds and said he was the better shooter.

Quite a few of these seem to be consequential topics. They vary in how much argumentation they seem to require, and this will depend on the people involved. The prayer argument, for instance, could be easily resolved or might generate thirty years of family theological disputes. The basketball conflict might be a serious one about dominance within the relationship, but it might also just be friendly banter, conducted as much to pass the time as to get anything settled. But in most of these examples we can immediately see how the relationship would be improved by a constructive solution, and how it might be damaged if the argument festered or escalated.

All these descriptions emerged from research solicitations that explained what a serial argument is and requested reports about one. People did not seem to have difficulty supplying examples, but that does not really testify to whether serial arguments are ordinary or rare. An indication of the commonness of serial arguments can be inferred from Coles and Samp (2013), who asked people merely to describe conflicts, not necessarily serial ones. However, they happened to ask respondents whether the reported conflict was one that had happened before. 77.5% of the participants said that their conflict topic was recurrent. This reminds us that eleven out of twelve of Trapp and Hoff's (1985) dyads reported a serial argument when they were only asked about relationally consequential disagreements. Furthermore, the conflicts in the Coles and Samp study were not rare. People estimated having a conflict with that relational partner 2.4 times a week. Serial arguments appear to be common threads in our relational lives.

Just to situate the possible importance of serial arguments, consider the results of a longitudinal study on the reasons for divorce (Amato & Previti, 2003). Seventeen years after interviewing married couples, Amato and Previti called them back to see how the marriage was going. Many of the couples were divorced by then. Here are the most common reasons people gave for their marriage having broken up: infidelity (18% of the couples), being incompatible (16%), drinking or drug use (9%), grew apart (8%), personality problems (8%), lack of communication (7%), physical or mental abuse (5%), and loss of love (4%). Is it even plausible that someone would dissolve a marriage based on a single argumentative episode on any of these matters? Even if a partner felt some issue was a cut and dried basis for divorce (e.g., infidelity, drug use), isn't it likely that the issue was brought up more than once before the lawyers were called? The decision to divorce or not, to continue in a romantic relationship or not, to keep a job or not, to stay in a friendship group or not—these are rarely instantaneous decisions. They will be made over the course of time, and some of that time will be occupied with recurring arguments. One of the reasons for having serial arguments in the first place is the goal of figuring out if the arguer wants to stay in the relationship (Bevan, 2010). In the case of a troubled marriage, those arguments will likely concern the sort of topics listed above—Are you faithful? Do you really love me? Can you control your drinking? An advocacy group obtained a research grant from the U.S. Department of Justice to conduct a telephone survey of 1,500 adults. They found that 56% of divorced people listed "too much conflict and arguing" as one of the reasons the marriage dissolved (National Fatherhood Initiative, 2005). Unresolved serial arguments may be crucially involved in marriages that break up. Resolving important serial arguments might be equally critical in preserving other relationships.

A serial argument's topic affects the conduct of the argument and its relational implications. My colleagues and I have collected more than 2,000 open-ended descriptions of serial arguments (Hample & Allen, 2012; Hample & Cionea, 2012; Hample & Krueger, 2011; Hample & Richards, 2015; Hample, Richards, & Na, 2012). Topics range from obviously important (marriage, sex, and addiction) to apparently superficial (tidiness, speech habits, and sports). The examples given above come from these studies.

Cionea and Hample (2015) classified the topics from these data sets into three categories, relying mainly on Johnson's (2002, 2009) distinction between personal and public topics (see Chapter 3). Personal topics are those that are internal to the relationship—its definition, its functioning, and its connections to the participants. Examples would be whether two people should become sexually intimate, who should cook on Tuesdays, and whether one person is habitually tardy. 63% of the serial arguments my colleagues and I collected had topics of that type. Public topics are external to the relationship. Even though the arguers may feel strongly about matters, the issues are not about the daily enactment or emotional definitions of the relationship. Examples include what sorts of movies are enjoyable, whether global warming is taking place, or whom to vote for. 12% of the topics were public ones. Because several of the data collections intentionally focused on serial arguments at work or in the classroom, a third topic category was added, called workplace. 22% of the reports were about serial arguments experienced at work, in high school classes, or in university classrooms. Most of the workplace topics (but not all) were reported in studies in which respondents were requested to tell about occupational or classroom serial arguments. Johnson, Averbeck, Kelley, and Liu (2010) reported that 55% of the serial arguments they collected from undergraduates dealt with public topics and 45% had personal topics. So the proportions of topic type are not yet clear, even from undergraduate samples, but all three sorts of issues are obviously common.

The personal topics are particularly involving and are associated with the participants experiencing more stress and health problems than with public topics (Johnson et al., 2010; Johnson, Averbeck, Kelley, & Liu, 2011; Johnson, Hample, & Cionea, 2014). More or less by definition, these are the serial arguments that have the most substantial relational consequences. These are the arguments about mutual responsibilities, about the nature of the relationship (e.g., cross-sex friendship or romantic?), debts and obligations, and matters that have to be handled as a couple (e.g., children, finances). Compared to public topics, personal ones usually have higher stakes. People have greater emotional involvement in them, and expect more potential benefit if the argument can be resolved. The workplace topics (occupational, classroom) seem to come in between public and private topics on most measures, but we have only a little evidence about that to this point.

So the topics for serial arguments are as variable as the people and their relationships are. Most of the issues that come to mind when people are first asked about serial arguments seem to be pretty important, but even simple arguments about sports or music can carry on for a while as part of the fabric of a friendship. Serial arguments appear to be common and to have considerable capacity to affect the nature of a relationship.

Consequences of Serial Arguments

In fact, prior research has established a number of important outcomes from serial arguments. In addition to the Johnson et al. (2010, 2011) papers mentioned earlier, research conducted by Roloff and his colleagues has also established that serial arguments can be personally consequential (Johnson & Roloff, 1998, 2000; Malis & Roloff, 2006a, 2006b; Roloff & Reznik, 2008). Serial arguments have been shown to increase people's stress levels, challenge both their physical and mental health, and lower their relational satisfaction. Many of these are not simple effects, however, since they may depend on how well the argument is going.

Relational satisfaction is perhaps the most common outcome variable in contemporary research. An initial suspicion was that satisfaction would be predicted by the frequency with which people argued about a particular topic, with the more frequent arguments expected to be the most damaging. But early work rather consistently showed either no connection at all between frequency and satisfaction, or such a small one that it obviously didn't make any real difference. Recently Morrison and Schrodt (2017) reported that frequency of arguing did have a little bit to do with relational uncertainty, up to 4% of the variance, depending on how relational uncertainty was measured. But more generally, researchers have found that satisfaction was associated with the perceived resolvability of the argument rather than its frequency (Johnson & Roloff, 1998, 2000; Miller, Roloff, & Malis, 2007). Even Morrrison and Schrodt reported that the effects of perceived resolvability on relational uncertainty swamped those of argument frequency.

The importance of resolvability for satisfaction, and the relative unimportance of episode frequency, has been well replicated. For example, combining all the data from three of my own studies (Hample & Cionea, 2012; Hample & Richards, 2015; Hample, Richards, & Na, 2012) to produce a sample of over 1,500 undergraduates, we get these correlations: between argument frequency and relational satisfaction, $r = -.12$, $p < .001$; between argument frequency and resolvability, $r = -.20$, $p < .001$; and between resolvability and relational satisfaction, $r = .40$, $p < .001$. The effect of argument frequency is significant with a sample size this large, but notice that only about 1% of the variance in satisfaction is statistically explained by episode frequency. Obviously, the more important effect is that of perceived resolvability, which accounts for about 16% of the variance in satisfaction. And, just to clarify the relative importance of resolvability, when the association between argument frequency and relational satisfaction is calculated as a partial correlation controlling for resolvability, the result is $r_p = -.01$, $p = .67$. Even with $df = 1,527$, the effect is not statistically significant. So high frequency of arguing is only a problem when the argument isn't seen as eventually resolvable. On the other hand, when argument frequency is partialled out of the association between resolvability and satisfaction, the original result is almost unchanged: $r_p = .39$, $p < .001$. Resolvability, the sense of optimism or pessimism about whether things will finally be settled, is what really affects satisfaction with the relationship that houses the argument.

Several other consequences of serial argument have also been explored. Civility, the politeness and apparent constructiveness of arguers' conduct while arguing, has been involved in my own research program. I will be reporting the somewhat complicated results about civility later in this chapter. I have participated in one study (Hample & Richards, 2015) that examined whether serial arguments made people take conflict more personally. We found that the way people argued was the key. When they argued integratively (openly, generously) people felt more positively about having been in the serial argument and made more optimistic projections about whether it would help the relationship. When either arguer was demanding (causing the other one to withdraw) people felt more stressed, more persecuted, took matters more personally, and were more pessimistic about the argument's effects on the relationship. When they argued distributively (selfishly) people actually enjoyed the conflict more, and were more optimistic about improving the relationship. Apparently the more mutual engagement there was (whether distributive or integrative), the better people felt about the serial argument episode. The more force-and-evasion there was, the more people took things personally.

No doubt there are many more consequences than these from being in a serial argument. These are consequential threads in interpersonal relationships, and an enormous variety of feelings and thoughts are connected with our relational lives. Even at this point, however, we can point to the importance of serial arguments in our physical health, our mental well-being, and our relational security.

Situational Effects and Intrapersonal Dynamics

In this section, I want to clarify the intrapersonal dynamics of serial arguments, and the effects of situational features on them. That is, why do people act in the way they do, and what feelings do they have afterwards? The situation-goals-plans-action model (Dillard, 1990, 2004; Dillard, Segrin, & Harden, 1989), summarized in Chapter 1, has been the frame for investigations of how serial arguments are produced. The general idea is that people come into contact with a situation that invites them to participate in another episode of the serial argument; they form particular goals for how to proceed; they prefer one or another tactic for arguing; and finally they generate their contribution to the episode. Several outcomes of the episodes have also been commonly studied: whether or not the person thinks the argument will ever be resolved, how civil the encounter was, and how satisfied the arguer is with the relationship that contains the serial dispute. I will start with some simple situational features, and then move to the dynamic relationships among the process variables. First, though, I should describe the data set I will be analyzing.

Data

The data I am reporting in this part of the chapter were cumulated from five independent studies, all making use of undergraduate respondents at the University of Maryland. Data were collected online. Hample and Allen (2012) studied serial arguments in organizations, with $N = 363$. Hample and Krueger (2011) examined serial arguments in the context of high school or college classrooms ($N = 342$). Hample and Cionea (2012, $N = 630$) studied romantic or friendship relationships among people of different ethnicities or national origins. Hample and Richards (2015) concerned themselves with romantic or friendship relationships, with $N = 698$. Finally, Hample, Richards, and Na (2012, $N = 213$) also dealt with romantic or friendship relationships. In the case of Hample, Richards, and Na, which traced serial arguments through several episodes, only the first episode's data are included here.

The details regarding measurements and procedures are to be found in the original papers. Scales ranged in value from one to five for every measure. Only common (but re-worded) versions of the climate/satisfaction items were used here in this report of the data, resulting in several items being dropped from the organizational and classroom studies. All designs included data on the seven goals developed by Bevan, four tactics, and three outcomes. In addition, these papers included measurements of general approach and avoid impulses, which were theorized to precede the more specific goals.

Serial argument goals have been identified and explored by Bevan and her colleagues (Bevan, 2010; Bevan, Finan, & Kaminsky, 2008; Bevan, Hale, & Williams, 2004; Bevan et al., 2007). This research has identified seven particular goals that explain why and how people argue in recurring disagreements. Two of these goals are positive ones: the commitment to a mutual agreement, and the impulse to express oneself positively. The other five goals are negative. These include the desire to express oneself negatively, the motivation to hurt the other person (benefitting self), the desire to change the other person's behavior or character, the goal of displaying one's dominance over the other person, and an interest in deciding whether or not to continue in the relationship. That last goal is perhaps not obviously negative, but it turns out to involve private surveillance and judgment of the relationship and the other person, and that sort of evaluative orientation is somewhat aggressive (see Gibb, 1961). This set of goals is in common use by most of the leading researchers with the notable exception of Roloff and his associates.

Serial argument tactics occupy the conceptual space for plans in the situation-goals-plans-action model. The tactics used by this research community are not particularly argument-centric, which is unfortunate. They do not, for instance, investigate common argument schemes or the quality of arguments made. Instead, they center on more general orientations. Three main tactical choices have been studied: distributive, integrative, and avoidant (Sillars, 1980). Distributive plans are those that seek benefits at the other person's expense. This orientation is consistent with a win/lose, zero-sum understanding of the disagreement. Integrative actions are those that endorse the other person's goals and needs. Here the orientation is win/win, and arguers seek a solution that satisfies both relational partners. Avoidance involves escape from the episode, perhaps with a topic change, obviously false claims or insincere agreements, or physical departure. Studied in this way, avoidance has not been a very useful variable but that may be because of the standard research plan, which asks respondents to recall an episode of a serial argument. Episodes that are actually recallable probably did not involve outright avoidance, and this may explain why avoidance has not participated with much vigor in the statistical analyses. Consequently, the idea of avoidance has been captured with two other measures, first applied by Roloff and his associates. These are demand/withdraw sequences. This tactic is measured in two ways: respondents are asked to remember whether they demanded and the other person withdrew, or whether the other person demanded and the respondent retreated. This has been a more fruitful approach to studying avoidance in serial arguments. Bevan's most recent work has used yet another set of tactics: avoidance, integrative, compromise, threat/insult, and criticize/blame (e.g., 2014). This might prove to be an interesting way to divide up the tactical possibilities, but not enough work has been done with this list to summarize it here. I will summarize the research centering on four tactics or plans: distributive, integrative, I demanded/other withdrew, and other demanded/I withdrew.

A set of three outcomes is well represented in the literature. The first of these, the estimate of whether or not the argument is resolvable, was an early contribution by Johnson and Roloff (1998, 2000). Like many others, they began with a curiosity about how many episodes of the serial argument had happened, and whether that made any difference. They found, as many others have since that time, that the frequency of episodes had little influence on people's feelings about the relationship. What did make a difference was whether or not the participants felt that the argument would eventually be resolved. Even in the face of an unsatisfactory episode if the arguers are optimistic about achieving agreement someday, their perceptions about the quality of their relationship remain unharmed. So measuring perceived resolvability has been a common element of research designs.

Roloff and colleagues also explored the second outcome, relational satisfaction. This concept was somewhat broadened in studies of classroom or workplace arguments (Hample & Allen, 2012; Hample & Krueger, 2011). Those investigations substituted classroom/workplace climate for satisfaction. The idea is that we should investigate the effects of the argument on people's essential satisfaction with the relational context in which the argument occurs. In a marriage, this would be marital satisfaction; in a friendship, relational satisfaction; in the workplace, occupational satisfaction; and at school, classroom satisfaction. Accordingly, relational satisfaction items were reworded to refer to job or educational matters, and the over-arching concept is climate or satisfaction with the contextualizing relationship.

The final outcome measure is civility. This is drawn from argument frames research (Hample, 2003; see Chapter 2). This measure refers directly to the conduct of the episode, and inquires whether it was polite, well-reasoned, and constructive. These three measures—resolvability, relational satisfaction/climate, and civility—certainly do not describe every interesting consequence of a serial argument episode. However, because they are both global and related to many other feelings and perceptions, they are useful indicators of the consequences of participating in a serial argument.

We will be examining cumulated results of several studies. Since the variables were measured on five point scales, a score of three is theoretically middling or neutral. The means themselves will show what scores were actually typical for each variable.

Situation

Available data give some information about the circumstances of the arguments. Data bearing on the situation involve a number of elements already mentioned. The relationship type (e.g., spouse, friend, boss) has an obvious influence on what might be at stake during a recurrent argument. The topic type (public, personal, workplace) is a well-established influence on how people argue and how they react to the fact of disagreement with a relational partner. The biological sex of the participants was also known, permitting us to see whether men and women differ in their approaches to serial argument episodes. Another key consideration is whether the respondent is the initiator or target of the episode.

My colleagues and I had enough data to offer some generalizations about five different relational contexts: romantic (dating or married), friendship, educational (almost always in the student role), family (including conflicts with parents and siblings), and occupational. Table 4.1 shows how type of relationship affected people's responses to questions about various features of serial arguments.

Table 4.1: Means of Serial Argument Measures by Relationship Type

	Romantic	Friendship	Educational	Family	Workplace
Sample Size	769	672	350	62	225
Motives and Goals					
Approach	2.79	2.88	3.04	2.74	3.05
Neg Express	3.50	3.16	3.26	3.34	3.27
Mutuality	3.80	3.49	3.22	3.62	3.43
Dominance	3.00	3.01	3.39	3.02	3.33
Rel Continue	2.94	2.51	2.51	2.08	2.80
Change Other	3.29	3.12	2.99	3.16	3.13
Pos Express	3.76	2.95	2.30	3.19	2.34
Hurt Other	1.77	1.84	2.17	1.52	2.13
Tactics					
Distributive	2.74	2.78	3.04	2.96	3.02
Integrative	3.56	3.39	2.99	3.39	3.25
I Demanded	2.71	2.46	2.62	2.44	2.54
O Demanded	2.48	2.39	2.35	2.58	2.42
Outcomes					
Satisf/Climate	3.07	3.09	2.93	3.19	2.89
Resolvability	3.09	3.07	2.74	3.23	3.07
Civility	2.92	3.02	2.75	2.86	2.91

Note. Analyses of variance (across each row) were statistically significant at $p < .001$ for each serial argument measure except Other Demanded, for which $p = .086$.

Analyses of variance showed that relationship type made a statistically significant difference on every measure except other demanded/I withdrew. Effects sizes were small, generally ranging from 1% to 3% of explained variance, with several exceptions. 4% of the variance in the mutuality and relational continuation goals was explained by relationship type, as was 7% of the variance in use of integrative tactics. Most notably, 22% of the variance in the positive expression goal was accounted for by relationship type. The means for positive expression show that people in romantic and family relationships were most motivated to say nice things, and they were considerably less inclined to do so in the other relational contexts. Use of integrative tactics followed a somewhat similar pattern, with people being more cooperative in their most emotionally satisfying relationships, with classroom and workplace settings trailing the others. Examining the other means in Table 4.1 might be interesting, but readers are reminded that the apparent differences are statistically small, even if they happen to be significant.

Table 4.2 summarizes analyses also reported by Cionea and Hample (2015). Here, the situational feature is topic type. The three types of topics were personal, public, and workplace, drawing mainly on the work of Johnson (2002, 2009; Johnson et al., 2014) for the distinction between personal and public (see Chapter 3). Personal topics are those that affect the relationship's definition, public topics are external to the relationship, and workplace topics refer to occupational or classroom issues.

Table 4.2: Means of Serial Argument Measures by Topic Type

	Personal	Public	Workplace	Effect
Sample Size	1411	258	494	
Motives and Goals				
Approach	2.79	3.15	3.00	.03
Neg Express	3.43	2.73	3.30	.05
Mutuality	3.69	3.08	3.36	.04
Dominance	3.03	3.20	3.31	.01
Rel Continue	2.78	2.16	2.63	.03
Change Other	3.26	2.72	3.12	.02
Pos Express	3.37	2.54	2.23	.15
Hurt Other	1.82	1.88	2.06	.01
Tactics				
Distributive	2.76	2.92	3.03	.02
Integrative	3.48	3.15	3.13	.05
I Demanded	2.61	2.31	2.61	.01
O Demanded	2.44	2.33	2.37	.00
Outcomes				
Satisf/Climate	3.04	3.25	2.91	.01
Resolvability	3.11	2.78	2.95	.02
Civility	2.93	3.06	2.83	.01

Note. Analyses of variance were statistically significant at $p < .001$ for each serial argument measure except Other Demands, for which $p = .123$.

All of the analyses of variance were statistically significant except for the one concerning other demanded/I withdrew. The effect sizes are in the table this time, and it is apparent that many of the significant topic effects did not control very much variance in the dependent measure. Exceptions were the impulses to express oneself positively or negatively and the use of integrative tactics. The means show that people were least motivated to express themselves negatively for the public topics; they most wanted to say positive things on serial arguments concerning personal topics; and they were most likely to use integrative tactics when they were dealing with a personal issue. These last two results suggest that people are aware of the importance of the personal topics to their lives, and act in a conciliatory way if they can.

The final situational factors considered here are the respondent's sex and role in the argument episode (initiator or target). Both sets of results are in Table 4.3. There, readers can see that biological sex had almost nothing to do with the experience of a serial argument. In fact, Table 4.3's results may well challenge some stereotypes about men being more aggressive in arguments and women being more nurturing. In spite of the healthy sample size, men and women did not differ significantly at all for several measures: the dominance goal, the desire for positive expression, the tactic of the respondent demanding, perceived resolvability, civility, and climate/satisfaction. Sex made no difference for any of these outcomes, in other words. Even for those measures that yielded statistically significant differences, Table 4.3 shows that the effect sizes were negligible across the board.

Table 4.3: Means of Serial Argument Measures by Respondent Sex and Role

	M	F	Effect	Initiator	Target	Effect
Sample Size	693	1553		1000	821	
		Motives and Goals				
Approach	2.95	2.87	.00	3.03	2.73	.03
Neg Express	3.15	3.40	.01	3.43	3.23	.01
Mutuality	3.40	3.60	.01	3.62	3.57	.00
Dominance	3.16	3.10	.00	3.01	3.14	.00
Rel Continue	2.60	2.72	.00	2.69	2.71	.00
Change Other	3.05	3.21	.00	3.39	2.98	.03
Pos Express	2.97	3.05	.00	3.21	3.14	.00
Hurt Other	2.02	1.85	.00	1.82	1.88	.00
		Tactics				
Distributive	2.93	2.81	.00	2.82	2.84	.00
Integrative	3.28	3.39	.01	3.45	3.39	.00
I Demanded	2.55	2.61	.00	2.81	2.37	.06
O Demanded	2.51	2.38	.00	2.19	2.72	.08

Table 4.3: Continued

	M	F	Effect	Initiator	Target	Effect
		Outcomes				
Satisf/Climate	3.05	3.02	.00	3.08	3.01	.00
Resolvability	3.03	3.03	.00	3.12	3.00	.01
Civility	2.93	2.91	.00	3.00	2.88	.01

Note. Analyses of variance on sex were statistically significant at $p < .001$ for each serial argument measure except Other Demands, for which $p = .123$. For argument role, non-significant results appeared for mutuality, rel continue, pos express, hurt other, distributive, integrative, and satisf/climate.

Respondents' role in the argument episode—whether the person initiated that episode or was the target of it—was only somewhat more important than sex. Quite a few results in Table 4.3 were not significant: for mutuality, relational continuation checking, positive expressiveness, hurt other to benefit self, distributive tactics, integrative tactics, and satisfaction/climate (but $p = .07$ there). However, several of the effect sizes for the significant analyses were noticeable: initiators had a higher level of general approach motivation for the episode, were more motivated to change the other person, and reported that they were more likely to have been demanding while the other person withdrew. By the same token, they were less likely to say that the other person demanded and that they withdrew. This all makes sense, because these respondents were initiating, after all. Argument role did not have any major effects on the outcome measures. One might have expected that initiator/target role would be more important than this on many of the measures, but we should remember that everyone was reporting on only a single episode of the argument. A person who initiated one episode might be the target for another, and this might lead us to expect that initiator/target differences would settle out over relational time. In fact, Johnson and Cionea (2016; Cionea & Johnson, 2014) reported that when both arguers brought up the topic from time to time, this improved relational satisfaction, reduced stress and protected against relational harm.

Goals, Tactics, and Outcomes

Now let us move on to the intrapersonal dynamics of participating in an episode of a serial argument. The SGPA model (see Chapter 1) alerts us to the connections between goals, plans, and action. Theoretically, there are causal connections here: goals lead to the tactics, and the tactics summarize the actions that produce the outcomes. These linkages can all be tested at once using an advanced statistical method called structural equation modeling, and that is the procedure I summarize here.

Kline (2015) is a recommended book-length introduction to structural equation modeling. I realize this procedure easily surpasses most readers' present level of education, so I will do my best to explain things clearly and put most of the technicalities in tables or in paragraphs that cry out to be skimmed. Unfortunately, this sort of statistical analysis is unavoidable if we want to talk about the dynamics of many variables at once, and these analyses are being reported here for the first time so they can't be checked in journals.

Each of the projects providing data for these analyses investigated the intrapersonal dynamics of serial arguing, but different statistical and sampling decisions were made for each of the original studies. Previous results are therefore not always comparable in detail. By collecting all the data into one analysis with only one set of statistical decisions in play, we should be able to obtain a clear picture of how serial arguments work for U.S. undergraduates (at least those at the University of Maryland). This should afford more confidence in the size and sign of various variable-to-variable relationships, and will permit smaller effects to be detected.

The general model being tested is conceptually represented in Figure 4.2. The theoretical idea is that general impulses become specified and implemented in the form of more precise interaction goals. The goals, alone or in combination, lead to tactical plans for how to conduct oneself during the disagreement. The tactics produce the outcomes. As Figure 4.2 implies, each panel of variables is expected to influence only the next panel. For example, impulses are not theorized to influence outcomes except insofar as their effects are mediated by goals and plans. The statistical analysis tests that theoretical restriction and corrects it where necessary.

Figure 4.2: Conceptual Representation of the Intrapersonal Dynamics of Serial Arguing Processes

Statistical Details. The first analytical step was to analyze the measurement model. This procedure evaluates whether the individual items actually congeal to produce a good estimate of the latent variables, which are linear composites of the indicators intended to measure them. A confirmatory factor analysis was conducted using

LISREL 8.8 with maximum likelihood estimation. Total sample size was 2,243. No variable transformations were performed and no cross-loadings were permitted. Due to poor R^2 with the latent civility variable, the last two civility indicators were dropped from this and the following analyses. All other indicators were retained. Results were acceptable: χ^2 = 14,370.25, df = 2,024, p < .001; *RMSEA* = .062 (90% *CI* was .061–.063), *CFI* = .94, and *SRMR* = .07. These results indicate that the individual items are doing a reasonable job of measuring the conceptual variables, and justify continuing the analyses to evaluate the theoretical model.

The idea in Figure 4.2 is that the panel of impulses (approach and avoidance) produces the values for the panel of specific goals (positive expression, etc.). The goals generate the tactics (distributive, etc.), and these result in the values for the outcome measures (resolvability, etc.). Thus, a causal flow is theorized, moving from the left panels in the figure to the right.

In the actual statistical model, every latent variable in each panel was freed to predict every latent variable in the next panel. So for example, mutuality's influence on distributive, integrative, I demanded, and other demanded were all tested. This resulted in many potential paths being evaluated. Only the significant paths will be reported, but the non-significant paths were still included in the model. That is, the structural equation model was not trimmed.

Analyses generate modification indices that indicate whether or not other important paths have been omitted. The model in Figure 4.2 systematically omits panel-skipping paths, for example the possibility that the approach impulse directly affects civility. When these omissions were statistically important, the modification indices were used as guides for revising the statistical model. Only theoretically sensible modifications were made. For instance, statistical suggestions that reversed the expected theoretical flow (e.g., an outcome causing a goal's value) were ignored. Suggestions consistent with the theorized causal direction were generally followed, because the theoretical critique amounts merely to saying that a variable's forward influence is direct and not completely mediated by the panel being skipped.

Latent variables within each panel were permitted to correlate. This means that each latent variable's error (the variance not accounted for by the causally prior latent variables' paths into it) was correlated with the parallel error for the other latent variables in that panel. For example, mutuality's error (i.e., its unpredicted nature in this model) was correlated with the error for hurt other, positive expression, and all the other goals. A statistical consequence of this is that even if a particular latent variable lacks a statistically significant path into the next panel, it might still be exerting some influence due to its correlation with some other variable, with which it shares variance. For example, the correlation between (the errors of) negative expression and change other was .44. So if one of the goals had a significant path into a tactic but the other goal didn't, some indirect influence would still be traceable to the goal without a statistically significant path.

The initial analysis tested Figure 4.2 exactly, without making use of the modification indices' suggestions. Results were largely acceptable, although the *SRMR* was a bit high: χ^2 = 17,576.80, *df* = 2,079, p < .001; *RMSEA* = .067 (90% *CI* was .066–.068), *CFI* = .93, and *SRMR* = .11. Modification indices suggested permitting several instances of direct influence from the approach and avoid impulses to particular tactics and outcomes. Once these suggestions were implemented, the model's fit improved slightly: χ^2 = 15,936.11, *df* = 2,065, p < .001; *RMSEA* = .066 (90% *CI* was .065–.067), *CFI* = .94, and *SRMR* = .09. This is the final model proposed and reported here.

Back to the Main Story. Tables 4.4 and 4.5 report the key results. Figures 4.3, 4.4, and 4.5 display the significant effects in various diagrams (all of which reflect the single model's test). Actual values for the significant effects are in Table 4.4.

Table 4.4: Significant Unstandardized Predictors of Latent Variables

Endogenous Variable	R^2	Predictor	Path Coefficient
		Serial Argument Goals	
Negative Expression	.36	Avoid	1.97
		Approach	1.93
Mutuality	.03	Avoid	.40
		Approach	.27
Dominance	.19	Avoid	1.31
		Approach	1.42
Relational Continuation	.61	Avoid	2.57
		Approach	2.44
Change Other	.24	Avoid	1.59
		Approach	1.61
Positive Expression	.12	Avoid	1.10
		Approach	.96
Hurt Other	.20	Avoid	1.31
		Approach	1.46
		Serial Argument Tactics	
Distributive	.43	Mutuality	–.11
		Dominance	.46
		Change Other	.07

Table 4.4: Continued

Endogenous Variable	R^2	Predictor	Path Coefficient
		Positive Expression	−.18
		Hurt Other	.11
Integrative	.38	Negative Expression	−.09
		Mutuality	.54
		Dominance	−.18
		Positive Expression	.22
		Hurt Other	−.10
I Demand	.51	Dominance	−.13
		Avoid	2.73
		Approach	3.07
Other Demands	.18	Mutuality	−.05
		Dominance	.07
		Relational Continuation	.14
		Change Other	−.13
		Positive Expression	.08
		Hurt Other	.26
		Approach	−.30
Serial Argument Outcomes			
Resolvability	.11	Other Demands	−.12
		Distributive	−.15
		Integrative	.22
Civility	.67	Resolvability	.20
		Satisfaction	.54
		Other Demands	−.13
		Distributive	−.08
		Integrative	.11
Satisfaction	.22	Distributive	.10
		Integrative	.25
		Positive Expression	.28
		Avoid	−1.29
		Approach	−1.14

Note. Modeling was conducted using Lisrel 8.8 with maximum likelihood estimation. Sample size was 2243. Model statistics: $df = 2065$, $\chi^2 = 15{,}936.11$, $p < .001$, RMSEA = .066 (90% C.I. .065–.067), CFI = .94, SRMR = .091.

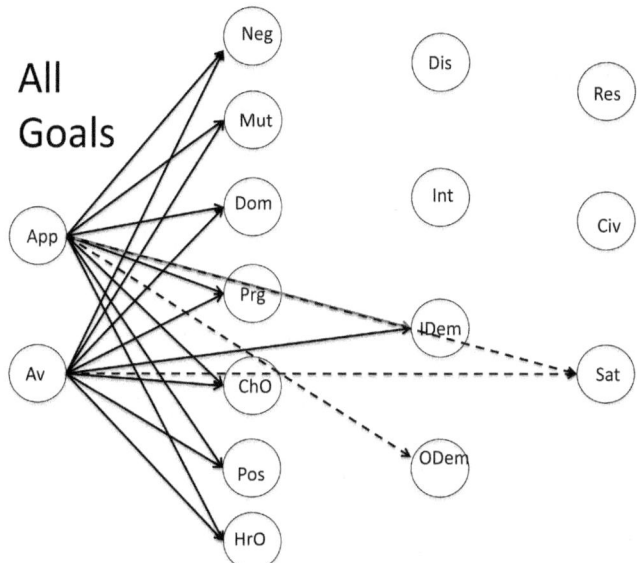

Figure 4.3: Effects of Approach and Avoid on Endogenous Variables. Solid Lines are Positive Paths, and Dashed Lines are Negative. App=approach; Av=avoid; Neg=negative expressiveness; Mut=mutuality; Dom=dominance; Prg=progress in the relationship; ChO=change the other; Pos=positive expressiveness; HrO=hurt the other; Dis=distribute; Int=integrative; Idem=I demanded, other withdrew; Odem=other demanded, I withdrew; Res=perceived resolvability; Civ=civility; Sat=satisfaction/climate

In Table 4.4 and Figure 4.3, we see the influence of approach and avoidance on the specific serial argument goals. The goals' variance accounted for by approach and avoidance varied from 3% to 61%. On the whole, the goal panel was substantially predicted by the two impulses. In fact, every goal was predicted at significant levels. Interestingly, approach and avoidance always both had positive associations with the goals (that is, the unstandardized path coefficients are all positive in Table 4.4). This is in spite of approach and avoidance being negatively correlated ($r = -.96$; see Table 4.5). This means that we are not observing goals being formed by a balance between approach and avoidance motivations. Instead, the *sum* of both impulses was the thing that was predictive. In other words, it was the total motivational energy that was leading to goal activation. This does not make very clear theoretical distinctions among the goals—after all, they each derived from the same impulses in Figure 4.2. Research exploring other precursor variables is obviously needed to explain why one goal is more highly activated than another.

128 | INTERPERSONAL ARGUING

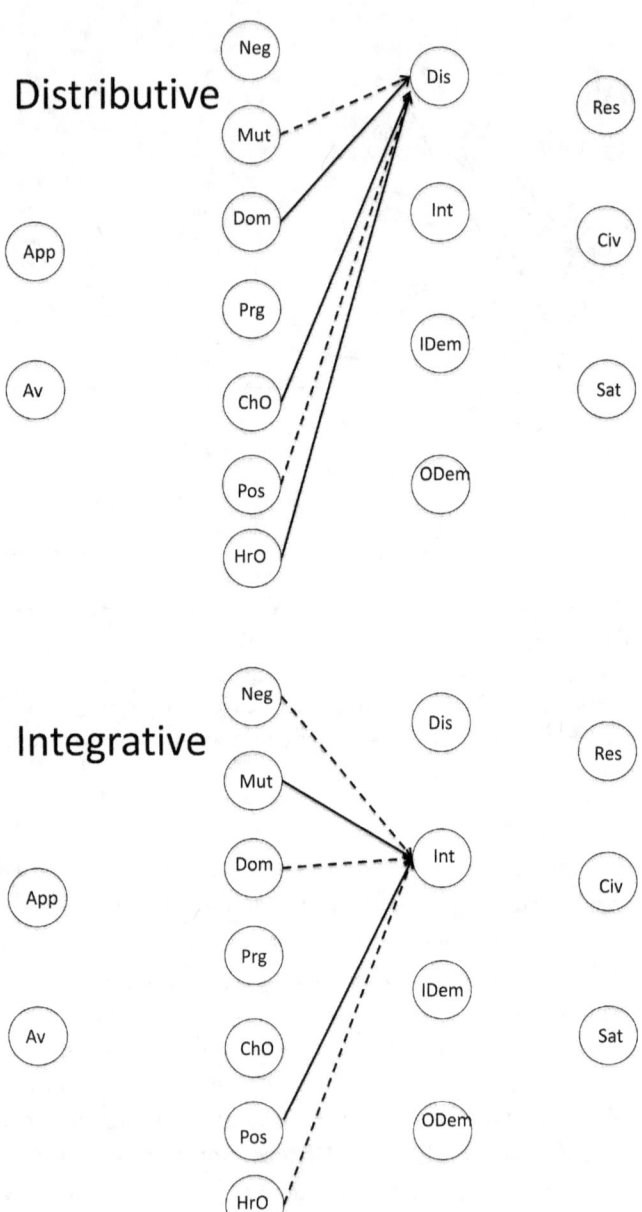

SERIAL ARGUMENTS | 129

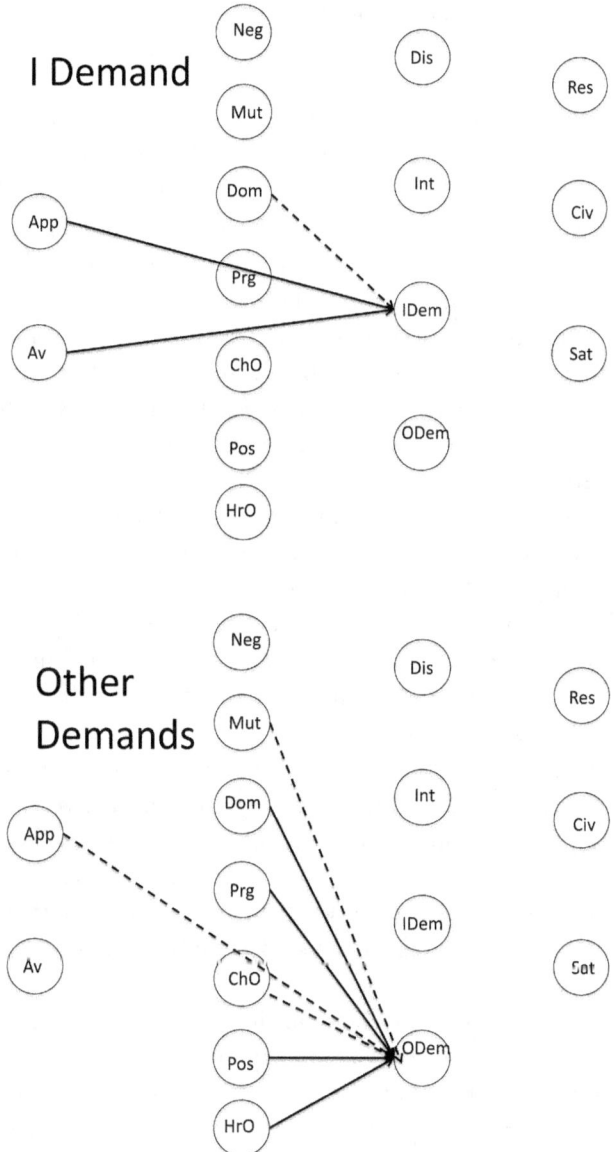

Figure 4.4: Effects of Goals on Tactics: Distributive, Integrative, I Demand, Other Demands. Solid Lines are Positive Paths, and Dashed Lines are Negative. App=approach; Av=avoid; Neg=negative expressiveness; Mut=mutuality; Dom=dominance; Prg=progress in the relationship; ChO=change the other; Pos=positive expressiveness; HrO=hurt the other; Dis=distribute; Int=integrative; Idem=I demanded, other withdrew; Odem=other demanded, I withdrew; Res=perceived resolvability; Civ=civility; Sat=satisfaction/climate

Table 4.4 and Figure 4.4 identify the latent variables that significantly predicted the four tactics. All four tactics were well predicted, with the lowest R^2 still being .18, for other demanded/I withdrew, and the other values ranging from .38 to .51. All of these were substantial effects. Approach and avoidance both skipped the goals panel to have direct effects on I demanded/other withdrew, and approach had a direct impact on other demanded/I withdrew. All seven goals had a direct path into at least one of the tactics. The goal of asserting dominance affected all four tactics, having its most substantial effects on the preference for distributive work. The two positive goals, mutuality and positive expression, were negatively related to the distributive tactic, strongly and positively related to integrative tactics, and had minor or absent effects on the demand/withdraw variations. Various negative goals positively predicted distributive tactics and had negative relationships to integrative work. Their relationships to the demand/withdraw tactics were somewhat mixed.

Outcomes were unevenly predicted (see Table 4.4 and Figure 4.5). Only civility had an impressive amount of variance explained (67%). This particular result had been improved by allowing direct paths from both resolvability and satisfaction. The nature of the statistical procedures implies that reversing those paths would have lowered the explained variance for civility and raised it for the other two outcomes, so it would be a mistake to assume that civility is more predictable than satisfaction or resolvability, apart from this statistical analysis. The causal dynamics among these three outcomes cannot be securely settled with the present data set. 11% of the variance in resolvability was accounted for, and 22% of satisfaction/climate. Both of these are very noticeable effects. Satisfaction was highly correlated with civility ($r = .68$; see Table 4.5), so it might be expected that anything that improves the civility of an encounter might also raise satisfaction/climate for the relationship. Civility and resolvability were also well correlated ($r = .44$).

Some of the significant influences on the outcomes were not quite anticipated by the theoretical model. Avoid and approach impulses skipped both the goals and tactics panels to assert direct effects on satisfaction, with both path coefficients being negative. Apparently high levels of motivational energy (the sum of approach and avoidance) indicate satisfaction problems. This suggests a frustration effect, although frustration is not a variable in the model of serial argument dynamics analyzed here. The positive expression goal also skipped the tactics panel, asserting a positive effect on satisfaction, independent of whatever tactics were in use.

Table 4.5: Correlations Within Panels of Latent Variables

	Exogenous Variables					
	1					
1 Approach						
2 Avoid	−.96					

	Serial Argument Goals					
	1	2	3	4	5	6
1 Negative Expression						
2 Mutuality	.18					
3 Dominance	.32	.03				
4 Relational Continuation	.33	.10	.31			
5 Change Other	.44	.05	.21	.38		
6 Positive Expressiveness	.12	.05	.12	.26	.15	
7 Hurt Other	.23	.03	.19	.31	.21	.12

	Serial Argument Tactics		
	1	2	3
1 Distributive			
2 Integrative	−.22		
3 I Demand	.34	−.06	
4 Other Demands	.00	−.02	.02

	Serial Argument Outcomes	
	1	2
1 Resolvability		
2 Civility	.44	
3 Satisfaction	.29	.68

Note. Sample size was 2243. Correlations among latent variables are essentially corrected for attenuation due to unreliability of measurement.

132 | INTERPERSONAL ARGUING

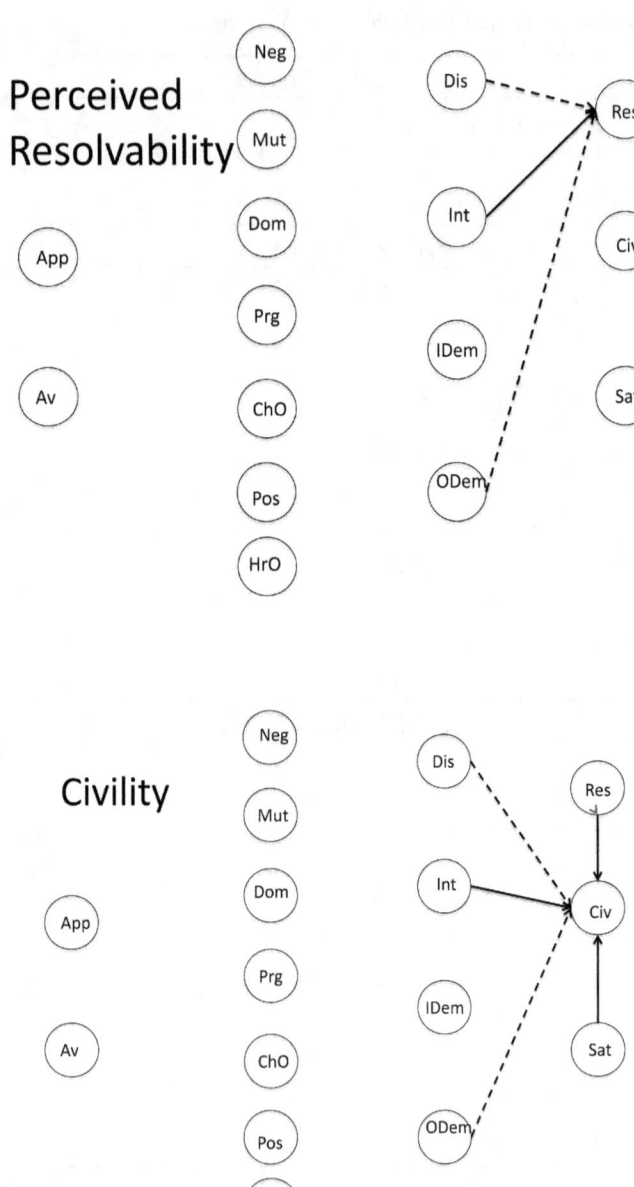

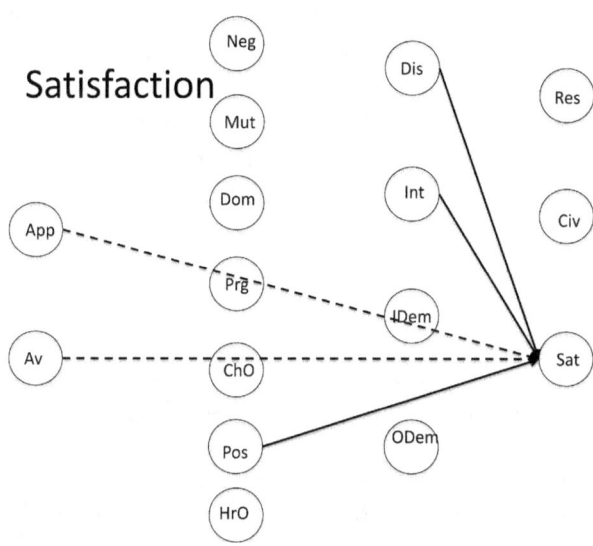

Figure 4.5: Effects of Tactics on Outcomes: Perceived Resolvability, Civility, and Satisfaction/Climate. Solid Lines are Positive Paths, and Dashed Lines are Negative. App=approach; Av=avoid; Neg=negative expressiveness; Mut=mutuality; Dom=dominance; Prg=progress in the relationship; ChO=change the other; Pos=positive expressiveness; HrO=hurt the other; Dis=distribute; Int=integrative; Idem=I demanded, other withdrew; Odem=other demanded, I withdrew; Res=perceived resolvability; Civ=civility; Sat=satisfaction/climate

All the other significant paths predicting outcomes were from the tactics panel, as the theoretical model proposed. I demanded/other withdrew was not a directly significant predictor of any outcome, but may have been indirectly involved due to its correlation with distributive tactics ($r = .34$; see Table 4.5). Distributive and integrative tactics predicted every outcome. They had path coefficients that were opposite in sign and comparable in extent for both resolvability and civility. Use of distributive tactics lowered ratings of both resolvability and civility, while integrative work improved them. In the case of satisfaction, however, they both contributed positively, with the distributive tactics being more important. Here we may be seeing a general effect of simply engaging in more work, whether distributive or integrative, and the more the effort, the higher the satisfaction. Or it may be that we are looking at two sorts of people, one that takes satisfaction from competition (distributive tactics) and one that prefers cooperation (integrative work).

The correlations among the latent variables are in Table 4.5, and some reference to those results has already been made. Among the goals, the correlations were all positive and ranged no higher than .44, with quite a few below .20. This suggests that there is very little redundancy in the goals list but that they all express the same motivational energy in some degree. The tactics panel showed similar independence, with other demanded/I withdrew having essentially no relationship to the other tactics at all. (The research design made it easy for respondents to indicate that tactics co-occurred—that is, they did not have to choose only one.) Distributive and integrative tactics seemed to be alternatives to one another ($r = -.22$), as one would expect. Distributive tactics tended to appear in concert with I demanded/other withdrew, which is a result also consistent with conceptual understanding of the aggressive element common to both tactics. The outcomes were all positively correlated. This suggests that they globally described somewhat similar recollections of the emotional flavor of a serial argument.

Section Summary. The purpose of this section has been to clarify the intrapersonal dynamics of serial arguing. Results of prior work have addressed this issue, but with somewhat inconsistent results. Those inconsistencies may have resulted from different sampling solicitations and different statistical decisions being made as the research program developed. Some data referred to serial arguments in the context of close relationships, and some to workplace or classroom relationships. Sometimes variables were transformed to promote normality, and sometimes not. Sometimes modification indices were used liberally, and sometimes not. Sometimes approach and avoidance were combined into a single latent variable, and sometimes they were dropped completely. Here, a consistent and fairly conservative set of decisions was applied to all the data together, resulting in results that are more generalizable and more securely interpretable than the previous individual-study results.

Results gave reasonably good support for the model conceptually displayed in Figure 4.2. A few important paths skipped panels, notably for the approach and avoidance impulses, but for the most part the significant effects were mediated in the way the diagram indicates. All the endogenous variables were predicted by at least some of the variables in the immediately prior panel, and many of those predictions accounted for substantial amounts of explained variance. Among the outcome variables, civility was far better predicted than either resolvability or satisfaction. Particularly in the case of satisfaction this is disappointing because satisfaction/climate is an important element of many relational dynamics. However, the result may have been due to the fact that respondents were describing a single episode, making civility perhaps more salient than overall relational satisfaction or eventual resolvability.

Results suggest that some additional variables be considered for inclusion in the theoretical system. The oddly consistent performance of approach and avoidance (that is, their consistent production of significant paths of the same sign) suggests that motivational energy is a more useful variable than the balance of approach and avoidance motivations. A similar thought has been tested in Hamilton and Hample (2011). The idea that opposing motivations should be combined into a simple estimate of motivational energy might be directly measured, or operationalized in terms of the felt stakes or importance of the serial argument's topic. Since personal and public topics are known to differ in importance, topic type might be used as a proxy for stakes, or the new stakes instrumentation could be directly used (Hample, Dai, & Zhan, 2016). The parallel (negative) effects of approach and avoidance on satisfaction also suggest that some measure of frustration be added to the model. Emotional energy, stakes, and frustration all seem to be similar constructs in the context of serial arguments, which concern important relational issues that have proved difficult to resolve.

The present analysis has been confined to the experiences of U.S. undergraduates. Serial arguments have also been studied in other cultures (Cionea & Hopârtean, 2011; Radanielina-Hita, 2010), and this is a welcome development. However, considering the likelihood that cultures differ in what they count as civil, resolvable, or satisfying, future work should probably segregate each culture until empirical analysis justifies combining them. A similar comment could be made about the differences between emerging, middle aged, and senior adults in the U.S., so future work should try to expand beyond the college campus in collecting data, in order to determine whether intrapersonal dynamics differ from culture to culture, or from one adult stage to another.

Conclusions

An argument that "just won't go away" can be a frustration, particularly when it doesn't seem to hold out much chance that it will ever be resolved. But the simple fact that it persists can be valuable information all by itself. A serial argument is like a relationship's reflection in a mirror. A list of all the recurring arguments in a relationship might be an interesting way to describe the relationship's content: its worries, its values, its commitments. (This would omit uncontroversial content, of course—important topics on which the partners' agreement never wavered.) When two partners continue to work on some issue, they are displaying their commitments to both that matter and to the relationship. Short-lived relationships may not even last long enough to have a serial argument, much less resolve one constructively.

The prospect of a constructive outcome to a serial argument can be encouraging, even though the argument hasn't yet been resolved. Serial arguments' topics are important and adults understand that sometimes it takes a while to work through a disagreement on a fundamental issue. Superficial agreements, the sort that we might express out of indifference or politeness, are out of bounds on many of these matters: Should we have children? Can I safely have only one drink? Should we regard gambling as harmless entertainment? Are you going to convert to my religion? Do you need a college degree? These things have to be settled properly, and arguers may have to change their lives to do so. Thinking that the argument will eventually be resolved strengthens the relationship during the time it takes to work through the disagreement or uncertainty.

The stakes of the argument depend on how much value one puts on the relationship that contains the argument. Even within the broad categories of "romantic," "friendship," and "occupational" there is considerable variability. A marriage is more important that a second-date romance, some friends are dearer than others, and some jobs are never more than career placeholders. The importance of the relationship and the closeness of the argument's topic to the relationship's heart—these are what combine to give a serial argument its importance, its urgency, and its decisiveness.

In short, insight into one's serial arguments leads to insight about one's life. Skill in resolving serial arguments should therefore lead to better experience. A particular moment might not be the right time to engage in another episode, but these issues should not be avoided as a matter of permanent policy. Approaching them is ultimately a good thing, even if it feels awkward in the instant.

References

Amato, P. R., & Previti, D. (2003). People's reasons for divorcing: Gender, social class, the life course, and adjustment. *Journal of Family Issues, 24*, 602–626.

Bevan, J. L. (2010). Serial argument goals and conflict strategies: A comparison between romantic partners and family members. *Communication Reports, 23*, 52–64.

Bevan, J. L. (2014). Dyadic perceptions of goals, conflict strategies, and perceived resolvability in serial arguments. *Journal of Social and Personal Relationships, 31*, 773–795.

Bevan, J. L., Finan, A., & Kaminsky, A. (2008). Modeling serial arguments in close relationships: The serial argument process model. *Human Communication Research, 34*, 600–624.

Bevan, J. L., Hale, J. L., & Williams, S. L. (2004). Identifying and characterizing goals of dating partners engaging in serial argumentation. *Argumentation and Advocacy, 41*, 28–40.

Bevan, J. L., & Sparks, L. (2014). The relationship between accurate and benevolently biased serial argument perceptions and individual negative health perceptions. *Communication Research, 41*, 257–281.

Bevan, J. L., Tidgewell, K. D., Bagley, K. C., Cusanelli, L., Hartstern, M., Holbeck, D., & Hale, J. L. (2007). Serial argumentation goals and their relationships to perceived resolvability and choice of conflict tactics. *Communication Quarterly, 55*, 61–71.

Brown, P., & Levinson, S. C. (1987). *Politeness: Some universals in language usage.* Cambridge: Cambridge University Press.

Cionea, I., & Hample, D. (2015). Serial argument topics. *Argumentation and Advocacy, 52*, 75–88.

Cionea, I. A., & Hopârtean, A.-M. (2011, November). *Serial arguments: An exploratory investigation in Romania.* Paper presented at the annual meeting of the National Communication Association, New Orleans, LA.

Cionea, I. A., & Johnson, A. J. (2014, May). *A new approach to examining serial arguments: The benefits of alternating initiator roles.* Paper presented at the annual meeting of the International Communication Association, Seattle, WA.

Coles, V. B., & Samp, J. A. (2013, November). *Nonverbal emotional management during relational conflict between dating partners: An examination of felt versus expressed emotions.* Paper presented at the annual meeting of the National Communication Association, Washington, DC.

Dillard, J. P. (1990). A goal-driven model of interpersonal influence. In J. P. Dillard (Ed.), *Seeking compliance: The production of interpersonal influence messages* (pp. 41–56). Scottsdale, AZ: Gorsuch Scarisbrick.

Dillard, J. P. (2004). The goals-plans-action model of interpersonal influence. In J. S. Seiter & R. H. Gass (Eds.), *Perspective on persuasion, social influence, and compliance gaining* (pp. 185–206). Boston, MA: Allyn & Bacon.

Dillard, J. P., Segrin, C., & Harden, J. M. (1989). Primary and secondary goals in the production of interpersonal influence messages. *Communication Monographs, 56*, 19–38.

Dillard, J. P., Solomon, D. H., & Samp, J. A. (1996). Framing social reality: The relevance of relational judgments. *Communication Research, 23*, 703–723.

van Eemeren, F. H., & Grootendorst, R. (2004). *A systematic theory of argumentation: The pragma-dialectical approach.* Cambridge: Cambridge University Press.

Gibb, J. R. (1961). Defensive communication. *Journal of Communication, 11*, 141–148.

Gilbert, M. A. (2014). *Arguing with people.* Peterborough, ON: Broadview Press.

Hamilton, M. A., & Hample, D. (2011). Testing hierarchical models of argumentativeness and verbal aggressiveness. *Communication Methods and Measures, 5*, 250–273.

Hample, D. (2003). Arguing skill. In J. O. Greene & B. R. Burleson (Eds.), *Handbook of communication and social interaction skills* (pp. 439–478). Mahwah, NJ: Erlbaum.

Hample, D., & Allen, S. (2012). Serial arguments in organizations. *Journal of Argumentation in Context, 1*, 312–330.

Hample, D., & Cionea, I. (2012). Serial arguments in inter-ethnic relationships. *International Journal of Intercultural Relations, 36*, 430–445.

Hample, D., Dai, Y., & Zhan, M. (2016). Argument stakes: Preliminary conceptualizations and empirical descriptions. *Argumentation and Advocacy, 52*, 199–213.

Hample, D., & Krueger, B. (2011). Serial arguments in classrooms. *Communication Studies, 62*, 597–617.

Hample, D., Paglieri, F., & Na, L. (2012). The costs and benefits of arguing: Predicting the decision whether to engage or not. In F. H. van Eemeren & B. Garssen (Eds.), *Topical themes in argumentation theory: Twenty exploratory studies* (pp. 307–322). New York, NY: Springer.

Hample, D., & Richards, A. S. (2015). Attachment style, serial argument, and taking conflict personally. *Journal of Argumentation in Context, 4*, 63–86.

Hample, D., Richards, A. S., & Na, L. (2012). A test of the conflict linkage model in the context of serial arguments. *Western Journal of Communication, 76*, 459–479.

Infante, D. A., Chandler, T. A., & Rudd, J. E. (1989). Test of an argumentative skill deficiency model of interspousal violence. *Communication Monographs, 56*, 163–177.

Johnson, A. J. (2002). Beliefs about arguing: A comparison of public-issue and personal-issue arguments. *Communication Reports, 15*, 99–112.

Johnson, A. J. (2009). A functional approach to interpersonal argument. Differences between public- and personal-issue arguments. *Communication Reports, 22*, 13–28.

Johnson, A. J., Averbeck, J. M., Kelley, K. M., & Liu, S. (2010). Serial arguments and argument type: Comparing serial arguments about public and personal issue argument topics. In D. S. Gouran (Ed.), *The functions of argument and social context* (pp. 211–218). Washington, DC: National Communication Association.

Johnson, A. J., Averbeck, J. M., Kelley, K. M., & Liu, S. (2011). When serial arguments predict harm: Examining the influences of argument function, topic of the argument, perceived resolvability, and argumentativeness. *Argumentation and Advocacy, 47*, 214–227.

Johnson, A. J., & Cionea, I. A. (2016). Serial arguments in interpersonal relationships: Relational dynamics and interdependence. In J. A. Samp (Ed.), *Communicating interpersonal conflict in close relationships: Contexts, challenges, and opportunities* (pp. 111–127). New York, NY: Routledge.

Johnson, A. J., Hample, D., & Cionea, I. A. (2014). Understanding argumentation in interpersonal communication: The implications of distinguishing between public and personal topics. *Communication Yearbook, 38*, 145–173.

Johnson, K. L., & Roloff, M. E. (1998). Serial arguing and relational quality: Determinants and consequences of perceived resolvability. *Communication Research, 25*, 327–343.

Johnson, K. L., & Roloff, M. E. (2000). Correlates of the perceived resolvability and relational consequences of serial arguing in dating relationships: Argumentative features and the use of coping strategies. *Journal of Social and Personal Relationships, 17*, 676–686.

Kline, R. B. (2015). *Principles and practice of structural equation modeling* (4th ed.). New York, NY: Guilford Press.

Kuhn, D. (1991). *The skills of argument*. Cambridge: Cambridge University Press.

Malis, R. S., & Roloff, M. E. (2006a). Demand/withdraw patterns in serial arguments: Implications for well-being. *Human Communication Research, 32*, 198–216.

Malis, R. S., & Roloff, M. E. (2006b). Features of serial arguing and coping strategies: Links with stress and well-being. In B. A. LePoire & R. M. Dailey (Eds.), *Applied interpersonal communication matters: Family, health, and community relations* (pp. 39–66). New York, NY: Peter Lang.

Miller, C. W., & Roloff, M. E. (2014). When hurt continues: Taking conflict personally leads to rumination, residual hurt and negative motivations toward someone who hurt us. *Communication Quarterly, 62*, 193–213.

Miller, C. W., Roloff, M. E., & Malis, R. S. (2007). Understanding interpersonal conflicts that are difficult to resolve: A review of literature and presentation of an integrated model. *Annals of the International Communication Association, 31*, 118–171.

Morrison, S., & Schrodt, P. (2017). The perceived threat and resolvability of serial arguments as correlates of relational uncertainty in romantic relationships. *Communication Studies, 68*, 56–71.

National Fatherhood Initiative. (2005). *With this ring…: A national survey on marriage in America*. Retrieved from www.fatherhood.org

Paglieri, F., & Castelfranchi, C. (2010). Why argue? Towards a cost-benefit analysis of argumentation. *Argument and Computation, 1*, 71–91.

Radanielina-Hita, M. L. (2010). Let's make peace! A cross-cultural analysis of the effects of serial arguing behaviors in romantic relationships: The case of Malagasy romantic partners. *Journal of Intercultural Communication, 39*, 81–103.

Rancer, A. S., & Avtgis, T. A. (2014). *Argumentative and aggressive communication: Theory, research, and application* (2nd ed.). New York, NY: Peter Lang.

Roloff, M. E., & Reznik, R. M. (2008). Communication during serial arguments: Connections with individuals' mental and physical well-being. In M. T. Motley (Ed.), *Studies in applied interpersonal communication* (pp. 97–120). Los Angeles, CA: Sage.

Sillars, A. L. (1980). Attributions and communication in roommate conflicts. *Communication Monographs, 47*, 180–200.

Trapp, R. (1990). Arguments in interpersonal relationships. In R. Trapp & J. Schuetz (Eds.), *Perspectives on argumentation: Essays in honor of Wayne Brockriede* (pp. 43–54). Prospect Heights, IL: Waveland.

Trapp, R., & Hoff, N. (1985). A model of serial argument in interpersonal relationships. *Journal of the American Forensic Association, 22*, 1–11.

Vuchinich, S. (1990). The sequential organization of closing in verbal family conflict. In A. D. Grimshaw (Ed.), *Conflict talk* (pp. 118–138). Cambridge: Cambridge University Press.

Wallenfelsz, K. P., & Hample, D. (2010). The role of taking conflict personally in imagined interactions about conflict. *Southern Communication Journal, 75*, 1–17.

Watzlawick, P., Beavin, J. H., & Jackson, D. D. (1967). *Pragmatics of human communication*. New York, NY: Norton.

Worley, T. R., & Samp, J. A. (2016). Serial argument goals and changes in perceived conflict resolution: A dyadic analysis. *Western Journal of Communication, 80*, 264–281.

CHAPTER FIVE

The Rationality Engine

It might be interesting to take a moment to consider some of the differences between one person trying to work through an argument alone, and two people trying to do it together. Let's suppose the argument itself is the same and that in both cases the person or dyad is simply trying to decide whether to accept the argument.

The single person is mainly thinking, and a lot of the thinking is probably unconscious. He or she has just been exposed to the argument, maybe in something overheard or posted online, and is occupied in comprehending the parts of the argument (maybe a couple of sentences that are giving evidence, or a story illustrating the importance of the evidence) and is trying to understand how they join together. The person alone is also remembering a lot of things, fitting the argument's material into his or her own life, including a virtual life acquired from television, reading, previous conversations, and so forth. We have noticed that arguments are generally based on something that is accepted or taken for granted, and then some additional material is added to propel recipients onto new ground. The person alone is trying out that movement from given to new, checking whether the sequence of ideas is sound, whether the starting points are solid, and whether the end point seems appropriate. He or she is not only working through the internals of the argument, but is also checking it against its externals (i.e., everything else in the world that is not already in the argument). The internals are what Johnson (2000) called the illative core of an argument, and the externals are what he called the dialectical tier. The chance that the person comes to the right conclusion is limited by his or her intelligence, experience, imagination, and—especially—the amount of effort that he or she puts into the whole operation of thinking.

Now suppose two people are doing the same thing together. One of them has just proposed the argument and the two of them are discussing it. Both people are acting individually, just as a person alone would. But something else is happening, too—they are doing public things, saying things out loud, reacting to what one another has said. To keep things simple, let us suppose that neither one of them is intentionally lying or trying to get one's way at any cost or generally just making things up. That means that what they say is reflective of what they are thinking. They are also making a special effort to explain things clearly for the other person, clarifications that we often skip over when we are alone. Their remarks are not perfectly reflective of their argument-centered thoughts, because both of them are editing things to make good impressions and to respect the other person's identity as well. But they each know this about one another and therefore they make some allowance for it. In short, both of them have reasonably full access to the other one's thoughts. This means that neither has to think of everything, neither is limited to his or her personal experiences, and if one of them misses some key point the other one might compensate for that.

This little pair of sketches is a bit unrealistic, of course. For one thing, people alone rarely go to all the work I described. Usually, they just check the conclusion to see if they agree with it (Nickerson, 1998). This is called "confirmation bias." If they do agree on first glance, they assume the argument itself was stellar without bothering to analyze it. If they think the conclusion is wrong, then they may scrutinize the argument critically, or just assume that it was terrible and still not do any real thinking at all. The two people together can also short-circuit their joint thinking with some sort of agreeability check (Janis, 1982; Schulz-Hardt, Jochims, & Frey, 2002). Or they can get carried away with impressing one another, leaping to agree with anything the other person says without waiting to see if there is any proof. But let us set aside these realities for now, and just think about people working at their best.

Even without looking at the research literature, which we will do momentarily, we can already see several things. The dyad is doing more things than an individual does—it is talking out loud, it is probably being a little fuller and more careful about what is being said so that the other person can understand, and it is doing interpersonal work along with interior psychological activity. In short, the dyad is thinking but is also acting socially (Boy & Witte, 2007). The solitary individual is probably quicker, but that might come at the cost of not really thinking beyond the first flash of an impression about the conclusion (Nickerson,

1998). The dyad may very well be slower, but that is because it is drawing on more resources than the person alone and addressing social responsibilities along with private thoughts. The dyad has both people's intelligences, it has two sets of experience and memory, it has double the prejudices and assumptions, and it has the shared commitment to work things out publicly.

This chapter is about the effects of having another person to argue with. The final section summarizes a series of studies that my colleagues, my students, and I did to test a hypothesis I had. That proposal was that intelligent, nicely motivated, and usefully informed conversation is the rationality engine. In other words, it is natural for two people who are ordinarily bright, well disposed toward arguing, and satisfactorily informed, to work through a complex argument properly, more or less rationally. People engaged in mature dialogue should set aside the awful arguments we have traditionally called fallacies, they should assess flawed arguments according to the weight they should really have, they should each nullify the other person's cognitive biases (Hastie & Dawes, 2010; Kahneman, 2011), and they should come to good conclusions. This is the hypothesis that I set out to test over a series of studies. Because academic writing doesn't really value suspense, I will say now that we largely supported the hypothesis. But another point of academic writing is to show readers the evidence, and that is what will happen as we move through the chapter.

Group Thinking

From the earliest days of research on small group processes, scholars were interested in comparing group outcomes to those of people working alone (Collins & Guetzkow, 1964; Laughlin, Bonner, & Miner, 2002; Steiner, 1972). Investigators wondered whether small groups did better or worse than the most capable group member would have done alone, better or worse than the average of members' individual abilities, better or worse than the most dominant member would have done alone, and so forth. As the (inconsistent) results rolled in, researchers realized that they had to explain their findings in terms of the task type, group processes, and information handling, not just some simple counting, choosing, or averaging of members (Laughlin et al., 2002; also compare Hinsz, Tindale, & Vollrath, 1997, with Levine, 1999). Whether groups were superior, inferior, or equivalent to some individual-related standard was best explained by what and how the groups did or didn't do. Those processes turned out to be affected by a great variety of task, motivational, identity, emotional, relational, and other influences, for better or worse (Kerr & Tindale, 2004). A problem with reading this literature is that there are few principled theories of what sorts of task there are, what kinds of information exist or what should be done with it, how people should be classified, and what kinds of thinking might occur, and many other things. This makes cumulation and summary of research quite challenging, and straightforward conclusions hard to come by.

So as this chapter develops, readers should remember that I am mainly aiming to explain things about dyads that have certain characteristics, and those features will guide our reading of the literature. We will eventually be examining how dyads deal with uncertain arguments, those that philosophers call "defeasible" ones. With a defeasible argument (one that can be reasonably objected to, or potentially defeated on its merits), we should not anticipate simple outcomes that are true or false, valid or invalid, larger or smaller. We will be examining how reasonable were the dyad's judgments, and we really cannot press much beyond "reasonable." And—this is particularly important—we will only be interested in certain sorts of dyads. We want to know if *intelligent*, *well-informed*, and *constructively motivated* dyads handle arguments well. Dyadic conversation is not magical enough to fix situations where the arguers are slow-witted, ignorant, or closed-minded.

Evolutionary Reasons for Optimism

We think that anatomically modern people (*homo sapiens*) probably appeared about 200,000 years ago, but those humans inherited genetic material and life practices from earlier sorts of creatures (the genus *homo* is about 3,000,000 years old). A great many of our "modern" behaviors and abilities evolved during the Pleistocene period, roughly 2.5 million years ago up to about 12,000 years ago. If you wonder what biological evolution has to do with arguing, bear in mind that people can only think or say things their brains are wired to accommodate, and our brains evolved. If you can't think it, you can't say it. Although we don't emphasize it very much, arguing has a biological basis, just as all sorts of social and communicative behaviors do (Floyd & Afifi, 2011). Brains, hormones, perceptual systems, voice box architecture, and skeletal and muscular abilities are all involved in conversational disagreements.

So pause briefly to imagine what life must have been like for our ancestors, because that's what directed our evolution. If you wanted meat, you had to kill it; if you wanted fruit, you had to pick it; if you wanted shelter, you had to find it; if you wanted better weather, you had to walk for a few years. Life was day to day because food could not be carried, stored, or protected for very long. We had a few tools, but sharp stones were at the top of our technological inventory for a long time. We were never the most fearful predator, nor did we have very good physiological protections against many of the conditions or animals that could kill us. We met those challenges with our intelligence, particularly the sophisticated languages that we eventually developed.

And we lived in groups, probably small families or kinship tribes. Someone else in the group might have meat if you did not; someone else might watch your baby or leave her toddler with you; someone else might know where tubers or water could be found. A solitary adult would not have survived for very long, much less a child, but a person living in a collective had some buffering against the inevitable ups and downs of a brute environment. Group life had to involve both giving and taking. An adult who was only parasitic would not be tolerated or permitted to remain (Cosmides & Tooby, 1992; Roos, Gelfand, Dau, & Lun, 2015). Cooperation, reliability, reciprocity, and trust were necessary. These were ultimately displayed via behavior, but they were negotiated and promised using language.

Mercier and Sperber (2011, 2017; Mercier, 2016) made an important claim about the connections between human evolution and human arguing. When students first start thinking about how we originally began to argue with one another, they naturally assume that people first learned to reason and then learned to say their reasoning out loud. Mercier and Sperber's "argumentative theory of reasoning" reversed that suggestion. They said that people first learned to persuade, and that reasoning abilities developed as a consequence of the interpersonal arguing.

Their views are still a little controversial, but they are quite plausible. We know that humans make systematic reasoning errors (e.g., confirmation bias, anchoring effects, atmosphere effects, and dozens of other well studied things; e.g., Falmagne, 1975; Hastie & Dawes, 2010; Revlin & Mayer, 1978; Wason & Johnson-Laird, 1972). These errors often result in inappropriate standpoints because flawed thinking generates unsupported conclusions. It is hard to make a case as to why evolution would have rewarded or ignored a private unwillingness to change one's mind in the face of new evidence, just to mention the example of confirmation bias.

But if we take Mercier and Sperber's view—that persuasion and arguing came first, and reasoning later—then it does start to make sense. In the most basic amoral respects, a persuader just wants to persuade, and would say just about anything that would result in the other person agreeing. So a persuader would be willing to make a bad argument if it would work. Reasoning, said Mercier and Sperber, developed as a kind of self-defense against this sort of exploitive argumentation. It was useful to be able to spot when the persuader was reasoning poorly and making demands that lacked support. Mercier and Sperber call this "epistemic vigilance." Consequently it also became useful to be able to anticipate when your audience would be able to see through your case. This process of defensive criticism nicely explains the prevalence of confirmation bias (the willingness to accept an argument that "comes out right," regardless of its merits). If someone gives you an argument that produces a conclusion you already approve, there seems to be no need to defend yourself against this persuasion and scrutinize the argument's details. So people are vulnerable to arguments that flatter them, that tempt them, that offer precious rewards. Thus, those fallacies flourished evolutionarily because accepting such arguments resulted in people doing what they wanted to do anyway. The sunk cost fallacy—persisting in some failing course of action because of a past investment in it, like finishing an awful meal even though you're not hungry any more—is also explicable in this theory (Mercier & Sperber, 2017). Persisting in a poor policy just for the sake of consistency makes you more predicable by others, which is a social benefit. Other sorts of arguments (e.g., "do it because it's better for you to die than for me to be hurt a little") would not match confirmation, sunk cost, or similar biases and so would be more carefully thought about by the receivers. Both the arguers and receivers would eventually develop a shared practice for good arguing whenever it was needed (e.g., when a naked appeal to self-interest would not suffice).

This theory has another implication for the present chapter. If reasoning developed as a sort of self-defense, as Mercier and Sperber said, then it has an essentially social origin, not a private interior genesis. We can certainly think when we are alone, but the natural site for reasoning was in interaction with other people, according to this theory. In other words, reasoning began in conversation and became cognitive as a consequence of social experience (Mercier & Sperber, 2017, p. 176). So this (very generally) supports the spirit of this chapter's hypothesis, that intelligent conversation is the engine that produces good arguing.

Besides the Mercier and Sperber idea, another line of evolutionary research also suggests a reason why a dyad might be expected to reason well together. Human evolved in groups, and Spoor and Kelly (2004) proposed that these collectives were clearly oriented to group affect (emotions or moods). Group affect could be homogenous (everyone has the same feelings) or heterogeneous (a variety of moods and emotions) and it served several functions. One was communicative, so that the sudden appearance of negative affect might alert members to the presence of danger and the necessity of fast, hard action. Spoor and Kelly said "affect in groups functions to alert the group to positive and negative aspects of the environment" (p. 405). This is an informative function.

Another function of group affect was bonding (Spoor & Kelly, 2004), and here is our particular relevance. Groups were held together in part by shared positive affect among the members, and various sorts of positive feelings constituted incentives to remain in the group. Perhaps the most commonly studied sort of group affect is cohesiveness, which Spoor and Kelly said includes three elements: interpersonal attraction, commitment to a task, and pride in one's affiliation to the group (pp. 405–406). When a decision's importance was low—that is, the people were not discussing how to distribute scarce food or something critical—they were just doing a task together, maybe selecting someone to gather nearby visible firewood. Two people working through a low stakes argument—exploring it, testing it, proposing and defending it—are engaged in a joint task, deliberating. Because it is low stakes, the process of arguing together is salient, perhaps more so than the actual joint decision. The arguers can take pride in having argued well together, and may enjoy one another's participation. Such an experience would seem to follow most immediately from cooperative arguing, rather than some sort of red-tooth competition for dominance. Cooperation involves loyalty, open-mindedness, and an acknowledgement that the other person's thoughts should be absorbed into one's own. Argumentative interaction takes place in the context of the bonds among the arguers, and the activity in turn can reinforce or otherwise modify the bond. The more cooperative, receptive, and other-oriented the relationships are, the better the arguments are likely to be, because they will tend to be civil, cooperative, and mutually open-minded.

These feelings of bonding and cooperation are natural because they reflect valued elements of our species' earliest socialization experience. Joint reasoning of the sort that should improve an interaction's processes and results would be a natural consequence of these fair-minded feelings. In other words, our natural need to bond with others generates some of the preconditions for good dyadic arguing, including openness to the other person, a cooperative attitude, the self-discipline of not saying untrue things for personal gain, and an easy engagement with the merits of the other person's arguments.

All of these evolutionary considerations are not pointed enough to be decisive for this chapter's main hypothesis (that conversation is the rationality engine), but they are suggestive. It is in our human nature to argue with one another, to learn to scrutinize what the other person says, and to value trust, loyalty, and mutual cooperation. Certainly we can do the opposite, and every reader of this book no doubt has plenty of experience in seeing people be closed-minded, naïve, and exploitive. But in a way, those undesirable behaviors take positive arguing behaviors as their background contrast. Confidence tricksters only succeed because they rely on others' trusting natures, amoral persuaders prevail only when listeners do not see any need to scrutinize the messages very closely, and people are more easily outmaneuvered when they expect the other arguer to be loyal and considerate. Our evolutionary inheritance—which follows from our earliest dependence on groups for survival—has also generated tendencies to argue cooperatively and carefully.

Contemporary Evidence

Let us advance some tens of thousands of years, and examine much more recent data bearing on how we reason together. Small groups (typically about half a dozen people) are larger and more complicated than dyads (two people, by definition), but in the present context small groups have been studied much more often than dyads, and they do involve a combination of private thought and social activity. So we will start there.

Kerr and Tindale (2004) wrote an extensive narrative review of research on group performance. They reported that groups can perform either better or worse than their members would have done alone. Overall, they believe that groups tend to do better than individuals (p. 642), but this effect is qualified by innumerable considerations and cannot be relied upon across the board. When groups do badly, part of the problem may be motivational, because when people can "hide" in a group they sometimes do what psychologists call "social loafing" (e.g., Smith, Kerr, Markus, & Stasson, 2001). Other difficulties involve bad information sharing, as when groups undervalue material that only one person possesses or when they issue a decision before everyone has been fully heard.

Interestingly, when face-to-face groups are compared with those using text-based computer mediated communication (i.e., texting and email, but not Skype or FaceTime), the face-to-face groups perform much better (Baltes, Dickson, Sherman, Bauer, & LaGanke, 2002). So we might be seeing an overall effect of personal presence here, with the most personally remote sort of interaction (text-based CMC) being worst, followed by groups in which one can be active or passive, or perhaps by individual work where there is no hiding. We might expect dyadic activity to be at the more involving end of this continuum, because the two arguers are each quite pointedly calling on the other person to consider, respond, and decide (cf. Kuhn, 2015). The immediacy of dyadic arguing might make the motivational weaknesses of group work less likely, and this in turn would lead to more activity in sharing information and responding to the other arguer's points. A dyad is a very small group, and its participants can hardly help but put themselves forward.

Particularly relevant to this chapter, Kerr and Tindale (2004) mentioned that groups are susceptible to many of the fallacies and cognitive biases that impede good individual thinking. For instance, groups are influenced by majority pressure (what we would call the *ad populum* fallacy; see their p. 634) and by anchoring effects (when the first-heard number "anchors" later numerical judgments, such as how much a jury should award in civil damages; see p. 645). Although groups and individuals are each vulnerable to the sunk cost fallacy (continuing on a bad line of action because you have already "sunk" substantial resources into it), groups were clearly less affected by it than individuals were (Smith, Tindale, & Steiner, 1998). Both whole juries and individual jurors can be influenced by officially irrelevant information (as when a judge rules some testimony out of order), but the conditions under which juries or jurors are better at this are quite complex (Kerr, MacCoun, & Kramer, 1996). So the same tempting reasoning shortcuts that can divert individuals from optimal thinking can also derail groups. Dyads will have no special vulnerability or protection from these cognitive heuristics. How well the argument proceeds and where it lands will depend on the actual arguing, not on how many people are involved (one, two, or half a dozen).

This brief review of the general question of whether groups or individuals make better decisions, consider the evidence more carefully, or reason better, has been somewhat inconclusive. I have spared readers the multitude of special circumstances (mediators and moderators) that can affect group versus individual relative superiority. For now, the point is that there is no overwhelming decision-making advantage either way, no generalization that can be expected to apply to most real-word situations. So now we change course a bit, to focus on special reasoning obstacles, and whether it helps to have someone else reasoning along with you.

Debiasing Arguments

The systematic threats to rational thinking are variously called cognitive biases, heuristics, cognitive shortcuts, material fallacies, cognitive illusions, sophistries, and perhaps some other terms depending on the researcher's academic field. The general topic is studied in economics, decision sciences, social psychology, cognitive psychology, philosophy, communication, and argumentation studies, among others. Certain researchers have become interested in the question of whether arguments can be made in such a way as to "debias" people's thinking, that is, to divert people away from their normal cognitive shortcuts (e.g., Zenker, Dahlman, & Sarwar, 2015).

We should begin by noticing that thinking shortcuts evolved naturally (Battersby & Bailin, 2013; Gigerenzer & Sturm, 2012). A basic principle in psychology is that people are "cognitive misers," that is, that people think as little as possible and are too limited and constrained to think with perfect rationality anyway (Cherniak, 1986). Intensive sustained thinking is not ordinary and has to be stimulated somehow. This human characteristic is reinforced by the reality that many problems are so computationally complicated that humans just cannot work through all the details even if they want to, and they recognize that. Once they have a solution that seems suitable to the stakes and the moment, they cease to contemplate (Simon, 1990). The issue is not whether humans have shortcuts, it is whether the shortcuts are useful or not, and in what circumstances.

There is some controversy about how awful these thinking patterns really are. These heuristics are only obviously irrational in the narrow sense of "rational" that refers to certain principles of logic and probability rather than to other principles (Cherniak, 1986; Gigerenzer, 1991). Technically, coming to an inductive conclusion after having seen only two examples of something is not very defensible. Neither is confusing an estimate about a particular case with a probability from a large sample. Nor is ignoring new information once you have a firm conclusion in mind. But in terms of saving overall cognitive resources, it might be rational *in a broad sense* to arrive at a conclusion quickly based on merely satisfactory or suggestive evidence (Cherniak, 1986; Cummings, 2014; Gigerenzer & Sturm, 2012; Zenker, 2013). Perhaps you lack the technical education to evaluate a particular bit of evidence, perhaps the information environment for your decision is complex and uncertain, perhaps there are huge consequences for a mistake in one direction and few for a mistake in the other, perhaps you have too little time available before action is necessary, or perhaps you simply don't care very much. In those circumstances, it is sensible to make a quick decision. Either relying on someone else's judgment rather than working everything out yourself or using a simple decision rule that ignores a multitude of fast-changing variables will not necessarily be less accurate anyway. In fact, there are actually specifiable circumstances in which trying to calculate everything that is technically relevant will generally result in a worse outcome than using a simple but intelligent decision rule (Cummings, 2014; Gigerenzer & Sturm, 2012).

But even with these thoughts in mind, it is still realistic to notice that people have been found to do some pretty terrible reasoning, errors that are quite clear once analysts have detected them. Many mistakes are just random, but some are systematic and appear in identifiable patterns of stimulus-and-reasoning. These are the things that have been identified as biases, studied, and been targeted with efforts to cure them.

"Debiasing" refers to some sort of intervention or restructuring of the problem that makes cognitive biases less likely to assert themselves. One idea seems to be that proper thought is somehow a naturally attractive system of cognition, and we merely need to remove the obstacles to it. While this isn't entirely evident to me—I personally find simple-minded thought pretty attractive on lots of topics—it does make sense that if we remove temptations, people might act in better ways.

Another approach is to force people to do something unnatural that will "cure" their ordinary reasoning patterns.

Several scholars suggest that debiasing efforts fall into three general classes (Heath, Larrick, & Klayman, 1998; Larrick, 2004; Zenker, Dahlman, & Sarwar, 2015). These three are *cognitive, motivational,* and *technological.* Cognitive interventions are intended to clarify and improve how people or groups think. As we will see momentarily, sometimes people are required to list pro and con arguments for their position, or groups are required to have a devil's advocate. Sometimes people are taught about proper statistical inference or warned against some common reasoning mistakes. Motivational interventions are generally intended to increase people's involvement in a group decision process or to increase their commitment to getting the right answer privately. They might be offered rewards for a right answer or punished for a wrong one. The last sort of intervention is called technological because many of these writers are group or organizational scholars who are interested in providing computer-aided processes, such as online databases. Often they study decision support systems (DSS), which is a well-researched topic in business and related disciplines. Our own interests are broader than that, however, so I will retitle this to "argument *design."* Arguments and argument settings can be designed to stimulate or restrict some kinds of participation and so we will consider whether design can debias arguments, whether the design involves technology or not.

Cognition

Let us begin by looking at some cognitive interventions. A very common one—and one especially pertinent to this book—is having counter arguments, that is, evidence and reasoning that disagree with a person's judgment. Inserting material that contradicts the participants is mostly aimed at countering confirmation bias (sometimes called "myside bias;" Sperber, 2017). This is one of the most basic of the cognitive biases (Nickerson, 1998; Schweiger, Oeberst, & Cress, 2014). It refers to looking for confirmation of your opinions, rather than truly wanting to test them. When they are instructed to look for more information on some topic, people influenced by confirmation bias seek out material supporting their view rather than information disagreeing with it, even though contradictory evidence would be more useful in evaluating their position. They look for "positive" evidence and avoid, ignore, or reinterpret inconvenient facts. They also under-weigh new information (possibly provided by the experimenter, introduced by another group member, or found by accident) when the new information conflicts with their opinion. They are not really open to genuine argument on the issue. Confirmation bias, in other words, represents stubbornness and closed-mindedness, which we all have to some degree. (When it refers to us, we call it conviction, firm resolve, and being steadfastly loyal.) Requiring people to list arguments for and against their position is an obvious method of preventing them from only thinking confirming thoughts (Battersby & Bailin, 2013, p. 8).

A basic idea in Western cultures and the legal traditions that emerged from them is that controversies have two sides and both need to be considered before making a decision (Kelly, 1964). Judges and juries are required to "hear the other side," or *audi alteram partem* in the old Latin texts. Huang, Hsu, and Ku (2012) had computers supply counter arguments to Chinese MBA students making investment decisions, and they found that the counter arguments reduced the effects of confirmation bias. The MBA students were less confident in their decisions (indicating that they knew that there were counter-considerations) and made less extreme decisions than when they did not get the counter arguments. Making an arguer generate material favoring both sides or countering one's own is another way of getting counter arguments into play. Koriat, Lichtenstein, and Fischhoff (1980) reported that having people list arguments that contradicted their choices reduced their confidence in their decision.

Zenker, Dahlman, Bååth, and Sarwar (2015) did a similar study using an outstanding research population: all of the municipal judges in Sweden (though only 40%, 239 of them, returned the surveys). In addition to these formally trained judges, the Swedish judicial system also makes use of lay judges, and over 350 of them participated in the study, too. They were all given a mock case in which a witness had a prior conviction, and they were asked whether this affected the witness's credibility (by Swedish law, it shouldn't). Some of the professional and lay judges were first asked to list reasons for and against the idea that the conviction should affect credibility, and the rest were not. The effect of giving reasons pro and con prior to making the decision was "miniscule," to quote the authors of the study. The judges pretty much followed the law regardless of whether they listed reasons or not, but there was a very small effect pointing to successful debiasing.

Another way of supplying counter arguments is to make use of a devil's advocate. This is a lovely term, originating in Catholic decisions about whether someone should be a saint or not. This is a very consequential matter for the Roman church, and enormous amounts of testimony and other evidence, often covering centuries, are gathered and evaluated. Eventually there are oral arguments in which evidence for the candidate's sanctity and ability to generate miracles is presented. One person is required to speak for the Devil—that is, to object to all the evidence of godliness, goodness, and saintliness, to propose that the miracles were faked, that witnesses had political ambitions, that scribes copied documents inaccurately, and so forth. Regardless of the person's genuine beliefs, he must serve publicly as the Devil's Advocate, an actual job. Outside the Vatican, we use the term metaphorically to refer to someone who is required to disagree with the rest of the group.

So some researchers have intervened into decision-making processes by creating a devil's advocate to create counter arguments. In fact, they contrasted the effects of genuine dissent with those of contrived dissent (the devil's advocate). They wanted to know how artificial generation of disagreement compared to natural disagreement. Schulz-Hardt et al. (2002) studied German managers in three person groups. Surveying the group members prior to the meetings, the researchers could tell whether everyone agreed in the first place or whether there was genuine dissent present in the group. Half the groups had someone publicly assigned to be a devil's advocate (that is, everyone knew the person was required to disagree). Genuine dissent (compared to everyone having the same view to start with) reduced confirmation bias, as measured by what sorts of information people searched for after the group made its decision. Groups without any preliminary disagreement were more likely only to look for confirming material. Contrived dissent—having a devil's advocate—did not have much effect on anything, but it did somewhat reduce the tendency of homogenous groups (members all initially agreed) to seek only confirming information. Nemeth, Connell, Rogers, and Brown (2001) suspected that devil's advocates in this sort of study would been seen as inauthentic and therefore not be taken very seriously. They put undergraduate women into "groups," but the other three "participants" in each group were actually computer-generated. They created three conditions: all four participants agree in the first place, one of them (a computer) genuinely disagrees, and one of them (a computer) is publicly assigned to be a devil's advocate. Participants typed their comments into their computers and saw others' comments onscreen. Authentic dissent was again more influential than devil's advocacy. In fact, genuine dissent had a significant effect on participants' decisions and thoughts, but devil's advocates did not.

Taken together, we see some evidence that counter arguments, which express the other side, do soften the confirmation bias. Fake arguments from devil's advocates do not seem to have much effect, but authentic dissent does, and having people generate their own pro and con considerations might. For the purposes of this book, genuine dissent expressed interpersonally is the most important condition in this research tradition, and it encourages us in the thought that intelligent well-motivated conversation may lead to better thinking. Face to face interaction with someone who disagrees with you is the sort of thing that can put you on top of your game, and it can have that effect on the other person, too.

Besides confirmation bias, another key cognitive factor is how people frame or understand the problem they are thinking about. Larrick (2009) generally recommended that decision makers need to broaden their frames to consider complications that we often skip over: the likelihood that decision-makers should pursue multiple goals, the chance that there may be many alternatives to the status quo, the reality that any decision will normally have many outcomes, and so forth. He argued that the simplifications involved in narrow frames (one choice, one goal, one cause, one effect) are actually what allow many of the cognitive biases to assert themselves.

However, I have something more specific in mind here. "Framing effects occur when logically equivalent redescriptions of objects or outcomes lead to different behaviors, and, traditionally, such effects have been seen as irrational" (McKenzie, 2004, p. 874). For example, as a parent you might hear "my sister made me hit her" or "I hit my sister first" and you seem to have very different things to think about, even though both statements summarize exactly the same event. Communication scholars have long realized that there is no neutral fact-language, and this means that we frame everything we say or think about. A particular framing choice is gain or loss framing (Kahneman, 2011; Kahneman & Tversky, 1979). A standard example is that a drug treatment can be described as saving 200 out of 600 people (the gain) or as resulting in 400 of 600 people dying (the loss). The math of these expressions is the same, but a great deal of research shows that people make different judgments about these circumstances. McKenzie gave evidence that a particular frame actually "leaks" information about the speaker and what the speaker thinks is particularly important, and this implies that math-equivalent statements may very well not be meaning-equivalent. If two things have different meanings, perhaps they should be thought about differently. I think this is an important point, and one that has been insufficiently appreciated.

Nevertheless, the fact of arithmetic equality is enticing, so most researchers have regarded as a bias any difference in how gain- and loss-framed materials are handled. Milch, Weber, Appelt, Handgraaf, and Krantz (2009) tried to counteract the usual effect, namely that gain framing leads people to be risk averse and loss framing leads them to take more risks. They appreciated McKenzie's point, and so they paid attention to the content of the arguments people made, either as individuals or group members, after they were given gain or loss framed information. Two decision topics were involved. Individuals were given a decision to make on one of them, framed either as gain or loss, and asked to write down their reasons for the decision. Then they were formed into three-person groups with people they knew (either from student clubs or work teams). The groups then made decisions on both topics. The groups reached consensus and then wrote down the group reasons for the choice. So there were three conditions: pregroup decision, naïve group (no one had seen that topic before), and group (everyone had seen that topic before). Frames (gain or loss) were the same in all three conditions for each group, but of course they varied within the whole study. Results showed that the frame clearly affected the individual decisions but did not affect the group choices strongly. They also found that the frames affected the reasons, although only for the drug and disease topic mentioned above, which is the standard one. So here we see some evidence that the different frames implied the different reasons people had, the things they were actually thinking about. And there was also evidence that face-to-face conversation made people more likely to treat the two arithmetically equivalent conditions in the same way.

These studies about cognitive interventions have therefore generated some grounds for optimism, but no clearcut case for any particular treatment. In fact, Zenker, Dahlman, and Sarwar (2015), in their review of more studies than I am summarizing, concluded that all interventions considered together fail about half the time. Still, we can see some encouragement: people can sometimes be jolted out of their cognitive furrows, and some of the best results were due to face-to-face disagreement, precisely the sort of thing that this chapter is about.

Motivation

The next sort of debiasing strategy is to alter participants' motivations. The idea is that argument stakes can be raised so that people will reason better. There are certainly limits to this kind of strategy. No matter how much money you offered me to hit Clayton Kershaw's slider, I simply couldn't do it. Ability and resources are always going to construct a firm ceiling for motivational effects. People who are so stubborn that they just cannot imagine that anyone could possibly disagree with them are never going to be able to generate arguments that respect the possibility of another point of view (see Kuhn, 1991). In fact, Kuhn gave evidence that many people have a private epistemology (an understanding of what counts as evidence and truth) such that no counter arguments will ever live in those people's psychological worlds. So motivational effects are always going to be limited to improvements on the margins of argument quality.

Most of the research on cognitive biases has tried to equalize motivations by offering everyone the same inducement to participate in the studies. In fact, researchers in this domain prefer to seek out respondents who are likely to take a professional approach to the task, for example the Swedish judges looking at a mock case, the MBA students practicing their investment decisions, the German managers, and so forth. This implies a fairly high level of motivation across the board, but since the motivation is equivalent from one condition to the next, we cannot see its effects very often.

One study is particularly interesting in this regard. Smith et al. (1998) asked 565 undergraduates to role-play being company owners or company managers while making a decision. The key motivational difference is that an owner does not have to explain himself or herself, but a manager will need to justify a decision to the board of directors. So in the owner condition, motivations could be entirely internal but in the manager condition participants had to make a decision that would satisfy other people. Some of the students did the task alone and others did it in five person groups. They were given a "sunk cost" problem. The sunk cost bias occurs when a person continues along a course mainly because of what has already been invested in it. For example, some people will watch a movie on Netflix to the bitter end even though they decided half an hour ago that it was the worst and most valueless experience they have ever had. The rational thing is always to ignore your previous investments ("what's past is past") and make a new decision on its own merits. In this study, groups were less susceptible to the sunk cost fallacy than individuals were, giving another bit of evidence that face-to-face arguing may be curative. Another supportive result was that managers (who had to justify themselves to others) were also less vulnerable to the bias than the owners were. Just imagining the interaction with the directors resulted in better reasoning.

Smith et al. (2001) did a study that dealt with motivation in more general terms. You may recall that earlier in the chapter I mentioned the phenomenon of "social loafing," which refers to letting other people in the group do all the work. Possibly you have encountered this while doing group projects in school. At any rate, social loafing is really only possible in a group. Individuals cannot hide from themselves. These researchers did a study with undergraduate respondents who worked either alone or in a group on a simple counting task (unlike the other work reviewed here, there was no decision-making or reasoning involved in this study). The key element to the design was that they measured participants' intrinsic motivation to solve problems, using a scale called Need for Cognition (e.g., Cacioppo, Petty, & Morris, 1983). People with high need for cognition want to work out intellectual things in detail and have real trouble leaving that sort of work undone. People with low need for cognition are more casual about their thinking and therefore should be much more prone to cognitive biases and easy choices. Respondents were divided into thirds based on their NFC scores, and only the top and bottom thirds were kept in the study. Students were also divided into two other conditions: whether their personal outcomes required "collective" work (the group working together) or depended only on their own contribution even if other people were present (the "coactive" condition). For people low in need for cognition, they did a lot of social loafing in the collective conditions where other people could "carry" them and were much more productive in the coactive conditions. But people high in need for cognition did not do any social loafing, and were even a little bit more productive in the collective condition. Need for cognition is an internal, intrinsic sort of motivation. It is unlike bonuses for good performance or the need to explain yourself to others because those are external. We see here that internal motivation affects the quality of performance.

So motivation is certainly important to how well one reasons. Just as your ability is an upper limit to how well you can do, your motivational energy can supply a floor as to how much you try.

Design

The last category of debiasing interventions is argument design (earlier writers restricted themselves to technological matters). In some families, arguments are designed so that everyone can argue, and in other families only the parents can talk. These two architectures exemplify how an argument's environment can be constructed to allow or censor points of view, voices, sorts of evidence, kinds of expression, and many other things.

A less personal example comes from the U.S. legislature. Much of the work done by the House and Senate occurs in committee hearings, in which various witnesses are called to testify. Today witnesses are sometimes present to publicize some issue or point of view, or perhaps to be publicly demonized. The legislators want to maintain control of what is said at the hearing. Witnesses must answer legislators' questions but cannot question them in turn. Witnesses, in a pretense of courtesy, are permitted to begin their testimony with a carefully prepared statement—but the legislators must be informed of its wording and content a full day before the public hearing. Here is how the Senate rule reads:

> Each committee (except the Committee on Appropriations) shall require each witness who is to appear before the committee in any hearing to file with the clerk of the committee, at least one day before the date of the appearance of that witness, a written statement of his proposed testimony unless the committee chairman and the ranking minority member determine that there is good cause for noncompliance. (Rule XXVI, 4b; http://www.rules.senate.gov/public/index.cfm?p=RulesOfSenateHome)

In other words, it is actually against the law to surprise a U.S. Senator in a hearing.

Of course, this sort of thing is not unique to U.S. legislatures. All systems of parliamentary procedure specify who can speak, and when, and on what topic. Most formal meetings have some rules, some patterns, or some customs that regulate the materials of argument. There will even be clear expectations in many informal settings, such as husband-wife disagreement, student-teacher consultations, explaining yourself to a police officer, and in most continuing interpersonal relationships.

Thus, some researchers have undertaken explicit analysis of argument design (Aakhus, 2003, 2007; Jackson, 1998; Jackson & Aakhus, 2014; Jacobs & Aakhus, 2002). Jackson (1998, p. 184) offers this definition: "Discourse design involves some sort of deliberate effort at management of talk." This can occur at the institutional level (as with law courts and their rules about allowable questions) or at the personal level (e.g., "Don't interrupt me").

Scholars have looked at how interpersonal situations can be designed to encourage or discourage types of arguing. Jacobs and Aakhus (2002), for example, studied how mediators in 41 community mediation sessions had three different models for how they tried to affect the flow of arguments in the sessions. Mediators could aim at critical discussion, bargaining, or therapy (Chapter 6 discusses choices such as these). By encouraging a critical discussion (van Eemeren & Grootendorst, 2004), mediators encouraged conversation that pointed to agreement based on the merits of the case, that is, its facts and the implications of that evidence. Bargaining, in contrast, refers to "meeting in the middle," and here the mediators tried to direct people toward a contract that provided maximum gain and minimum loss to both parties, given the circumstantial constraints. Finally, some mediators steered participants toward a therapeutic discussion that explored each person's sense-making and identity, and aimed at mutual affirmation of one another by both parties. Different things are going to be said in these three sorts of mediations, to say the least (the Jacobs and Aakhus paper is full of conversational excerpts). Each sort of mediation has its own implicit rules, and therefore its own model of what counts as rational and what is irrelevant. Consequently, various arguments are going to be required or gently discouraged from one type of interaction to the next. In fact, the bargaining orientation actually points participants away from what we would otherwise regard as rational argumentation: "It is not at all uncommon for mediators to say things like, 'It's not a matter of who's right or wrong or good or bad or moral or immoral or any of those things; I don't care'" (Jacobs & Aakhus, 2002, pp. 197–198). The idea is to meet halfway, not to come to the most justifiable conclusion. Mediators tried to keep the participants within the boundaries of the particular mediation model being used in each session, and so we would say that the three models were being used as argument designs.

For those environments in which we actually want to have full rational argumentation, one important design feature is the quality of feedback arguers receive. Larrick and Feiler (2015) explored the constructive effects that unmistakable feedback has on weather forecasters, contract bridge players, and serious horse betters, in contrast to the lack of clearly interpretable feedback received by political pundits and clinical psychologists. Weather forecasters clearly realize if they were right about the rain, but pundits rarely have any sharp evaluations of whether their interpretations were correct or not. When circumstances cannot supply plain feedback (e.g., "He's off his meds, but which of his many confusions led to that choice?"), people's reasoning cannot easily be improved. Providing feedback to arguers is something that can be done well or neglected, and people cannot learn to bring their judgments into conformity with the world unless they know how the world reacted to their previous choices. Managers and parents, to take two common examples, can provide plain feedback to subordinates and children, or can make consequential information hard to find or can "spin" it until it is no longer obvious what it means.

Johnson et al. (2012) took up the idea of "choice architecture" and suggested that decisions can be productively designed in two respects: structuring the decision task, and describing the choices. Considerations involved in structuring the decision task include determining how many alternatives will be considered, what technology to provide participants, and what time constraints to supply. The choice options can be listed separately or collected into groups, the alternatives can be described simply or in great detail, and a common metric can be provided (or not) for evaluating all the alternatives. These sorts of structural issues, resolved before the decision-making even begins, can affect what sorts of arguments are made and how they are weighed.

All arguing is situated, and situations can be designed or altered to hinder or stimulate various kinds of thoughts and reasons. Defining an issue, specifying goals, managing information, controlling participation—these are only a few of the ways that arguments can be directed, dammed, or let loose. So argument design takes its place alongside cognitive and motivational interventions in efforts to debias arguments and improve their quality.

Understanding Debiasing

This triad of cognitive/motivational/design is not the only way to think about improving people's arguing. As we have examined researchers' efforts to discourage people's natural heuristics (that is, to "debias" them), an important distinction has begun to appear. In principle, an intervention could be debiasing in two different ways.

The first way is internal, by manipulating the premises or terms of the argument itself. One could draw people's reasoning into naturally unbiased patterns.

To comprehend such an argument would be to think clearly. For instance, when a person hears "all men are mortal; Socrates is a man; therefore Socrates is mortal," he or she naturally thinks in simple deductive terms and is not entertaining any possibly tempting shortcuts that would interfere with the argument as stated. The argument scheme is both sound and completely absorbing. A related approach is to present the same argument in a particularly useful way, for example the diagrammatic representation that made a base-rate fallacy disappear (unpublished work by Cosmides and Tooby reported by Gigerenzer, 1991). These internally-oriented actions would be classified as cognitive interventions.

The second main possibility is external work. The debiasing argument can be internally ordinary, but can be presented in a context that encourages open-mindedness, genuine scrutiny of the argument's content, and cooperation with the other arguer. This external action (i.e., external to the argument content) can happen in two ways, by intervening with the individuals or by strategically rearranging their circumstances.

At a couple of points in this book, we have noticed the importance of people's orientation to the interpersonal episode that contains the arguing. People can be competitive or cooperative, or civil or nasty, for instance, or they can be flexible or stubborn. These are motivational matters in some respects, but cognitive in others. An important element of pragma-dialectical theory is that in addition to high quality give and take during an argument, people should also satisfy higher-order conditions for good arguing, such as being open-minded, willing to balance multiple considerations, committed to equal rights for all participants, and other things of this general sort (van Eemeren, Grootendorst, Jackson, & Jacobs, 1993, ch. 2; also see Burleson & Kline, 1979). People can be encouraged to take on these sorts of views or their opposites, and this encouragement can take on the character of cognitive (how to think about arguing), motivational (what relationship to have with the other person), or design matters (does everyone have equal access to the key information?).

The other external approach is careful arrangement of the decision-making environment. This refers to argument design, of course. So as we consider how to improve people's arguing behaviors, we can think about things in two general but interrelated ways: as cognition, motivation, and design, or as internal versus external interventions. This chapter's general hypothesis—that good argumentative conversation is the rationality engine—implies that the combination of several people's motivations, abilities, and orientations is what protects the quality of their thinking, and that the arguers' circumstances can affect how these personal attributes assert themselves.

How Good Conversation Improves Argumentation

We have now arrived at the studies that my students and I did to explore the possibility that good conversation is the rationality engine. By that last phrase, we never intended to connect to the very technical definitions and controversies about "rational" that take place in the discipline of philosophy (e.g., Bermejo-Luque, 2016). We did not especially mean "valid," as logicians would, or "profit maximizing," as economists would, or "mathematically proved," as statisticians would. We only meant that rational was equivalent to "well reasoned," where that in turn refers to arguments that are sound, cogent, or well supported. Informal logicians evaluate naturally occurring arguments with three criteria: the premises must all be *acceptable*, each premise must be *relevant* to the conclusion, and the premises must be collectively *sufficient* to sustain the conclusion (e.g., Johnson, 2000). These three standards are all matters of degree and therefore they require good thinking and judgment for their application. Arguments that satisfy those conditions are what we mean by rational. We propose that the basic engine or process that generates this sort of rationality is intelligent, well-informed, and well-motivated conversation.

We gave some thought to how to encourage that sort of conversation, that is, how to design it. Over the years I have done a lot of studies in which I brought two undergraduate students into the lab, asked them to indicate their opinions on several controversial topics, and then discuss the topic that I noticed they disagreed the most on. I got a lot of argumentative conversations about capital punishment, abortion, gay rights, and whatever political topics were current at the time of the study. When I reviewed and analyzed the videotapes of those dyadic arguments, I noticed a lot of really bad argumentation. It turns out that people can have truly extreme opinions about capital punishment without actually knowing very much about it, for instance. They know what capital punishment is, of course, and what the Bible says, but that's about where it stops. They don't know if two adjoining states have different murder rates when they have different capital punishment laws, whether or how many people have been found to be innocent after being executed, how different nations compare on their laws and murder rates, or whether there are changes in murder rates when the same state or nation changes its laws in one direction or the other. The resulting arguments were full of sincerity but empty of evidence. They were poor arguments, in other words. They really weren't engines for anything except a little extra credit.

So we designed these arguments in a way that encouraged good content. All our respondents were undergraduates and we used roughly the same argument architecture in each of the studies. The arguments were all dyadic and they were all about gun control, except for the first study when we were still clarifying our procedures and used several topics. We selected the gun control topic because there is division on it and everyone knows there is disagreement, so that the presence of argumentation on both sides would be seen as realistic.

We wanted to make sure that everyone was actually knowledgeable about the topic, so we prepared fairly elaborate briefing materials for participants. When they arrived at the lab site, participants received about four pages (single spaced, but including some graphs and tables) of briefing information. The briefing packet was composed of quotations and witness-supplied material, mainly from some hearings on gun control held by one of the U.S. House of Representatives committees. The quotations represented both sides of the central question, which was whether or not gun ownership should be more tightly restricted in the U.S. A great deal of factual information was provided, covering the different gun laws in various U.S. cities along with those cities' crime rates, some historical information about whether crime rates changed when gun laws did, some factual information about some other nations, and other reasonably high quality material. Participants were given as much time as they wanted to study this information and were told that they could quote from it during their arguments if they wished. Students seemed to take this seriously, and many highlighted sections or made marginal notes as they read. In the actual face-to-face arguments, many students did refer to the material or read from it.

We told everyone that they were to role-play being a U.S. Senator. The pretense was that they were meeting with another Senator who had a very different view on gun control than they did, and they were supposed to try to work out some compromise legislation that they could both agree on. When students were brought into the conversation room, they each had nameplates ("Senator Smith" and "Senator Jones") and were asked to address each other that way (some did). They sat on opposite sides of a table, facing each other. We did this to introduce a little bit of formality into the experiments. Students did seem to be reasonably serious in their conversations, and we attribute this in great part to the fact that they had quality information to support their views and to rebut what the other "Senator" said. Here are the actual instructions we used:

> Please pretend that you and the other person are both U.S. Senators who have differing views about gun control. You have come together to see if the two of you can agree on some national policy regarding guns. This is a private behind-the-scenes conversation between the two of you.
>
> As Senators, you would naturally have been briefed by your own staff before such an important meeting. These materials constitute that briefing.

Some of the material in your briefing has also been given to the other Senator. However, we have "arranged" the briefing materials so that you each mainly have information on one side of the issue that the other Senator wasn't given, so that you will tend to have opposing views. Please try to argue in conformity with the briefing materials that you have been given.

Your position is that private citizens should be permitted to own handguns. Your briefing materials mostly support this view.

You should discuss the issue for 5–10 minutes.

Here is the key to the studies. One of the undergraduate students was a confederate, a member of the research team. In addition to the same briefing materials we gave the genuine participant, we also supplied the confederate with a number of arguments and remarks that we wanted to be inserted somewhere into the conversation. These were always bad or at least questionable arguments. The idea in all the studies was to see what happened to these inserted materials. Confederates were trained to keep the prepared insertions on the floor only for as long as the real participant was discussing them, and to drop the matter as soon as the participant did. So the genuine participants were in complete control of how long the questionable arguments were discussed and what was said about them, if they were discussed at all. Different studies had different sets of questionable materials, as you will see.

The genuine participant was always assigned to argue that more restrictive gun control laws should not be adopted. This was simply a control decision. It kept advocacy position constant across the study and let us make sure that each participant could be exposed to questionable arguments from the same list. In most of the studies, we measured participants' attitudes toward gun control both before and after the conversation.

We videotaped the conversations. The confederates, who worked very hard for their independent study course, also transcribed and coded the conversations. They only transcribed the parts of the conversations that included and followed the inserted material. Then they coded how the genuine participant dealt with each of the questionable arguments. Here is the coding system that we used.

Use the highest available code for each argument sequence. For example, if the initial response is a 4 but later there is a 3 in the same argument sequence, code it as 4.
1. **Accept.** Explicitly or implicitly indicate agreement with the confederate's argument. "I agree," "Oh, I see." For something like, "well, I see what you mean, but" it's the "but" that's important. If the "but" leads into a disagreement, don't use this

code. If the "but" leads to a change in topic, code it as 2. "I see what you mean" by itself would be coded here.
2. **Ignore.** No explicit or apparent uptake of the argument. There might be a pause or not, but the participant's next turn is a new topic.
3. **State Irrelevance, but with No Reason.** The person just says, "That's wrong," but doesn't say *why* it's wrong.
4. **Rebut.** The participant refutes the argument by giving a reason that it's a bad argument. "One example doesn't prove anything." Even if the participant's reason is itself awful, code the response here.
5. **Repaired.** Take up and improve the argument. "Well one example doesn't prove much, but didn't you say it happened in Chicago, too?" The participant takes up the confederate's argument and either changes it or adds something to it, to make it better. Even if the participant's "improvement" is not very impressive, code it here.

Just record the number of the code.

A number of actual examples from the conversations then followed to illustrate each of the codes. The fifth category was almost never used after the first study.

Fallacies

The first study was about outright fallacies (Hample, Jones, & Averbeck, 2009). This was the only study in which we did not have everyone argue about gun control. We used two different topics: what the U.S. Navy's policy toward ocean piracy should be, and how the U.S. should define "poverty" in connection with its various welfare policies (e.g., what the income for a family of four needed to be before the family was not classified as being in poverty). We gave all the genuine participants briefings on their topic, and otherwise followed the general procedures described above.

For both topics, we composed six fallacious remarks for the confederate to introduce somewhere into the conversation. The fallacies were *equivocation* (using a word's other meanings, for example, referring to music piracy in the ocean piracy topic), *ad hominem* ("against the man;" directed against the source of a piece of evidence that the genuine participants read in their briefings and which many used in the conversation), *anecdotal evidence* (using a single vivid and personal example that may well be atypical), *slippery slope* (the idea that if we do the first thing, we will be unable to stop from doing a series of related and more extreme things), *sweeping generalization* (going well beyond the available evidence to make an unqualified conclusion), and *appeal to pity* (getting someone to focus on their feelings of sympathy rather their knowledge about frequency or typical seriousness). Obviously, the content of the fallacies was different from one topic to the other.

We had 68 genuine participants in the study, all undergraduates. The confederates got better and better at inserting the fallacies into the conversations, and the average number of fallacies per conversation was 2.3 overall. The coding system mentioned above was applied to how the genuine participants handled the fallacies: they could accept it, ignore it, refuse to accept it without really saying why ("that's irrelevant"), refute it with a reason, or repair the argument to make it less fallacious.

We did not have a control group of any kind. In retrospect, it would have been much better to have also given the fallacies to people who weren't engaged in any sort of conversation and see how they reacted to the bad arguments. But we weren't really thinking in quite those terms when we planned the study. We generated fallacies that we felt were tempting and realistic. We just wanted to see how people dealt with them, and whether some fallacies were more misleading than others.

Let me show you some of the fallacies, how people responded to them, and how we coded them. I have organized them by code (see the coding system above) and have included examples from both topics. After the code I have indicated which conversation it was in the data set, the name of the fallacy, and the beginning and ending times for the material quoted. C is the confederate and P is the genuine participant. They are different people in different conversations, of course. In the first example, the reference is to a (fictitious) person that P has just quoted from the briefing sheet. The first contribution from C in each example is the fallacy.

1 **Accepted**, Conversation 48 (Ocean Piracy), Ad Hominem, 2:50–3:41
C: I happen to know that Caitlin Harrington works for Foreign Affairs. She works for them and she has two DUI's and has been in rehab.
P: Really?
C: Yeah.
P: Well I mean I don' know about her. We might have to look at this for some better evidence because I had no support for who works at Foreign Affairs but that's what they told me but um yeah I guess you're right on that. Cuz uh yeah. So let's not trust that evidence.

2 **Ignored**, Conversation 65 (Poverty), Sweeping Generalization, 3:40–3:58
1.C: The poor people of America are simply lazy and they're just expecting a handout from Uncle Sam.
2.P: Alright, well since since you're sitting here um wanting to know exactly all the positions I have and everything, well uh, how do you feel about this welfare and everything? What do you think we should do as far as the poverty line?

3 **That's Irrelevant**, Conversation 45 (Ocean Piracy), Anecdotal, 0:41–2:07
C: Well like I guess I could like where the problem's at and like exactly like what's going on uh cuz here as a Senator in the United States like I mean like my grandparents go on a cruise every year and they've never been attacked by any pirates

P: Well what do where do your grandparents go? I mean do they go to the Bahamas? Do they go do they I mean what area are they are they traveling around so if you look at the map right here cuz you see we have I mean first where do they go?
C: They go all over the place. Different areas and
P: Well I mean right now we are talking about Southeast Asia

4 **Refuted with Reason**, Conversation 4 (Poverty), Slippery Slope, 2:04–2:52
C: But, I mean, if we keep raising the poverty line every time the cost goes up or every time people can't afford something then it will just go up and up and up and we'll have to raise it all the time and it will never stop and eventually we'll all be in poverty, right?
P: Not necessarily, no, not at all. Uh, because, uh, studies um from Professor Michael Kline of the Chronicle of Higher Education August 11, 2006. Uh you can see that his studies found that people on welfare do actually strive to get off welfare and use their aid and stuff like that like towards education and stuff like that so they won't have to rely on the welfare system and have better education.

5 **Repaired**, Conversation 10 (Ocean Piracy), Slippery Slope 1:30–2:42
C: I just think that if like we start monitoring the strait for like large boats then we have to start monitoring for little boats then like if we do that we have to start monitoring like little fishing boats even and if we do that we'll have to start monitor
P: Why do you think that?
C: Just because like if we are going to watch like all like the boats aren't we going to have to watch all of them?
P: Well you can tell the difference between a small little fishing boat and a large piracy boat.
C: Yeah, I guess you're right. Um
P: I don't think you necessarily even have to monitor all of the boats
C: Isn't that being fair?
P: That's being fair as in to who?
C: To everybody like are we just going accuse people of being pirates.
P: No that's why you're monitoring the waterways.
C: But how do we know unless we board their boat.
P: You're going to board? You don't have to board any boat first of all. You can watch each boat I mean, uh, special boats have to have special tags on each side saying what the size is what it is and uh you could monitor it that way. You could I guess go into each boat. I don't think you necessarily have to unless you have suspicion to go into that boat.

Besides seeing the fallacies and how we coded replies, I hope you also agree that the conversational arguments were fairly intelligent (by the way, no one seems like they've ever seen a sentence when you transcribe their conversation, so you have to set that aside), in spite of the fact that prior to the briefings no one really knew anything about ocean piracy (it showed up in the news a year or two after we did the study) and probably didn't have much detailed knowledge about defining poverty statistically. Providing people with the briefings so that they had quality information to use was really important. In fact, across all the studies, we never had anyone ignore the material we gave them and just express ungrounded opinions over and over again, as I used to see in arguments about capital punishment and gay rights. If you want to have a truly productive interpersonal argument with someone, perhaps the most important design advice I have is this: make sure that everyone is provided with the information they need, even if it means delaying the start of the actual conversation.

The object of coding people's replies instead of just examining them qualitatively was to generate a statistical summary of what happened. The key information is in Table 5.1, organized to feature the fallacies and the codes.

Table 5.1: Crosstabulation of Fallacy Type and Response to Fallacy, Both Frequencies and Column Percentages

	equivocation	ad hominem	anecdote	slippery slope	sweep general	appeal to pity
Accept 15.5%	3 (9.4%)	5 (20.8%)	2 (7.4%)	5 (19.2%)	3 (12%)	6 (28.6%)
Ignore 6.5%	2 (6.3%)	2 (8.3%)	3 (11.1%)	1 (3.8%)	2 (8%)	0 (0%)
Irrel 5.8%	4 (12.5%)	2 (8.3%)	1 (3.7%)	1 (3.8%)	0 (0%)	1 (4.8%)
Refute 58.1%	22 (68.8%)	15 (62.5%)	18 (66.7%)	8 (30.8%)	16 (64%)	11 (52.4%)
Repair 14.2%	1 (3.1%)	0 (0%)	3 (11.1%)	11 (42.3%)	4 (16%)	3 (14.3%)
Total	32	24	27	26	25	21

The key result is that very few of the fallacies actually seemed to fool anyone. Out of all 155 fallacies, only 15.5% of them were accepted. Overwhelmingly, the most common response was to refute the fallacy (58.1%), with quite a few more people simply ignoring it (6.5%) or remarking that the confederate's comment was irrelevant (5.8%). We also found that 14.2% of the fallacies were repaired—that is, the genuine participant actually improved the confederate's argument before integrating it into the conversation. (In later studies, we did not find much repair, often none.)

Five of the six fallacies had pretty much the same pattern of responses, but slippery slope stood out. It was the only fallacy that was not refuted most of the time (only 30.8%), and it was by far the one that was most often repaired by the genuine participant (42.3%). I think that this is because the slippery slopes we used had some initial plausibility and only had to be toned down a little bit to become reasonable arguments (see the examples for codes 4 and 5, above). In contrast, there wasn't much to be done about the irrelevant *ad hominem* attack that some foreign policy writer had DUI convictions (code 1 example above) or the argument that music piracy over the Internet really should be handled the same way as we respond to homicidal ocean piracy.

These results were encouraging. Textbook writers who cover fallacies often seem to regard them as truly dangerous threats to good thinking. The authors imply that only the people privileged enough to have instruction like their textbook provides have much chance of surviving exposure to the exploitive, feral arguments that politicians, advertisers, and editorial writers generate in order to trick us. Here we found that the simple circumstance of having a pleasant, informed, and intelligent conversation with another person made most of the fallacies evaporate. In fact, our results may even understate the corrective effects of conversation because even an accepted fallacy would have been only one of the many arguments in the conversation and might have ended up having no weight at all in the arguers' eventual conclusions. Just talking to another person, paying attention and actually replying to what he or she says, seems to generate pretty good thinking. The fallacies we wrote were good enough, I think, that a person sitting alone and thinking loosely about the topics might well have been misled. The presence of another person and the consequent need to communicate in a socially positive way puts us on our best (cognitive) behavior.

Convergent Arguments

Thus encouraged, we slightly altered our aims. Instead of studying awful arguments—fallacies—we began to study arguments that were only flawed. These defeasible (possibly refutable) arguments don't have much argumentative force one at a time, but they have some. When several of them are combined, they might add up to something that deserves serious consideration.

This idea of combining various arguments together to justify one conclusion goes under various names in the argumentation literature (conductive arguments: Wellman, 1971; coordinately or subordinately compound argumentation: van Eemeren, Grootendorst, Jackson, & Jacobs, 1993). I follow Henkemans (2000) in calling this convergent argument because this title seems to be the simplest phrasing for what happens. Figure 5.1 illustrates what I mean, which is pretty straightforward. The idea there is that the arguer has one conclusion to support, and he or she has three different reasons for it. When we finally try to decide whether or not the conclusion is a good one, we have to take all three arguments into account simultaneously. Perhaps argument 2 is so convincing that arguments 1 and 3 can be terrible without affecting our support for the conclusion. Perhaps all three arguments are incoherent, so that even together they don't support the conclusion. And perhaps—this is the key possibility for what we studied—maybe all three arguments are individually flawed, but they reinforce each other enough so that the conclusion should be accepted anyway. In other words, the first argument doesn't satisfactorily justify the conclusion, and neither does argument 2 or argument 3, but when we combine them—let them converge—they are collectively sufficient to justify the conclusion.

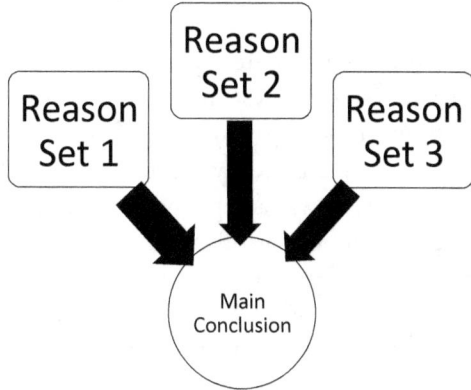

Figure 5.1: Convergent Argument (from Hample, 2011a)

Along with dozens of undergraduate research assistants enrolled in independent study courses, I did several studies along these lines. My idea was to insert as many of these flawed arguments into the conversations as we plausibly could, and see how the genuine participants responded to them. When they heard the first poor argument, we supposed they ought to be very critical. When they heard the second one, they should also be pretty critical. But as the flawed arguments piled up they might converge, we thought. If this happened, we would see this when we coded the genuine participants' responses: they should become more accepting and less critical of the flawed arguments as they were exposed to more of them. We made sure that the flawed arguments were inserted in very different orders, so that we could not accidentally put the best arguments later in the sequences.

Just to be explicit: the idea of these studies was to see if we could observe convergent arguments. This idea of convergence appears in quite a number of philosophical and rhetorical theories, but the examples in those writings are carefully chosen and sometimes just constructed by the authors. We wanted to determine if we could actually observe arguments converging.

I did several separate studies. One was on examples (Hample, 2011b). Using a single example to justify a general conclusion is a fallacy (variously called hasty generalization or anecdotal evidence). But using a lot of cases to justify a general conclusion is an induction, which is not only *not* fallacious but which is also regarded as the basis of empirical science. So we gave people example after example to see when they began to regard the evidence as possibly converging on some conclusion, as opposed to being insufficient evidence by itself.

We had 102 undergraduates participating genuinely in the study and used the gun control topic. Another 17 undergraduates served as confederates. We wrote 9 examples for them to insert, and we ended up with an average of 4.2 examples in each conversation.

When the genuine respondents were exposed to the very first example, they were the most critical, with typical codes almost halfway between stating that the example was irrelevant but not saying why, and refuting it with a reason (often something like "one example doesn't really prove very much"). We regarded the codes as being actual numbers (1 was accept and so forth: see the coding manual a few pages ago), which is not very justifiable in technical statistical terms, but it does give us some guidance here. For the first example in the conversation the mean response was 3.4, for the second example it was 3.2, for the third it was 2.9, and it stayed below 3 (state irrelevant, but give no reason) all the way through the seventh example. In other words, people were less critical and more accepting of the later examples than of the earliest ones. They were permitting the arguments to converge, just as we thought we might see.

We explored this more generally in the next study (Hample, 2011a). This time we focused on cause-effect arguments in particular. Causal reasoning is some of the most fundamental thinking we do, because it helps us understand why things happen and what might happen next. In fact, the natural response to a "why" question is "because." So in this study we selected a number of flawed reasons for thinking that some cause-effect conclusion was justified. Some of those flawed reasons were examples, because one example isn't enough to prove a general causal connection. But there were others, too. For instance, you have surely learned that "correlation is not causation:" just because two things happen in sequence does not mean that one caused the other. This is one of the most important fallacies, *post hoc ergo propter hoc* ("after this, therefore because of this"). However, correlation actually is *relevant* to causation; it just isn't *sufficient*. So correlational evidence is flawed but not valueless. These were the kinds of flawed arguments we used in the study, and again we wanted to see if they would converge.

This time, we had 72 undergraduates as genuine participants and 11 undergraduates as confederates. We generated 10 weak causal arguments to work into the conversations, and had an average of 4.3 flawed arguments put into the conversations.

We obtained a pattern of results that was roughly similar to what we found in the examples study. Exposed to the first weak argument, participants were highly critical (3.6 on the scale where we suppose that the coding system's numbers can be averaged), and the following arguments had similar but declining averages: 3.5 for the second insertion, 3.3 for the third poor argument, 3.6 for the fourth (we regarded this as a blip in the data), and 3.1 for the fifth. As with the examples study, we saw respondents becoming less critical and more accepting as they were exposed to more and more arguments that were flawed but not valueless. In other words, we saw convergence.

Results for both the examples and weak causal arguments studies match what we would expect for converging arguments. Individual arguments can be disregarded because they are each insufficient to justify the conclusion. But as those arguments collect and build up as they might in a real discussion, they converge on the conclusion as being the best explanation for how all those things could be true at once. This makes the conclusion more acceptable in people's minds. This is a good thing, because our theories of convergent argument indicate that the conclusions are also more rationally justified as more evidence accumulates for them.

I have mentioned more than once in the book that informal logicians have developed the standards of acceptability, relevance, and sufficiency to evaluate arguments. What we see in the case of convergent argument is the idea of collective sufficiency. Each individual argument has to have acceptable premises and needs to be relevant to the conclusion, but it does not have to be sufficient by itself. The sufficiency can be collective, even though the acceptability and relevance still need to be evaluated an argument at a time.

Analogies

But there is another possible explanation for this pattern of results. The conversations took 5 to 10 minutes, occasionally longer. Maybe after several minutes of being battered by bad arguments the genuine participants just started being more agreeable out of weariness. Maybe that's why they became less critical and more accepting. To test this possibility against the one we favored (that the arguments converge) we needed some sort of weak but not valueless argument that wouldn't converge. Analogies were what we needed.

Analogies are an interesting phenomenon. Quite a number of important argumentation theorists are reserved, to say the least, about whether analogies can actually be good arguments (Bermejo-Luque, 2012; Botting, 2012; Perelman &

Olbrechts-Tyteca, 1969, p. 372; Walton, Reed, & Macagno, 2008). The conclusion Walton et al. (p. 61) offered seems reasonable: "argument from analogy is best seen as a defeasible argumentation scheme that is inherently weak and subject to failure, but that can still be reasonable if used properly to support a conclusion."

Perelman and Olbrechts-Tyteca (1969, pp. 372–373) gave an excellent explanation of what an analogy is, and how it works. They said that the essential argument scheme is that of a ratio: A is to B as C is to D. The idea is that the A/B relationship is similar to the C/D relationship. It is the relationships that are being compared, not the individual parts. Perhaps one day you will tell your son, "A boy eating his vegetables is like a rocket ship getting refueled." You would be saying that boy/vegetables is like rocket/fuel. This is not a very good reason to eat vegetables, of course, and if it worked it would probably be because you got your son to start daydreaming about being a rocket ship heading to the Hot Dog Planet or something. So analogies can work, but they seem to do so by highlighting and emphasizing and framing, just as clever phrasing does, rather than by generating pointed evidence that contributes clearly to a linear argument.

And so there is really no reason at all to suppose that analogies might converge. Here are some of the analogies we inserted into the gun control conversations in the analogy study (Hample, 2016).

- Taking guns away from citizens is like declawing a cat. It's fine if you're going to keep the cat inside all the time. But you can never let the cat outside because it can't protect itself. We want people to feel free to go outside and do what they want.
- For regular citizens, guns are just for defending yourself. They're sort of like alarm systems. It wouldn't be right for the government to make it illegal to install an alarm system in your house or business. And it isn't right for the government to take away people's guns.
- Gun control is like Prohibition. Outlawing booze because a small fraction of people got sloshed was punishing to responsible drinkers as well. Why deprive responsible gun owners because a few people use guns irresponsibly?
- There is so much crime in the streets that people must protect themselves. Gun ownership for people in dangerous areas is a tool of necessity like a paintbrush for a painter.

These are indifferent arguments against gun control, as were the arguments by example or correlation. The critical question is, should these converge? I see no reason to imagine that they could. How could being like Prohibition strengthen the idea of being like declawing a cat? How could the paintbrush analogy make the alarm system comparison any stronger? So we have arguments that are weak but should not converge. If we see the usual convergence effect in our results, it had to have been because we wore out our genuine participants by making them put up with so much bad arguing.

We had 166 genuine participants in this study and two dozen confederates (this was a two-semester study, and the confederates changed in the second semester). Every conversation had at least three analogies inserted, with an average of 5.1.

The results did not show evidence of convergence. For the first analogy, people's mean response was 3.1, which was the same as their response to the second. For the third, their mean was 3.0, for the fourth 3.0, and for the fifth 3.0. The statistical test for this trend did not return a significant value (whereas it did for the two previous convergence studies on examples and weak causal arguments). The power for this non-significant result was .88, assuming an effect size of .15. This is enough power (the usual standard is .80) to constitute some genuine evidence in favor of the null hypothesis (which was no convergence over time). The analogy-ridden conversations did not converge.

Figure 5.2 graphs the results of the examples, weak causal arguments, and analogies studies all together. Our codings of people's reactions are graphed against the ordinal positions of the insertions in the conversation. For example, the first analogy we inserted had ordinal position 1, the second one had ordinal position 2, and so forth. The analogies data (the filled circles) are fairly level across the graph. The examples (the squares) fall off in criticism from the first to third example and then level off. The weak causal arguments (the diamonds) fall off from the first to the third argument, have that (frankly annoying) jump at the fourth insertion, and then drop again.

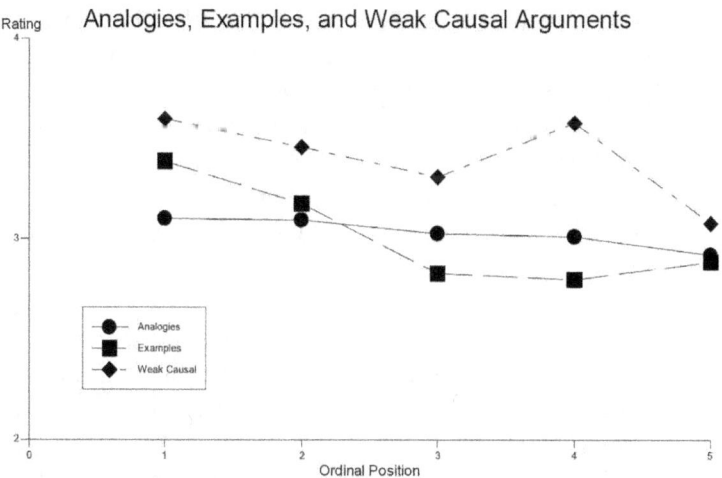

Figure 5.2: Coding of Genuine Participants' Responses to Examples, Weak Causal Arguments, and Analogies by Ordinal Position in the Conversations (from Hample, 2016)

If the earlier results had been because our participants lost patience with our confederates' poor arguing, we would have seen a convergence-like pattern for analogies, and we did not. In short, the two sorts of argument that were supposed to converge did, and the kind of argument that wasn't supposed to converge didn't. This is what good arguers ought to have done in all three instances. It supports the idea that good conversation is the rationality engine.

Conclusions

This chapter has covered a lot of ground, from the Pleistocene era to some contemporary communication laboratories. The theme connecting everything is the question of whether arguing with another person improves your thinking and conclusions. This issue is so broad that you should be skeptical about any unqualified conclusion, but the evidence we reviewed here is generally encouraging.

We found evolutionary reasons to suppose that social arguing ought to be fairly good. The evolutionary theory of reasoning indicates that arguing was a social phenomenon to begin with, so that good arguing should be especially natural in conversations. We also noticed that the emotional and motivational dimensions of early group life encouraged (and maybe required) some of the interpersonal bonds that ought to encourage good dyadic arguments. These included trust, cooperation, and valuing for the other person.

When we turned to group decision-making, we noticed that the more individual presence there was (e.g., in-person versus online), the better the group thinking. Particular group vulnerabilities such as social loafing and inadequate information sharing became less likely as individuals were more important and exposed. Highly motivated people worked harder.

Several strategies for improving thinking were explored here. These were cognitive, motivational, and design matters. Once we looked at them, we also noticed that we could classify the interventions as aiming at either the internal or external elements of arguments. Genuine disagreement was a consistently beneficial thing to have in a group, but of course the dissenter has be respected rather than shunned. We also noticed that because all arguments are situated, they are also all designed. Often the design is not done deliberately, but sometimes it is, as when an agenda is written, when speakers are given limited time on the floor, when informational materials are passed out beforehand, at the meeting, or not at all, or when voting procedures are settled beforehand.

The studies that my students and I did displayed some of the dynamics of arguing with another person. We took some care to make it likely that the participants would be well informed and reasonably well motivated. We saw these dyads discard fallacies, let examples and weak causal arguments converge, and treat analogies with an appropriate arms-length attitude. This is why we call dyadic argument the rationality engine.

In sum, we can all think better than we normally do. We need to try harder and be more mindful of the argument—to control our biases, to pursue ideas that annoy us, to consider points of view that aren't immediately obvious. A lot of this hard work seems to come more naturally when we are arguing face to face with someone else who is also trying a little harder than usual.

References

Aakhus, M. (2003). Neither naïve nor critical reconstruction: Dispute mediators, impasse, and the design of argumentation. *Argumentation, 17*, 265–290.
Aakhus, M. (2007). Communication as design. *Communication Monographs, 74*, 112–117.
Baltes, B. B., Dickson, M. W., Sherman, M. P., Bauer, C. C., & LaGanke, J. S. (2002). Computer-mediated communication and group decision making: A meta-analysis. *Organizational Behavior and Human Decision Processes, 87*, 156–179.
Battersby, M., & Bailin, S. (2013). Critical thinking and cognitive biases. In D. Mohammed & M. Lewiński (Eds.), *Virtues of argumentation. Proceedings of the 10th international conference of the Ontario Society for the Study of Argumentation (OSSA), 22–26 May 2013* (pp. 1–9). Retrieved from http://scholar.uwindsor.ca/ossaarchive/OSSA10/papersandcommentaries/16
Bermejo-Luque, L. (2012). A unitary schema for arguments by analogy. *Informal Logic, 32*, 1–24.
Bermejo-Luque, L. (2016, May). *What should a normative theory of argumentation look like?* Paper presented at the meeting of the Ontario Society for the Study of Argumentation, Windsor, Ontario.
Botting, D. (2012). The paradox of analogy. *Informal Logic, 32*, 98–115.
Boy, R., & Witte, E. H. (2007). *Do group discussions serve an educational purpose?* (Hamburger Forschungsbericht zur Sozialpsychlogie Nr. 79). Hamburg: Universität Hamburg, Arbeitsbereich Sozialpsychologie.
Burleson, B. R., & Kline, S. L. (1979). Habermas' theory of communication: A critical explication, *Quarterly Journal of Speech, 65*, 412–428.
Cacioppo, J. T., Petty, R. E., & Morris, K. J. (1983). Effects of need for cognition on message evaluation, recall, and persuasion. *Journal of Personality and Social Psychology, 45*, 805–818.
Cherniak, C. (1986). *Minimal rationality*. Cambridge, MA: MIT Press.
Collins, B. E., & Guetzkow, H. (1964). *A social psychology of group processes for decision-making*. New York, NY: Wiley.
Cosmides, L., & Tooby, J. (1992). Cognitive adaptations for social exchange. In J. H. Barkow, L. Cosmides, & J. Tooby (Eds.), *The adapted mind: Evolutionary psychology and the generation of culture* (pp. 163–228). New York, NY: Oxford University Press.
Cummings, L. (2014). Informal fallacies as cognitive heuristics in public health reasoning. *Informal Logic, 34*, 1–37.

van Eemeren, F. H., & Grootendorst, R. (2004). *A systematic theory of argumentation: The pragma-dialectical approach.* Cambridge: Cambridge University Press.

van Eemeren, F. H., Grootendorst, R., Jackson, S., & Jacobs, S. (1993). *Reconstructing argumentative discourse.* Tuscaloosa, AL: University of Alabama Press.

Falmagne, R. J. (Ed.). (1975). *Reasoning: Representation and process.* Hillsdale, NJ: Erlbaum.

Floyd, K., & Afifi, T. D. (2011). Biological and physiological perspectives on interpersonal communication. In M. L. Knapp & J. A. Daly (Eds.), *The SAGE handbook of interpersonal communication* (4th ed., pp. 87–127). Los Angeles: Sage.

Gigerenzer, G. (1991). How to make cognitive illusions disappear: Beyond "heuristics and biases." *European Review of Social Psychology, 2,* 83–115.

Gigerenzer, G., & Sturm, T. (2012). How (far) can rationality be naturalized? *Synthese, 187,* 243–268.

Hample, D. (2011a). Convergent causal arguments in conversation. In F. Zenker, (Ed.). *Argument cultures: Proceedings of the 8th international conference of the Ontario Society for the Study of Argumentation* (OSSA), May 18–21, 2011. Windsor, ON: Ontario Society for the Study of Argumentation.

Hample, D. (2011b). How many examples is an induction? In R. C. Rowland (Ed.), *Reasoned argument and social change* (pp. 121–128). Washington, DC: National Communication Association.

Hample, D. (2016). Analogies in conversation. In R. Von Burg (Ed.), *Dialogues in argumentation* (pp. 53–72). Windsor, ON: Windsor Studies in Argumentation.

Hample, D., Jones, A. K., & Averbeck, J. M. (2009). The rationality engine: How do arguers deal spontaneously with fallacies? In S. Jacobs (Ed.), *Concerning argument* (pp. 307–317). Washington, DC: National Communication Association.

Hastie, R., & Dawes, R. M. (2010). *Rational choice in an uncertain world: The psychology of judgment and decision making* (2nd ed.). Los Angeles, CA: Sage.

Heath, C., Larrick, R. P., & Klayman, J. (1998). Cognitive repairs: How organizational practices can compensate for individual shortcomings. *Research in Organizational Behavior, 20,* 1–37.

Henkemans, A. F. S. (2000). State-of-the-art: The structure of argumentation. *Argumentation, 14,* 447–473.

Hinsz, V. B., Tindale, R. S., & Vollrath, D. A. (1997). The emerging conceptualization of groups as information processors. *Psychological Bulletin, 121,* 43–64.

Huang, H.-H., Hsu, J. S.-C., & Ku, C.-Y. (2012). Understanding the role of computer-mediated counter-argument in countering confirmation bias. *Decision Support Systems, 53,* 438–447.

Jackson, S. (1998). Disputation by design. *Argumentation, 12,* 183–198.

Jackson, S., & Aakhus, M. (2014). Becoming more reflective about the role of design in communication. *Journal of Applied Communication Research, 42,* 125–134.

Jacobs, S., & Aakhus, M. (2002). What mediators do with words: Implementing three models of rational discussion in dispute mediation. *Conflict Resolution Quarterly, 20,* 177–203.

Janis, I. L. (1982). *Groupthink: Psychological studies of policy decisions and fiascoes.* Boston, MA: Houghton Mifflin.

Johnson, E. J., Shu, S. B., Dellaert, B. G., Fox, C., Goldstein, D. G., Häubl, G., et al. (2012). Beyond nudges: Tools of a choice architecture. *Marketing Letters, 23,* 487–504.

Johnson, R. H. (2000). *Manifest rationality: A pragmatic theory of argument*. Mahwah, NJ: Lawrence Erlbaum.

Kahneman, D. (2011). *Thinking, fast and slow*. New York, NY: Macmillan.

Kahneman, D., & Tversky, A. (1979). Prospect theory: An analysis of decision under risk. *Econometrica, 47*, 263–291.

Kelly, J. M. (1964). Audi alteram partem. *Natural Law Forum, 9*, 103–110.

Kerr, N. L., MacCoun, R., & Kramer, G. P. (1996). Bias in judgment: Comparing individuals and groups. *Psychological Review, 103*, 687–719.

Kerr, N. L., & Tindale, R. S. (2004). Group performance and decision making. *Annual Review of Psychology, 55*, 623–655.

Koriat, A., Lichtenstein, S., & Fischhoff, B. (1980). Reasons for confidence. *Journal of Experimental Psychology: Human Learning and Memory, 6*, 107–118.

Kuhn, D. (1991). *The skills of argument*. Cambridge: Cambridge University Press.

Kuhn, D. (2015). Thinking together and alone. *Educational Researcher, 44*, 46–53.

Larrick, R. P. (2004). Debiasing. In D. J. Koehler & N. Harvey (Eds.), *Blackwell handbook of judgment and decision making* (pp. 316–337). Oxford: Blackwell.

Larrick, R. P. (2009). Broaden the decision frame to make effective decisions. In E. A. Locke (Ed.), *Handbook of principles of organizational behavior* (2nd ed., pp. 461–480). Chichester: John Wiley.

Larrick, R. P., & Feiler, D. C. (2015). Expertise in decision making. In G. Keren & G. Wu (Eds.), *The Wiley Blackwell Handbook of judgment and decision making* (pp. 696–721).

Laughlin, P. R., Bonner, B. L., & Miner, A. G. (2002). Groups perform better than the best individuals on letters-to-numbers problems. *Organizational Behavior and Human Decision Processes, 88*, 605–620.

Levine, J. M. (1999). Transforming individuals into groups: Some hallmarks of the SDS approach to small group research. *Organizational Behavior and Human Decision Processes, 80*, 21–27.

McKenzie, C. R. M. (2004). Framing effects in inference tasks—and why they are normatively defensible. *Memory & Cognition, 32*, 874–885.

Mercier, H. (2016). The argumentative theory: Predictions and empirical evidence. *Trends in Cognitive Sciences, 20*, 689–700.

Mercier, H., & Sperber, D. (2011). Why do humans reason? Arguments for an argumentation theory. *Behavioral and Brain Sciences, 34*, 57–111.

Mercier, H., & Sperber, D. (2017). *The enigma of reason*. Cambridge, MA: Harvard University Press.

Milch, K. F., Weber, E. U., Appelt, K. C., Handgraaf, M. J. J., & Krantz, D. H. (2009). From individual preference construction to group decisions: Framing effects and group processes. *Organizational Behavior and Human Decision Processes, 108*, 242–255.

Nemeth, C. J., Connell, J. B., Rogers, J. D., & Brown, K. S. (2001). Improving decision making by means of dissent. *Journal of Applied Social Psychology, 31*, 48j–58.

Nickerson, R. S. (1998). Confirmation bias: A ubiquitous phenomenon in many guises. *Review of General Psychology, 2*, 175–220.

Perelman, Ch., & Olbrechts-Tyteca, L. (1969). *The new rhetoric: A treatise on argumentation.* (J. Wilkinson & P. Weaver, Trans.). Notre Dame, IN: University of Notre Dame Press.

Revlin, R., & Mayer, R. E. (Eds.). (1978). *Human reasoning.* New York, NY: John Wiley.

Roos, P., Gelfand, M., Dau, D., & Lun, J. (2015). Societal threat and cultural variation in the strength of social norms: An evolutionary basis. *Organizational Behavior and Human Decision Process, 127,* 14–23.

Schulz-Hardt, S., Jochims, M., & Frey, D. (2002). Productive conflict in group decision making: Genuine and contrived dissent as strategies to counteract biased information seeking. *Organizational Behavior and Human Decision Processes, 88,* 563–586.

Schweiger, S., Oeberst A., & Cress, U. (2014). Confirmation bias in web-based search: A randomized online study of the effects of expert information and social tags on information search and evaluation. *Journal of Medical Internet Research, 16,* e94.

Simon, H. A. (1990). Invariants of human behavior. *Annual Review of Psychology, 41,* 1–19.

Smith, B. N., Kerr, N. A., Markus, M. J., & Stasson, M. F. (2001). Individual differences in social loafing: Need for cognition as a motivator in collective performance. *Group Dynamics: Theory, Research, and Practice, 5,* 150–158.

Smith, C. M., Tindale, R. S., & Steiner, L. (1998). Investment decisions by individuals and groups in "sunk cost" situations: The potential impact of shared representations. *Group Processes & Intergroup Relations, 1,* 175–189.

Sperber, D. (2017, June). *Inference, reasons, and argumentation.* Paper presented at the meeting of the European Conference on Argumentation, Fribourg, Switzerland.

Spoor, J. R., & Kelly, J. R. (2004). The evolutionary significance of affect in groups: Communication and group bonding. *Group Processes and Intergroup Relations, 7,* 398–412.

Steiner, I. D. (1972). *Group process and productivity.* New York, NY: Academic Press.

Walton, D., Reed, C., & Macagno, F. (2008). *Argumentation schemes.* Cambridge: Cambridge University Press.

Wason, P. C., & Johnson-Laird, P. N. (1972). *Psychology of reasoning: Structure and content.* Cambridge, MA: Harvard University Press.

Wellman, C. (1971). *Challenge and response: Justification in ethics.* Carbondale, IL: Southern Illinois University Press.

Zenker, F. (2013). Commentary on Mark Battersby and Sharon Bailin's "Critical thinking and cognitive biases." In D. Mohammed & M. Lewiński (Eds.), *Virtues of argumentation. Proceedings of the 10th international conference of the Ontario Society for the Study of Argumentation (OSSA), 22–26 May 2013* (pp. 1–6). Retrieved from http://scholar.uwindsor.ca/ossaarchive/OSSA10/papersandcommentaries/17

Zenker, F., Dahlman, C., Bååth, R., & Sarwar, F. (2015). Giving reasons pro et contra as a debiasing technique in legal decision making. In D. Mohammed & M. Lewinksi (Eds.), *Proceedings of the First European Conference on Argumentation, vol. 1,* Lisbon, June 2015 (pp. 807–820). London: College Publications.

Zenker, F., Dahlman, C., & Sarwar, F. (2015). Reliable debiasing techniques in legal contexts? Weak signals from a darker corner of the social science universe. In F. Paglieri (Ed.), *The psychology of argument: Cognitive approaches to argumentation and persuasion.* London: College Publications.

CHAPTER SIX

Relational Dialogues

This chapter is about dialogues within relationships, usually dyadic ones. "Dialogue" is a common word that often means no more than "nice conversation" or something along those lines. However, it is an old word in philosophy and it has often taken on technical meanings. Plato's main writings, for instance, are called *The Dialogues*, and scholars have written many books and articles about how Plato portrayed the philosophical discussions that he offered to the newly literate world (e.g., Robinson, 1953). Sometimes "dialogue" and "dialectic" are treated more or less as synonyms, but I will not do that here. To me, a dialectic is a careful philosophical inquiry in which all personal attributes except knowledge, reasoning ability, and a desire for truth are scraped away from the arguers, and I think it is useful to have a word that means only that. For our purposes, a dialogue is an argumentative conversation. It might aim at dialectical purity but might also have lesser or more personal goals.

Since this whole book concerns that sort of interaction, you might wonder why I have pulled out the idea of dialogue for its own chapter. It is because of a particular line of philosophy that has been just as specifically adapted to the study of interpersonal communication. The philosophical work was done by Douglas Walton (1998; Walton & Krabbe, 1995; also see Reed & Tindale, 2010). The connection to empirical research on face-to-face communication was developed by Ioana Cionea (2011, 2012).

Before we move into the details of Walton's and Cionea's work, some preliminary points may be helpful. First, a dialogue is an activity type. Other activity types include ordering food in a restaurant and learning to thank your aunt for a tee shirt you will never wear. As you will soon learn, dialogues can be for persuasion, negotiation, information exchange, and several other things. Each of these is a type of social activity (persuading, negotiating, sharing information). Another way of saying this is that each dialogue type has a particular structure. Dialogues are constituted by messages, and these messages (and their relations to one another) are the structure of the particular episode.

Walton says that the wellspring of each dialogue type is a particular goal, and this goal naturally points us toward certain message behaviors. This book has been full of talk about goals, but these are a little different because they are about dialogue types. They are not goals such as "get a ride to the airport." Instead, these are more abstract goals that indicate a desired sort of argumentative dialogue: to persuade (the other person), to find out (what the other person knows), to come to an accommodation (with a competitive co-worker), and things like that. Dialogues may not be consciously planned out the way an architect designs a building, but people do aim themselves toward these sorts of interactions even if they do not have Walton's vocabulary for them.

Details will follow, but for now it is useful to realize that a person's goals lead him or her into a *kind* of interaction, and that an interaction type is a thing of its own. Just as you can play basketball in a gym but not in a janitor's closet, some things are natural in one dialogue type but inappropriate in others. Every dialogue type has its own expectations, affordances, and constraints. For the dialogue type to happen purely, both people have to be participating in the same sort of activity so that it becomes co-constructed. Walton sometimes assumes this and Cionea tests it.

When we move to Cionea's work on dialogues within interpersonal relationships, it will be helpful to realize that some of the things I've just said about dialogues are also true of interpersonal relationships. Relationships are also constituted by messages, and can be understood as continuous message systems. Pairs of people—maybe friends, romantic partners, or siblings—often develop one or more patterns of interaction. These are recurrent message patterns (joke/joke, accusation/outburst, compliment/kissing, etc.). These repeating message configurations can be so magnetically attractive that people can become trapped in them even though neither person consciously wants that sort of interaction (Cronen, Pearce, & Snavely, 1979). Other patterns, equally inviting, are much more pleasant and so we look forward to spending time with the other person.

But a relationship is a much larger thing than a particular conversation. A relationship is the sum of all the interactions two people have ever experienced together. It has a history and a future, and most of all, it has a characteristic feel (ethos) to it. That feel might be one of friendship, romantic affection, sisterly rivalry, security, combativeness, annoyance, or hundreds of other things. We tend to reproduce those feels and patterns when we are in the other person's company, and the other person does as well. Where Walton said that goals cause dialogue types, here we can see that a relationship's ethos causes its interaction patterns. Actually, the connection is bidirectional, so that the message patterns and ethos reinforce, reproduce, and help recreate each other.

Relationships contain all sorts of communication and not all of it is argumentative. By definition, argument dialogues mainly contain argumentative moves (along with various niceties such as facework, noncommittal acknowledgements, and little digressions). Argument dialogues normally take place within relationships. Gilbert (2014) emphasizes that nearly all our arguments are with familiars, people we know. So in this chapter we will be trying to see how the dialogue patterns fit within the relationship patterns. First I will summarize Walton's theory, and then I will move on to the empirical research initiated by Cionea.

Walton's Theory of Dialogue Types

The grandfather of Walton's theory is probably Hamblin (1970), a book many of the informal logicians regard as a foundational classic. In his chapter 8, Hamblin began working out what he called dialectical games. These games, not unlike chess or contract bridge except without the tactics or cleverness, were defined by a small number of formal rules, perhaps a dozen. These rules specified a very limited number of things that could or must be said in a dialogue, mainly consisting of things like asserting S, asking why S is so, retracting S, or refusing to commit to S. Hamblin worked them out to show how a finite set of formal rules could define a dialectical system that could prevent certain reasoning mistakes, such as the fallacy of many questions or begging the question.

An enduring contribution of this development was Hamblin's idea of a commitment store. This is a list of all the statements that a participant is obligated to regard as true. These commitments, for Hamblin, occur because the statements have been asserted or conceded at some point in the game or agreed to at the beginning of the interaction. He also mentions the possibility that commonly accepted statements might be in one's commitment store even if they have not yet appeared in the dialogue (e.g., coffee and tea are not the same drink), though he is unenthusiastic about permitting this sort of external influence on the games. These commitments grow in number as the conversation continues, until sometimes (depending on the particular set of rules being played) a conclusion becomes inescapable and must be endorsed. Perhaps a commitment is the negation of what is presently being asserted, or perhaps some conclusion is logically implied by a combination of commitments.

Hamblin's own dialectical games (he actually made one of them into a card game that he played with a friend in what I imagine must have been one of the longest evenings in human history; Hamblin, 1970, p. 282, n. 1) are not of much interest to us here, but they introduce the idea of a definable system of interactive reasoning, along with the very useful concept of commitment stores. If you are interested in these formal approaches and their history, van Eemeren et al. (2014, ch. 6) provide a good summary of several approaches, including Hamblin's.

In Hamblin's analysis, the commitment store essentially consisted of propositions, more or less sentences that express some understanding of the world (e.g., "Jane prefers tea to coffee"). Walton and Krabbe (1995) expanded this idea to include commitments to some course of action (e.g., "I am committed to paying off my student loans"). They also developed the initial descriptions of Walton's (1998) dialogue types. They believed that fallacies were especially likely to be located when an arguer shifts from one dialogue type to another, because, as we will see, a move that is appropriate in one sort of dialogue can be a fallacy in another.

For Walton and Krabbe (1995, p. 12), commitments are not psychological things at all. They are simply argumentatively usable things that go into a commitment store, like cards you hold in your hand in a game of contract bridge. You don't need to be emotionally involved with the ten of clubs to play it. Some commitments are shared, or at least publicly known, but others are unilateral—known by one party but undiscovered by the other. When we get to Cionea's work, we will certainly take a psychological point of view repeatedly, but for now it is important to understand Walton and Krabbe on their own terms. One commits to something by saying it or accepting it, not necessarily by believing it or wanting it.

Some of the commitments they analyze are like Hamblin's—propositional matters that are stated or accepted during the dialogue game. But they also analyze "dark-side" commitments, which are not necessarily stated (in fact, probably not) but that underlie an arguer's statements and other game moves. Unlike simple propositional commitments, these are quite hard to retract during the dialogue because they connect to so many other things that they can pull down a whole argumentative edifice. Finally, Walton and Krabbe study action commitments, which naturally give some direction and real-world application to an interactive argument. A dialogue is a joint activity and if it moves forward at all, it will be because both arguers decide to share some of the other's commitments, possibly including some dark-side ones. The arguers must find common ground so they can proceed to a common conclusion.

When a person commits to some statement or proposition, two sorts of things are involved in that commitment. If you announce that you think tea is better than coffee (and you meet no opposition on this point), you are entitled to use that idea later in the argument, perhaps as a bit of evidence or something. That is like playing a card. But there are other, more interesting, consequences of your statement. By saying that tea is better than coffee, you become bound to defend that idea if it is challenged, you become bound to provide evidence or supportive reasoning for that statement, you are not allowed to suddenly say that coffee is better than tea, and perhaps some other things. These latter consequences of your simple commitment about tea being better than coffee have to do with how you are supposed to argue in a dialogue. We begin to see how dialogue rules emerge from commitments: if you say something you must stand by it; if you say something you must be able and willing to prove it; if you say something you are not permitted to contradict it. These, in fact, are probably common rules in most dialogue games. If you violate these sorts of rules, you are out of bounds in the dialogue and being out of bounds becomes the definition of a fallacy in this particular approach to argumentation. It would be like picking up another player's ace of diamonds from the table and setting it on fire. That would not be a bad play, like deciding not to put down a trump card. Instead, it would place you out of bounds and therefore be a card game fallacy.

Perhaps it is time to identify Walton's (1998; Walton & Krabbe, 1995) six kinds of argumentative dialogue. These six activities can be distinguished in several ways and we will get to several of them soon. For now, however, I want to concentrate on their goals. Two sorts of goals need to be kept track of: the dialogue's goals and the arguers' goals. Each dialogue has a unique purpose, and when I refer to those I will call them Dialogue goals. By capitalizing Dialogue, I mean to imply that you should think of it as its own thing, having an almost personal agency. When I talk about arguers' goals, I will be using "goals" in a more familiar way. To illustrate the difference between these sorts of goals, consider the U.S. criminal justice system. A criminal court has its own goal, to generate a decision of guilt or innocence, that is, to settle the immediate issue of whether someone should be punished. If you are generous, you might want to say that the Court's goal is justice, but in any event we can agree that the essential Court goal is decision. We can see that the system itself, the Court, capitalized, has a goal that contextualizes and generates the specific rules participants must obey to stay in bounds (here, a fallacy might involve going to jail for contempt of Court). The attorneys, on the other hand, have the more mundane goal of winning. The arguer's goal, to win, operates within the context of the Court's goal of rendering a decision. In fact, the Court's goal and associated rules actually makes a place for the individual goal of winning. In a similar way, we need to distinguish the Dialogue's goal from the arguer's goal.

The six dialogues are persuasion, inquiry, negotiation, information-seeking, deliberation, and eristic (from the Greek word that means "strife"). These each have a distinct Dialogue goal and imply different arguer goals. Some of the goal distinctions may appear subtle but they are real and important.

In a persuasion dialogue, at least one of the arguers is trying to change the other's mind. The Dialogue goal is to resolve the arguers' initial conflict in points of view, using verbal means to reach a permanent agreement. The initiator's goal is to persuade the other person, that is, to use persuasive arguments to impel a change in view on the part of the other person. The second person can have a variety of goals, such as to resist, to listen open-mindedly, or to counter-persuade. The initiator has a dominating goal, even if it derives from a genuine intention to improve the other person's views, and is restricted only by the quality of available arguments.

The inquiry dialogue is different, of course. Where the persuasion dialogue began with at least one of the participants having a clear position and an equally clear intention about where the dialogue should conclude, in inquiry neither arguer begins with a position. Instead, they both begin with awareness of an intellectual problem that they both want to resolve in the most justifiable way possible. For instance, they might want to know whether free speech or separation of powers is the most important element of American democracy, or whether beef or pork makes a healthier meal. The Dialogue goal is to generate knowledge that both arguers eventually accept. The arguers' goal is to generate a proof in favor of a conclusion, or to refute a proof. Here, the arguers have the same goal. They are not competing with one another in the way a persuader and listener compete. The inquiry dialogue is only successful if both of them genuinely endorse their final mutual thinking. Scientific investigation should be an example of inquiry.

Third is the negotiation dialogue. Some limited thing lies between the two arguers, and they try to divide it. Perhaps a married couple is trying to decide whether to use their modest surplus of money to buy new coats or new cooking pans. The Dialogue goal is to make a deal, simply to achieve some allocation of the limited good. The arguers' goal is to get the most for oneself. The dramatic distinction between negotiation and persuasion is that persuasion operates by arguing on the merits of the case (What is fair? What is traditional? What is most just?), but negotiation operates by bargaining ("I'll give you this if you give me that"). The negotiated agreement does not have to be justified on the merits of the issue. It only has to be acceptable to both parties. The parties might have the attitude that they would like to divide things equitably (perhaps because they will be negotiating again due to being married), but they might also have the attitude of trying to get everything they can. Power dynamics become very important here, whereas in persuasion only the force of arguments is supposed to matter.

Information-seeking is the next kind of dialogue. Here one arguer believes that the other has information that the first person would like to have, and inquires after it. It might be a simple question/answer session, but it might also be something like a police interrogation where the police officer has to track the suspect's commitments very carefully to test whether they are consistent or contradictory, plausible or unlikely. The Dialogue goal is to spread information, perhaps in the interest of discovering someone's actual position on a question. The initiator's goal is to gain knowledge. The other person's goal might be to share information, to withhold it, or to obscure it. This dialogue can have a variety of relationships between the arguers, varying from police officer/suspect to librarian/patron. The information that is being sought might be a conclusion of its own ("Aha! So you did steal the diamonds!") or might only generate a bit of evidence, a card to be played later in another dialogue.

Deliberation is the fifth dialogue, and the last one that is very likely to be productive. Deliberation is very easily confused with persuasion, inquiry, or negotiation, so close attention may be needed here. In deliberation, the Dialogue goal is to reach a decision on a future course of action. The arguers' goal is for the individual's preferred decision to be chosen. Deliberation is oriented to the future: Where should we go on vacation? Should local taxes be raised? Where should our new office building be built? Persuasion has no particular time orientation, and neither does inquiry. Negotiation is also future oriented, but negotiation functions at the level of deal making, and deliberation operates by means of argument on the merits. So deliberation dialogues involve careful arguing on the best grounds, aimed at selecting a future action. Imagine a legislative body that acts seriously and thoughtfully, the way we were taught legislatures worked when we were children. They would deliberate and then pass the most justifiable law, to implement the wisest available program.

The last kind of dialogue is called eristic. This is verbal combat, pure and simple. It often involves insults, name-calling, and accusations. It may call out the same in response, along with defensiveness and self-protection. The Dialogue goal is to have a verbal fight, and the individual arguers' goal is to win, probably by hurting the other person. (Here I am following Walton, 1998, ch. 7, in preference to Walton & Krabbe, 1995, ch. 3, but am perhaps going somewhat beyond either book.) The prototypical case of eristic dialogue is the angry shouting match, the sort of awful interaction that people (or people who haven't read a book like this one) often call an argument (as in, "I'm upset because I had an argument with my friend today"). Perhaps I should point out that this sort of episode actually contains arguments, even if they are nasty ones. "You are an awful person" is a claim that can be supported with reasons (e.g., "Because you eat toast wrong"—I'm going to leave the real examples to the reader). Walton actually holds out some hope for this sort of dialogue, proposing that it might clear the air and possibly improve the relationship. He and Krabbe also point out that a playful aggressive exchange between two friends about what football team is the best can be eristic, and harmlessly so. But I think the nasty version is the most common.

In distinguishing the six dialogues I have emphasized their goal differences. Some other features are worth noticing. They differ in their formal rules of operation and commitment management, but these are quite technical and frankly we do not need them for our present purposes (see Walton & Krabbe, 1995, ch. 4, for various persuasion rules, or van Eemeren et al., 2014, ch. 6, for other formal theories). More relevant to us is that the relative status of the two arguers differs from dialogue to dialogue. The initiator claims a superior position in the persuasion dialogue ("you need to think what I want you to"), the information-seeker assumes a subordinate position in the information-seeking dialogue ("teach me, master"), and the initiator assumes a superior position in the eristic dialogue ("you're a worse person than me or anyone I've ever met"). But in the inquiry, negotiation, and deliberation dialogues the two arguers begin with a more or less symmetrical position in the dialogue. (Naturally, reality may intervene to make one of the arguers richer, or older, or better educated, or something else that seems to award status in that culture. But Dialogue doesn't.) As a consequence of these differences in status and goals, the mutuality of the dialogues' endings seems to vary as well. In persuasion and eristic, one arguer is trying to pressure or coerce the other, probably more gently in persuasion than in eristic. In inquiry and deliberation, both arguers seek a genuinely mutual decision on the merits of the case. Information-seeking and negotiation seem to be in between. Negotiators are both striving to push the other around, but they usually understand that they need to end in livable agreement. The information-seeker aims at personal gratification, which might be agreeable to some information-providers (e.g., a librarian) but not to others (e.g., a criminal suspect). These considerations of status and mutuality raise issues of about interpersonal behaviors, which are outside the scope of what Hamblin, Walton, and Krabbe study but which are congenial to the interpersonal work led by Cionea.

But before moving to Cionea's work, a final important matter remains. This theory of argument dialogues is normative, which is to say it prescribes rules and defining characteristics of various kinds of Dialogue. It is rarely descriptive. But one empirical reality is so stark that it required philosophical treatment: the fact that people do not purely stay within the bounds of a single dialogue type. Walton's theory includes treatment of "mixed" dialogues, which inherently combine two or more sorts of dialogues, but our concern here is mainly with what he calls dialogue shifts. That happens when one or more of the arguers slide spontaneously from one sort of dialogue to another.

Sometimes this is productive. For instance, two deliberators can digress from their main dialogue to do some inquiry and then use that result to go back to their deliberation and continue it. Or in the middle of a persuasion dialogue, one arguer may seek information about the other's commitments, and then go back into the original persuasion dialogue with another bit of information that they might both agree about. In an inquiry, one arguer might figure out a conclusion first and then have to persuade the other person to accept it. These are all useful argumentative moves that involve dialogue shifts.

Other dialogue shifts are "illicit." That is, the movement into a second dialogue type violates the nature of the original dialogue type. These shifts are called fallacies (also see Macagno, 2008). Before giving a few examples, however, a key element of dialogue theory needs to be emphasized: that a particular argument scheme can be appropriate in one dialogue type but not in another. For instance, threats are fine in a negotiation ("Give us a raise or we will go on strike") but not in persuasion ("Agree that Smith is a better candidate or I will steal your bicycle"). Many eristic dialogues are full of ad hominem attacks, and weirdly this is a dialogue-appropriate thing to do in an eristic shouting match. It is not appropriate in a deliberation (the U.S. Senate has a rule forbidding one Senator from insulting or impugning another Senator on the floor, for instance: https://www.rules.senate.gov/public/index.cfm?p=RulesOfSenateHome, Rule XIX, paragraph 2). Bargaining is fine in negotiation, but it is a fallacy in inquiry ("I'll give you Hume having a better epistemology if you'll give me Kant having a better moral philosophy").

Problems can therefore occur when one arguer diverts into a different dialogue than the one the other person thought was under way. In most people's experience, the most common problem is when a persuasion (or deliberation or any of the others) devolves into eristic. What had been an exchange of reasons becomes an exchange of intemperate remarks. Or a deliberator suddenly offers a deal rather than a counter argument. Or an information seeker begins to counter the information-provider's answer. What has happened is that the arguer is out of bounds, the bounds being defined by the nature of the original dialogue type. On this theory, we can see why certain argument schemes are often identified as fallacies. The fallacies of bargaining (when bargaining isn't called for), ad baculum (threats), and ad hominem have already been mentioned here. Walton (1998) and

Walton and Krabbe (1995) discuss others that have this same general character: they are fallacies because they are out of place. They are in the wrong sort of dialogue.

Finally I should mention that a dialogue type is a mutual choice. One arguer may have wanted that dialogue type more than the other person, but if they are both participating in it, they both chose it in some measure. Neither left the room, for example. But very possibly, one arguer might try to initiate dialogue type 1 and the other arguer heads toward dialogue type 2 instead. In the next sections of the chapter, we will find that interesting.

I do not assume that ordinary arguers have the sort of perceptiveness and formal knowledge of different dialogue types that I have discussed here, but they do have a basic understanding of what they are doing. They can tell the difference between seeking truth and making a deal, and they certainly recognize that deliberation and eristic are different experiences. Being in a particular sort of dialogue is an implicit endorsement of that Dialogue goal and it puts the personalized arguer goals into play as well. It makes some sorts of argumentative contributions appropriate and declares others to be out of bounds. In other words, being in one sort of dialogue rather than another is consequential in many ways. Some of these are normative and philosophical, but quite a few are empirical and social.

Cionea's Theory of Dialogues in Relationships

Cionea (roughly pronounced *cho-nya*) has applied dialogue theory to interpersonal relationships (Cionea, 2011, 2012). Her key insight was the realization that we might be able to distinguish relationships by their preferred sort of dialogue. For instance, one couple might fight eristically all the time; another pair might deliberate quietly; and yet another might begin with the assumption that any disagreement they have must inevitably be due to them not having the same initial information. That people in close relationships develop repeating interactional patterns is not controversial. The new idea is that the dialogues, with their interactionally distinct goals, might be a suitable way to describe some of those patterns.

Recall that Walton and Krabbe (1995) discussed the idea of action commitments. Normally these are things like "I promise to pay you $5 if you buy me a milkshake now." This is an action commitment whether the promise is sincere or not: it merely needs to be said in order to enter the commitment store. However, action commitments might be more abstract than that. In particular, volunteering to participate in a specific kind of argumentative interaction can be understood as an action commitment (we could say the same about joining a joking match or a cuddling episode, but those are outside the scope of this book). Again, joining the dialogue might be half-hearted, but the action commitment is straightforwardly inferred from the action, and so once you have begun to deliberate or negotiate (for example) you are officially committed to continue in that activity. Your private action sincerity does not matter, and you will be correctly accused of a fallacy if you abandon the dialogue without proper participation. Since these sorts of commitments seem especially interesting, let us distinguish them by calling them dialogue commitments. Freely engaging in a mutual inquiry implies a commitment to the inquiry dialogue, with all its rules and other characteristics, and similar things can be said about the other dialogues.

Couples might only prefer one sort of dialogue, but that frankly seems unlikely. Instead, people in a stable relationship might favor two or three sorts of dialogue and might systematically avoid the others or only engage in them randomly. They might even generate their own private sort of mixed dialogue—maybe deliberation with some information-seeking about the other's feelings, for instance. This could have to do with how the two people most comfortably think together, it might have to do with what sort of status relationship they desire (symmetrical or asymmetrical), or maybe it is strongly influenced by what approach to argumentation has most often worked well for them. At this point in the chapter, notice that it is only a hypothesis that couples will have similar dialogue preferences. I will summarize some empirical data later, and it will suggest that the hypothesis has merit.

Recall that both dialogues and relationships are constituted by the messages that occur within them. These messages have some sort of remark-to-remark coherence and therefore can be said to be structured. Both relationships and dialogues (once under way) also have histories. The histories include messages that have been said earlier (maybe a few minutes ago or maybe a few years ago), and these things go into the people's commitment stores. In a thorough dialogue or a long-term relationship, those commitment stores become public, that is, exposed to both parties. Those commitments—the propositional ones, the action ones, and perhaps even the dark side ones—all become available for use in interactions, and most of them will be mutually known, especially in an enduring relationship. People can be held to what they just said or what they promised when they became engaged. Commitments can be retracted, too, and this action has different ease and consequences depending on the dialogic or relational context. The dialogues we are thinking about in this chapter occur within the context of a close interpersonal relationship, and that means that years-old commitments can be in the commitment stores of a dialogue that only began a moment ago. Where Walton's theory was unconcerned about the psychological status of a commitment—only whether or not it was said—when we begin thinking about interpersonal communication it becomes important to consider the sincerity of the remarks as well. This moves us from philosophical work to psychological application.

Cionea (2011) proposed to conceive of close interpersonal relationships as ongoing "meta-dialogues." This phrasing nicely indicates that an argumentative dialogue will be encased within a larger relationship system, which we can think of as a dialogue of dialogues. The nature of the relationship has implications for how people can (non-fallaciously) argue within it. "In a relationship, the recurrent exchanges between the two partners create a system of messages and meanings that accumulate over time. These repeated dialogues define the relationship, nuance it and give it its characteristics and also provide the anchoring point for partners' understanding of their relationship" (p. 96). Just as dialogues have rules and goals, so do relationships. Several students have told me over the years that their family has a rule that every argument has to end with both arguers saying, "I love you" to the other person. Other families have rules like "father decides" or "quit when anyone becomes upset." One can immediately see that rules like these are derived from fundamental relationship goals (love, authority, or consideration) and have the effect of affording, requiring, or forbidding certain kinds of arguing moves.

Sometimes a relationship's commitments are only exposed by violating them. Thus it was natural for Cionea (2012) to explore these ideas in the context of relational transgressions. She asked more than 400 undergraduates and nearly 300 married people to imagine that there had been a transgression within their romantic relationship, committed either by themselves or their partner, and that they might need to discuss this with their partner. The transgressions involved things like breaking a promise or being insensitive. People provided data on many elements of the transgressive situations and how they felt about them, but our concern is mainly with their preferences for dialogue type and how they thought the interaction would turn out. Based on pilot testing, Cionea found that respondents really weren't inclined to use deliberation and inquiry, so she only collected data on persuasion, negotiation, information-seeking, and eristic dialogues.

Cionea found that the positivity or negativity of people's goals in the imagined interaction pointed toward the type of dialogue they most wanted. She learned that eristic dialogue was more preferred when relational partners were especially concerned with their own negative feelings and wanted to dominate their partner. Desire for either a persuasive or information-seeking dialogue rose when people concentrated on positive feelings. Wanting to maintain a positive image in the relationship led to persuasive, negotiation, and information-seeking dialogues, but being worried about the other person constraining one's freedom to think or act freely was associated with wanting an eristic encounter.

Dialogue preferences were associated with how people thought their interactions would end. They thought the conflict would be more resolvable if they oriented to using persuasion, negotiation, and information-seeking dialogues. Choice of the negotiation dialogue also produced more anticipated satisfaction with the encounter. Cionea was unable to give a data-based explanation for why eristic dialogues did not affect ratings for expected resolvability or satisfaction, but she speculated that perhaps eristic exchanges are short-lived (maybe outbursts that fizzle out) and the real work would be done with the other dialogues.

The biggest lesson from this initial empirical work is that dialogue types do have a place in relationships, specifically in how people talk about transgressions of the relationship's mutual commitments (or perhaps commitments that were thought to be mutual but turned out not to be). For the dialogue types to have returned different results, one from another, means that people actually are sensitive to the differences in the goals and rules for the different dialogues. We can also see confirmation that undergraduates and married people, not just philosophers, can clearly see that some dialogues (persuasion, negotiation, and information-seeking) are constructive and that one dialogue (eristic) is not. When people had positive goals for the conversation, they chose the productive dialogues, but when they had negative goals or were worried about being pushed around they aimed themselves at eristics. The eristic dialogue, as we said earlier, is a verbal fight aimed at catharsis. But persuasion, negotiation, and information-seeking are argumentative activities that aim at a mutually acceptable outcome.

Cionea's earliest work on the place of argument dialogues within personal relationships points to some fundamental ideas. Dialogues can be seen as relatively short-lived message structures that are enclosed within a particular relationship, which is a longer-lived message structure of its own. Both have goals, rules, and commitments, but a relationship tends to have more general and enduring ones. The relationship gives context to the argument and also imposes various rules, goals, and meanings on the dialogue, so that a particular argument is a temporary instantiation of the relationship's general ethos. The relationship's history supplies commitments (propositional, action, dark side, and dialogue commitments) that may be used in the course of an argument between the relational partners. The fact that there are dialogue commitments within a relationship leads to the idea that a relationship is a meta-dialogue, that is, an ongoing structure that prefers some sorts of argument activity more than others.

Investigating Argument Dialogues in Relationships

Cionea continued her empirical investigations and expanded the research domain to include all of the dialogue types, not just the four studied in Cionea (2012). I will summarize all that more recent work in this section of the chapter, and will divide it into several parts. First I will explain how the dialogues are measured in Cionea's research program. Then I will indicate which dialogues people most approve, and how those preferences connect to other argument-relevant constructs.

Operationalizing the Dialogue Types

In order to study how people actually participate in argument dialogues, and what they think they are doing while they argue persuasively, deliberatively, and so forth, a fundamental first step was to figure out how to measure these things (Cionea, 2012; Cionea & Hample, 2014; Cionea, Hample, & Fink, 2013). Collecting actual data on argument dialogues required that the dialogue types be "de-philosophized" a little bit. The basic constructs remain those that Walton developed, of course, but Cionea needed to develop specific survey items that ordinary people could use to indicate their judgments about the various kinds of arguing activities.

This required some simplifying of nuanced philosophical ideas, and inevitably there is a bit of slippage in projects like this. Walton (2013) himself wondered why phrasing about "explaining" was included in Cionea's scales about arguing. Explaining and arguing are quite different things to philosophers (e.g., Bex & Walton, 2016), but we felt that those nuances probably would not be registered by respondents. It even seemed possible that they might more immediately understand "explain" than "argue," given the widespread confusion about whether arguing is always a nasty explosive sort of interaction. In fact, the word "argue" and its relatives do not even appear in the items, even though argumentation is certainly what is being studied.

Furthermore, reflection suggested that a seventh "dialogue" be added, information-giving. This is not really a seventh dialogue, of course, but it seemed possible that some people might be very interested in receiving information but not in providing it. Precise measurement therefore seemed to require separate assessment of people's interest in information-seeking and information-giving. These additional measurements bearing on the information-seeking dialogue permit people to indicate, for example, that they encourage other arguers to share information with them but are not especially inclined to expose their own knowledge and commitments, or that they are happy to offer information but are not much interested in listening to any in return.

In the end, scales were developed to measure people's endorsement (approval) of each dialogue type (Cionea & Hample, 2014; Cionea et al., 2013). People read items representing some possible approach to dialogic arguing (e.g., "I weighed the options with the other person"), and indicate how much they agree with that orientation. The entire instrument for measuring the dialogue orientations is in the Appendix of this book.

The persuasion dialogue, as you remember, takes place when one arguer sets out to change the views of the other. Here, items include "I try to make a case for my position," and "I try to give the other person reasons for my position." The Dialogue goal is for the two participants to end up in agreement, so we also ask people to give their approval or disapproval to "I try to make sure the other person and I are on the same page." As in the scales for the other dialogues, our focus is on the individual goals but we try to make room for the Dialogue goals as well.

In negotiation, the two arguers bargain with one another. So we ask people to say if these are characteristic impulses: "I try to make a deal with the other person," and "I try to make concessions hoping the other person would make some concessions, too." Another item is "I try to make sure that what we both want is accomplished." This last item represents the Dialogue goal, to come to a mutual accommodation.

Information-seeking and information-giving are separately operationalized in the item set. To assess people's interest in receiving information, we use "I try to ask the other person for the whole story," and "I try to ask for more information from the other person." Information giving items are parallel: "I try to offer the other person the whole story," and "I try to let the other person know more information." The Dialogue goal is for the two arguers both to have possession of the relevant data. This idea is represented by "I try to make sure I know everything the other person knows," and "I try to make sure the other person knows everything I know."

Deliberation involves careful argumentation aimed at selecting the best available choice of future behavior. Here we invite people to say whether these ideas typify their arguing behavior: "I try to weigh the options with the other person," and "I try to work with the other person to solve the matter." The idea that "we" will jointly choose appears in several of the items, for instance, "I try to decide with the other person how we should proceed."

Inquiry is our closest approximation to pure philosophical dialectic. The arguers try to discover the truth, or at least to get as close as possible to it. They estimate the degree to which these things are typical of how they argue: "I try to find the truth," and "I try to establish the facts before concluding anything." Inquiry, too, has a joint Dialogue goal, finding the truth, that in this case is pretty close to the individual goals. The arguers commit to making sure that both of them argue well. So people indicate a judgment about "I try to make sure we don't make any mistakes when reasoning."

Finally, we offer items about inclinations toward eristic dialogue. We simplified this idea to omit the potential positive elements of eristic (e.g., cathartic release, playful competitive joking), and concentrated on the possibility of nasty ad hominem exchanges. We asked people to say how much these things were true of them: "I try to use words to attack the other person," and "I try to blame the other person." Even eristic dialogues involve some level of contact (hence cooperation) with the other arguer. Thus, one item states "I try to take the opposite position from the other person." This at least envisions that even eristic remarks are responsive to what the other person says.

These items were developed over several studies. They can be rephrased as the researcher needs. I have just given items that are worded to solicit people's general orientations to interpersonal arguing. To make more specific assessments about arguing with one's spouse, we might preface all the items with "When arguing with my romantic partner...." If we were asking about people's reflections on an argument they had just had, or perhaps one they had just seen recorded on a video, we can put the items in past tense and say things like, "I [or the person on the left] was trying...." These minor wording changes can be applied to all the instruments in the Appendix, by the way. Across several data collections and several minor rewordings, Cionea's dialogue scales have proved to be satisfactorily reliable.

Connecting Dialogue Preferences With Other Argumentation Measures

Although a major objective of this research program has always been to see how these dialogues appear within relationships, we needed to begin by understanding the constructs. One step was learning how to measure them. The second step was discovering how people's ownership or disavowal of the dialogue types connected to their other views about arguing. That is the work I will review in this section. The idea is that we will have a better empirical understanding of the dialogues if we can see how they connect to other matters that we know a lot about, such as argumentativeness or argument frames. The results I report in this section are from the data collections of the previous studies, but much of what I summarize here had to be recalculated from those data sets because the original papers were focused on different matters.

General Preferences for Dialogue Types. An initial question is whether people prefer one or two dialogue types to others. We would hope that the eristic dialogue would be recognized as least productive and so liked the least, but is there a preference for information sharing over persuasion? For negotiation over deliberation? To answer this question, I have collected the mean levels of endorsement from the same three studies that I will be concentrating on in this subsection of the chapter: Cionea and Hample (2014), Cionea et al. (2017) and Hample and Cionea (2016).

Table 6.1 reports the means from each study. You may want a little background on the samples in those studies. Therefore I have included some descriptive data about the respondents on the top of the table. This will be useful throughout the rest of the chapter.

Table 6.1: Mean Intentions to Use Argument Dialogue Types

Sample:	ugrad	adults	ugrad	ugrad
Relationship:	n/a	married	strangers	friends
N:	286	214	142	140
Mean Age:	19.7	45.5	20.7	19.7
% Males:	36	51	48	54
		Dialogue Means		
Persuasion	82.3	7.6	5.3	5.3
Negotiation	72.8	7.4	4.6	5.0
Info Seek	72.6	7.8	5.2	5.5
Info Give	76.9	7.9	5.4	5.5
Deliberation	74.3	7.7	5.2	5.2
Inquiry	73.3	7.5	5.3	5.6
Eristic	35.2	3.2	3.0	3.3

Note. Data from the first column is from Cionea and Hample (2014) and a magnitude scale was used. The second column is from Hample and Cionea (2016), using a 1–10 point scale. The last two columns are from Cionea et al. (2017), and a 1–7 point scale was used.

Comparing the means from column to column is inconvenient because different measuring scales were used in the studies (see the table's note). Furthermore, in the first two data columns people were reporting their general preferences, and in the last two, respondents were indicating how they intended to act in an argument they were about to have in the lab. But it is useful to inspect each column on its own. Generally, the six productive dialogues seemed to be about equally preferred. These include persuasion, negotiation, information seeking, information giving, deliberation, and inquiry. The only truly striking difference is for eristic, which was always and distinctly the least preferred.

The results in Table 6.1 indicate that people were pretty approving of the productive dialogues. On a scale with a maximum value of 10 (column two), their preferences were close to 8. On a 1–7 scale (the last two columns), they were also well above the midpoint of the scale, 4. Eristic dialogue seemed to be commonly recognized as undesirable, with mean endorsements below the scales' midpoints.

Argumentativeness and Verbal Aggressiveness. Argumentativeness is the inclination to present a controversial claim or to attack the other person's case, evidence, or reasons (Infante & Rancer, 1982). Verbal aggressiveness is the predisposition to attack the other person, particularly his or her character, habits, background, and so forth (Infante & Wigley, 1986). Both measures have subscales (argument-approach and argument-avoid; verbal aggressiveness-antisocial and verbal aggressiveness-prosocial). For decades one of the subscales has been subtracted from the other one to get a single summary score, but now the better procedure is to report the subscale scores separately (Hample, 2017; Chapter 7 will make it clear why this is preferable).

Here we want to know if argumentativeness and/or verbal aggressiveness are associated with any of the dialogue preferences. Several of the studies collected relevant data (Cionea & Hample, 2014; Cionea et al., 2017; Hample & Cionea, 2016) but for the most part the particular results I am giving here were not reported in those papers, so I have recalculated things for this book.

Table 6.2 shows the correlations between people's preferences for each dialogue type and their self-reports of their predispositions toward argumentative and verbally aggressive behavior. The table, like the others in this section, reports analyses from three studies combined (Cionea & Hample, 2014; Cionea et al., 2017; Hample & Cionea, 2016) and the total sample is 782. Virtually all the correlations in Table 6.2 are statistically significant, but with a sample so large that is not really a special accomplishment. Instead of worrying about statistical significance, we need to read the table for the *size* of the correlations. Here is some interpretive advice. Correlations below |.10| should be regarded as constructive evidence for a *zero relationship* (because of the large sample). Correlations in the teens are pretty much *uninteresting* until they begin to approach |.20|. Correlations in the .20's are *noticeable*; those in the .30s are *substantial*; and those in the .40s or higher are *very strong*. These interpretations are advice, not standard rules.

Table 6.2: Correlations Among Dialogue Types, Argumentativeness, and Verbal Aggressiveness

	Arg-Approach	Arg-Avoid	VA-Prosocial	VA-Antisocial
Persuasion	.19	−.08	.09	.05
Negotiation	−.05	.19	.31	−.13
Info-Seek	.04	.06	.26	−.12
Info-Give	.05	.09	.28	−.11
Deliberative	.08	.04	.35	−.17
Inquiry	.19	−.03	.21	−.05
Eristic	.29	−.03	−.25	.50

Note. Sample size is 782. Data are from Cionea and Hample (2014), Cionea et al. (2017) and Hample and Cionea (2016).

Are dialogue preferences related to argumentativeness and verbal aggressiveness? Inspection of the table shows that by far the best predicted dialogue preference was for eristic. The two aggressive subscales, approach and antisocial, were directly related to eristic orientation and the two relatively avoidant subscales were negatively associated with it. Negotiation was somewhat associated with argument avoidance and prosociality, implying that perhaps people regard bargaining as a way out of actually confronting the other person's detailed position. As a matter of fact, a key thing to notice is the prosocial column. Prosociality basically means being nice during arguments (e.g., "I try very hard to avoid having other people feel bad about themselves when I try to influence them"). Prosociality was clearly associated with all the dialogue preferences except persuasion, with positive connections to the productive dialogues and a negative correlation with eristic orientations. The strongest associations between dialogue preferences and these measures of arguing motivation were for prosociality and eristic orientation. Preference for persuasion dialogues, which Walton felt are the prototype for argument dialogues, was not especially related to different kinds of argument motives. That might mean that persuasion is equally relevant and available to anyone, regardless of their motivational orientation toward arguing.

While the results for argumentativeness and verbal aggressiveness are somewhat uneven, we do learn some interesting things from Table 6.2. Eristic dialogue preferences were strongly predicted by these very basic arguing motives, and persuasion was almost completely unrelated to them. The most potent motive was prosociality, which strongly aimed people at productive dialogues and away from the corrosive one. Table 6.2 helps us pass conceptually between the domains of personal goals (e.g., being antisocial) and Dialectical ones (e.g., verbal fighting).

Argument Frames. Results from the study of argumentativeness and verbal aggressiveness were mostly informative about prosociality and eristic. We can continue learning about how dialogue preferences fit into people's general understandings of interpersonal arguing by comparing dialogue endorsement with scores on argument frames instruments (see Chapter 2; the frames measures are also in the Appendix).

The frames, you may remember, contain people's basic goals for arguing, their understandings of the social relationships arguers can have, and their general sophistication about arguing. The goals include utility, projecting a desired personal identity, asserting dominance, and arguing for play. Social relations are captured by measures of blurting, cooperation, and civility. Professional contrast is the final subscale, and it indicates the level of people's sophistication about the abstract nature of interpersonal arguing. As in the last subsection, I will present correlations that combine data from Cionea and Hample (2014; Cionea et al., 2017) and Hample and Cionea (2016). However, Cionea and colleagues (2017) did not have data for two of the frames, cooperation and professional contrast, so the sample size for those frames' correlations is 500, not 782. But N = 500 is still large enough to make statistical significance routine, so again we will want to interpret the results mainly by reference to the correlations' magnitudes.

Table 6.3: Correlations Among Dialogues and Argument Frames

	Util	ID	Dom	Play	Blurt	Coop	Civil	ProfCon
Persuasion	.14	.19	.06	.08	.08	.18	.07	.15
Negotiation	.02	.00	−.18	−.14	−.10	.35	.13	.18
Info Seek	−.03	.06	−.18	−.08	−.07	.31	.11	.19
Info Give	.04	.05	−.11	−.09	−.07	.36	.07	.17
Deliberative	.06	.08	−.16	−.06	−.10	.40	.16	.21
Inquiry	.07	.21	−.06	.05	−.10	.29	.20	.17
Eristic	.28	.25	.42	.36	.41	−.21	−.22	−.10

Note. N for the cooperation and professional contrast correlations is 500, and is 782 for the other results. Data are from Cionea and Hample (2014), Cionea et al. (2017) and Hample and Cionea (2016).

Not much seems to be going on in Table 6.3, with two key exceptions. Most of the correlations were relatively minor, and at this sample size they should be pretty stable. The first exception is that preference for eristic dialogues was pretty well associated with the argument frames. All of the goals for arguing (utility, identity, and so forth) were positively associated with eristics, as was blurting. The positive social relations measures—cooperation, civility, and professional contrast—were all negatively related to eristic preference. Of the frames, cooperation was clearly the most important correlate of dialogue preferences, and this is the second constructive pattern in the table. The more cooperative a person thought interpersonal arguing was, the more he or she oriented to the productive dialogue types and the less attractive was an eristic experience. Professional contrast and civility showed patterns similar to cooperation, but not as strongly. The primary reasons for arguing (the four goals) did not distinguish which sort of dialogue a person preferred, except for eristic. A minor exception to this last statement is that persuasion dialogues were somewhat associated with interest in utility or identity-displaying reasons for arguing.

Still, the cooperation (and other positive social measures) results here are consistent with the prosocial results we saw in Table 6.2. The dialogue types that have the greatest potential for positive personal and subject matter outcomes were predicted by prosocial and cooperative orientations to interpersonal arguing. The eristic dialogue was mainly associated with aggressive, nasty motives (Table 6.2) and strong self-oriented goal commitments (Table 6.3). Though many of the results in these two tables are negligible, what does come through is consistent and sensible.

Correlations Among the Dialogue Types. The final thing I'd like to share here as fundamental information about how people see these dialogue types is how the dialogues associate with one another. In the first part of the chapter we reviewed Walton's explanations of why the dialogues are distinct, but I also mentioned that I've had trouble getting students to see all of the differences clearly. It seems more than possible that the respondents in our studies were not making stark distinctions, either.

I should mention that the dialogue types and their contributing items (the ones listed in the Appendix) have been tested with an advanced statistical procedure called confirmatory factor analysis (Cionea, 2012; Cionea & Hample, 2014). You read one example of this sort of statistical analysis in Chapter 4, where the measurement model for the serial argument variables across several studies was evaluated. The favorable results of these analyses on the dialogue scales indicate that the item groups themselves are statistically distinct. So our question here has to do with how ordinary people see things, not with whether or not the scales are statistically distinguishable.

Table 6.4 presents the correlations among the dialogue types, combining data from the three studies I have been using throughout this part of the chapter. Total N size is 782, so we will again be ignoring statistical significance and concentrating on the size of the correlation coefficients.

Table 6.4: Correlations Among the Dialogue Types

	Pers	Negot	I-Seek	I-Give	Delib	Inquiry
Negotiation	.37					
Info Seek	.45	.51				
Info Give	.44	.43	.57			
Deliberative	.48	.61	.66	.56		
Inquiry	.47	.48	.61	.56	.66	
Eristic	.12	−.06	−.01	−.01	−.10	−.00

Note. N = 782.

The most striking thing about Table 6.4 is the very high correlations among the productive dialogue types. All of them were quite substantially associated with one another. This suggests that perhaps people simply set out to be constructive in their arguments, and are willing to follow the dialogues wherever they go—to persuasion, to negotiation, to information exchange, to deliberation, or to inquiry. All the productive dialogue intentions have a persuasive flavor, they all share some orientation to inquiry, and so forth.

One of those correlations is particularly interesting, the one between information seeking and information giving (r = .57). This means that seeking and giving were symmetrical. If a lot of people wanted to receive information but not to share it, or if a lot of people wanted to convey information but didn't want to listen to any in return, that correlation would have been near zero or maybe even negative. The high positive correlation coefficient means that these dialogue types seemed to be a balanced information party, with both people seeking, sharing, and listening.

Of course, the line reporting the correlations with eristic dialogue is intriguing. Eristic intentions were essentially unrelated to preference for any of the productive dialogues. As we've noticed before, eristic is pretty unique in this set of measures and its results are often set off from all the others. One worry throughout dialogue theory, whether philosophical or empirical, is that the good dialogues can degenerate into eristic exchanges. This certainly happens, but the near-zero correlations in Table 6.4 means that eristics were not particularly associated with any of the other dialogue activities. For example, if persuasion were the one particularly vulnerable to derailing into ad hominem attacks, we would have seen a large positive association between persuasion and eristic rather than the negligible r = .12 in the table. Or if inquiry were well insulated against nastiness, we would have seen a substantial negative correlation. None of that sort of thing is apparent in the table.

Eristic derailing was not associated with any of the other kinds of interpersonal arguing, for good or ill.

Summary. The point of this part of the chapter has been to enlarge our understanding of the dialogue types. By reviewing the philosophical work and the research on scale construction, you should have gotten a general idea of what was *intended* by the scholars studying the dialogue types. But in this portion of the chapter, we also began to see how the dialogues are put into use by regular people. What kinds of distinctions do they make, what do they think the different dialogues actually mean, and how do their intentions to do one dialogue type or another connect with other predispositions they have about arguing?

We saw that people preferred the productive dialogues over eristic, which is what the philosophers would recommend. However, we did not see any real preference distinctions among the productive dialogues. People basically seemed to be distinguishing between eristic encounters and the other kinds. We did not see much evidence of people being able to say that deliberative and persuasive experiences are very different, for example. The correlations among the dialogue preferences told the same story: the dialogues basically ended up being in two groups, eristic and all the others.

When we compared dialogue preferences to the arguing frames, we only got a little insight. The cooperative frame was pretty important in predicting which dialogue people would rather experience, but the other frames were unhelpful. Even though we saw in Chapter 2 that the argument frames are fairly informative about the personal experience of arguing, only the eristic dialogue was particularly associated with those basic understandings of face-to-face arguing.

The same sort of pattern, but with different variables, appeared when we compared dialogue intentions with argumentativeness and verbal aggressiveness. The main associations were with prosociality, the intention to be polite and nice during arguments. And again, eristic stood out as being the only dialogue to attract very substantial correlations. For eristic, however, we noticed a very positive correlation with willingness to be antisocial (being insulting, personally aggressive) during interpersonal arguments. This and the other results flesh out our understanding of how these dialogues might function in ordinary discourse, and prepare us to look at the place of dialogues in interpersonal relationships.

Couples and Their Dialogues

Finally, we are ready to approach the core of Cionea's ideas, namely her notion that relationships are meta-dialogues. That is, she proposed that dialogue structures are seated within relationship structures, such that a particular relationship might call out a particular pattern of argument dialogues. To study this, we need to examine *pairs* of people. Therefore, we collected data on married couples (Hample & Cionea, 2016) and undergraduates involved in friendship relationships (Cionea et al., 2017). As a contrast group for the latter study, we also solicited data from undergraduates who were paired with strangers.

The basic statistical hypothesis is that we will see correlations between husband and wife or between friends. Anticipating that this might be so, we can imagine two reasons for it. One is that over time the partners *teach* each other how to argue. As a 30-year marriage or a one-year friendship moves along, the partners learn how best to argue with one another. The other main possibility is that people *select* their partners based in part on how they argue. Every involving relationship has conflicts, and the relationships that survive have navigated those disagreements successfully. In the beginning of a relationship, the two people size up one another in a number of respects. One of those might be whether the other person disagrees or responds to disagreement in the same way you do. A technical term for the selection hypothesis is assortative mating.

Because we asked people how long they had been married, we can do a test of whether any observed associations between spouses were due to teaching or selecting. Teaching takes time, so if that is what is going on, we should see the partners moving together more as they spend more time in the relationship. A longitudinal study would really be required to get precise information, but even in a cross-sectional study like these, we can see whether we get the same level of associations from people in the early months or years of their marriage, compared to people who have been together longer.

The key information is in Table 6.5. We correlated the dialogue preferences of one spouse/friend to the preferences of the other. For the married couples, they each filled out a survey on which they indicated their general orientations to arguing *with their spouse* (Hample & Cionea, 2016). For the friends, they were scheduled to have an argument with one another in the laboratory and reported how they intended to act during it. The strangers, included as a kind of no-relationship baseline, also had an argument scheduled in the lab, but they were assigned to argue with another undergraduate they didn't know beforehand (Cionea et al., 2017).

Table 6.5: Correlations of Dialogue Preferences From One Partner to the Other.

	Strangers	Friends	Spouses
Persuasion	.02	−.18	.02
Negotiation	−.00	.21	.27**
Info Seek	−.02	.06	.03
Info Give	.08	−.13	.08
Deliberative	.09	.03	.19
Inquiry	.08	.04	.29**
Eristic	−.01	.18	.44***

Note. Data are from Cionea et al. (2017) and Hample and Cionea (2016).
** $p < .01$; *** $p < .001$.

Table 6.5 shows essentially zero relationship between strangers' dialogue preferences. This is a baseline result, and shows that people who don't know one another do not, by accident or shared culture, prefer the same dialogues. It is actually a little bit interesting that there were no local or national norms that inclined people toward one dialogue type or another, or that (at least in this sample of undergraduate strangers) there was no cultural prohibition of eristic exchanges. Just as interestingly, the undergraduate friends did not show statistically significant associations with one another either, although a couple of the correlations (for negotiation and eristic) were getting close to $p < .05$, the usual standard for statistical significance.

Only with the married couples did we find clear connections. Spouses matched one another in their preferences for negotiation, inquiry, and eristic. All of these correlations were positive, which means that both of the partners synchronously either liked or disliked the same dialogues. (A negative correlation might have meant, for example, that husbands loved to persuade but the wives hated it. We didn't find anything like that.) The high correlation for the eristic dialogue is interesting. It means that both spouses either enjoyed eristic or that both of them assiduously avoided it. So marriages either tended toward high-energy fighting or careful mutual restraint. Either way, the spouses matched.

We collected data on the length of the marriages. When we took that information into account with partial correlations (which essentially produce correlations that control for, or nullify, the effects of length of marriage), we got essentially the same results as in Table 6.5. The partial correlation for the deliberative dialogue rose slightly to .20, and that became statistically significant ($p < .05$). The previously significant correlations for negotiation, inquiry, and eristic remained essentially identical (the correlation coefficients differed by .01, if at all), with the same significance levels. Length of relationship didn't really affect the degree to which spouses had synchronous dialogue orientations.

What Table 6.5 shows us is this. Among strangers, dialogue preferences did not match. Individual undergraduates had individual argumentative orientations, and these appeared more or less randomly within that sample. The correlations between these recent acquaintances were essentially zero. For undergraduate friendships, the correlations were still statistically non-significant. But when we compare their column to the strangers', we can see some small evidence of movement toward some sort of matching or compensating (the negative correlations for persuasion and information-giving would suggest that maybe one friend does the activity and the other doesn't, if the correlations were significant). Only when we arrive at the most involving and longest-lasting relationships did we see any real evidence that people matched on their dialogue preferences. There, for the spouses, we found significant positive correlations for several of the dialogue types.

For the married couples, the only ones who really displayed connections with one another on these measures, we have some evidence that the matches appeared because of *selection* and not *teaching*. If the shared dialogue preferences occurred because the spouses had taught one another what sort of arguing worked best in that marriage, we would have seen higher correlations for longer-married couples than for just-married ones (these long-term relationships varied from having existed for one year to 58 years, with an average of about 19 years). The partial correlations tested that possibility by taking length of marriage into account. Length of marriage made no difference in the level of associations in spouses' dialogue preferences.

I see two possible explanations for this. First, perhaps the teaching was very quick and was essentially complete before the marriage began, so that no more mutual instruction was needed during the course of the marriage. This seems extremely unlikely to me, because I have tried to teach all this to reasonably bright and attentive students without seeing dramatic shifts in their attitudes during the semester. And many marriages begin as friendships, and we saw no effects among the friends. Besides, surely the learning would have been initially imperfect and spouses would polish the dialogue agreements over the years. But that would have shown an effect for length of marriage, which we did not observe.

The second possibility is that people chose their mates partly based on how they conduct themselves during disagreements. Interestingly, the dialogues that showed spousal associations have particular symmetry features. Negotiation and inquiry are dialogues between equals, and both spouses agreed as to whether or not those are good ideas. Eristic is remarkably asymmetrical, with one partner being the aggressor and the other the intended victim. Spouses agreed on the goodness or badness of this idea, and given the means for eristic in Table 6.1, they were probably agreeing that it is a bad idea.

So we found evidence in marriages but not in friendships that the relationships made preferred space for certain sorts of argumentative dialogues. Although the evidence was not completely decisive, it pointed to the likelihood that people selected partners who are likely to support the kind of dialogue that they both want in the first place.

We have been reviewing results that indicate some of the dialogues were better received than others. People preferred the productive dialogues about equally, and clearly judged those to be better than eristic. If people are right about this—and I have no reason to disagree with them—then dialogue preferences might well predict relational satisfaction. Productive arguers should find a more congenial place in the meta-dialogue that is their relationship. Partners who prefer eristic might not be relationally welcome.

We collected data relevant to these possibilities for the spouses and the friends. We asked the married people to say how satisfying their relationship was. For the friends, we asked how much intimacy they felt was present in the friendship. (The strangers had no real relationship except for their shared laboratory experience, so we felt this was a silly question for them and did not ask it.) Using these as rough indications of how happy people were in their marriages or friendships, we can test whether dialogue preferences had anything to do with relational satisfaction. Table 6.6 has the relevant results.

Table 6.6: Correlations Between Dialogue Preferences and Relational Quality

	Friends	Spouses
Persuasion	.13	.19**
Negotiation	.16	.22***
Information Seeking	.10	.25***
Information Giving	.18*	.27***
Deliberation	.14	.34***
Inquiry	.07	.13
Eristic	.14	−.31***

Note. Data are from Cionea et al. (2017) and Hample and Cionea (2016).
*p < .05; ** p < .01; *** p < .001.

In the friendships, we see only a little bit of connection between intimacy and preferences about how to conduct an argumentative exchange. Only one dialogue, information giving, gave a significant correlation, and it was not very high. The sort of arguing behaviors reflected in the dialogue measures did not have much to do with how intimate these friendships were.

The story is different for the marriages. There, the productive dialogues were almost uniformly associated with greater relational satisfaction. The more the spouses intended to argue productively with one another, the happier they were in their marriages. Eristic intentions produced a substantial negative correlation. The greater the temptation to argue aggressively, personally, and nastily, the less satisfying the marriages were.

I think it is not a coincidence that the married people (compared to the other samples) were most likely to agree on how arguments ought to be conducted and that they were also the ones who connected arguing intentions with relational satisfaction. Of the relationships we studied, the marriages were the most involving, complex, intricate, and long-lasting. These were the relationships in which people were most committed and most cemented. Some college friendships are casual and evaporate when one person graduates or even just moves to another apartment. Friendships can also fly apart and dissolve far more easily than marriages can: a single bad conflict, a wrong glance at someone else's girlfriend, or a nasty remark about someone's appearance can end a college friendship, especially if it mainly existed for convenience. Not so a marriage, one hopes. Marriages ought to be more resilient than that.

Marriages, where we see the most strongly developed relational identities, are also the sites for the greatest dialogue coordination. The data I have summarized here clearly show that strangers' temporary connections did not constitute a meta-dialogue. We can see some tantalizing but non-significant hints that this began to happen in friendships. And marriages gave the most support to the idea that as a relationship structures itself, it includes preferred substructures for interpersonal arguing.

Summary

In this chapter, we have studied a relatively new idea in argumentation studies, namely dialogue types. Dialogues are argumentative exchanges, and there are several varieties of them. They are mainly distinguished by their goals. We have reviewed both the Dialogue goals and the individual arguers' goals within each sort of argumentative activity. Sharply distinct philosophically and statistically, the dialogue types did not seem to be especially separate for ordinary arguers. They clearly saw the difference between the productive dialogues and the eristic one, but they did not distinguish the productive ones from one another. Those were dialogues aimed at persuasion, negotiation, information seeking, information giving, deliberation, and inquiry. Eristic dialogue was the final type, and evidence indicated that people clearly understood that this was quite a different sort of arguing.

The central motivating idea for the research summarized here was that interpersonal relationships are meta-dialogues. Relationships are complex message structures, with commitment stores that can span decades. Within any developed relationship, the partners find themselves participating in many sorts of mutually constructed patterns. These can be patterns of affection, of task sharing, of financial responsibilities, and of arguing, among others. Arguing is necessary in a complex relationship because conflict is inevitable and the partners need to work things out in a way that preserves (and perhaps strengthens) the relationship. Relationships that cannot do this are unhappy and unstable. When we notice that two people are in a years-long relationship of some sort, a reasonable inference is that they have learned to argue in such a way as to settle disagreements without damage to their shared life.

By saying that a relationship is a meta-dialogue, Cionea meant that all the arguments contained in a relationship's history congeal into a way of arguing, or perhaps a couple of ways. We thought that dialogue types might well describe those ways of arguing, because all the dialogue types together seem to describe the main mutual activity goals that arguers can have.

We found evidence that people's preferences for dialogue types had some connection with their other views about arguing. We saw that argumentativeness and verbal aggressiveness predicted dialogue preferences to some degree. Mainly the prosocial scale of verbal aggressiveness and the eristic preference stood out as having key associations across the collection of argument motivations and dialogue preferences. We also examined the connections between dialogue preferences and argument frames. There, we learned that the cooperative frame was especially important in predicting the dialogue that people preferred. And again, we discovered that the eristic dialogue was distinctive in its predictability and in its pattern of associated variables.

When we finally turned to the examination of the place of dialogue preferences within ongoing relationships, we found some encouraging evidence bearing on the idea of meta-dialogues. Among strangers, where we never expected to see anything like a meta-dialogue, we found no real connections from one person to another. We also didn't see much when we compared one friend to another. But when we examined marriages, by far the most developed relationships on which we have data, we found that spouses do share mutual preferences and disinclinations for various dialogues. We also discovered that dialogue preferences were associated with relational satisfaction in marriages.

This research program is young, as you may have gathered. Only a few studies have been conducted to test and empirically evaluate the more considerable body of philosophical work. Results are generally encouraging, but the research needs to expand to cover more sorts of interpersonal relationship and to move into other cultures as well.

References

Bex, F., & Walton, D. (2016). Combining explanation and argumentation in dialogue. *Argument & Computation, 7*, 55–68.

Cionea, I. A. (2011). Dialogue and interpersonal communication: How informal logic can enhance our understanding of the dynamics of close relationships. *Cogency, 3*, 93–105.

Cionea, I. A. (2012). *A dual perspective on the mangement of relational transgressions in romantic relationships* (Unpublished dissertation). University of Maryland, College Park, MD.

Cionea, I. A., & Hample, D. (2014). Dialogue types and argumentative behaviors. In B. J. Garssen, D. Godden, G. Mitchell, & A. F. Snoeck Henkemans (Eds.), *Proceedings of the 8th international conference of the International Society for the Study of Argumentation* (pp. 245–256). Amsterdam: Sic Sat.

Cionea, I. A., Hample, D., & Fink, E. L. (2013). Dialogue types: A scale development study. In D. Mohammed & M. Lewiński (Eds.), *Virtues of argumentation: Proceedings of the 10th international conference of the Ontario Society for the Study of Argumentation (OSSA)* (pp. 1–11). Windsor, ON: OSSA.

Cionea, I. A., Hample, D., Mumpower, S. W., Bostwick, E., Piercy, C., & Foutch, C. (2017, June). *Argumentation traits, frames, and dialogue orientations*. Paper presented at the European Conference on Argumentation, Fribourg, Switzerland.

Cronen, V. E., Pearce, W. B., & Snavely, L. M. (1979). A theory of rule-structure and types of episodes and a study of perceived enmeshment in undesired repetitive patterns ("URPs"). *Communication Yearbook, 3*, 225–240.

van Eemeren, F. H., Garssen, B., Krabbe, E. C. W., Snoeck Henkemans, A. F., Verheij, B., & Wagemans, J. H. M. (2014). *Handbook of argumentation theory*. Dordrecht: Springer.

Gilbert, M. A. (2014). *Arguing with people*. Peterborough, ON: Broadview Press.

Hamblin, C. L. (1970). *Fallacies*. London: Methuen.

Hample, D. (2017, July). *Argumentativeness and verbal aggressiveness are two things apiece*. Paper presented at the biennial NCA/AFA Argumentation Conference, Alta, UT.

Hample, D., & Cionea, I. A. (2016). *Couples' dialogue orientations*. In P. Bondy & L. Benacquista (Eds.), *Argumentation, objectivity, and bias: Proceedings of the 11th international conference of the Ontario Society for the Study of Argumentation (OSSA), 18–21 May 2016* (pp. 1–13). Windsor, ON: OSSA.

Infante, D. A., & Rancer, A. S. (1982). A conceptualization and measure of argumentativeness. *Journal of Personality Assessment, 46*, 72–80.

Infante, D. A., & Wigley, C. J. (1986). Verbal aggressiveness: An interpersonal model and measure. *Communication Monographs, 53*, 61–69.
Macagno, F. (2008). Dialectical relevance and dialogical context in Walton's pragmatic theory. *Informal Logic, 28*, 102–128.
Reed, C., & Tindale, C. W. (Eds.). (2010). *Dialectics, dialogue and argumentation: An examination of Douglas Walton's theories of reasoning and argument.* London: College Publications.
Robinson, R. (1953). *Plato's earlier dialectic.* Oxford: Oxford University Press.
Walton, D. (1998). *The new dialectic: Conversational contexts of argument.* Toronto: University of Toronto Press.
Walton, D. (2013). Commentary on: Ioana Cionea, Dale Hample, and Edward Fink's "Dialogue types: A scale development study." In D. Mohammed & M. Lewiński (Eds.), *Virtues of argumentation: Proceedings of the 10th international conference of the Ontario Society for the Study of Argumentation (OSSA)* (pp. 1–4). Windsor, ON: OSSA.
Walton, D. N., & Krabbe, E. C. W. (1995). *Commitment in dialogue: Basic concepts of interpersonal reasoning.* Albany, NY: State University of New York Press.

CHAPTER SEVEN

Arguing and Culture

For various historical reasons, modern argumentation studies have been mainly a North American discipline, although this has lessened in the last several decades. Being place-bound has been partly because rhetoric and communication were more commonly studied in American university departments than in other parts of the world, and partly because a particular philosophical approach, informal logic, happened to develop in Canada. Another distinctive modern theory, pragma-dialectics, appeared in the Netherlands at about the same time informal logic was born, but pragma-dialectics was largely restricted to one university for several years and has only flowered globally in the last quarter century. In the final decades of the 20th century, however, argumentation's merit and value became apparent throughout the world. Today, we have standing conferences in Tokyo, Amsterdam, Venice, and Santiago; a movable conference in Europe; and North American conferences in Ontario, Canada and Alta, Utah. These are all meetings dedicated just to argumentation. Other global conferences in communication, rhetoric, linguistics, philosophy, and artificial intelligence also make some room for argumentation studies. All of these meetings have substantial representation of scholars from various parts of the world, not just the host country. Programs that award a Ph.D. in argumentation have recently been started in Canada and Switzerland, and Portugal, Switzerland, and Poland all have special concentrations of argumentation scholars to go along with those in Canada and the Netherlands. Argumentation has clearly become an international topic of investigation.

The sort of interpersonal approach to argumentation that this book expresses, however, stubbornly remained American until the last decade or two (I have written a history of the U.S. developments, if you're interested: Hample, 2016). The theories and measurement scales that dominate this book were almost all developed in the U.S., and the interesting results nearly all came from American respondents (usually university undergraduates, a problem all by itself: Henrich, Heine, & Norenzayan, 2010). North America is not like other parts of the world in many obvious ways: not everyone prefers our sort of government; some resist our large-scale corporations, agriculture, and finance industry; other nations have starkly different religious affiliations or none at all; romantic and other personal relationships involve different expectations and roles; higher education is not a realistic expectation in many nations; families are structured in other ways; freedom of speech is encouraged to different degrees; and many other differences. Even though the last two generations have seen globalization, McDonaldization, and a world shrunk by trade, travel, and the Internet, nations and places are still very different from one another. It is more than reasonable to wonder whether American interpersonal argumentation theories apply at all or to what degree to arguing elsewhere in the world. That is the question this chapter pursues.

To explore it, we first need to discuss what a culture is. Then we will examine the somewhat limited amount of material that describes arguing throughout the world. The various ideas that have been discussed in this book—argumentativeness, argument frames, and so forth—will be used to compare various cultures to one another. Because the U.S. is solidly at the base of all this academic research, I will often use the U.S. as a calibrating point to help organize the comparisons.

Culture

"Culture" is one of the more important words in modern social science. Perhaps because of its acknowledged importance to social life, it is sometimes used a little loosely or defined a little bit too conveniently just to suit the writer's purposes. Thus we commonly see references to things like "the Chinese culture," "the war between men's and women's cultures," "the cultural divide," "progressive and alt-right cultures," "the two cultures," "the culture wars," and many other things that readers may well have views about. Some of these uses come fairly close to a technically defensible use of the word "culture" but others are rhetorical flourishes, used mainly so that the writer can expound energetically on some difference that he or she thinks is important.

Definitions and approaches vary to a noticeable degree even within standard academic literature, so perhaps we should not be too hard on people who may be using "culture" as some sort of metaphor for any discernible experience or outlook shared by some group of people. I can make sense of writing that contrasts "a football culture" with "a baseball culture" or "a mathlete culture" even if I don't think that these distinct social experiences rise to the level of "culture." But we should probably have a clear basis for thinking about culture if we are going to try to connect arguing to it, as this chapter intends to do.

I think that there is really one general idea of culture but two different academic approaches to studying it. The general idea is the one developed in the early and continuing study of anthropology. Kroeber and Kluckhohn (1952) undertook an elaborate survey and critique of various definitions of culture, and found that a fundamental idea was "patterns." When a human group's social life displayed a pattern that was distinguishable from those in other groups, one could begin to build a case for that pattern being an element of the group's culture. A culture might even be thought about as a collection of these patterned behaviors and values. If one could exclude biological or physical environmental causes (e.g., persistent drought) for the pattern, one's argument that the pattern was "cultural" would be strengthened. So early anthropologists comparing a particular social group to some implicit European standard could see different kinship systems, different cooking practices, different male and female roles, different religious rituals, and many other things. But when studying a culture empirically, actual culture is too abstract to see directly. One can mainly see the people (nicely concrete and observable people) performing the pattern.

After discussion of many definitions and descriptions, Kroeber and Kluckhohn tried to pull things together. This is from their conclusions about the various ideas they found in early anthropological and sociological research:

> Culture is not a mystical "force" acting at a distance. *Concretely*, it is created by individual organisms and by organisms operating as a group. It is internalized in individuals and also becomes part of their environment through the medium of other individuals and of cultural products. Acts take place: (a) in time between persons, (b) in space in an environment partly made up of other persons. But because acts take place in time the past continues to influence the present. The history of each group leaves its precipitate—conveniently and, by now, traditionally called "culture"—which is present in persons, shaping their perceptions of events, other persons, and the environing situation in ways not wholly determined by biology and by environmental press. Culture is an intervening variable between "organism" and "environment." (Kroeber & Kluckhohn, 1952, p. 186; italics original)

In this general statement, we see indications of what has developed into the two main approaches to culture in the communication literature.

One of these has to do with the "precipitate." These are the practices that solidify and clarify through the decades and centuries. A group's language, its religion, its priorities among basic values, its preferences for government and economics, its laws and customs, its art and music, its system of family duties and affordances—all these and more constitute a persistent social system. This is the group's history, the elements of social life that the group enacts, endorses, and transmits to new generations. It is as though the social system has slots that people can fill, so that if someone wants to be a musician, he or she will compose that particular sort of music, or if someone has the ambition to acquire many possessions, he or she will gather these particular properties using these particular methods. Families are also formed according to the precipitated instructions. Perhaps arguments are conducted in a prescribed way as well: With whom is one allowed to disagree? How should disagreement be conveyed, if at all? Does one plead a case at law, or quietly submit oneself to an elder for judgment?

The second sort of investigation concerns "internalized" culture. As the quotation indicates, culture is imported into the humans who inherit it, and therefore they become the organisms that perform, reenact, and recreate it. According to this point of view, externally observable cultural patterns appear because of the people's internal impulses and shapings. You can't speak Japanese without having it in your head, you can't approach a person to marry you without knowing how it is done, and you can't enjoy Italian opera without having learned how to listen to it. So from this point of view, a researcher would investigate what values different persons held, how they believed people should act toward one another, how they understood various social episodes, and similar things. Culture exists to the degree that it is expressed within individuals. This seems relevant to arguing as well: What is your personal threshold for speaking up or remaining silent? How deferential should you be to a higher executive as opposed to a subordinate? Do you think it is disrespectful to object to another person's reasons?

In contemporary scholarship, both approaches appear. The "precipitate" is investigated by people who identify and then study particular cultures (e.g., Israeli culture by Katriel, 1986, or Columbian culture by Fitch, 1998). The "internalized" approach is carried out by those who are interested in the degree to which people are individualistic or collectivistic, competitive or harmonious, face-saving or face-threatening, and to what degree (e.g., Cai & Fink, 2002; Ting-Toomey, 2005). Several years ago, one of our journals invited proponents of the two orientations to write about them side-by-side, and two nice essays resulted, by Philipsen (2010) and Ting-Toomey (2010). Philipsen showed how someone might try to figure out the speech code being used in a particular culture, and Ting-Toomey discussed why one might want to explore the culture-relevant value dimensions (e.g., individualism-collectivism) that are internalized by individuals.

These two academic orientations are not contradictory. Those who study a particular culture, say Schiffrin's (1984) Jewish community in Philadelphia, end up investigating what the particular people think and do. Those who wonder how individualized values affect interaction (e.g., how the acceptance of power distance affects organizational expressiveness; Farh, Hackett, & Liang, 2007) need to find some place where the value might be expected to assert itself in an interesting way (China, in the Farh et al. example). Readers certainly find a difference in emphasis in these sorts of investigations. Schiffrin found that urban Jews' religious traditions encouraged an interesting pattern of arguing behavior, whereas Farh and colleagues discovered that people with more tolerance of status inequality believed that their employer was more supportive of them. One conclusion is about the group and its precipitate (Jews in Philadelphia, with their religious traditions) and the other conclusion is about how one internal variable affects another (power distance and its correlation with perceived organizational support). But the two approaches clearly speak to each another, if one cares to listen. So it seems to be mainly a matter of focus, rather than one research ideology ruling the other one out.

A few more points—warnings, really—need to be made at the beginning of this chapter. The first is that nations are not cultures. The development of intergroup studies (e.g., Lewin, 1935; Tajfel, 1982; Tajfel & Turner, 1986) has made it obvious that many distinctive groups live within one larger collective, and that diplomatic boundary lines on a map may not be decisive in this respect. In the U.S., for example, we study groups such as African-Americans, LGBTQ people, Catholics, seniors, farmers, and so forth, and often notice how their personal identities can be tied up in those group affiliations. Some of these identities might be different if the Americans moved to Ireland, but others would be unchanged. Malaysia and India also have distinctive religious and linguistic groups, as do other nations. Almost a third of all people living in China do not speak Mandarin, for example (Beijing, 2013). In fact, it is hard to think of an homogenous nation, even historically. Nonetheless, nations are often used as convenient proxies in the study of cultures. There are, after all, lots and lots of Chinese people in China, so that's a good place to look for the effects and expressions of Chinese culture(s). But we need to remember that China is not homogenous and that what we are describing as Chinese culture may very well be present elsewhere in the world, and perhaps not everywhere in China.

The second main warning is that people have many traits, many values, and many patterns of action, thought, and feeling. No researcher looks at more than a handful at once. To say that French and Malaysian people differ on some measure is a pretty limited statement about the possible differences and commonalities of French and Malaysian culture. So we should be wary of the temptation to say that people in one nation are radically different (or similar) compared to people in another part of the world just because we found that they have different (or similar) argument frames or something else as specific as that.

Mapping the Globe: Initial Considerations

For the past few years I have collaborated with a number of scholars throughout the world to gather information about interpersonal arguing in their home countries. Our idea has been to map the world on some basic measures that are important in our theories of face-to-face arguing. We certainly are not close to a complete map, but in this chapter you will read about our studies in the U.S., Chile, Portugal, France, the Netherlands, the United Arab Emirates, India, China, and Malaysia.

In spite of the considerable amount of work we've done, we aren't in a position to offer any generalizations about groups of countries—not about Europe, not about nations that speak Romance languages, not about East Asia. But we are able to give some initial ideas about how much variability seems to exist throughout the world, and this in turn offers an initial estimate of the degree to which American theories and findings can be expected to cross national boundaries. I will say right here that our results indicate that no one should assume that an American finding, no matter how basic, applies elsewhere in the world. We found many small discrepancies from U.S. results, and several very fundamental ones. At this point, I am inclined to say that every nation needs its own description, and perhaps even its own theory, of interpersonal arguing.

At any rate, we conducted very similar studies in all those countries. In several (U.S. and India) we collected data in English, in others all the instruments were translated (Chile, Portugal, Netherlands, France, and China), and in several we offered respondents a choice between English or a local language (United Arab Emirates and Malaysia). Some samples were university students (U.S., Chile, and China) and others were non-university adults or mixtures of students and adults (U.S., Portugal, France, Malaysia, and India). We collected data on the same set of instruments in every nation, although a few scales are missing here and there in the earliest studies because the U.S. scales hadn't been finalized at that point.

You have been reading about those scales throughout this book, but perhaps a brief review would still be in order. The instruments were argumentativeness, verbal aggressiveness, argument frames, and conflict personalization.

We selected argumentativeness (Infante & Rancer, 1982) and verbal aggressiveness (Infante & Wigley, 1986) because we felt that these two instruments gave basic information about *motivations for arguing*. Argumentativeness is the impulse to attack the other person's case, evidence, and reasons, or to offer a controversial case of your own. It has two subscales, argument approach and argument avoid. In the U.S. these have always been understood as opposites, so that avoid could be subtracted from approach to give an overall argumentativeness score. That doesn't work elsewhere in the world as you will soon see, so we will be reporting approach and avoid scores separately. Verbal aggressiveness is the impulse to attack the other arguer's character, background, personal characteristics, or personal history. In other words, verbal aggressiveness is the motivation to engage in ad hominem attacks. Verbal aggressiveness also has two subscales, prosocial (the motivation to be polite and considerate while disagreeing) and antisocial (the motivation to initiate personal attacks). These, too, are opposites in U.S. theory and results, so that prosocial scores are normally subtracted from antisocial ones to give an overall verbal aggressiveness score. Similarly to argumentativeness, this doesn't work everywhere in the world so we will report these two scores separately as well. Argumentativeness and verbal aggressiveness are both kinds of interpersonal aggression (Rancer & Avtgis, 2014), but the targets of the aggression differ: high argumentatives attack the other arguer's argument, but high verbal aggressives attack the other arguer. These, we felt, were two fundamental arguing motivations and would be informative about various nations.

The argument frames instrument (see Chapter 2) is a collection of measures that we felt would describe nations' *understandings of the activity of interpersonal arguing* (Hample, 2005; the English scales are in the Appendix of the present book). The first four scales deal with a person's primary goals for arguing. These are utility (arguing to obtain or protect some benefit), identity display (arguing to show off some valued aspect of the arguer's self or identity), dominance display (arguing to show that one is superior or higher in status compared to the other person), and play (arguing for the entertainment of having a disagreement with the other person). The second set of frames concerns the degree to which the arguer respects and accounts for the other person. These are blurting (saying whatever one thinks without regard to how the other person will receive the remark), cooperation (arguing in a way that respects and supports the other person's immediate needs), and civility (arguing in a polite, considerate way). The last "set" of frames only has one instrument, which is designed to assess people's sophistication about interpersonal arguing. This measures how closely people agree with the judgments of North American and European argumentation scholars, and so is called professional contrast. A high score means that the respondents agree with the scholars. Altogether, the frames measures summarize people's basic understandings of interpersonal arguing—why someone might argue at all, how people value the other arguer, and general sophistication about the constructive affordances of interactive arguing.

Finally, we chose the taking conflict personally instrument (TCP) to get an estimate of people's *feelings about interpersonal arguing* (Hample & Dallinger, 1995; these scales are also in the Appendix). The TCP measure involves several subscales. The first is called direct personalization, and it indicates pretty straightforwardly whether or not people take conflicts personally. Stress reactions are the second scale, and these items allow people to say if conflicts result in psychological or physiological pressure, and how much. Persecution feelings refer to whether respondents think that the other arguers are "out to get them," perhaps picking fights just to do interpersonal damage. The next two subscales are a pair, positive and negative relational effects. These ask for estimates of how conflicts can affect ongoing interpersonal relationships. Finally, the TCP battery includes a measure of like/dislike valence, which asks whether people enjoy or dislike participating in conflicts. It is scored so that high scores indicate enjoyment of conflict. The positive and negative relational effects scores reflect cognitive expectations about conflict's effects, and the other subscales gather fundamental expectations about the emotional experience of arguing face to face.

We felt that this collection of instruments would give us basic information about motives for arguing, understandings of arguing, and reactions to arguing, from nation to nation. Certainly we could have chosen some other scales that would have provided parallel information of equivalent merit, and we hope that others will do so in the future. One thing that recommended all these instruments to us is that they have fairly extensive empirical records in the U.S. (Hample, 2005; Hample & Cionea, 2010; Rancer & Avtgis, 2014). We have very good information about the scales' reliability and internal associations in the U.S. A related consideration was that all that empirical literature documented many connections between these scales and other measures, and these associations offer a large number of clues about what to investigate next if something interesting is found. Each of these instruments originated in clear theoretical reasoning (at least it was all clear in the U.S. context), and so the results of individual studies connect back to basic understandings of human motivation, social perception, and emotional life.

As we move forward in this chapter, we will deal with two basic questions. The first is, how do different nations compare on their scores for these instruments? We will be examining average scores for each scale, and considering which nations have the highest and lowest values. As we do this, we will begin to notice some similarities between a few pairs or groups of countries. The second question is, do all nations have the same relationships among the measures? For instance, if certain nations have high scores on X, does that mean that they will all have high scores on Y, too? We will examine the correlations among the measures to see if the same associational patterns appear throughout the world. In dealing with both questions, we will start by looking at the U.S. results because those are the outcomes that have driven our theoretical understandings of these matters to this point.

I am fully aware that this chapter is no more than a progress report on what will need to be a much larger community project over many more years. More nations need to be surveyed, more groups within countries need to be distinguished, and more measurements need to be taken. Soon we will need to move away from the present reliance on self-report measures, and establish some internationally comparable way to observe actual behavior during face-to-face arguing. But at least we are beginning to build a foundation for these foreseeable improvements. Let us explore that platform.

Mean Differences: Nations High and Low

With all these basic ideas out of the way, let us look at the average scores of different nations on our instruments. We should have some reserve about this, especially about noticing small differences from one country to another. Some people read the items in English and some in translation; some samples were all undergraduates and others were not; people in some nations were obviously more comfortable responding to social science surveys than people in others; some people did the surveys online and others filled out papers. It is even possible that people in various nations use Likert scales differently (Harzing, 2006). But frankly, there is no way to equalize our methodologies on every relevant consideration since we are studying people *in different nations* to start with, and those national contexts supply some interpretive meaning to various details of any survey methodology. Samples and procedures are just going to be somewhat incomparable no matter what we do. So it lies with us to be conservative in our judgments and weightings of any one result, and to support the idea that anything interesting should be reinvestigated with triangulating methods in the future.

I will divide up the results by general topic. First we will examine the national averages for argumentativeness and verbal aggressiveness, to get an idea of the extent and direction of motivations. Then we will move to the argument frames results, and this should give us information about nation-to-nation understandings of the experience of interpersonal arguing. Finally we will examine the taking conflict personally results, thereby getting clues about how people in different nations react to the prospect of an argument. Most of the data reported in this chapter are from the same set of studies, so some of their key characteristics are listed in Table 7.1, for easy reference.

Table 7.1: Characteristics of the World Argumentation Studies

	N	Mean Age	Percent Female	Languages
US Undergrads	460	20.3	71	English
US mTurk	256	35.8	54	English
Chile	384	20.6	53	Spanish
China	235	–	63	Mandarin
Portugal	252	35.2	64	Portuguese
India	307	30.6	33	English
Malaysia	230	–	53	Malay/Eng
United Arab Emirates	156	24.1	78	Arabic/Eng
Netherlands	130	20.6	68	Dutch
France	223	39.3	61	French

Note. Age was not collected in the China study. In the Malaysia study it was collected in wide intervals: 50% were in the range 20–30 years, 29% were less than 20 years old, and the remainder were older than 30.
Sources. US Undergraduates: Hample and Irions (2015); US mTurk: Hample and Anagondahalli (2015); Chile: Santibáñez and Hample, 2015; Portugal: Hample, Lewiński, Saàágua, and Mohammed (2016); India: Hample and Anagondahalli (2015); Malaysia: Waheed and Hample, 2016; United Arab Emirates: Rapanta and Hample (2015); Netherlands: Labrie, Akkermans, and Hample (2017); France: Dufour and Hample (2017).

Argument Motivation

The argument motivation results are in Table 7.2. This displays national means on the four subscales. As is true of all the means reported in this chapter, data are on a 1–10 metric, which means that 5.5 is the theoretical neutral point. The nations are compared within each column to show what countries were especially high or low. (Remember the cautions about assuming that, say, a 6.40 score means the same thing in every nation.) As a variable, "nation" was statistically significant for each of the four dependent variables at $p < .001$.

Table 7.2: National Means for Argumentativeness and Verbal Aggressiveness

	Argument Approach	Argument Avoid	Verb Agg Prosocial	Verb Agg Antisocial
US Undergrads	5.76 b	5.77 e	6.36 b	4.58 e
US mTurk	5.27 a	5.71 e	6.60 b,c,d	3.77 b
Chile	6.56 d	3.74 a	6.42 b,c	3.91 b,c
China	5.91 b,c	5.31 d	7.38 e	4.14 c,d
Portugal	6.78 d	3.74 a	6.40 b,c	3.04 a
India	6.66 d	6.22 d	6.75 d	5.70 f
Malaysia	5.72 b	5.86 e	5.97 a	5.50 f
UAE	6.09 c	5.60 e	6.74 d	4.68 e
Netherlands	5.99 b,c	4.92 c	6.61 b,c,d	4.71 e
France	6.07 c	4.48 b	6.68 c,d	4.28 d

Note. The letters appended to each mean represent results from Duncan follow-up tests, and indicate homogenous subgroups at $p < .05$. Thus every nation sharing a letter *within a column* is statistically indistinguishable from other nations with that letter, on that variable. So for argument-approach, China, UAE, Netherlands, and France have comparable scores because they all share a "c."

First, consider argumentativeness, the first two columns. Looking mainly at the extreme results in Table 7.2 (the highest and lowest nations on each variable), we can see some interesting patterns. Nations that were most eager to enter into arguments (i.e., high on approach) were Chile, Portugal, and India. Countries with the highest avoidance scores were the U.S., Malaysia, and the U.A.E. Based on the original American understanding that approach and avoid are opposites, we would expect the high approach nations also to be the low avoid countries. This was actually true of Chile and Portugal, and India was close. But we would also expect the high avoid nations to be the low approach ones. This was only true for the U.S. mTurk sample and clearly not the case for the U.A.E. Based on the first two columns of Table 7.2, if we look for the patterns of high approach/low avoid and low approach/high avoid, we can tentatively conclude that the nations that found arguing most attractive were Chile and Portugal, and the most avoidant nations were the U.S. and maybe Malaysia. However, argument approach and avoid scores did not give precisely opposite results, and we will be returning to this issue later in the chapter.

Next let us examine the verbal aggressiveness results. The most prosocial (i.e., most polite, most considerate) nations were China, India, the U.S. (mTurk sample), the Netherlands, and France. The nations with the highest antisocial scores (those most willing to initiate ad hominem attacks) were India and Malaysia. However, although Malaysia was the least prosocial nation, India had the second highest prosocial score. The prosocial and antisocial subscores did not display precisely opposite results, as American theory would have supposed. Still, we can see that Malaysians tended to be pretty antisocial, compared to the other nations we studied.

Some cross-measure results justify a little reflection, too. The two subscales that most clearly assess aggressiveness are argument approach and the antisocial scale for verbal aggressiveness. True, the attack targets differ (other's case versus other's person), but in the U.S. we expect aggressiveness to predict aggressiveness. As we have noticed, the nations highest on argument approach were Chile, Portugal, and India. The nations highest on antisocial aggressiveness were India and Malaysia. Only India appeared on both lists. The more nonconfrontational subscales are argument avoid (U.S., Malaysia, and U.A.E.) and prosociality (Malaysia and India). Only one nation appeared on both of these lists. Again, we are seeing reason to be suspicious that U.S. understandings of interactive motivations should not automatically be projected onto other cultures.

These conclusions about particular nations need to be replicated with other instrumentation and should also be followed up with textured qualitative investigations before we depend very much on the results of just these few studies. For one thing, we would like to be confident that the observed patterns of results can be traced to something within these nations' broader cultures, perhaps their religious, communitarian, or linguistic backgrounds. However, one thing that is already apparent is that we found considerable variability from country to country. Travelers, businesspeople, diplomats, and people studying abroad should expect that those in other nations might well have different thresholds for when to argue and how aggressively to do it. The remarks in this paragraph apply to the rest of this section's results as well.

Argument Frames

Let us build on this general finding of variability by proceeding to Table 7.3. Here we see the national means on the argument frames instruments. These include people's recognition of particular motives for arguing (utility, identity, dominance, and play), their orientations to other arguers (blurting, cooperation, and civility), and their level of sophistication about the abstract nature of interpersonal arguing (professional contrast). The variable "nation" made a significant difference for each of the dependent variables at $p < .001$.

Table 7.3: National Means for Argument Frames

	Utility	Identity	Dominance	Play
US Undergrads	5.32 b	6.57 e	4.44 c,d	4.44 b,c
US mTurk	5.16 b	6.17 c,d	4.18 b,c	3.92 a
Chile	–	7.55 h	3.98 b	5.49 d
China	–	6.36 d,e	3.97 b	4.80 c
Portugal	5.14 b	6.90 f	3.92 b	5.52 d
India	6.59 d	6.95 f	6.13 e	6.07 e
Malaysia	6.27 c	7.21 g	4.75 d	6.33 e
UAE	5.09 b	5.79 b	4.12 b,c	4.33 b
Netherlands	5.37 b	5.93 b,c	4.42 c,d	5.50 d
France	4.39 a	5.22 a	2.95 a	4.10 a,b

	Blurting	Cooperation	Civility	Prof Contrast
US Undergrads	5.11 b,c	6.83 b,c	6.26 c	6.29 a
US mTurk	5.17 b,c	6.99 c,d	6.04 c	6.69 b,c
Chile	–	7.85 e,f	7.23 d	–
China	–	8.05 f	5.24 a	6.93 c,d
Portugal	4.20 a	7.76 e	7.82 e	8.09 e
India	6.42 d	7.13 d	5.70 b	6.91 c,d
Malaysia	5.41 c	6.88 b,c,d	6.18 c	7.23 d
UAE	5.03 b	6.76 b,c	5.72 b	6.51 a,b
Netherlands	5.01 b	6.60 b	6.06 c	6.89 c,d
France	4.27 a	5.57 a	8.12 f	7.05 c,d

Note. Utility data were not collected for Chile or China. Blurting data were not collected in Chile and China, and the professional contrast instrument was not used in Chile. See note to Table 7.2 for an explanation of the Duncan follow-up tests.

The argument goals are in the first part of Table 7.3. The most utilitarian nation was India, and the nation least likely to see interpersonal arguing as a way to get or protect resources was France. Using argumentation to promote or display some valued part of the arguer's identity was a possibility most apparent to people in Chile, Malaysia, India, and Portugal, and seemed most odd to the French. Dominance displays through the vehicle of arguing (e.g., picking a verbal fight just so the other person has to give in) was most familiar to Indians and least common in the worldviews of the French. The most playful nations were India and Malaysia, and the least were the U.S. (mTurk sample) and the French. This part of the table shows that there were quite different understandings of arguers' goal sets from nation to nation. The French appeared particularly deserving of some additional focused study, and India and Malaysia seemed to stand out a bit as well.

The other portion of Table 7.3 reports how arguers in different countries regarded their argument partners (or opponents?), and their levels of reflective awareness about the process of arguing in general. Blurting indicates a disinclination to take the other person into account at all, and the nations who said they blurt the most were India, Malaysia, and the U.S. The Portuguese and French were most careful about thinking before they speak. Cooperation was most evident to the Chinese and Chileans. The least cooperatively oriented nation was France. However, they also believed that their arguments were quite civil, because France had the highest civility score, followed closely by Portugal. Finally, the nation with the highest sophistication about interpersonal arguing as an abstract activity was Portugal. The least reflective sample was U.S. undergraduates. The French were particularly interesting in this portion of the table, too. They didn't report much blurting and they were quite civil, but they didn't claim to be very cooperative. Apparently the French believe that they are able to be competitive without any sacrifice of politeness. This bears investigation because it would be a valuable pattern of argumentation to learn, if we can confirm that it actually describes how the French disagree.

Personalizing Conflict

Finally, how do people in different nations react emotionally to interpersonal disagreements? Our data on this point concern taking conflict personally. The country means are in Table 7.4. "Nation" was a statistically significant factor in predicting all the personalization scores at $p < .001$. Readers should be alerted that the TCP scales were not adequately reliable in Malaysia, but the means are reported here anyway in the hopes that the random noise of messy measurement was self-cancelling enough that we might at least get some idea of where Malaysians rank on these measures (Waheed & Hample, 2016).

Table 7.4: National Means for Taking Conflict Personally

	Direct Personal	Stress Reaction	Persecution Feelings
US Undergrads	5.82 c	5.70 d,e	4.59 b
US mTurk	5.82 c	4.93 a	4.94 c,d
China	4.57 a	5.55 c,d,e	4.91 c,d
Portugal	4.78 a	5.24 a,b,c	4.15 a
India	5.98 c	5.75 e	6.08 f
Malaysia	5.85 c	5.09 a,b	5.65 e
UAE	5.15 b	5.59 c,d,e	5.16 d
Netherlands	5.36 b	5.32 b,c,d	4.66 b,c
France	5.73 c	5.85 e	3.91 a

	Positive Relationship	Negative Relationship	Positive Valence
US Undergrads	6.02 b,c	6.06 c	4.12 b
US mTurk	5.41 a	6.85 f	3.78 a
China	6.59 d	4.83 a	4.99 c,d
Portugal	5.11 a	6.78 f	5.28 d
India	6.12 c	6.59 e,f	5.01 c,d
Malaysia	5.79 b	6.05 c	5.03 c,d
UAE	6.04 b,c	6.19 c,d	4.69 c
Netherlands	5.99 b,c	5.67 b	5.24 d
France	5.17 a	6.46 d,e	5.04 d

Note. Taking Conflict Personally was not collected in Chile. See note to Table 7.2 for an explanation of the Duncan follow-up tests.

The first part of Table 7.4 presents results for direct personalization, stress reaction, and persecution feelings. These are so closely connected in U.S. research that they have sometimes been combined into a single index called "Core TCP." Direct personalization is the simplest report of whether people take interpersonal conflict personally. Nations who reported doing so the most were the U.S., India, Malaysia, and France. The countries that said they did it the least were China and Portugal. Stress due to conflict was said to be highest in the U.S. (undergraduates), China, India, the U.A.E., and France. It was a lesser problem in the U.S. (the mTurk sample), Portugal, and Malaysia. The sense that others are engaging in an argument in order to victimize you is captured by "persecution feelings." This reaction to conflict was most apparent in India and Malaysia.

The other portion of Table 7.4 gives reports on two cognitive estimates about conflict: whether it can improve or damage the relationship between the two arguers. This table also gives an overall evaluation of the experience of being in a conflict. The expectation that conflicts can have positive effects on relationships was most evident in China, although the U.S. (undergraduates), India, the U.A.E., and the Netherlands were also somewhat optimistic. The negative estimates were most pronounced in the U.S. (the mTurk sample), Portugal, and India. We might expect that results for positive and negative projections would be opposite, and there is some support for that in the table (China, Portugal). But why would we expect that? Isn't it possible that conflicts have the potential to both harm and help a relationship, or neither? The table gives some support for the appearance of those views as well (India, Netherlands). Finally, the table indicates an overall valence for being in conflicts. U.S. respondents reported noticeably low enjoyment for conflict interactions, whereas the Netherlands, France, China, India, and Malaysia had higher scores. Even those latter scores, however, did not rise to 5.5, the theoretical midpoint of the measurement scale.

There are a lot of details in Tables 7.2 to 7.4. It would be a nice exercise to try to connect a particular nation's scores on one or two variables to its scores on one or two others. There are so many possibilities for little essays like that, though, that it isn't feasible to undertake anything like that here. And as I have said before, it is too early to be certain about these scores down to their decimal points. However, I can indicate some general points of interest.

Most obviously, these nations differed with each other on every one of these measures. Some of the differences were more marked than others, and in every table you can find pairs or groups of nations with similar scores. But the same patterns did not persist through every table, at least in detail. The most general finding of all in this work was our discovery of variability. Even though readers should be clear by now that every human society uses interpersonal arguing to do important social business, different cultures do it differently, understand it differently, and have different reactions to it. This is not a small conclusion. Interpersonal arguments are not controlled only by their premise-to-conclusion relationships—they reflect their cultural environment as well. Face to face arguing displays how people reason, how they reason together, how they draw together or push apart, how they treat one another when they clash, and how they organize and conduct their inevitable disagreements.

Another point is the possibility of readers locating themselves in these tables. I suppose that most of my readers are U.S. undergraduates. You might enjoy noticing the divergences and commonalities between the undergraduate sample studied here and the mTurk sample of adults, who were about 15 years older. A decade and a half after you graduate you are pretty likely to have married, you might have children, and I hope you will be well started on your career and have a continuing job that you value more than any you have had to this point. Your personal identity will probably be much more settled than it is now, along with your relational and economic lives. Some of the data in these tables suggest that you are also likely to have different connections to interpersonal disagreement than you do now. (It is also statistically possible that we are seeing cadre effects such that the mTurk respondents were always very different sorts of people than the undergraduates, but my intuition is that the differences are due to more and different life experiences.) How, if at all, do you suppose you will be a different arguer in 15 years?

Finally, it might be interesting to reflect on why these theories and instruments happened to develop in the U.S. Social scientists tend to choose social problems as their research topics—the social problems that they immediately see in their own lives and communities. What about interpersonal arguing seemed to demand research attention to U.S. investigators? How might the world's research on face-to-face arguing have developed differently if it had originally begun in France or China? This chapter is going to give considerable evidence that the nature of interpersonal arguing differs from nation to nation, with the implication that scholars in other countries need to develop their own theories rather than assuming that U.S. work is going to apply with any precision. If those communities of scholars choose their own issues freely without allowing U.S. research to set the agenda, we may eventually have the challenge of trying to integrate theories and findings that are not entirely comparable in their assumptions.

Sex Differences

In conducting these studies we naturally collected basic demographic information about our respondents, such as their age and sex. We had no real research agenda for doing so. We mainly wanted to understand our samples better so that we could describe them. At a couple of points, this demographic data turned out to have substantive importance. For example, we divided our India sample by age to get a better understanding of whether generational differences affected our results (Hample & Anagondahalli, 2015). But the demographic variable that began to assert itself most urgently was sex of respondent.

Sex differences on these argumentation measures have been consistent in the U.S., and have frankly become uninteresting because of their predictability. American men in study after study showed themselves to be more aggressive, less perceptive, and blunter than American women. Female respondents, in contrast, were more empathetic, more nurturing, and more perceptive about interpersonal life than men. So men have been more argumentative and verbally aggressive, more motivated to argue for any of the four argument frames goals, less cooperative and civil, less stressed about conflict, and so forth. These are consistent empirical results, but as I say, they became boring to many of us a long time ago. Men are pushy and aggressive; women are polite and aware; and the sexes act and think that way in arguments, too. But not everywhere, it turns out.

In each of the studies, we compared men's scores with women's. At first we did this out of a general sense of following routine, but we soon began to notice that all the studies did not come out in the same way. And here, those differences have a little more credibility than in the first part of this chapter. Instead of comparing scores across languages and oceans, here we were comparing men's and women's scores in the same nation, under the same conditions. Table 7.5 summarizes what we found.

Table 7.5: Sex Differences by Nation, Indicating Which Sex Had Higher Scores

	US Undgr	China	Portugal	India	Malaysia	US Adults	UAE	Chile	France	Netherlands
Arg-Appr	M***	M	F	M	M	M***	M	M	M	M*
Arg-Avoid	F***	F	F	F	F	F***	F	F	F***	F***
VA-Anti	M***	M***	M***	F	F	M***	M	M**	F	M**
VA-Pro	F**	F**	F	M	M	F	M	F*	M	F*
Utility	M**	–	M	M	M	M***	M	–	F	F
Identity	M*	M	M	M	M	M***	F	F	M	M
Domin	M***	M	M	M	M**	M**	F	M***	M	F
Play	M***	M*	M*	M	F	M***	F	M***	M**	M***
Blurt	M	–	M	M	M	M	F	–	F	F
Coop	F**	F***	F	M	F	F	M*	F**	M	F
Civil	F*	M	F	M	M*	M	M	F*	M	M*
ProfCon	F	F*	F	F	M*	M	M	–	M	F
Direct	F***	F	F	F	F	F***	F*	–	F***	F***
Persec	F	F	F	F	M	F	F	–	F**	F
Stress	F***	F***	F***	F	M	F***	F	–	F***	F***

Table 7.5: Continued

	US Undgr	China	Portugal	India	Malaysia	US Adults	UAE	Chile	France	Netherlands
PosRel	M**	F	M	M	M	M***	M	-	F	M
NegRel	F***	F	F*	F	M*	F**	F	-	F	F
Valence	M***	M*	M	M	M	M***	M	-	M***	M***
Percent	83	44	22	0	22	67	11	67	33	50

Note. All *t*-tests were two-tailed. These were adjusted for unequal group variances when necessary. Empty entries appear because those scales were not applied in that nation. Only the Ms and Fs with asterisks were statistically significant, and those are reflected in the final row of the table.
* $p < .05$; ** $p < .01$; *** $p < .001$

As you browse the table, you can see the sex differences pattern I described earlier. With almost no exceptions, if there was a sex difference, it was in the direction I mentioned. Men were more aggressive, women were more polite and other-oriented, and men were less worried about being in disagreements. But what is striking is that sex differences appeared at different rates from nation to nation. The last row in the table indicates the percentage of statistically significant sex differences for each nation. It varies from 83% (U.S. undergraduates) to 0% (India), with a lot of intermediate values in between those extremes.

I wondered about this for quite a while, particularly which nations were which. The status of women has changed quite a lot during my lifetime, with American women gaining access to more educational, political, and economic possibilities over the years. They have been less and less chained to their kitchens and vacuum cleaners, and getting outside assistance with child care (e.g., daycare and prekindergarten) has become less often condemned, even if we still tend to think of it as the woman's responsibility when we are not being careful. Similar things happened in other economically advanced nations after World War II. Surely women's equality explains our results, I thought. Well, not obviously. The nations you might suppose were delivering the most general equality would be the U.S. and Europe (Chile is officially a developed economy, too), but those were not necessarily the nations with the fewest sex differences.

I could make no sense of this, so I asked some friends. One of them suggested an academic article to me (yes, that's the kind of friends professors have). It proved to be enlightening (Charles & Bradley, 2009; I first wrote about this in Hample, 2015, but have more data here). Charles and Bradley looked at women's choices of college major in 44 nations. Some majors are sex-typed. For instance, education and nursing are stereotypical "women's majors," and engineering and business are more associated with men. Charles and Bradley compared the proportions of women choosing those majors, and compared those choices to whether the nation was Westernized (i.e., economically advanced, sort of modern European) or not. They found more sex-typing in the Westernized nations. You should read their paper to see their own phrasing, but essentially they concluded that when the struggle for equality has more or less succeeded, women feel free to make gendered choices, and so they do. Charles (2017) has reported similar results, finding that in 32 countries eighth grade girls were less and less likely to aim themselves at STEM careers as their nations became more economically advanced.

I wondered if that theory might explain what we found across all these argumentation studies, too. Rather than just classify the nations as Charles and Bradley did, however, I downloaded national data on a couple of points. I will convey more about those two data sources in a few pages, but what I did here is simple and so I will not complicate it now.

First I got Hofstede's (2001; Hofstede, Hofstede, & Minkov, 2010; Hofstede & Minkov, 2013) results for power distance for as many of our nations as he had in his database (http://geert-hofstede.com/countries.html). Power distance is a measure of people's tolerance for status differences in society. The women's equality movement can be understood as a rejection of the traditionally higher status for men. I correlated those national power distance scores with the percentages of sex differences in Table 7.5. I obtained $r = -.73$, $p = .017$, $N = 10$. Figure 7.1 displays the scatterplot for these data. In other words, the less tolerant a nation is of status differences, the more sex differences it produced in our studies. More equality was associated with more sex difference. This generally supports the Charles and Bradley idea: nations that are more insistent on people's social equality yielded more differences between men and women.

I followed up on this by collecting scores from the World Values Survey (e.g., Inglehart & Baker, 2000; Welzel, 2013). The WVS, too, has a browsable website (http://www.worldvaluessurvey.org/WVSOnline.jsp) that reports nation-level scores for many of the countries in the argumentation project. I used their Wave 6 data, covering 2010–2014. One of their measures is "equality," which assesses each nation's self-reported progress on eliminating oppressive status differences. I correlated that result with the percentages of sex differences in Table 7.5. The correlation was $r = .88$, $p < .009$, $N = 7$; Figure 7.2 shows the scatterplot. I also formed my own measure for women's equality in particular (adding their items 50 through 53) and found $r = .89$, $p = .008$, $N = 7$. This means that the more a nation's survey respondents advocated equality, the more sex differences that nation produced on argumentation measures. This, too, is consistent with the Charles and Bradley view that nations socially develop to a point that women again feel free to accept and express their gendered natures.

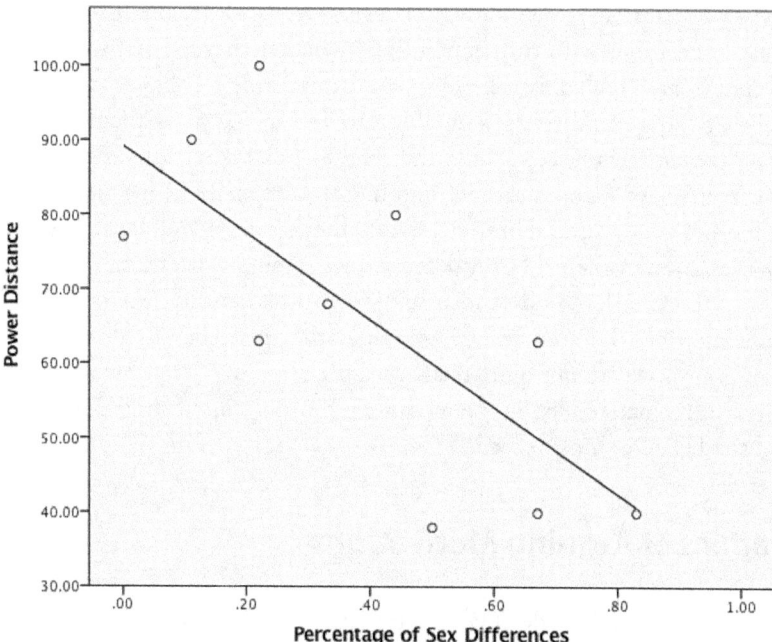

Figure 7.1: Scatterplot and Regression Line for Power Distance and Percentage of Sex Differences

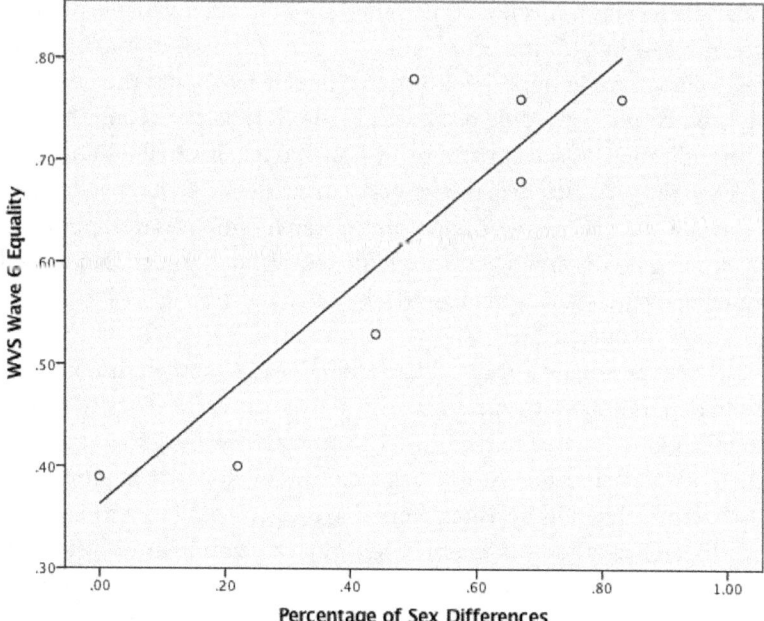

Figure 7.2: Scatterplot and Regression Line for Equality and Percentage of Sex Differences

These conclusions are tentative for several reasons. For one thing, we ought not trust correlations with tiny sample sizes whether they are statistically significant or not (search on "statistical power" or "capitalizing on chance" to learn why). For another thing—and this is something to be very cautious about—the analysis I have presented is susceptible to the charge of cherry-picking. Both Hofstede and the WVS have many measures, and many more could be gleaned by picking through other cross-cultural projects. Surely they would not all be consistent with the Charles/Bradley theory. In my defense, I went looking for things that did seem relevant to the Charles/Bradley idea, and they turned out to be supportive. But I quit looking when I found what I wanted. Still, this certainly deserves further scrutiny, even if we are not quite ready to settle anything yet. Obviously, international sex differences ended up being quite a bit more interesting than they have been in the U.S. empirical record.

Dynamics of Arguing Motivations

The two previous sections dealt with national means on various measures. This allowed us to compare country to country, and then men to women. Now we change interests from means to correlations. When we examine the correlation between two variables, we are asking whether they change their values in a coordinated way. If one variable increases (decreases) its value, does the other variable do the same? This would result in a positive correlation (Figure 7.2 is an example). If the two variables' values move in opposite directions (one increases and the other decreases), a negative correlation would result (see Figure 7.1). If we examine correlations, we get an indication of social patterns in how groups of variables affect one another. We see the variables' dynamic associations with one another, in other words.

In the U.S., one of the most important research initiatives dealing with interpersonal arguing is concerned with two basic motivations arguers can have. These are argumentativeness and verbal aggressiveness, and they have been important throughout this chapter.

These two personality traits differ dramatically in their implications for people's lives. Argumentativeness is constructive because it leads to testing and defense of arguments on their merits. In principle, two argumentative people are well-motivated and have a good chance to conclude their joint argument with a substantively good decision. Verbal aggressiveness leads to ad hominem attacks, which do not address the merits of the case and instead just amount to nasty accusations that often cause angry defense or withdrawal. A vast amount of research in the U.S. has shown that high argumentativeness makes positive contributions to people's relational satisfaction, educational success, occupational status, and many other outcomes. High verbal aggressiveness has opposite results and is caustic to many things that lead to personal happiness (Rancer & Avtgis, 2014). It has proved quite important, both theoretically and practically, to understand these variables.

The Opposites Theory

As I have been careful to point out, both of these constructs are actually composed of two subscales, and the relationships among those subscales are a key topic here. Argumentativeness is measured by an argument approach subscale (e.g., "I am energetic and enthusiastic when I argue") and an argument avoid subscale (e.g., "I try to avoid getting into arguments"). Traditionally, the overall argumentativeness score is computed as approach minus avoid. Verbal aggressiveness has a similar structure. Here the two subscales are antisocial (e.g., "When individuals are very stubborn, I use insults to soften the stubbornness") and prosocial (e.g., "When others do things I regard as stupid, I try to be extremely gentle with them"). The composite verbal aggressiveness score is computed as antisocial minus prosocial.

These computations—subtracting one score from another—seemed obviously appropriate to U.S. researchers. ("Reverse-coding" is the same thing as doing these subtractions.) But notice that the procedure really only makes sense if the two subscales are opposites. For example, one way to measure your performance on an academic test would be to subtract your number of wrong answers from your number of right answers. That would give a clearly interpretable score, because wrong is the opposite of right. But suppose someone calculated your exam score by subtracting the number of correct true-false answers from the number of correct multiple-choice answers. That score wouldn't make any sense at all because getting a true-false question correct is not the opposite of getting a multiple-choice question right.

This idea of "opposite" is statistically represented by negative correlations. For a classroom of students, the number of correct exam answers will be negatively correlated to the number of mistaken answers (the higher the score for one variable, the lower the score for the other). In the U.S., argument approach and argument avoid have consistently correlated negatively, and the correlations have been of substantial size. Similarly, antisocial and prosocial have correlated negatively and at high levels—in the U.S.

Research in other nations calls into question the idea that arguing motivations always work this way. Table 7.6 shows what happens to the relations among these scales once we cross the oceans. The first two columns of correlations show us whether the subscales are actually opposite, from nation to nation. I have ordered the nations by reference to their correlation between argument approach and argument avoid.

Table 7.6: Correlations Among Argumentativeness and Verbal Aggressiveness Subscales, by Nation

	Approach Avoid	Antisocial Prosocial	Approach Antisocial	Avoid Prosocial
Germany	−.64			
US, mTurk	−.54	−.43	.46	.28
China	−.40	−.31	.26	.08
France	−.40	−.26	.11	.06
US, undergrads	−.35	−.31	.32	.30
Portugal	−.34	−.21	.12	.03
Japan	−.34	−.24		
Turkey	−.31			
Netherlands	−.31	−.28	.17	.13
Chile	−.16	−.16	.26	−.14
UAE	.02	.15	.35	.51
Malaysia	.16	.20	.43	.40
India	.17	.27	.45	.44

Additional Sources: Japan: Suzuki and Rancer (1994), and these correlations are between latent variables (i.e., are corrected for unreliability of measurement). Turkey: Croucher et al. (2013). Germany: Blickle (1995, Study 3).

For the argumentativeness scales, the approach and avoid measures correlated very negatively in many nations, but they actually had a positive correlation in India and Malaysia. They had no discernible correlation in the United Arab Emirates, and their negative correlation in Chile was too small to make us comfortable in saying the subscales were really opposites there.

For the verbal aggressiveness scales, antisocial and prosocial scores had their U.S.-expectable negative correlations in many of the countries, but the U.S. correlations seemed to stand out as being high. The supposedly opposite subscales actually had positive correlations in India, Malaysia, and the United Arab Emirates. Some of the negative correlations were not especially high.

In other words, the oppositeness that was obvious in the U.S. and has been basic to the theory and measurement of argumentativeness and verbal aggressiveness did not characterize every nation in the world. In fact, the U.S. may actually be exceptional in the degree to which these pairs of scales are opposite to one another.

The immediate implication for researchers is that the scales cannot be confidently subtracted to create meaningful overall scores for argumentativeness or verbal aggressiveness. This will be easily handled in the future—results simply have to be reported separately for each subscale, as I have done throughout this book. For data collected in nations where the "opposites" theory seems plausible, old research can still be straightforwardly interpreted. However, for other nations, any results involving the summary measures (e.g., approach minus avoid) are pretty much unintelligible at this point. It may even make sense to *add* the subscales, to get something like measures of argumentative or verbally aggressive energy and involvement (see Hamilton & Hample, 2011). By far the safest course is just to regard the subscales as separate measures, each having its own intrinsic empirical information and construct integrity.

The Basis for the Opposites Theory

But the really interesting issue is conceptual: How can we understand argument approach and avoidance as being anything but opposites? How can antisocial and prosocial impulses not be clear contradictions? Perhaps the place to begin is to recover the original thinking in Infante and Rancer (1982).

First of all, I should reassure readers that I am not distorting anything about the basic conceptualization by talking about a theory of opposites. On the first page of the first article, Infante and Rancer (1982, p. 72) introduce their idea of argumentativeness:

> Some individuals seem to argue more than others about controversial issues. They seldom ignore the opportunity to argue, seem to find it pleasurable, challenging, and, at times, a form of recreation or amusement. Other people seem to have an opposite reaction to arguing.

Infante and Rancer point out that even argument-averse people may understand that arguments can be constructive in reaching good decisions. These people just don't enjoy the activity, in the same way that someone might think that physical exercise is good but unpleasant. Infante and Rancer develop their idea of opposites carefully, saying that argumentativeness (i.e., approach minus avoid) represents the resolution of an approach-avoidance conflict for people. An approach-avoidance conflict occurs when a person simultaneously has impulses both to do a thing and not to do it. For example, a person on a diet might suddenly be frozen in front of the doughnut case at a convenience store. The dieter wants a doughnut, but also knows that this would be a very bad idea. According to Infante and Rancer, argumentativeness is a trait that represents a person's stable balance between approaching and avoiding arguments. Verbal aggressiveness is a parallel personality characteristic, representing the compromise between a person's desire to be nice to others and the impulse to attack (verbally) without restraint.

A further development of the idea of opposites was in Infante and Rancer's (1982) connection of their argumentativeness theory with Atkinson's (1957, 1966) theory of achievement motivation. Atkinson said that human motivation is the result of seeking satisfactions on one hand, and minimizing pain on the other. These correspond to approach and avoidance, and have been thoroughly explored by means of expectancy-value models in psychology and behavioral economics. In the decades since Atkinson's original work, something closely resembling this theory has been confirmed to have clear biological bases in humans, in both our genetic inheritance and our brain structures (e.g., Corr & McNaughton, 2012; Enter, Colzato, & Roelofs, 2012). The motivational theory of approach and avoidance (attraction and aversion) is basic and continues to be well regarded.

However, Infante and Rancer (1982) did not make very precise use of the theory. They originally said only that Atkinson's theory was an "analog for the present conceptualization" (p. 73), and even today it is described as no more than a "model" and "analog" for the theory of argumentativeness (Rancer & Avtgis, 2014, p. 45). So throughout the community research program on argumentativeness, it has never been directly tested in Atkinson's terms. Argumentativeness theory has only been represented as having ideas that are analogous to those in Atkinson's motivation theory. It has never been evaluated as a version, an implementation, or an implication of Atkinson's theory (Infante, 1987, is to my knowledge the closest thing to a direct implementation of Atkinson's theory, and it is very approximate). This was not a problem for American researchers, because both theories made sense, their correspondence was obvious, and their unity seemed intuitive and uncontroversial. So the "opposites" that are well established in motivational theories were easily assumed to have the same quality of support in argumentativeness theory.

To be clear: I have no doubt that approach and avoidance are human motivational systems, and that they are generally in play when people decide on their behaviors. But this can be so without assuming that any particular behavior always has opposing motivations that need to cancel each other out to some degree in order to leave a resulting motive vector. Furthermore—and this may be the crux of the matter—what looks like a negative outcome to me, something that should be avoided, doesn't need to register as negative for you. For example, just because one culture is immediately cynical about their government officials' statements doesn't mean that another culture will have the same reflexive negative valuation for their leaders' public views. Two cultures could also have divergent views about if and when interpersonal arguments ought to be avoided or sought with energy. Or some muscley undergraduate might actually enjoy exhausting exercise, whereas I have evolved beyond that view. Things that would customarily be avoided in the U.S. might be sought out in India.

So the fact that argument avoidance seemed (in the U.S.) to be the opposite of argument approach, doesn't mean it is also opposite elsewhere in the world. Can you be happy to keep an argument from happening (an avoidance item) and also enjoy defending your point of view (an approach item)? Those two items make approach and avoid look a little less opposite, but other items seem more obviously contradictory: "I feel excitement when I expect that a conversation I am in is leading to an argument" (approach) versus "Once I finish an argument I promise myself that I will not get into another" (avoid).

Trying to Understand the Presence or Absence of Opposites

Some readers may feel like I do right now: It is very hard not to be American when I think about all this, and it is really difficult to imagine any other way to absorb what these subscales could mean. Perhaps it is time to begin looking at external data for clues. Again, I will consider Hofstede's research and the World Values Survey, but in a little more detail than in the sex differences section.

Hofstede Values. One of the best-known research projects concerning national values is Hofstede's (2001; Hofstede et al., 2010). In the 1970s he obtained data that IBM had already collected on its employees around the world and then designed further studies. This work produced, among other things, summaries of the employees' values. Some other values were added to the list over the decades. Although the original data were collected some time ago, Hofstede (2001) argued that these values persist for centuries within nations, and he emphasized that by surveying only people who worked at IBM, a huge number of other variables were matched and controlled for, leaving "nation" as the most plausible explanation for any observed differences.

He identified several values that differentiated how people from various nations deal with inherent social problems. In terms of the concepts I mentioned early in the chapter, he dealt with "internalized" culture. He felt that responses to problems were particularly revealing about national character. The first value, power distance, relates to how nations react to the inherent status differences within a society. People with high power distance scores are accepting of these status differences, and populations with low scores are more insistent on equality among people. Individualism/collectivism is relevant to how people integrate themselves into larger groups. Highly individualistic nations contain people who are reluctant to give up too much individuality to their family or employer, and highly collectivist nations freely commit to the groups that are important in their lives. Uncertainty avoidance is connected to the inherent unknowability of the future. High uncertainty avoidance scores mean that national populations have a lot of rules, rituals, and procedures that must be followed to structure their personal or organizational lives, giving them more stability. Low uncertainty avoidance scores imply less structuring and more willingness to adapt creatively to whatever happens. Masculinity has always seemed a little misnamed to me because it doesn't directly assess the salience of gender identities. Instead, high masculine scores are due to a nation having preferences that Hofstede associated with masculinity, such as striving for recognition at work and wanting a chance for a promotion. These are contrasted with priorities that Hofstede connected with feminine identity, such as wanting pleasant co-workers and living in a desirable area. Next is long-term orientation, which summarizes whether a nation more naturally does long-term or short-term thinking. The last national value is indulgence, which refers to whether a nation's people prioritize immediate gratification or easily practice disciplined restraint. Current nation-by-nation data are available for many countries across the world at Hofstede's website, http://geert-hofstede.com.

I took that information for the countries in Table 7.6 and correlated those national scores with the correlations in the table. It may seem odd to correlate correlations, but the coefficients in Table 7.6 are numbers themselves, and like more traditional variables, they have their own conceptual meaning. In this case, the correlations in the first two columns of Table 7.6 are measuring the degree of oppositeness in national understandings of either argument approach/avoid or prosocial/antisocial verbal aggressiveness.

Having only a few data points makes doing these correlations very tentative because one peculiar score can really throw things off. As with my application of the Charles and Bradley (2009) analysis of sex differences, we should be careful in depending very heavily on these results. However, they may well suggest hypotheses that can be evaluated systematically in more precisely designed work. The small sample also restricted me in what analyses I could do, since there simply aren't enough degrees of freedom to conduct multiple regressions, canonical correlations, or structural equation models. So I restricted myself to simple analyses, done step by step.

My first step was to evaluate some control variables. These are not very interesting theoretically, but since they might plausibly control variance in the oppositeness correlation coefficients, they needed to be evaluated. For each nation, I evaluated whether national per capita income affected the oppositeness (I used https://www.cia.gov/library/publications/the-world-factbook/rankorder/2004rank.html for my income data). This is because Hofstede (2001) reported that per capita income is often strongly associated with his national values measures, presumably because wealthy nations tend to have different value profiles than nations with smaller economies. I also compared the correlations to the percentage of female respondents in the studies that generated the correlations in Table 7.6 (percentage of female respondents was taken from Table 7.1 or was obtained from the studies mentioned in the footnote of Table 7.6). This is because biological sex is often a predictor of the mean scores for approach, avoidance, prosocial, and antisocial, as we have seen. I knew that the studies did not have the same proportions of men and women, so I wanted to be sure that the differences in oppositeness correlations was not somehow due to that. Finally, I correlated the samples' average age to the correlations, because there is some evidence that older adults have different scores than undergraduates (e.g., Hample & Anagondahalli, 2015).

None of the control variables produced significant correlations with the oppositeness coefficients. Per capita income was fairly close, producing correlations of about $r = -.33$ (p's were .25 and .34) for both oppositeness coefficients, but neither age nor percentage of female respondents yielded anything that large in absolute value. National wealth may be somewhat relevant, with wealthier nations having more negative coefficients. That is, the larger and more vigorous a country's economy, the more sharply the population sees approach/avoidance and prosocial/antisocial as clearly demarcated opposites, but it is worth emphasizing that this result was not statistically significant. Data from quite a few more nations will be required to evaluate this possibility, since it is presently dominated by U.S. and German results at one end, and Indian and Malaysian results at the other.

Tentatively setting the control variables aside, I therefore moved on to correlating Hofstede's (2001) national values with the correlations in the first two columns of Table 7.6. The only significant predictor was power distance. It predicted oppositeness for approach/avoid at $r = .76$ ($p = .002$, $N = 13$), and for prosocial/antisocial at $r = .77$ ($p = .006$, $N = 11$). Most of the other predictions from Hofstede's values were negligible, but individualism produced correlations of about $-.50$ (the higher the individualism, the sharper the oppositeness; but this was not statistically significant, with p's around .10 and N's of 13 and 11). Since per capita income was almost statistically relevant (see above), I then partialled it out of the power distance correlations and still had a significant result for approach/avoid

($r = .72$) and for prosocial/antisocial ($r = .74$). The predictions from individualism weakened when per capita income was partialled away.

So the Hofstede-based analyses suggest that power distance might be an important nation-level characteristic to think about in connection with the "opposites" theory. The correlation was positive, meaning that as power distance (acceptance of status inequality) increased in the nations studied, the correlation between the "opposites" was higher, that is, more positive. So the more accepting a nation is of differences in authority, wealth, and status, the less opposition is felt between approaching and avoiding arguments or between being nice and being nasty. Equally, the result also means that the less a nation accepts power distance, the more it insists that approach and avoid are opposites and that prosocial and antisocial are opposites.

World Values Survey. Another effort to map the world's values is a long-term project by teams of social scientists to survey people in different nations to ascertain their basic values. The initiative, called the World Values Survey (WVS), began in the 1980s, and new surveys have been conducted once or twice a decade. About 100 nations are now included. Background information and nation-by-nation data are available at http://www.worldvaluessurvey.org/. Based on the many questions in the survey, the WVS researchers have determined that national values have two large-scale dimensions, secular and emancipatory values. Each has some subscales.

Secular values (the opposite is traditional values) represent the degree to which a nation is not dominated by religious and other traditional teachings. Nations with high ratings on this composite index are secular (i.e., relatively non-traditional). Elements of secularity include defiance, disbelief, relativism, and skepticism, and all of these have separate measures. The other large collection of values is called emancipation, which contrasts self-expression with survival values. The more a nation is oriented to personal emancipation, the more it values self-expression and self-determination. Subordinate values here include autonomy, equality, and choice. I downloaded measures from the 2010 to 2014 data collection for most of the nations in Table 7.6, and followed the same procedures as for the Hofstede analyses above.

The overall measures of secular and emancipatory values did not predict either of the opposites measures (that is, the first two columns in Table 7.6). The summary of secular values was not very close, giving correlations only around $r = -.20$. But the emancipatory measure was close to being significant, with $r = -.58$ ($p = .08$, $N = 10$) for approach/avoid, and $r = -.68$ ($p = .06$, $N = 8$) for prosocial/antisocial. If these last correlations had been statistically significant, they would mean that when nations commit more and more fully to individual emancipation, they see the opposites even more clearly. I therefore looked at the subsidiary emancipation goals. Voice was clearly unrelated to the opposites measures, and choice generated non-significant correlations of about $r = -.45$. The key predictor was equality, which significantly predicted both opposites measures: $r = -.67$ ($p = .033$, $N = 10$) for approach/avoid, and $r = -.81$ ($p = .015$, $N = 8$) for prosocial/antisocial. This suggests that as nations increase their valuing of equality, they perceive opposites more starkly.

When I partialled out the effects of per capita income, the overall emancipation correlations dropped a bit ($r = -.53$, $p = .143$, $N = 7$ for approach/avoid, and $r = -.74$, $p = .058$, $N = 5$), and equality predictions kept their statistical significance. One of the points of the World Values Survey project has been to see what happens to national values as the countries become more Westernized and economically developed, so it is no surprise that per capita income is sharing variance with the values measures.

Thus we might conclude that as nations become more Westernized, with their economic production increasing along with their commitment to personal equality, they see clearer opposition between approaching versus avoiding arguments, and between being pleasant versus being verbally aggressive. This is somewhat consistent with what we found when using Hofstede's instruments. There, we noticed that when nations became less accepting of power differentials, the opposites became more pronounced. This is not a pure result because we didn't see similar things happening as individualism increased, as masculine striving decreased, or as commitment to individual voice and the merit of individual choice rose.

How Strong a Conclusion Should Be Drawn? The key results here are that as a nation commits more strongly to equality, and as it becomes less tolerant of power differentials, it sees argument approach and argument avoidance as more clearly opposed, and similarly with prosocial and antisocial impulses in interpersonal conflict. These two findings are consistent with one another. However, they weren't theorized. They were just found. This makes them a proper basis for hypothesizing but not for concluding. And we should notice that the egalitarian effect (pro-equality and intolerance for power distance) was not strong enough to include individualism (which correlates with both power distance and equality in this data set), nor choice, voice, or any of the other measures that we might imagine could connect with equality and power distance. So matters are complex and tentative.

However, they are also quite important. The idea of opposition between argument approach and argument avoid, and the parallel idea of opposition between being prosocial and antisocial when arguing, is a fundamental basis for our American understanding of arguing motivations. Important differences in the motivational dynamics of different cultures really require that interpersonal arguing be re-thought from the ground up, from one nation to the next. In an important sense, motivation to argue is the first thing, and it controls how the constructive and destructive potentials of arguing are understood and how they can be important for a culture's system of social life.

Comparing Dynamics in Detail

To this point, the only correlations we have examined are those among the subscales of argumentativeness and verbal aggressiveness. I pulled those out for special examination because I think they are unusually important. But all the other correlations can be compared from country to country as well. Some of those differences might be stimulating, and if there are similarities, those would reassure us that U.S. results could, with modification, be helpful in exploring other nations' arguing behaviors. This can be done for every pair of nations and every pair of variables.

Frankly, that would just be too tedious and repetitive to do here. So for the sake of illustration, I have chosen just two nations to compare: France and India. If you review Tables 7.2 through 7.4 you will notice that these two nations frequently had statistically different national means, and often they had almost opposite values in the context of the other countries.

But just because their means were different, that does not necessarily indicate that their internal correlations will be different, too. One nation could be very low on both X and Y and another nation could be high on both, but X and Y could have the same association with one another in both countries. Relatively high X could imply relatively high Y in both places, with the only difference being what each nation means by "relatively high." On the other hand, two nations that are observably different in one statistical aspect might be distinct in another, too, so France and India might be interesting to compare. You can use the original research reports to compare pairs of countries or variables yourself by following this model.

Argument Motivations

Let us begin with the correlations among the argumentativeness and verbal aggressiveness subscales for the two nations. I have already presented those in Table 7.6. For the "opposites" measures (the first two columns), France was −.40 and −.26, and India was .17 and .27. This is a pretty stark difference. The subscales really were opposite in France but were consistent with one another in India. France had the U.S. understanding that a person does one thing *or* the other, but Indians saw no special problem with wanting to approach and avoid disagreements at the same time.

Nor were the two nations any more comparable for the other two correlations in Table 7.6. Argument approach and verbal aggressiveness antisocial are the respective aggressive subscales: the impulse to attack the other's case or the other's person. In France, these were weakly associated ($r = .11$), but in India the association was considerably stronger ($r = .45$). The other two subscales, avoid and prosocial, are the nonconfrontational subscales. In France, they were almost completely uncorrelated ($r = .06$), but in India their association was clear: $r = .44$. For the last two columns of Table 7.6, the Indian associations are like the U.S. ones, and the French scores are different. The four measures correlated in Table 7.6 had systematically different systems of interconnection in the two countries.

Table 7.2 showed that France and India had different means on these measures, too. India was in the highest category of scores for all four variables, but France was sort of middling. We now understand that these were not the only differences between the countries on those measures. Not only did France and India have different mean scores, they also experienced the connections among these variables in different ways.

Argument Frames

Let us move on to the argument frames. Table 7.3 reported that France had very low scores for the first six measures, but fairly high ones for civility and professional contrast. India, on the other hand, was in the highest score category for the first six measures. India was lower than France for civility, but they were about the same for professional contrast. How did their correlations compare? Table 7.7 gives the results.

Table 7.7: Correlations Among Argument Frames Measures for France and India

	Util	Ident	Dom	Play	Blurt	Coop	Civil	ProfCon
				France				
Utility	–							
Identity	.23	–						
Dominance	.40	.41	–					
Play	.01	.26	.42	–				
Blurting	.17	.14	.25	.27	–			
Cooperation	.08	.08	–.03	–.03	–.06	–		

Table 7.7: Continued

	Util	Ident	Dom	Play	Blurt	Coop	Civil	ProfCon
Civility	−.35	−.16	−.51	−.17	−.32	.10	–	
Prof Contrast	−.09	−.11	−.37	−.08	−.13	.10	.38	–
India								
Utility	–							
Identity	.63	–						
Dominance	.60	.55	–					
Play	.59	.55	.65	–				
Blurting	.58	.47	.58	.51	–			
Cooperation	.52	.54	.24	.33	.37	–		
Civility	.04	.08	−.25	.01	−.28	.20	–	
Prof Contrast	.06	.09	−.06	.06	.04	.30	.36	–

Note. For France, correlations of |.14| or higher are statistically significant at $p < .05$. For India, the figure is |.11|.

The most striking thing about the French versus Indian correlations is how high the India results were. In fact, they were higher than just about any nation we have studied. The first five frames—the four goals and blurting—generally correlate positively among themselves in the U.S., and they also did so for both France and India here. But the correlations from the India data were about twice as large as those from France. This means that those five variables, which cluster together for many nations, were very tightly connected in India but pretty loosely in France. This result could be expressed in several ways: we could say that India was more disciplined and internally consistent, or that France saw more conceptual divergence among the constructs, or something else. But it is very clear that the two nations had quite different dynamics. If you know one score about an Indian, you can pretty much predict his or her scores on the other four measures. The same is not true of a French person, at least with the same level of precision.

The last three frames—cooperation, civility, and professional contrast—also tend to have positive connections among themselves. These are the last three correlations, a little triangle of results in the bottom parts of the table. We do see the positive associations for both nations but not all the French ones were statistically significant (see the note to the table). And again, the India results were higher, except for the civility-professional contrast association, which is about the same.

We could examine the rest of Table 7.7 to see the correlations between the first five frames and the last three. The table shows some further differences, but they seem a little miscellaneous to me. The conclusion I draw at this point is that the Indian respondents were far more coherent and interconnected in the patterns of their responses than were the French participants. These measurements reflected a more cohesive system of variables in India than in France. If some intervention could change how people in the two nations felt about playful arguing, to take an example, we would expect that change to ripple out to other goals to a much greater degree in India than in France.

Personalizing Conflict

Finally, let us perform the same exercise for taking conflict personally. The correlations are in Table 7.8.

Table 7.8: Correlations Among Taking Conflict Personally Measures for France and India

	Direct	Stress	Persecution	Pos Relat	Neg Relat	Valence
			France			
Direct	–					
Stress	.67					
Persecution	.49	.49				
Pos Rel Eff	.00	−.14	−.08			
Neg Rel Eff	.41	.48	.43	−.27		
Valence	−.46	−.57	−.35	.14	−.37	–
			India			
Direct	–					
Stress	.70					
Persecution	.72	.66				
Pos Rel Eff	.27	.17	.37			
Neg Rel Eff	.51	.48	.64	.09		
Valence	−.11	−.15	−.08	.49	−.37	–

Note. For France, correlations are significant at $p < .05$ if they are $|.14|$ or higher. For India, the figure is $|.12|$.

In the U.S., the first three variables tend to be positively associated, and negative relational effects is also part of that cluster. These four ratings—direct personalization, stress, persecution, and relational damage—describe different facets of taking conflict personally. In both France and India, Table 7.8 shows very strong associations of that type. The correlations were a little bit higher in India, but the difference was not as obvious or important as we saw in the argument frames data.

The table implies that the effects of arguments on relationships might be particularly interesting to researchers. Positive relational effects and valence are positively correlated in the U.S., and tend to have negative correlations with the other variables. That is because relational improvement and enjoyment of conflict are inconsistent with the idea that conflicts are nasty and personal. Here we see some nation-to-nation divergence. The correlation between positive relational effects and valence was .49 in India, consistent with American theorizing, but it was only .14 in France. Positive and negative relational effects had a different relationship in the two countries, too. Positive and negative effects correlated at $r = -.27$ in France but only .09 in India. In India, people were apparently quite comfortable with the idea that conflicts can have both positive and negative consequences for a relationship, or neither, but the French tended to expect one or the other. In addition, we see that positive relational effects had the expectable negative connection to the first three TCP scales for France, but not for India. So Table 7.8 alerts us that France and India had pretty different understandings of how interpersonal disagreements affect the relationship between the two arguers. The national means for these measures (Table 7.4) did show differences in the two nations' ratings for these subscales, but only the positive relational effects scores put the two countries in different score categories. Arguing and relational satisfaction appeared to have different connections in France than in India. Do people in these nations argue differently? Do they conduct relationships differently? Both?

In other words, France and India differed on more than just their national averages for the argumentation measures. Our analysis shows that the variables also had different patterns of influence and connection in the two countries. Correlation is not causation, but it is an important clue about possible cause-effect relationships. Argumentation theories feature statements about causality. We can now see that it would be productive to investigate the causal systems that produced the correlations we have just been studying. Techniques such as experimentation, quasi-experimentation, and structural equation modeling can be used to get a better focus on causality, reducing our natural temptation to use correlational evidence to imply causal connections.

You might suspect that I chose France and India to discuss because their contrasts were especially large, and you would be right. But doing this sort of thing for two countries that do not differ very much would be productive too, because it might suggest that we would not be going too far wrong if we described both of those nations using the same theories. That is just as important as finding the nations (or groups of nations) that need their own theories, potentially quite independent from the original U.S. work.

Conclusions

This chapter has mainly summarized the results of a cross-national research program that has been going on for several years. The chapter is called "Arguing and Culture," but you should be able to evaluate that title pretty carefully. Nations have been used as proxies for cultures, and you know how approximate that is. As to "culture," you surely realize that this chapter has had very little to do with the "precipitate" of culture and has concentrated almost exclusively on its "internalized" nature.

To get a better grasp of cultural precipitates and how they connect to interpersonal arguing, I think we need good qualitative work to be done. People who speak the language, who understand what is implied but not said, who can see things that are obvious to natives but invisible to visitors—they need to be the investigators who explore how different cultural groups argue. Many qualitative researchers prefer methodologies that are data-driven, where the scholar just dives into a cultural experience and eventually notices particular things that need to be pursued. But there is absolutely nothing wrong with qualitative researchers having a starting point, a conceptual target that they want to explain. Studies like the present one can be used to suggest agendas for qualitative work. The points we made about France and India would be good candidates for in-depth work, using interviews, participant observation, conversation analysis, focus groups, or other qualitative methods. It takes a lot longer to do a good qualitative study than it does to do a survey, so it makes sense to me that the scholarly community might want a division of labor like this.

Even the quantitative work needs to get deeper. For example, we will ultimately want to move away from self-reports about intentions and impressions, and toward observation of actual arguments. Those arguments might be controlled to improve their comparability, or they might be naturally occurring to improve their external validity.

Understanding how face-to-face arguing operates (or doesn't) in various cultures is quite important. Conflict is inherent to human social life, and it is a civilized advance to be able to "use your words" to resolve disagreement. Regulating possession, insults, debts, identities, needs, and many other things—how is that regulating done? Do the participants have to do it themselves? If so, they may very well need to argue (alternatives include physical violence, third party adjudication, or accepting the harm). Even if a dyad can carry a dispute to a third party (a judge, an elder, one's mother), the participants are still likely to need reasons and to make a case. Think about how much of your own social life involves mutual decisions, disagreements, discussions, and arguments. That's how basic interpersonal arguing is to the social life of a community, group, or culture.

Even though I think we are only at the beginning of this research, we can already see several encouraging things. First, we should be willing to mistrust American theory whenever we are thinking about some other culture or nation. Some of what is true in the U.S. happens in (some) other nations too, but not always with the same strength or insistence. Sometimes the opposite happens. Second, we should expect variability from one country to another, even regarding basic phenomena like argument motivations. Third, we ought to be looking for nations that seem to be similar in their argument understandings and behaviors, so that we might eventually come up with cultural groupings. We might find that one social group in China is very much like one in the U.S., and that neither of them is very similar to the dominant cultures in those nations. This will smooth out international life, which is becoming a much more prominent part of the modern world than it ever was in previous centuries.

For me, and now perhaps for you, this project has been a lesson in recognizing my own cultural inheritance and how I have naturally been assuming that it was a universal human experience. Of course I knew better, and so did you, but *which* details can we trust and which should we set aside? Research projects like the one I have described here are very important in teaching us what to assume or question about our own worldviews.

References

Atkinson, J. W. (1957). Motivational determinants of risk-taking behavior. *Psychological Review, 64*, 359–372.

Atkinson, J. W. (1966). *An introduction to motivation*. New York, NY: Van Nostrand.

Beijing says 400 million Chinese cannot speak Mandarin. (2013, September 6). *BBC News*. Retrieved January 11, 2017 from http://www.bbc.com/news/world-asia-china-23975037

Blickle, G. (1995). Conceptualization and measurement of argumentativeness: A decade later. *Psychological Reports, 77*, 99–110.

Cai, D., & Fink, E. (2002). Conflict style differences between individualists and collectivists. *Communication Monographs, 69*, 67–87.

Charles, M. (2017). Venus, Mars, and math: Gender, societal affluence, and eighth graders' aspirations for STEM. *Socius, 3*, 1–16.

Charles, M., & Bradley, K. (2009). Indulging our gendered selves? Sex segregation by field of study in 44 countries. *American Journal of Sociology, 114*, 924–976.

Corr, P. J., & McNaughton, N. (2012). Neuroscience and approach/avoidance personality traits: A two stage (valuation–motivation) approach. *Neuroscience & Biobehavioral Reviews, 36*, 2339–2354.

Croucher, S. M., Otten, R., Ball, M., Grimes, T., Ainsworth, B., Begley, K., & Corzo, L. (2013). Argumentativeness and political participation: A cross-cultural analysis in the United States and Turkey. *Communication Studies, 64,* 18–32.

Dufour, M., & Hample, D. (2017, June). French interpersonal argument: Fundamental understandings. Paper presented at the European Conference on Argumentation, Fribourg, Switzerland.

Enter, D., Colzato, L. S., & Roelofs, K. (2012). Dopamine transporter polymorphisms affect social approach–avoidance tendencies. *Genes, Brain and Behavior, 11,* 671–676.

Farh, J. L., Hackett, R. D., & Liang, J. (2007). Individual-level cultural values as moderators of perceived organizational support–employee outcome relationships in China: Comparing the effects of power distance and traditionality. *Academy of Management Journal, 50,* 715–729.

Fitch, K. (1998). *Speaking relationally. Culture, communication, and interpersonal connection.* New York, NY: Guilford.

Hamilton, M. A., & Hample, D. (2011). Testing hierarchical models of argumentativeness and verbal aggressiveness. *Communication Methods and Measures, 5,* 250–273.

Hample, D. (2005). *Arguing: Exchanging reasons face to face.* Mahwah, NJ: Lawrence Erlbaum Associates.

Hample, D. (2015). Orientations to interpersonal arguing in Chile and around the world. *Cogency, 7,* 61–80.

Hample, D. (2016). The psychological approach to interpersonal argumentation in the U.S. argumentation community. In F. Paglieri, L. Bonelli, & S. Felletti (Eds.), *The psychology of argument: Cognitive approaches to argumentation and persuasion* (pp. 257–274). London: College Publications.

Hample, D., & Anagondahalli, D. (2015). Understandings of arguing in India and the United States: Argument frames, personalization of conflict, argumentativeness, and verbal aggressiveness. *Journal of Intercultural Communication Research, 44,* 1–26.

Hample, D., & Cionea, I. A. (2010). Taking conflict personally and its connections with aggressiveness. In T. A. Avtgis & A. S. Rancer (Eds.), *Arguments, aggression, and conflict: New directions in theory and research* (pp. 372–387). New York, NY: Routledge, Taylor, and Francis.

Hample, D., & Dallinger, J.M. (1995). A Lewinian perspective on taking conflict personally: Revision, refinement, and validation of the instrument. *Communication Quarterly, 43,* 297–319.

Hample, D., & Irions, A. (2015). Arguing to display identity. *Argumentation, 29,* 389–416.

Hample, D., Lewiński, M., Saàágua, J., & Mohammed, D. (2016). A descriptive and comparative analysis of arguing in Portugal. In D. Mohammed & M. Lewiński (Eds.), *Argumentation and reasoned action: Proceedings of the 1st European Conference on Argumentation, Lisbon, 2015* (vol. 1, pp. 135–157). London: College Publications.

Harzing, A.-W. (2006). Response styles in cross-national survey research: A 26-country study. *International Journal of Cross Cultural Management, 6,* 243–266.

Henrich, J., Heine, S. J., & Norenzayan, A. (2010). The weirdest people in the world? *Behavioral and Brain Sciences, 33,* 61–83.

Hofstede, G. (2001). *Culture's consequences: Comparing values, behaviors, institutions, and organizations across nations* (2nd ed.). Thousand Oaks, CA: Sage.

Hofstede, G., Hofstede, G. J., & Minkov, M. (2010). *Cultures and organizations: Software of the mind* (3rd ed.). New York, NY: McGraw-Hill.

Hofstede, G., & Minkov, M. (2013, May). *Values survey module 2013 manual*. Retrieved from http://www.geerthofstede.nl/vsm2013

Infante, D. A. (1987). Enhancing the prediction of response to a communication situation from communication traits. *Communication Quarterly, 35*, 308–316.

Infante, D. A., & Rancer, A. S. (1982). A conceptualization and measure of argumentativeness. *Journal of Personality Assessment, 46*, 72–80.

Infante, D. A., & Wigley, C. J. (1986). Verbal aggressiveness: An interpersonal model and measure. *Communication Monographs, 53*, 61–69.

Inglehart, R., & Baker, W. E. (2000). Modernization, cultural change, and the persistence of traditional values. *American Sociological Review, 65*, 19–51.

Katriel, T. (1986). *Talking straight: Dugri speech in Israeli Sabra culture*. Cambridge: Cambridge University Press.

Kroeber, A. L., & Kluckhohn, C. (1952). Culture: A critical review of concepts and definitions. *Papers of the Peabody Museum of Archaeology & Ethnology, Harvard University*. Cambridge, MA: Peabody Museum.

Labrie, N. H. M., Akkermans, A., & Hample, D. (2017). *Arguing in the Netherlands*. Manuscript in preparation, Universities of Amsterdam and Maryland.

Lewin, K. (1935). Psycho-sociological problems of a minority group. *Journal of Personality, 3*, 175–187.

Philipsen, G. (2010). Some thoughts on how to approach finding one's feet in unfamiliar cultural terrain. *Communication monographs, 77*, 160–168.

Rancer, A. S., & Avtgis, T. A. (2014). *Argumentative and aggressive communication: Theory, research, and application* (2nd ed.). New York, NY: Peter Lang.

Rapanta, C., & Hample, D. (2015). Orientations to interpersonal arguing in the United Arab Emirates, with comparisons to the United States, China, and India. *Journal of Intercultural Communication Research, 44*, 263–287.

Santibáñez, C., & Hample, D. (2015). Orientations toward interpersonal arguing in Chile. *Pragmatics, 25*, 453–476.

Schiffrin, D. (1984). Jewish argument as sociability. *Language in Society, 13*, 311–335.

Suzuki, S., & Rancer, A. S. (1994). Argumentativeness and verbal aggressiveness: Testing for conceptual and measurement equivalence across cultures. *Communication Monographs, 61*, 256–279.

Tajfel, H. (1982). Social psychology of intergroup relations. *Annual Review of Psychology, 33*, 1–39.

Tajfel, H., & Turner, J. C. (1986). The social identity theory of intergroup behavior. In S. Worchel & W. G. Austin (Eds.), *Psychology of intergroup relations* (2nd ed., pp. 7–24). Chicago, IL: Nelson-Hall.

Ting-Toomey, S. (2005). The matrix of face: An updated face-negotiation theory. In W. B. Gudykunst (Ed.), *Theorizing about intercultural communication* (pp. 71–92). Los Angeles, CA: Sage.

Ting-Toomey, S. (2010). Applying dimensional values in understanding intercultural communication. *Communication Monographs, 77*, 169–180.

Waheed, M., & Hample, D. (2016, June). *Argumentation in Malaysia and how it compares to the U.S., India, and China.* Paper presented at the annual conference of the International Communication Association, Fukuoka, Japan.

Welzel, C. (2013). *Freedom rising: Human empowerment and the quest for emancipation.* New York, NY: Cambridge University Press.

CHAPTER EIGHT

The Processes of Interpersonal Arguing

Research on interpersonal arguing has been going on for about fifty years. It began in the 1970s but has really accelerated in the last quarter century (see Hample, 2016, for a history of the study of face-to-face arguing). The research has almost all been very specific to a particular topic, such as serial arguing or verbal aggressiveness, and not much generalizing and stocktaking has been going on. I think that both this book and the field in general are now in a position where there is enough raw material to justify trying to organize the empirical projects into some sort of coherent outline. This final chapter is my effort to do that. If some parts of this book have been interesting to you and others have left you unenthused, this chapter may help you to locate yourself and see what sorts of directions you might like to pursue in the future.

One of the striking things about face-to-face arguing is how many things are going on at once. Each of those things can become a scholar's entry point. One's first motivating question is both essential and irrelevant at the same time. I have told my students for years that "It doesn't really matter where you start. If you follow the evidence, eventually you end up everywhere." For example, you might begin with an interest in understanding the emotional experience of arguing, but soon find that people have different affective reactions to different topics, that their expressed emotions lead to different attributions by the other person, that displaying or disguising emotions leads to saying different things, that those things stimulate different thoughts in the other person and therefore different replies, and so on. You could understand all this by viewing arguing as a personal emotional experience, or as an interactive accomplishment, or as a way of structuring the other person's argumentative context, or as frames for self and/or other, and so on. Your initial question would end with you addressing just about every issue implied in this book if you stayed with your emotions-based research program long enough. Or, as another example, you might not begin with any interest in emotions at all, but start out instead with a commitment to analyzing what is said publicly. In a similar way, you would end up everywhere, including notice of emotional feelings and displays—provided that you follow the evidence wherever it points. There are very real limits to what you can do in a single study or a single essay, of course, and so we should remember to respect a paper that is restricted to some phenomenon that we don't happen to feel is central. Eventually it will all connect, or at least that is my experience.

So in drawing things together in this chapter, it would obviously be foolhardy for me to try to say what is the right perspective, the right set of theoretical commitments, or the right research topics. It is unavoidable that some of my own perspectives will be involved because I can't write about this or any topic without proceeding from my own intellectual foundations. But what I can do is to try to generate a description of the field that will be at least recognizable and at best expressive for scholars who produce a variety of research projects.

Multiple Simultaneous Processes

For me, the key to this chapter is the idea that interpersonal arguing is several different sorts of processes at once. Of course, arguing involves cognitive processes, nonverbal processes, verbal processes, perceptual processes, performative processes, and things like that, but I mean something much more general here. I want to convey that arguing involves processes that move on different levels of human experience, and that these movements are simultaneous. This might actually be easier to understand in outline rather in abstract description, so let me display the diagram that will organize the whole chapter.

Figure 8.1: A Sketch of Three Simultaneous Lines of Experience

Processes	Situation	Goals	Plans	Actions
Observable	Reasonably Apparent	Social Expectations	Negotiation of Practice	Arguments
Individual	Traits and Thresholds	Goals, Frames	Editing, Plans	Unilateral Arguing
Shared	Climate, Constraints	Shared Goals, Dialogue	Shared Plans	Bilateral Arguing

Figure 8.1 shows the kinds of processes that happen simultaneously and inevitably during a face-to-face argument. I have labeled these processes observable, individual, and shared. These labels are already somewhat prejudicial for our thinking, because they make certain questions unnatural to ask (e.g., what do individuals think about shared arguing rules?). But the labels seem to be fairly clear and useful, and as the chapter progresses we will see how far we can get with them.

The observable processes in the first line are those that the pragma-dialecticians and conversation analysts would call externalized and available for reconstruction (van Eemeren & Grootendorst, 1983; van Eemeren, Grootendorst, Jackson, & Jacobs, 1993; Jackson & Jacobs, 1980). These are public matters. Everything studied here is observable, or at least can be immediately inferred from public behaviors. To understand things at this level, no one needs to interview or survey any of the arguers. This work can be done from video, from transcripts of trials or hearings by Congressional committees, or even from centuries-old correspondence. Scholars only need to notice obvious features of the situation (the apparent topic, the setting, people's relational history, etc.), notice the constraints of that sort of situation (stay quiet in church, answer a teacher's questions, be respectful of a courtroom judge, etc.), try to figure out if the participants have negotiated any special procedural rules (father speaks last, witnesses cannot interrogate lawyers, etc.) or simply use the standard ones (be relevant, be truthful, etc.), and of course analyze what is said or written or publicly gestured (the externalized argument itself). Notice that I have cross-classified all these matters as pertaining to situation, goals, plans, and actions, a theoretical approach described first in Chapter 1. This is one of my own intellectual foundations.

The second line of Figure 8.1 represents the individual-level processes that also move forward during interpersonal arguing, or at least are in a state of constant agitation and relevance. Here, a key element of the situation is the arguer's own readiness to argue. His or her traits (e.g., argumentativeness) and thresholds (e.g., what does it take for this person to turn aggressive?) are important to an understanding of what is happening and how the arguer registers it. We should acknowledge that the arguer's knowledge is also relevant here, since we noticed in Chapter 5 that arguers who lack a nice fund of information tend to produce insistent but nearly content-free assertions. The goals portion of this process involves individual motivations—an intention to change the other person or to express one's keenest feelings (several of the serial arguing goals from Chapter 4), or perhaps the sort of primary goals we studied under the heading of argument frames (instrumental, dominance, identity, and play; Chapter 2). These goals are distinguished from those at the observable level because the observable goals are imposed by social structures (e.g., car salespeople are required to try to sell cars regardless of how they feel that day), but at the individual level the goals just arise spontaneously from the depths of what a person wants. The plans at the individual level are private intentions, which might be pursued simply or edited and revised before committing oneself to public action. Finally, the argument may be just as observable as in the Observable line, but here we take note that the public action is essentially unilateral because we are only considering a single person at a time. However, this analytical stance encourages us to consider that what a person thinks may not correspond exactly to what he or she is saying or admitting. We can also notice that even if the arguer is actually engaged in a dyadic conversation, this perspective still regards his or her actions as proximally caused by internal cognitions and motivations. Any influences from the situation or the other arguer are understood as distal causes that have to pass though the individual to have any effects.

The last line in Figure 8.1 is called shared, and by this I mean that these processes are intersubjective, emergent, and jointly experienced. You getting angry and me growing afraid of you is not "shared" in this sense—it is just two individual processes that happen to be colliding in the moment. By shared I mean that we each see and experience the same thing in the same way. We understand the situation similarly, for instance. Perhaps we both know that the climate is competitive or charming. We might disagree as to who started the striving or who is more suave, but we both directly understand that the climate is combative or warm. The climate is outside of both of us; it is a thing that we can both perceive; and we consider that it emerged because of how we interacted (not because of how I acted or because of what you invited). Two people can also share a goal or a commitment to a dialogue type (see Chapter 6). In a competitive disagreement, it is me against you. In a cooperative episode, it is us against the problem. "Us against the problem" is an example of two people sharing the same goal. The sharing does not necessarily happen because they have negotiated an agreement about what they will pursue. The sharing happens because it is natural for them to be a two-person agent in a single enterprise. Their plans and intentions can be shared in the same way—not always through explicitly achieved agreement, but more through a common experience of what they are doing. Notice, by the way, that the idea that an argument always has two "sides" can start to look odd once we begin to focus on how two people can share the experience of interpersonal arguing. We saw something like this in the chapter on dialogue types (Chapter 6), where we found one dialogue (eristic) was very combative, but that the others had greater degrees of joint action and shared experience. In the figure I have called these actions "bilateral," and by this I mean that the argument emerges in the interactive space between the two people. It is not half your argument and half mine—it is something that we created together, something that only exists because we worked jointly to generate the conversation.

This is the organization that I am going to pursue for the rest of the chapter, but it might be interesting for you to experiment with other ways of cutting things up. Maybe you would like to consider classifying arguments as destructive, neutral, or productive. Perhaps you might find it interesting to distinguish arguments as personal or public, as liberal or conservative, as literally or figuratively expressed, as expressing privilege or oppression, as private or corporate, as scientific or humanistic, or something else. Just as the three processes that I've chosen happen simultaneously, you may also choose several theorizing stances that can operate at the same time. By this point in the book you have surely realized that arguments are all around us and pretty much constitute whatever we think about nearly everything. Consequently whatever you care about can be a vantage point for the study of conversational arguing.

Even though all the processes happen simultaneously and nearly instantaneously during an actual interpersonal argument, we can separate things analytically and examine them individually. This makes them seem more independent than they really are, so we will need to remind ourselves periodically that everything is happening at once. Let us study each process line of Figure 8.1, one at a time.

Observable Arguments

Arguing is—among other things that happen simultaneously—a public thing. Interpersonal arguing (as opposed to people talking to themselves, imagining what they would say to someone, or writing arguments in term papers) is a mutual accomplishment. Two or more people work together to create a public product. They take positions, they express disagreement, they prod one another to expand their reasoning, they give evidence themselves, and so forth. All this has to happen in public because interpersonal arguing is responsive: each person answers the other. An arguer can only respond to something that the other person has expressed publicly. Thus the scholar taking this perspective is restricting himself/herself to exactly the information available to an arguer about the other person. If someone keeps things private, thinks things but doesn't say them, those are not elements of the observable conversational argument.

Figure 8.2: Scholarship Oriented to the Observable Processes in Arguing

Processes	Situation	Goals	Plans	Actions
Observable	Reasonably Apparent	Social Expectations	Negotiation of Practice	Arguments

Many scholars who write about argumentation praise it because they believe it expresses democracy, individual freedom, and truth, and is a path toward mutual understanding and social enlightenment. Aristotle (*Rhetoric*, 4th century BCE) and van Eemeren and Grootendorst (2004) are useful beginning and contemporary time points for this idea, but it can be found in just about every era of Western intellectual history. It has been pretty consistently expressed for more than two millennia. The proposal is that an argument improves as it is tested and revised, either immediately in a cooperative dyad or over centuries as a tension between great ideas such as personal freedom versus the divine right of kings. This process is traditionally called "clash." When one person makes an argument and the other objects to it without giving a counter reason, we fault the second person for not really clashing (see Kuhn, 1991, for a depressing study of how often this probably happens). But when the second person objects to the evidence, or points out an exception, or gives an opposing reason, we say that the two arguers have clashed. Even at that point, the mutual argument has improved, and if the first person then clashes in response, their interpersonal argument has become even more sophisticated. Jackson (2017) proposes that this sort of responsiveness is a fundamental normative standard for evaluating interpersonal arguing.

Since all this is public, quite a lot can be learned about interpersonal arguing without asking the arguers how they felt, what they really thought about the other person, and whether or not they were lying. This work can even be done when the arguers are inaccessible to scholars, perhaps because they have been dead for centuries but left a correspondence or transcribed debate behind.

For example, a nice idea from the studies of conversation and dialogue is the notion of commitment: that once you say something, you are committed to it (and all its implications) regardless of how sincere and thoughtful you were (see Chapter 6; in fact, commitment/obligation is a very old idea in the theory of logic: see Stump & Spade, 1982). When scholars of the observable analyze arguments, they generally need to begin by doing what is called argument reconstruction because people do not express themselves completely when they talk. If a friend asks if you want to go to lunch together and you don't want to, you might say, "Sorry, not hungry." Nothing in your reply actually mentions lunch or the proposal to share it, but we understand that you are refusing and giving a reason for doing so. The "sorry" shows that you care at least a little about the other person, that you acknowledge a social obligation to spend time with your friend, and that you appreciate the politeness norms that are associated with an invitation. The "not hungry" is a reason for the unstated refusal, and expresses the idea that a person who isn't hungry should not eat lunch. The refuser, who gave an argument for not going to lunch, is committed to all the things I have just listed, and more besides. He or she intentionally said "Sorry, not hungry," and is therefore committed to everything that this utterance implies, whether the arguer happened to think about those things or not (van Eemeren, Grootendorst, Jackson, & Jacobs, 1993, pp. 92–94). Perhaps your instinct is that it seems odd to conclude that the refuser "cares for" the inviter without asking him or her about this privately, but the idea here is that by being polite the refuser has enacted being considerate, and so is committed to it.

In U.S. civic life, we do this all the time. Many people are very cynical about whether political candidates mean anything they say. But even those citizens who didn't believe the politician in the first place can get angry when they discover that once elected, the politician doesn't make much effort to deliver what he or she promised. It is natural and justifiable to hold that a person is committed to what was said, even if we are doubtful that the person ever meant it. Often politicians are exactingly careful about what they say explicitly, but as citizens we reconstruct their statements to be clear and we hold our leaders to commitments that the leaders often deny they ever quite made. Deniability is in conflict with commitment, and the common-sense requirements of commitment are more important than the pedant's deniability. If people were only responsible for what they said explicitly, human communication would be essentially unworkable. Just review how many large ideas were implicit in "Sorry, not hungry," and how long it would take to say all them at every turn of an interaction.

Thus, an important idea about argumentation scholarship has quietly become evident. Studying observables is not just another route to figuring out people's private thoughts. Analysis and reconstruction of observables is an entirely different enterprise than psychological approaches. Your private feelings are one thing and your public expressions are another. They both count, and neither trumps the other. Obviously, it would be a fundamental mistake to confuse interior thought with public commitment.

Perhaps it is time to examine Figure 8.2 in more detail. The first notation is about situation. All arguments are situated, as I have emphasized repeatedly. That is, they each occur in a particular time and place, with particular people, pursuing particular aims, and so forth. In Chapter 3 we took note of the differences between reasonably apparent features of an interactive situation in contrast to the subjective ones. Reasonably apparent features, we saw, are those that can be pretty straightforwardly noted by an ordinarily informed observer. Such an analyst would have very little chance of error in saying whether the arguers were male or female, approximately how old they were, whether they were in public or in a private setting, whether they were talking face-to-face or texting, what the apparent topic of their disagreement was, and (assuming some background knowledge) what the personal relationship between the arguers was.

Along with these reasonably apparent features come structural norms, goals, affordances, and expectations (Brown & Levinson, 1987; O'Keefe, 1988, 1992). By "structural" I mean that these things originate in our social system, in the social organization that we live within and that is observable to any competent adult. An example is that in elementary school you might have been taught that boys aren't allowed to hit girls. "Girl" is a reasonably apparent feature of some interactive situations and the norm ("can't hit") has everything to do with external social rules and regrettably little to do with a particular boy's immediate temper and motivations.

Argument-relevant constraints and affordances can be like that, too. If you are asked to give reasons for some theoretical position during a classroom discussion, the immediate social situation calls on you to use scholarly evidence for your position, to express it in formal terms, to respect any opposing point of view, to regard any controversy as being about the topic and not being about any person in the classroom, to speak politely to others, and many other things that you probably take for granted now (see O'Keefe, 1992, for a general theoretical exposition of structural requirements for interpersonal communication). You may not approve of all these requirements and restrictions—perhaps you think that a teacher's authority is hegemonic or creativity-stifling, for instance. But if you act out your objection, it is apparent to everyone that you are rejecting the situational constraints. You might look like a crusader or a boor depending on the other students' views, but either way you will have taken on that identity because you have contrasted your own behavior with what everyone understood was required. We are supposed to act in particular ways to pastors and mothers-in-law, we are supposed to express ourselves in different ways in bars and in classrooms, we are supposed to use different sorts of evidence in temple and on subways, we are supposed to express ourselves one way in person and another way while leaving a phone message, we are supposed to use different vocabulary while texting than when writing a term paper, and so forth—the examples can be multiplied for as many reasonably apparent situation features as we can think of. More or less objective circumstances restrict our freedom of argument and action. We can often resist those structures, and the force of the situation's demands will be revealed by the degree to which our resistant behavior is censured (Garfinkel, 1967).

Thus, observable features of the situation lead naturally to the next idea in Figure 8.2, goals. For many people the word "goal" immediately refers to an internal motivation, as in "the child's goal was to eat as much ice cream as possible." That isn't what is meant when studying arguments observably. A goal is simply an end point, a target, the thing that actions aim toward. For this line of Figure 8.2, the goal is required by the situation and may or may not be the private goal of the arguer. For example, legal trials impose the goal of telling the truth on witnesses, but some of them lie anyway. An essay exam imposes the goal of getting a top grade, but sometimes a student is fatigued or bored and really doesn't try. Mature, responsible arguing imposes goals of mutuality and cooperation, but many interpersonal arguments go off the rails and degenerate into eristic exchanges. Particular levels of politeness are always expected (Brown & Levinson, 1987) and if you are pointedly impolite, you will be socially punished in some way, proving that the politeness goal was there all along, regardless of what you preferred. Therefore when working on the observable processes, we consider goals to be social expectations or requirements, not individual motives.

So if people don't always implement structurally required goals, what use is the concept? The answer is simple: knowing the goals inherent to the situation puts us in a position to evaluate what and how well the arguers did. We can see that an observable argument was or was not moving toward a particular goal to some degree. We can say that a witness lied and should go to jail, that a student did indifferently and should be given a C, or that a boyfriend was nasty and does not deserve to have his way. We can compare the situation's observable goals with the equally observable argumentation to make normative judgments. Evaluation has to happen in a very different way when we assume that goals are private. We can see that someone was abusive and perhaps discover independent evidence that he or she had the goal of being awful, but our critique has to be that the goal was wrong, not that the behaviors didn't pursue it. Here on the Observable line, we observe the goal so we can then take it for granted and measure the actions against it.

Plans are the ways that goals are pursued. Normally we would express this by saying that "people use plans to pursue goals." This isn't technically wrong here but it does obscure what we are doing when we only study observables. In restricting ourselves to publicly noticeable processes, we are looking to see how text (or gesture or music, etc.) responds to situation, relates to social expectations, and implements standard practices to generate public argument. This is the sort of thing that is meant by "intertextuality," a word that captures the idea of how texts talk to texts. To give examples of intertextuality, we might say that one remark in a Presidential debate called out the next remark, or that Reformation rhetoric stimulated Rome's Council of Trent reform proclamations, or that a particular set of public demonstrations advocating gun control was answered by NRA statements, and so forth. People are actually doing all this, but by concentrating only on the observables we put the people well into the background—tiny little footnotes, if you will—and speak metaphorically of person-independent texts saying this, doing that, and responding to the other. The idea is that the people are not really very relevant to what is happening: given what one text expresses or what a situation requires, only a few things could have been done in reply regardless of what particular people were involved. This is a way of attributing agency to the argument rather than the arguers.

So if arguing plans are not personal accomplishments or intentions, what does "plan" mean when we are working only on observable processes? In Figure 8.2, I have labeled this cell "negotiation of practice." The essential idea is that the scholar looks at the text and analyzes where the text is pointing, what its targeted end point seems to be. Although we normally think of a plan as being something that we project into the future, in this sort of work we detect plans after the fact. For example, here is a little snippet of an argument from an historical mystery novel that I like:

"Have you ever seen a drowned man?" William asked.

"Many times," Severinus said. "And if I guess what you imply, they do not have this face: the features are swollen."

"Then the man was already dead when someone threw the body into the jar." (Eco, 1980, p. 105. The "jar" is actually a large pottery vessel in which the corpse was discovered.)

The interesting thing here is the first question: "Have you ever seen a drowned man?" On the face of it, it is just a question that could have been asked almost aimlessly out of simple curiosity. But in the context of what happens immediately after, we see that this was the beginning of a plan to generate a conclusion ("the man was already dead"). The question was textually designed to make space for a yes or no ("many times" was a yes) that would either directly constitute evidence for the conclusion (as it did here) or would necessitate an intervening explanation ("people's faces swell up when they drown," or something like that). In retrospect, we can see that there was a textual plan: seek evidence, agree on evidence, and use evidence to support a conclusion.

"Retrospect" is an important word here. If we were trying to do the same analysis while listening to the conversation in real time, we would still have to wait for a few moments to see what happened. The observables-oriented study of interpersonal argument is clearly in the domain of pragmatics, which refers to the effects that words have on people. Pragmatics is a division of semiotics, the study of signs. Semiotics includes semantics, syntactics, and pragmatics. Semantics is the relation between words and the world ("dog" to a type of animal), syntactics is the relation between words and other words (adjectives require nouns), and pragmatics is the relation between words and people ("your email made me laugh"). This is a very simple summary: see Arundale (2005), Cooren (2005), or Levinson (1983), for instance. To understand the effects that a text has on people, we have to wait to see how the people reacted. To distinguish between a joke and an offensive remark, we need to observe whether the second person laughed, ignored, or criticized. Even in the example above, Severinus could have taken offense that William might think that Serverinus was not a man of the world who had seen things, and then the snippet would not have moved so easily to its conclusion.

So plans become apparent to the analyst when the text and its consequences can be seen. This is what I mean by "negotiated" in Figure 8.2. The two arguers do not need to negotiate like ambassadors. They just act in response to one another, and each action carries meaning. If I smile at your remark I am proposing that you joked a little, and if you smile back we have negotiated: that you joked, I got it, you know I got it, and we are both pleased. In public arguments, we can see agreement, hesitation, avoidance, disagreement, and many other things that we can use to characterize the pragmatic nature of the talk. All these observations take place in the context of having seen where the text was supposed to go or apparently went, its plan. To say that a person disagreed, for instance, requires that in the first place, we could tell that the text was aimed at a different conclusion that the one expressed by the "disagreement."

If the conversation goes smoothly, analysts generally assume that the text went as it was supposed to go. Thus, its apparent direction was also the textual plan. But scholars can also observe people getting messed up in conversation. When materials are transcribed closely enough, we can see people mispronounce words, say one phrase when the context called for another phrase that sounded similar, hesitate in the middle of an expression, lose confidence in what is being said, trail off before the thought is finished, self-correct halfway through an inappropriate remark, and so forth. People's responses can also show uptake, avoidance, or confusion. In these cases, it can be harder to reconstruct what the plan was, but careful thinking can still produce very credible analyses of failed or flawed plans.

Before leaving this idea of plans in the observable processes of arguing, I should emphasize that most of the plans are standard and that the negotiation mainly consists of implicitly agreeing that we will both do what is expected. Conversation is a very structured thing and we have to acknowledge its constraints in order to be coherent (Grice, 1975; Jackson & Jacobs, 1980; Sacks, 1992). Questions are so insistently followed by answers, for example, that anything said after a question will be understood as answering it even if that meaning cannot be tracked to the exact wording (e.g., Question: "Can I borrow $100?" Response: "I think my car isn't running right.") We take turns, we speak responsively, we signal when we are changing topics, and thousands of other things that are part of known patterns, typically only unconsciously known. Conversational argument patterns have been identified, as we saw in Chapter 1 (e.g., Muntigl & Turnbull, 1998). These patterns have been absorbed by competent adults and so there is not much explicit negotiation needed when they are used. It is the departures that need to be brought to the surface for explicit consideration: "Excuse me, but I have to go back to an earlier point here, to clarify what I meant." One needs to be excused because he or she has intentionally violated the structural framework of conversation, in this instance the expected timing involved in being coherent.

So in Figure 8.2, the negotiation of plans is a text-to-text negotiation, with the background rules mainly provided by social and conversational convention. In pragma-dialectics we find specifications of the roles of protagonist and antagonist, allowable and irrelevant speech acts, standards for agreement or abandonment of standpoints, and many other things (van Eemeren & Grootendorst, 1983, 2004). These rules can be mutually rejected but this is much more likely to require explicit discussion than the far more ordinary acceptance of rules, patterns, and sequencing conventions.

Because many people find this idea odd, I want to emphasize that the plans are not individual behavioral intentions, just as the goals in Figure 8.2 were not personal impulses. Analysts are trying to understand the text, not the people, and are really trying to develop a theory of text rather than a generalizable theory of people and their behaviors. The latter projects occur later in Figure 8.1.

The final entry in Figure 8.2 is the action, which I have simply called the argument. This is an observable thing, constituted by text. It is not assumed to be a complete expression. As we have seen throughout this book, beginning in Chapter 1, arguments are enthymematic and many of their elements and meanings are implied rather than explicit. Scholars committed to studying observable processes do not want to ask the arguers what they meant by their utterances. Instead, these scholars "reconstruct" the argument (van Eemeren, Grootendorst, Jackson, & Jacobs, 1993). The text is the first set of clues, of course, but then the scholars identify assumptions, things that were noticeably not said, social conventions, previous statements, and many other things that lead to an inventory of the arguers' commitments, which I mentioned earlier. These commitments are just as arguable as the explicit statements are. If you imply a thing, you cannot dodge a criticism by replying, "I didn't say that." If you implied it, it is reconstructed as having exactly the same commitment status as if you had said it clearly. These commitments are not directly observable but they are direct inferences from things that are public matters, and so I count them as observable. The key point of contrast with the rest of Figure 8.1 is that all the evidence is drawn from the public performance of text and none from surveys or interviews involving the arguers.

Having reconstructed the argument, scholars can then go on to classify the argument's type (e.g., Walton, Reed, & Macagno, 2008). Various kinds of classification systems are available as we saw in Chapter 1. The oldest is induction/deduction (abduction was later added to this list), but today we prefer to use "argument schemes," such as argument from authority, cause to effect reasoning, analogy, practical reasoning, and so forth. Once having identified the argument scheme, the scholar can then point to critical questions that match each scheme (e.g., "Is the authority an expert in the field of study that the argument is in?"). This allows normative evaluation of the textual argument. We have noticed the general standards of acceptability, relevance, and sufficiency that can be applied even if the scholar finds that the text doesn't quite fit one of the standard schemes. The Toulmin model is a general analytical system that does not depend on being able to label some text as an example of a particular argument scheme. In the face-to-face context we are studying in this book, the idea of clash or responsiveness is an important standard. Scholars can also make broader (i.e., non-argumentative) evaluations of the text—for example, saying that the argument followed or violated social conventions. These sorts of things also have a bearing on how effective an argument can be.

It is at once odd and amazing that we can learn so much about interpersonal arguing when we do our best to ignore the people and their subjective experiences. Working along this line of Figure 8.2, we can see elements of the situation that funnel behavior, we can see that standard types of social interaction impose certain objectives, we can see sequencing and patterns built into kinds of text exchanges, and we can see how these things get expressed in public arguments. Taking this point of view does not deny that people have subjective experiences, impulses, intentions, or weird understandings. This observables scholarship just brackets those things as being someone else's research problem, and tries to see what we can learn without worrying about such matters.

Individual Arguments

As we move down a line in Figure 8.1 we encounter the arguers themselves, in all their individuality, peculiarity, and even their self-deceptiveness (see Hample, 2007). In the Observables line of Figure 8.1 we were trying to understand text. In the Individual line, we will be investigating psychology and cognition. Instead of regarding text as our primary research topic and source of data, now we will only consider it as a set of clues. We want to know what arguers are thinking and why they think it; what they want and how they intend to accomplish it; and what they think they did when they argued. Our now-restricted idea about text is that what a person says is some sort of hint about what he or she was thinking, and that what the other person said is a possible indication of what needs to be thought about. For Observable research, text is the point. For Individual research, text is only a symptom or stimulus. Here is the relevant part of the chapter's organizing figure:

Figure 8.3: Scholarship Oriented to the Individual Processes in Arguing

Processes	Situation	Goals	Plans	Actions
Individual	Traits and Thresholds	Goals, Frames	Editing, Plans	Unilateral

The most basic idea in this sort of inquiry is that individual people have all of the agency in face-to-face arguing. They produce each bit of behavior, and they generate it in conformity to their interior lives. They do things because they want to, they feel things because that is how they react, and they intend things because that is how they know how to accomplish what they want. The observable things we examined in the previous section still exist of course, but now we consider that they are all channeled through a person and only affect behavior after the individual has processed and made sense of them. Here is a simple example. Perhaps an instructor tells the class to form into five-person discussion groups. This would be an observable feature of the situation and its goal. Most students will probably react to this situational element by moving into five-person groups. But perhaps one student is tired of what s/he thinks is pointless peer discussion, perhaps a second student is too depressed to want to talk with anyone, or perhaps another student has already been ordered around enough that day and just refuses. The same situational demand is present in all these cases, but it results in different thoughts and behaviors because it has moved through different individual psychologies. In statistical or causal vocabulary, we would say that situational elements are completely "mediated" by individual processes when we are trying to explain arguing behaviors.

Therefore scholars pursuing this sort of inquiry work very hard to figure out the terrain of people's interior lives. Because we are only studying arguing, our interest is compressed to things that we suppose might affect people's interpersonal disagreement behaviors and experiences. This is still a large expanse of research topics, but sometimes beginning scholars need to be reminded that not everything that is relevant to personal psychology is guaranteed to have any connection to argumentation. A link between arguing and a particular facet of psychology is a necessary element to doing this kind of argumentation research.

What sorts of things have proven to be relevant? You have already learned that some personality traits, some impulses, some beliefs, and some orientations affect people's experience of being in a face-to-face argument. "Some" is obviously important. You might have a personal interest in a particular theory from social psychology, such as an account of how people understand close relationships, but you would still have to make a case for its relevance to argumentation. (In this case, attachment style, Toews, Catlett, and McKenry, 2005, might get you started on a rationale.) In another case, you might find nothing already done and so you would have to build the case for a connection yourself. One cannot simply assume that everything important to psychology will also be important to arguing. Among the things that argumentation scholars study in regard to human psychology are personality traits, cognitions, feelings, and intentions. In Figure 8.3, traits and thresholds are listed as pertaining to "situation."

A personality trait is a general predisposition to behave in a particular way across situations. So if a person is shy (the trait), he or she will act quietly or passively in a lot of social contexts, compared to other people who are less shy. Traits and states are different. A trait is the general inclination and a state is the immediate one. So a generally shy person (trait) can still be very aggressive in a particular moment (state). States are temporary and traits are relatively enduring. Roberts and DelVecchio (2000) explored the stability of personality traits over the life span and found noticeable periods of consistency from college age to about 50, and another from 50 to 70. Even in the age range 3 to 18 years, they found predictability from year to year, though there was more change than in later life stages. So traits are consistent over time.

Over the decades, psychologists have explored hundreds, maybe thousands, of personality traits. In the last quarter of the 20th century they undertook an empirical simplification of their huge inventory of variables, and concluded that altogether they represented either three or five "supertraits." Actually, psychology has coalesced on the conclusion that there are five, but communication research started down this path by using the three. The Big Three are psychoticism (being cold, unfeeling, or hostile toward others), neuroticism (being anxious, worried, or nervous), and extraversion (being outgoing, sociable, or friendly). The Big Five, which summarize the same specific traits with a different organization, are openness (curiosity, interest in exploring new things), conscientiousness (being careful, being duty-bound), extraversion, agreeableness (friendliness, acquiescence), and neuroticism; sometimes the acronyms OCEAN or CANOE are used as memory aids for the Big Five.

These supertraits have been connected to some key argument-relevant traits, such as argumentativeness, verbal aggressiveness, and communication apprehension (e.g., McCroskey, Heisel, & Richmond, 2001). These supertraits are part of our genetic inheritance from our biological parents, since research shows that they are about 50% heritable (e.g., Jang, Livesley, & Vernon, 1996; Polderman et al., 2015). Biology is not destiny: even if you are born with aggressive tendencies, you can learn to be polite and diplomatic, for instance. But our inclinations are often our social reflexes and it can take a long time to retrain. In Chapter 7 we also saw that people's traits (argumentativeness, etc.) varied from nation to nation, implying that cultural context might also affect our social orientations. The implication of all this is that being high or low in argumentativeness, verbal aggressiveness, personalization of conflict, indirect interpersonal aggression, or shyness (to name a few personality characteristics that have been connected to the heritable supertraits and/or to nation of origin) is likely to be a persistent feature of someone's personality.

One way to understand traits is to regard them as thresholds. A highly aggressive person has a low threshold for losing his or her temper. A person with low anxiety can endure a lot of uncertainty before feeling nervous. A highly argumentative person needs very little opening to argue, and a shy person needs to be encouraged to express disagreement. So once we have found a personality trait to be relevant to argumentation, we should be able to predict something about how the person is inclined to act in a situation that invites arguing (Chapter 3 discussed argument situations).

The idea of threshold reminds us that neither personality nor situation affect behavior alone. Both are always present, but something more than that is meant here. Behaviors and emotional reactions result from some combination of person and context. Two people can react differently to similar situations because they have different personalities, and two people with similar personalities will act differently if they are confronted with different circumstances. The interaction of personality and situation is far more likely to be an explanatory resource than either personality or situation in isolation. If you should read a paper saying that some trait affected arguing all by itself, you should examine the study carefully to see if perhaps situational variables were kept constant. You should do parallel thinking if you find a study saying that everyone acts the same way in a particular kind of conflict: were they all the same sort of people in some important respect? Keeping a variable constant allows us to see other effects more clearly, but does so at the cost of covering up interactions between constructs.

All these considerations were what led me to identify the "situation" as traits and thresholds in Figure 8.3. The idea is that a person's arguing originates within the person—that is, it is energized internally. Thus its proximal originating situation must be interior—what a person thinks, how he feels, what she wants to have happen. Cognitions (perceptions, beliefs, information) should also be included as part of the individual situation, since this material guides interpretation of circumstances and points the way to expression of traits. External events, including what the other person just said, are the raw materials that one's personality acts upon to start the individual argument production process. Thus on this thinking, when we ask, "Where is the cauldron for this argument?" our answer will be, "Within."

The next entry on the Individual process line of Figure 8.3 is goals. Goals are desired end states. In that cell, I have mentioned goals and frames. Both goals and frames are intimately connected to the arguer's personality (see Chapters 2 and 6), and so we have an easy transition from situation to goal for individual processes. The basic idea here is that personality projects itself onto what one desires, and vice versa. A set of personality predispositions represents the person's social values and priorities. So a highly aggressive person will easily form an aggressive goal, an apprehensive person will tend toward avoidance goals, an argumentative person will want to clash, and so forth.

In contrast to how we thought about goals in connection to observable text, here we see them as expressions of interior desire. They are aims, ambitions, targets, and preferences. Goals are personal things that express what we want to be true. If my goal is to be friendly, it is because I want us to be friends; if my goal is to persuade you, it might be because I want you to acknowledge my superiority or maybe because I want you to have more useful opinions. Researching individual processes leads us to see goals as originating within people rather than as being imposed by circumstances. Circumstantial forces exist, but here we insist that they must be processed through the person before they can exert themselves.

We have already studied many particular goals in this book, perhaps most explicitly in Chapter 4, which explored Bevan's set of serial arguing goals (e.g., Bevan, Hale, & Williams, 2004), or in Chapter 6 where we examined dialogue preferences (e.g., Cionea, 2011). Serial argument goals included positive and negative personal expression, seeking mutuality, trying to hurt or change the other person, surveilling the relationship to decide whether to stay, and getting one's own way. Dialogue goals included persuasion, negotiation, information exchange, finding the truth, deliberating, and eristic fighting. These are not the only possible lists of goals (Dillard, Segrin, & Harden, 1989 have another one, and so do Clark & Delia, 1979). In fact, a list is not a very satisfactory theory, and so other theorists have created general accounts of motivation that involve approach and avoidance, cooperation and competition, individualism and collectivism, and other simpler organizing ideas.

In both Chapters 4 and 6 we reviewed work that connected those goal lists to several personality traits, notably argumentativeness, verbal aggressiveness, and personalization of conflict. While we found some connections, the evidence was not overwhelmingly strong. We certainly did not conclude that we only needed to know someone's personality to be confident about that person's interaction goal in a particular episode. Very possibly that was because we were looking for gross relationships between personality and goals, thus omitting situational variables for the most part. The relationships that we did discover, combined with our conceptual understanding of how traits and thresholds project engagement impulses, still encourage us that we will end up with a good account of how goals emerge from individual psychologies.

Frames, the other element in the "goals" cell in Figure 8.3, were the topic of Chapter 2. They are also connected to personality, as we repeatedly saw there. Frames are cognitive: they represent thoughts, construals, and perspectives. Goals, in contrast, express desires and impulses. With the frames entry in Figure 8.3 I mean to acknowledge a variety of beliefs and sense-making systems that are pertinent to arguing. Naturally, while working on the Individual line of processes, we will be considering that all these beliefs and frames are individual accomplishments, rather than being the possessions of social collectives or being submerged in a text's commitments. Research has discovered that several personality traits such as argumentativeness and verbal aggressiveness lead to different beliefs about arguing (e.g., Rancer, Kosberg, & Baukus, 1992) as well as different frames for arguing (e.g., Hample & Irions, 2015). As with the goals lists, we again have a simple transition from situation-as-personality to the Goals stage in Figure 8.3.

In what sense can we understand frames and beliefs as goals? Neither is immediately a set of desired end states, but they both imply motivations. Particular beliefs connected to argumentativeness include seeing the activity of arguing as beneficial to one's intellect and as providing enjoyment. Frames for arguing include obtaining some personal benefit, displaying one's identity, cooperating with one's partner, and being civil. These understandings—that arguing can improve one's mind or social life—carry the easy implications that arguing can be intentionally used in service of such purposes. Seeing that arguing can be initiated to dominate implicitly acknowledges that you or another person might have the goal of domination when arguing.

Frames, in other words, describe the affordances of arguing from one person's point of view. An affordance is a possibility, a capacity of something. So when we say that arguing can be for play, we are saying that play is an affordance of arguing, that arguing has the capacity to provide entertainment. A person's argument frames collect and summarize his or her survey of interpersonal argument's potentials. If someone cannot see that arguing can be civil (one of the frames in Chapter 2), then that person cannot intentionally move toward civil interaction during verbal conflict. If someone's frames are so limited that he or she thinks the only reason for disagreeing is to start a fight, then that person is going to have a lot of fights. Frames, in other words, collect our goals into cognitively organized systems. These organizations are our personal theories of interpersonal arguing—what it is, what it is for, and what it feels like.

Frames are simultaneously expressions of our personalities and our experience. When a person describes his or her frames for arguing, that person is summarizing a life history. We cannot simply tell a person, "No, arguments are really cooperative so quit being stubborn," and have any real expectation of changing the other person's understanding of the social world. We are shaped by biology and history. If someone says that arguing is always competitive then we should assume that for that person it has been, and we should probably expect a confrontational display if we argue with him or her. Our frames constrain us in the goals we can conceive and therefore pursue. Thus, frames are part of the "goals" cell in Figure 8.3.

The next entry, of course, is Plans. In that cell I have included planning and editing. Plans are projected lines of action intended to deliver us to our desired end states, our goals (Berger, 1997; Hample, 1997, 1999). Editing is a planning process in which a person changes plans to improve them, just as writers should revise rough drafts of their papers. In the Observables orientation to the study of argumentation, we found plans by noticing how the discourse proceeded, and identifying efficient movements as having been the textual plans. Here in the individual approach, we seek plans within people's private experiences. Plans are intentions or projections. They do not need to be conscious. As adult members of society we have learned to do many things automatically, and we may only think about our plans when they suddenly go wrong.

As with traits and goals, we can discover a person's plans by asking (there is danger is assuming that we are getting all the information, and getting it exactly right, but we will pass over those problems here; see Hample, 1984). A standard procedure is to provide a person with some interaction goal—maybe asking a friend for a financial favor—and then requesting the respondent to list out what he or she would say in order (e.g., Berger, 1997; Bower, Black, & Turner, 1979; Schank, 1982). Actual plans are quite specific and so we will want to provide the respondent with at least a brief description of the situation and of course the goal. So I might ask you, "How would you talk your roommate into changing his or her major? List the things you would say or do, in order." This will produce a draft of your intentions, a map of how you would try to achieve your aims. Some of the steps in your plan will probably be argumentative and others will establish an interactional context for your reasons. By carefully selecting and phrasing situations and goals, we can restrict our studies to arguing as opposed to other kinds of communication (e.g., comforting or forgiving).

Meyer (1997) has worked out a nice explanation of how we do this sort of private planning, whether we do it consciously or unconsciously. She says it is a two-stage process.

First we absorb the social situation (including its goal) and let it connect itself to our long-term memories. This connects situational features ("it's my Mom;" "she thinks I messed up") with our memories of how we have dealt with this before (denial, giving an excuse, or perhaps admitting it with apparent sincerity). This is automatic, in Meyer's theory. She says that we simply register associations between situations and messages. Considering how quickly we communicate during conversation, this makes sense. This first stage generates a rough draft of what we will say. It gives our reflexive arguments, our message impulses, our blurts.

The second stage—which is optional—involves possible suppression, revision, and replanning. This is what I mean by "editing." In this stage, we snag what we were about to say and compare it to a second set of long-term memory stores before we say anything at all. In particular, we compare the draft message's features to the consequences we remember for that sort of utterance. The consequences are those that we care about, so they reflect interaction and other social goals. So we might notice that Mom gets mad when we deny, or that this person will actually expect evidence before being convinced. Therefore we might abandon that draft of our argument. We could revise it a little or drop it entirely. We would cycle back to the situational stimulus and develop a second draft message, and then evaluate that according to its likely consequences. This is the editing process. It happens very quickly unless we encounter major problems and actually have to think about our argument consciously. Some people do not edit very often or very well. We call these people blurters (Hample, Richards, & Skubisz, 2013).

Notice that when studying individual processes, we assume that all this happens inside one person's head. As a child you were certainly taught what you should say and what you must not say, and these were social processes that possibly represented your cultural heritage. But here we consider that those things only affect individual arguing after they have been completely mediated by the individual's interior life. A considerable amount of research has connected editing choices to personality (Hample, 2005, ch. 6). This means that we have a nice set of empirical relationships moving directly from situation to goals to plans, in the context of Figure 8.3.

It only remains, then, to explain why the Actions cell in Figure 8.3 is called "unilateral." The word means one-sided, and indicates that the arguer is acting alone. Naturally, we do sometimes argue alone, as when we work out the reasons we give in a term paper or email. This is what O'Keefe (1977) called argument$_1$. But even then, we should have an audience in mind and be imagining how that person will react to whatever we are writing (Honeycutt, 2003). This book is more focused on the other main possibility, interpersonal arguing, in which two or more people go back and forth in what they say. Even here, however, we can conceive of one person saying simply what he or she wants to say. Such a person may very well register what the other arguer has said and react to it. But it is still a case of action by one person at a time. Earlier in the chapter I contrasted the case of one person against another and the case of two people against the problem. For two people, A and B, and one mutual problem, the first case produces a sequence like A → B → A → B, and the second a sequence like AB → problem. The first sequence is the unilateral one. The second sequence will be taken up in the next part of the chapter, where we examine the shared processes.

In unilateral arguing, the individual acts from his or her private interior life. This may be done politely, cooperatively, responsively, and helpfully, but it is still done alone (by scholarly assumption for this sort of research). Two people can be doing it together but the argument is still unilateral, just doubly so. We will encounter the other possibility, bilateral or joint action, momentarily.

Taking on a commitment to studying the individual processes in interpersonal argument does not deny the existence of observable or shared phenomena. It just directs attention away from them. The agency of the individual is the premise and focus of this sort of theory. We see individuals construing their circumstances, reacting with the instantaneous creation of goals, quickly producing revisable intentions, and finally acting back on that environment. In this perspective, we see each person trying to navigate and shape his or her social world.

Shared Arguing

Nearly everyone can immediately see the competitive element of interpersonal arguing, but very substantial cooperation is also needed for an argument to take place. Quite a bit of this is obvious: people must use the same language, must take turns speaking, must have common assumptions, must acknowledge similar standards for what counts as evidence, must maintain an open channel of communication, and so forth (e.g., Brockriede, 1975; van Eemeren & Grootendorst, 2004; Sacks, 1992). Some cooperation is optional or more subtle, however, and those possibilities are the topic of this part of the chapter.

The key idea for this sort of research is that face-to-face arguing is an *interactive* accomplishment. For Observables research, we found agency in the text; for

Individual research the agency was within a single person. The Shared viewpoint sees agency *between* the people, in their emergent interaction. Just as a newborn baby is not half-father and half-mother but its own thing, emergent properties have their own nature.

Suppose we witnessed this little argumentative exchange:

> A: Gasoline powered cars can get 40 or more miles per gallon now, so I don't see the need to buy hybrids.
> B: But hybrids can get about 50 miles per gallon. And an electric-only car doesn't use gas at all, so it gets something like infinity per gallon.
> A: Wow. Maybe we should be looking at electricity or hydrogen powered cars.
> B: Yes.

We can see A changing his or her position as the dialogue moves on, and we can see the importance of B's contribution to that change. But who does the conclusion belong to? Or the reasons? B was the first to propose some clash with A's original gasoline-only position, but A obviously endorsed that reason ("Wow"), so it belongs to both of them from that moment onward. And the conclusion was first expressed by A but B immediately indicated that it was agreeable ("Yes"), and in our fictional little context, B might even have believed that before the exchange began. And where did "hydrogen powered" come from? It appears in the conclusion and is presented as though it had been argued for, but it is nowhere in the explicit reasoning.

This dialogue can be analyzed for its observables or for its individual elements because as we noticed early in the chapter, all three sets of processes are always present. But seeing the episode as shared has some advantages. First, it allows people into the picture, instead of restricting agency to text. We could wonder why A and B were having the exchange, what they individually knew about the topic, whether they had any hidden agendas for the conversation, and so forth. Text might reveal some of this, but it would be much more straightforward just to ask A and B these questions. However, the second main advantage of studying shared processes is that we are no longer required to trace every element to a single person's agency, as in Individual approaches. We have already noticed the problems of deciding about authorship of the various public elements of the argument in the automobile exchange above. Even if we learned that A had some positive views about electric powered cars before the conversation, could we be certain that A would have expressed those views as B did in the second turn, or even as A eventually did in the third turn?

The automobile argument was birthed between A and B. They both can claim parentage and influence, but neither can say they authored it. More subtly, neither can say they half-authored it either. The argument is not simply "what A said" plus "what B said." The sum is more than its parts, and the coherence and direction of the exchange cannot be completely accounted for by its components. That is the idea animating research on shared arguing processes.

Here is the pertinent part of Figure 8.1 for this section of the chapter:

Figure 8.4: Scholarship Oriented to the Shared Processes in Arguing

Processes	Situation	Goals	Plans	Actions
Shared	Climate, Constraints	Shared Goals, Dialogue	Shared Plans	Bilateral Arguing

We have the same categories (Situation, Goals, Plans, Actions) as in the earlier approaches, but this time we will concentrate on their nature as joint productions. All these things will be treated as accomplishments, as things emergent in interaction, rather than given (as with textual approaches) or subjective (as with individual approaches).

Figure 8.4 mentions climate and constraints as elements of the shared situation. Sometimes climate is understood subjectively ("I felt unwelcome at the dinner") but here we are regarding it as something that both arguers sense and endorse equally. They can both feel that an episode is competitive or happy. They may have different explanations for why it feels that way, but they both see it. What is more, they both participate in it. By reacting to it they are each endorsing its existence, and so are extending it further into the future. They accomplish it. Not only does the climate initially seem to exist independent of the two people, but their actions jointly confirm that climate and help it to persist.

As an example of climate, consider the Supreme Court of the United States. It was established by the U.S. Constitution, which came into effect in 1789. More than 100 judges have been on the court, and obviously almost none of them are still alive and serving. I do not know how many attorneys have appeared, but it must be in the thousands, and nearly all of them have passed away as well. But in spite of all the people repeatedly changing every few years or decades, and the original room having been repurposed and replaced, the Supreme Court's proceedings continue to have a particular climate: structured disagreement, respectful refutation, automatic subservience of any lawyer to any justice, unquestioned time limits, and so forth. I once went to watch the court in action (you just find out the schedule of oral arguments and get there on the outside steps early in the morning: the proceedings are public). I have no trouble believing that the climate inside the courtroom is little changed over the last two centuries. I could observe the climate from the visitors' seating. It was not due to any one or two of the attorneys or judges I saw, and still less by any of the visitors, security personnel, or other court officials in the room. No one in particular created that climate, but everyone respected and so reinforced it. For that day, the climate was a shared accomplishment by everyone present, and its historical persistence is not due to any individuals in particular.

Relationships have climates, too. Perhaps you have attended an extended-family Thanksgiving dinner where everyone was happy to see everyone else: all the adults were funny, all the children were cute, mistakes were always tiny and entertaining, weird uncles were just eccentric, and everything was instantly forgiven and enjoyed. Or maybe you have been to the other kind of Thanksgiving dinner: jokes failed because they were stupid or insulting, disrespect and prejudice were apparent everywhere you looked, children had no discipline or common sense, uncles were Neanderthals, and every moment of conversation was another little beating. You didn't create either climate, but neither did anyone else. It was just there, available for everyone to experience. By responding to it (were you smiling or frowning at everything you heard? were you stone-faced?) you were re-enacting it, and the joint recreation of it from moment to moment was a real thing that cemented the climate's person-independent existence. It was, in a word, shared.

Dyads also have climates. From the individual point of view, we might call these expectations. But a climate is enacted as a message system, and those messages both follow from and invite the perception of climate. So if you and your relational partner are going through a bad time, when you talk you both feel nervous and uncertain about what to say and how it will be taken. So you both hold yourselves back a little and you both notice that about the other and feel it within yourself. The climate emerges from your interaction. In this way, a climate can force itself into existence even though neither individual wants it (e.g., Cronen, Pearce, & Snavely, 1979).

Besides having a "feel" about them, climates have the communicative function of encouraging or hindering certain kinds of actions (Hample, 1997, 1999). A cooperative climate makes it easy to trust and share. A competitive climate stimulates the reflex of disagreeing and pushing back. Climates can be characterized in many ways, and I do not know of a defensible theory that classifies all the possibilities. So here is a partial list of climate types. Climates can be safe, happy, abusive, boring, racist, forgiving, encouraging, damaging, hurtful, hilarious, and many more things. Imagine how people might be inclined to argue in each of them. Suppose in each of them, someone said to you, "Do you like wearing expensive clothes?" You would interpret the remark in the context of that climate, and probably reply in different ways. Sometimes you would move in an argumentative way, taking offense, making an attack, or defending yourself, but sometimes you would act cooperatively, maybe smiling, returning a little joke, or saying something quietly thoughtful. The question is the same, but encased in jointly experienced climates it projects different mutual meanings. Different arguments will result, but not because either individual was aiming at that sort of exchange.

Sometimes the climate is routine, ordinary, and unnoticed, but there is always a climate. It focuses us on certain choices and therefore closes off others. That is why I have combined the ideas of climate and constraints in Figure 8.4. Climates can be enduring or temporary, or a particular relationship can have its own climate so that a set of feelings and behavioral tendencies is imported whenever that other person is near you. The climate affords a particular "set" so that arguers are guided toward being agreeable, or reactive, or generous, or defensive in how they listen and what they say.

Thus climate suggests the goals and dialogue types for the episode, and this brings us to the next things in Figure 8.4. Here the goals are labeled "shared" to distinguish them from the subjective impulses of the individual processes and the textual paths of observables scholarship. Ideally, shared goals partake of the "us against the problem" orientation. The two people become one actor, moving jointly to achieve their emergent aim.

We explored these possibilities most explicitly in Chapter 6, on dialogue types. Remember that we distinguished between Dialogue goals (the shared commitment, such as inquiry or information-sharing) and personal goals (like those on the Individual line of Figure 8.1). Some of the research reported there explored the possibility that spouses or friends might share dialogue orientations for their disagreements. Recall that the different dialogues proceed differently (featuring persuasion, or negotiation, or cooperative information exchange, and so forth), but that they do so because they begin with different shared goals—to persuade, to negotiate, or to exchange information. Long-term sharing of dialogue preferences happens either because people choose partners who understand conflict management in a similar way or because people grow more argumentatively compatible as their relationship goes on. But the point is that the most over-arching goals are shared. They are not negotiated in the moment because they are not at issue at any point during a routine argument. "That's just the way we argue."

People can share either productive or destructive goals. Eristic goals can be shared, just as deliberation or information exchange goals can be. Spouses and romantic partners can fall into awful interaction patterns that they both regret but cannot seem to escape. Cronen, Pearce, and Snavely (1979) called these URPs, "undesired repetitive patterns." No matter how a disagreement—or when things are really bad, a simple conversation—begins, it can devolve into blaming, accusing, denying, insulting, and the whole inventory of reciprocal aggressive and defensive things that can make relational life almost unendurable. These patterns are shared. The fact that the partners may very well regret those patterns simply means that their interactional system is complicated and probably needs third party intervention if it is to be helped.

Happier are the relationships sharing goals that have more potential to be productive and civil. The civility probably originates in a shared substratum of mutual respect and trust, and this permits the sharing of goals that depend on the other person. I can't share information with you if you won't respond in kind, because a one-way transaction misses the idea of "sharing." Some people maintain power in a relationship through information control, and this obviously discourages mutual goals about self-disclosure and having similar beliefs about the world. We cannot share a deliberation goal if one of us is unwilling or unable to listen open-mindedly and expose beliefs to change. Some of the dialogue goals are unilateral: persuasion and eristic struggle, for example. Other dialogue goals are more naturally mutual: deliberation, information sharing, inquiry, and negotiation. Any of the goals can be shared in some sense. Two people can pound away at one another, trying to persuade or hurt each other. Those goals and behaviors are still shared, though not in a recommendable way. People who share the orientations that they should deliberate, inquire, inform, and negotiate obviously have a better chance to achieve genuine argument resolution at the same time they pursue relational health.

Perhaps more clearly than on the other lines of Figure 8.1, we can see here how arguing goals are part of a larger context of relational goals. In a book about argumentation, it has been inevitable that I give special attention to argument-centric goals like having acceptable premises, relevant premises, and collectively sufficient premises; that I emphasize doing quality work on the illative and dialectical tiers; and that I praise cogent arguments and discourage weak argument schemes (see Chapter 5). But this is also a book about *interpersonal* arguing, and so it is well to be reminded that all arguments do not have to be "won," and that concentrating on a goal like that might cost something more highly valued. It is a matter of perspective: which is more important, the argument or the relationship? Many people have a problem remembering this when they are caught up in a disagreement. A relational danger sign is the feeling that there are two "sides" to the disagreement.

Shared goals lead to shared plans. If a pair of people is free to act, their impulses will naturally be expressed in their behavior. We have already noticed that dialogue goals lead to the performance of dialogue types, and that unhappy shared impulses lead to undesired repetitive patterns. These patterns of argumentative interaction are therefore emergent, with neither party especially or uniquely responsible for how things move along. The idea here is that the people are background elements of a social system. The system is actually composed of messages that fall into system-required patterns (Watzlawick, Beavin, & Jackson, 1967).

Your family of origin is probably a familiar example of this. A simple but productive way of classifying families is to say that they have either a conversational or a conformity orientation to communication (Ritchie & Fitzpatrick, 1990; see Baumrind, 1966, for parenting styles). These are both systems, sets of shared plans, for family communication. In the conversation orientation, families award voice to everyone, even the children. People are encouraged to be open about their feelings and thoughts. Children are permitted to disagree with their parents. In the conformity-oriented families, parents have authority to settle disagreements, and may do so without having to give reasons. The parents, or perhaps one of them, are the final arbiters of disputes, and children are not allowed to object. Obviously, interpersonal arguing has different roles and takes different forms in these two kinds of families. The conversational families have a clear place for elaborated arguing in their interactional patterns, but the conformity families do not. A conflict can certainly appear in a conformity family, but its development may be cut off because it could be summarily judged. Koerner and Fitzpatrick (1997) reported that conformity-oriented families were characterized by conflict avoidance (as well as venting feelings and depression, by the way), but that conversational orientation was associated with approaching conflict (and valuing social support).

Like climates and goals, shared plans make arguing more or less likely, and permit it to be fully developed or quickly squelched. You have probably been in classes that encouraged student disagreement and easy exploration of alternatives, and in other classes where the student's proper role was to record what the teacher said. It is simple to attribute this entirely to the instructor, just as you might be inclined to praise or blame your parents for the atmosphere of your youthful home. But the students and the children participated in those systems. One way of thinking about that might be to say that they voluntarily gave up their personal agency and let the system control the interactions. I once went on a whitewater-rafting outing with my wife and young children. The water was not very white, and after a while the guide invited us to slide off the raft and just float along in the river. I did. It was odd just to lie back in the water and realize that I was effortlessly moving right along with the raft. That is often how we react to message systems. We cooperate with them, reinforcing and reproducing them. Good systems benefit us, and destructive systems capture us. But all the systems project, require, and exclude particular kinds of argumentative action, and that is why I call them shared plans.

Finally we have arrived at the last entry in Figure 8.4. Here I have called the Actions bilateral arguing. Actually, this is a little hopeful because the idea of bilaterality is a normative one and it is not always achieved. The basic idea is a contrast between the forceful, self-centered, and closed-minded actions of a propagandist or advertiser, and the cooperative, other-oriented, and open-minded actions of a bilateral arguer (Johnstone, 1982). The term "bilateral" is Johnstone's. He wrote that proper arguing (that is, arguing aimed at finding the truth; Johnstone was a philosopher) required that each arguer occupy the other's position. He meant more than just empathy and simple acknowledgement by this. He meant that each person needed to learn how to think as the other thinks, how to value what the other values, and how to react to arguments as the other does. This fundamental respect for the other person is a basic principle in many approaches to moral philosophy (e.g., Buber, 1958). The other arguer's whole nature has to be occupied before one can argue toward it without misunderstanding. A further consequence of this view is that each arguer has to be open to the other. Therefore, intending to persuade or correct the other person is inherently unilateral, the coercive attitude of the propagandist. Offering arguments with openness to being corrected and improved by the other person's reasoning is the bilateral attitude. These attitudes will obviously result in different actions, especially once the other person has doubted, or answered, or clashed.

As I said, bilaterality is not often achieved in practice. We normally argue because we want something for ourselves—perhaps a practical benefit, a chance to show off, or the fun of verbal competition, as we saw in Chapter 2. But as we also saw in that chapter, people believe that arguments can be cooperative and civil, too. So the self-oriented elements of arguing can be modified or balanced by other-oriented matters. Spouses pretty clearly share their utility, identity, and play frames for arguing, but they share their civility and cooperation understandings as well, although more weakly (Hample & Cionea, 2016).

Pure bilaterality—Johnstone's philosophical idea—is a normative standard, but not one that any of us meets very often. So for practical purposes, bilaterality is really a matter of degree. It happens when we trust one another to such an extent that we move together in a cooperative and respectful way. We seek a conclusion, one that was not shared jointly when we started to argue. One of us may actually have privately secured that conclusion before the episode began, but it is not offered forcefully or insistently. Sharing your actual reasons for believing something is an honest and trusting move in an interpersonal argument. It becomes even more bilateral if, at the same time, you are open to having your thinking improved and changed by the other person.

Bilaterality is only possible if both arguers participate in it, so it can be regarded as shared in the same way that we were able to identify shared plans, goals, and situations earlier in this section. A key point is that if anything like bilaterality appears to any degree, it had to have been emergent. One person cannot create bilaterality. That is why it can be a shared feature of arguing.

When we try to study shared argument processes, we look for emergent argument products. If we think we see one arguer defining the argument, we immediately stop to realize that the other person implicitly agreed to be guided. We may find activity endorsed by passivity, information by agreement, and reasoning by elaboration. One cannot do an interpersonal argument alone. There will always be sharing, if only we look for it. Ideally, it will be bilateral with an "us against the problem" flavor. But we might also find a series of mutual aggressions and ambushes, anticipatory defenses and attacks, and unwanted repetitive patterns. These, too, are shared.

Conclusions

This chapter has tried to give an overall perspective on the various things that have been presented in this book, as well as some things that were a little out of the book's focus. I definitely have a point of view about studying interpersonal arguing. Not everyone in the field is particularly oriented to the situation-goals-plans-actions description of voluntary human behavior, only a handful of us has any interest in gathering arguers' own impressions of what they are doing, and many scholars restrict their attention to the textual argument without examining consequences such as relational satisfaction and emotional state. I encourage readers of this book to seek out that other work. But for now, I have tried to pull things together (from my point of view) in Figure 8.1, which I will repeat here for convenience.

Figure 8.1: A Sketch of Three Simultaneous Lines of Experience

Processes	Situation	Goals	Plans	Actions
Observable	Reasonably Apparent	Social Expectations	Negotiation of Practice	Arguments
Individual	Traits and Thresholds	Goals, Frames	Editing, Plans	Unilateral Arguing
Shared	Climate, Constraints	Shared Goals, Dialogue	Shared Plans	Bilateral Arguing

The three lines of Processes are inherent to interpersonal arguing. The scope of the whole phenomenon is so vast that inevitably a particular study will only try to capture one bit of Figure 8.1, maybe a line of it, maybe a column, or maybe only part of one cell. All these things are always going on, however. An interpersonal argument will produce text (the Observables line), thought (the Individual line), and mutuality (the Shared line). All interpersonal arguments are situated, intended in some respect, planned to some degree, and public (or conceived as being public, in the case of an imagined interaction). These things can vary quantitatively from substantial to minimal: the text might only be a grunt, the thought might be superficial and distracted, and the mutuality can be only pro forma. But even the negligible events are interesting—Why won't he talk more? Is she even paying attention to me? Am I supposed to regard that as sincere?

Possibly one line, column, or cell is more interesting to you than the rest. That's fine. It is probably true of every scholar working in the argumentation community. You can acknowledge that something else is going on without being interested in pursuing it yourself. As I said in the beginning of the chapter, I think that if you work on these matters long enough, you will find yourself wandering all through Figure 8.1. That certainly summarizes the work I've done for more than forty years.

Figure 8.1 is more than merely descriptive of the various processes and actions that occur when two or more people argue together. It also indicates the things that need to be theorized, it points to possible weaknesses in the structure of particular episodes, and it might even imply intervention targets if we want to improve people's interpersonal arguments and lives. It functions to outline description, theory, and intervention, depending on the uses to which it is put.

It also hints at the kinds of normative evaluations that we might want to attempt. At the textual level, our main choice is to evaluate the reconstructed argument. We would identify its argument scheme and the associated critical questions. In different forms, this means that we will be asking of the premises whether they were each acceptable and relevant, and whether they were collectively sufficient to sustain the conclusion. In the textual dialogue, we can also notice legitimate and derailing moves, and so we can praise or criticize the various public acts. At the individual level we can repeat all those evaluation systems but we would apply them to people's interior experiences of the argument, recognizing that one's private thoughts and feelings might differ from what was publicly expressed. Notice that just as we can reconstruct underlying values and ideologies from public text, we can also discover moral beliefs within individuals. We can discover prejudice and tolerance, selfishness and generosity, and individualism and collectivism within a person, and connect those general world orientations to what the person thought and said. We can find the broad views that provide the psychological context for a particular position, and can then critique them if we are so inclined. Finally, for the shared processes we have bilaterality as an obvious normative standard. Bilaterality implies a fundamental joining of the two people, respecting the other as much as self and insisting that any conclusion be equally suitable for both. This is, as I said earlier, a matter of degree. So we would look for evidence of self, other, and joined orientation when we work within this scholarly tradition.

Though it may be most evident in the shared perspective, in all three scholarly orientations we should be thinking about both arguing and relational considerations as we evaluate the episodes. Sometimes one seems more important than the other, and the people will then naturally act that way. External critics are entitled to ask whether they made the right choice: Should the argument have been pursued or dropped? Or should the relationship have been temporarily set aside so that a better answer could have been obtained? These sorts of questions can be prompted by text, by private thoughts, or by emergent actions. Attention to the relational reality that situates a particular argument is one of the ways in which the study of interpersonal arguing is distinct from the study of argumentation in general.

These final remarks reinforce the original aim of this book. Arguments are commonplace in our social lives. Relationships are constituted by the messages they contain, and the argumentative messages create meanings for people. Repeated arguments can summarize important themes in a relationship. Resolution of a high-stakes argument can redefine a relationship and make it more secure. Realizing that an important argument is not being mutually settled can be either an opportunity or a danger sign. Being more conscious and educated about the nature of interpersonal arguing will not automatically make you a better relationship citizen, but it can be a first step. People sometimes need to do meta-communication and discuss what they are doing together. Education and clear vocabulary can help in that.

References

Aristotle. (1984). *Rhetoric* (W. R. Roberts, Trans.). In J. Barnes (Ed.), *The complete works of Aristotle* (2 vols). Princeton, NJ: Princeton University Press.

Arundale, R. B. (2005). Pragmatics, conversational implicature, and conversation. In K. L. Fitch & R. E. Sanders (Eds.), *Handbook of language and social interaction* (pp. 41–63). Mahwah, NJ: Lawrence Erlbaum.

Baumrind, D. (1966). Effects of authoritative parental control on child behavior. *Child Development, 37*, 887–907.

Berger, C. R. (1997). *Planning strategic interaction: Attaining goals through communicative action*. Mahwah, NJ: Lawrence Erlbaum Associates.

Bevan, J. L., Hale, J. L., & Williams, S. L. (2004). Identifying and characterizing goals of dating partners engaging in serial argumentation. *Argumentation and Advocacy, 41*, 28–40.

Bower, G. H., Black, J. B., & Turner, T. J. (1979). Scripts in memory for text. *Cognitive Psychology, 11,* 177–200.

Brockriede, W. (1975). Where is argument? *Journal of the American Forensic Association, 11,* 179–182.

Brown, P., & Levinson, S. C. (1987). *Politeness: Some universals in language usage.* Cambridge: Cambridge University Press.

Buber, M. (1958). *I and thou.* New York, NY: Charles Seribner's Sons.

Cionea, I. A. (2011). Dialogue and interpersonal communication: How informal logic can enhance our understanding of the dynamics of close relationships. *Cogency, 3,* 93–105.

Clark, R. A., & Delia, J. G. (1979). *Topoi* and rhetorical competence. *Quarterly Journal of Speech, 65,* 187–206.

Cooren, F. (2005). The contribution of speech acts theory to the analysis of conversation: How pre-sequences work. In K. L. Fitch & R. E. Sanders (Eds.), *Handbook of language and social interaction* (pp. 21–40). Mahwah, NJ: Lawrence Erlbaum.

Cronen, V. E., Pearce, W. B., & Snavely, L. M. (1979). A theory of rule-structure and types of episodes and a study of perceived enmeshment in undesired repetitive patterns ("URPs"). *Communication Yearbook, 3,* 225–240.

Dillard, J. P., Segrin, C., & Harden, J. M. (1989). Primary and secondary goals in the production of interpersonal influence messages. *Communication Monographs, 56,* 19–38.

Eco, U. (1980). *The name of the rose* (W. Weaver, Trans.). New York, NY: Harcourt, Brace, Jovanonich.

van Eemeren, F. H., & Grootendorst, R. (1983). *Speech acts in argumentative discussions.* Dordrecht: Foris.

van Eemeren, F. H., & Grootendorst, R. (2004). *A systematic theory of argumentation: The pragma-dialectical approach.* Cambridge: Cambridge University Press.

van Eemeren, F. H., Grootendorst, R., Jackson, S., & Jacobs, S. (1993). *Reconstructing argumentative discourse.* Tuscaloosa, AL: University of Alabama Press.

Garfinkel, H. (1967). *Studies in ethnomethodology.* Englewood Cliffs, NJ: Prentice Hall.

Grice, H. P. (1975). Logic and conversation. In P. Cole & J. L. Morgan (Eds.), *Syntax and semantics, vol. 3: Speech acts* (pp. 41–58). New York, NY: Academic Press.

Hample, D. (1984). On the use of self-reports. *Journal of the American Forensic Association, 20,* 140–153.

Hample, D. (1997). Framing message-production research with field theory. In J. O. Greene (Ed.), *Message production: Advances in communication theory* (pp. 171–192). Hillsdale, NJ: Erlbaum.

Hample, D. (1999). The life space of personalized conflicts. *Communication Yearbook, 22,* 171–208.

Hample, D. (2005). *Arguing: Exchanging reasons face to face.* Mahwah, NJ: Lawrence Erlbaum Associates.

Hample, D. (2007). The arguers. *Informal Logic, 27,* 163–178.

Hample, D. (2016). The psychological approach to interpersonal argumentation in the U.S. argumentation community. In F. Paglieri, L. Bonelli, & S. Felletti (Eds.), *The psychology of argument: Cognitive approaches to argumentation and persuasion* (pp. 257–274). London: College Publications.

Hample, D., & Cionea, I. A. (2016, May). Couples' dialogue orientations. In P. Bondy & L. Benacquista (Eds.), *Argumentation, objectivity, and bias: Proceedings of the 11th international conference of the Ontario Society for the Study of Argumentation (OSSA), 18–21 May 2016* (pp. 1–13). Windsor, ON: OSSA.

Hample, D., & Irions, A. (2015). Arguing to display identity. *Argumentation, 29*, 389–416.

Hample, D., Richards, A. S., & Skubisz, C. (2013). Blurting. *Communication Monographs, 80*, 503–532.

Honeycutt, J. M. (2003). *Imagined interactions: Daydreaming about communication*. Cresskill, NJ: Hampton Press.

Jackson, S. (2017, June). *Naturally occuring argumentation*. Paper presented at the meeting of the European Conference on Argumentation, Fribourg, Switzerland.

Jackson, S., & Jacobs, S. (1980). Structure of conversational argument: Pragmatic bases for the enthymeme. *Quarterly Journal of Speech, 66*, 251–265.

Jang, K. L., Livesley, W. J., & Vernon, P. A. (1996). Heritability of the Big Five personality dimensions and their facets: A twin study. *Journal of Personality, 64*, 577–591.

Johnstone, H. W., Jr. (1982). Bilaterality in argument and communication. In J. R. Cox & C. A. Willard (Eds.), *Advances in argumentation theory and research* (pp. 95–102). Carbondale, IL: Southern Illinois University Press.

Koerner, A. F., & Fitzpatrick, M. A. (1997). Family type and conflict: The impact of conversation orientation and conformity orientation on conflict in the family. *Communication Studies, 48*, 59–75.

Kuhn, D. (1991). *The skills of argument*. Cambridge: Cambridge University Press.

Levinson, S. C. (1983). *Pragmatics*. Cambridge: Cambridge University Press.

McCroskey, J. C., Heisel, A. D., & Richmond, V. P. (2001). Eysenck's BIG THREE and communication traits: Three correlational studies. *Communication Monographs, 68*, 360–366.

Meyer, J. R. (1997). Cognitive influences on the ability to address interaction goals. In J. O. Greene (Ed.), *Message production: Advances in communication theory* (pp. 71–90). Mahwah, NJ: Lawrence Erlbaum Associates.

Muntigl, P., & Turnbull, W. (1998). Conversational structure and facework in arguing. *Journal of Pragmatics, 29*, 225–256.

O'Keefe, B. J. (1988). The logic of message design: Individual differences in reasoning about communication. *Communication Monographs, 55*, 80–103.

O'Keefe, B. J. (1992). Developing and testing rational models of message design. *Human Communication Research, 18*, 637–649.

O'Keefe, D. J. (1977). Two concepts of argument. *Journal of the American Forensic Association, 13*, 121–128.

Polderman, T. J. C., Benyamin, B., de Leeuw, C. A., Sullivan, P. F., van Bochoven, A., Visscher, P. M., & Posthuma, D. (2015). Meta-analysis of the heritability of human traits based on fifty years of twin studies. *Nature Genetics, 47*, 702–709.

Rancer, A. S., Kosberg, R. L., & Baukus, R. A. (1992). Beliefs about arguing as predictors of trait argumentativeness: Implications for training in argument and conflict management. *Communication Education, 41,* 375–387.

Ritchie, L. D., & Fitzpatrick, M. A. (1990). Family communication patterns: Measuring intrapersonal perceptions of interpersonal relationships. *Communication Research, 17,* 523–544.

Roberts, B. W., & DelVecchio, W. F. (2000). The rank-order consistency of personality traits from childhood to old age: A quantitative review of longitudinal studies. *Psychological Bulletin, 126,* 3–25.

Sacks, H. (1992). *Lectures on conversation* (2 vols). Oxford: Blackwell.

Schank, R. C. (1982). *Dynamic memory*. Cambridge: Cambridge University Press.

Stump, E., & Spade, P. V. (1982). Obligations. In N. Kretzmann, A. Kenny, & J. Pinborg (Eds.), *The Cambridge history of later medieval philosophy* (pp. 315–341). Cambridge: Cambridge University Press.

Toews, M. L., Catlett, B. S., & McKenry, P. C. (2005). Women's use of aggression toward their former spouses during marital separation. *Journal of Divorce & Remarriage, 42,* 1–14.

Walton, D., Reed, C., & Macagno, F. (2008). *Argumentation schemes*. Cambridge: Cambridge University Press.

Watzlawick, P., Beavin, J. H., & Jackson, D. D. (1967). *Pragmatics of human communication*. New York, NY: Norton.

APPENDIX

Instrumentation

The Appendix contains the usual wording for the instruments that I have had a part in developing. Other scales mentioned in the book need to be found in those authors' own publications.

Minor rewording of the items can be done to fit the study. For instance if you were investigating someone's recollections of an argument, you might put everything in past tense. To illustrate this, two versions of the dialogue scales are given. Or if you wanted to restrict your question to how people argue with their siblings, you might preface each item with "When I argue with my siblings, …." Sometimes you can handle this simply by changing the instructions for the scales. For instance, you might say, "Respond to the following items in terms of how you argue with your grandmother," if that's what the study was about.

Unless otherwise noted, all the instruments use a Likert format in which people choose numbers to represent the degree to which each statement applies to them "as you generally are." The choices range from "strongly disagree" to "strongly agree." Any number of response choices can be used at the researcher's discretion, but the most common decisions are 1–5, 1–7, or 1–10 scales. Make a note as to what the higher numbers mean (e.g., more stress or less stress?) to save yourself trouble later on. The standard procedure is to make sure the higher numbers mean more of what the scale name is.

Only the Taking Conflict Personally scales have a standard mixed-up order. The other scales tend to be presented in chunks, with all the items intended to measure some subscale presented together.

Some of the items are marked **reverse code**. This means that you reverse the item scoring. If you were using a 1–5 scale, you would recode all the 1's to be 5, all the 2's to be 4, leave the 3's alone, recode the 4's to be 2, and recode the 5's to be 1. A quicker way to do this for a 1-n scale is to add 1 to n and then subtract the obtained score from that. So for a 1–7 scale, subtract the scores that you intend to reverse code from 8. It is a good idea to keep the original scores as well as the recoded ones, because in a few days you may forget whether or not you have recoded. Do not include **reverse code** on the actual survey instrument. Similarly, if parts of the instrument are marked off by the subscale name (e.g., [UTILITY]), don't include that on the questionnaire either.

All these scales and subscales have generated acceptable reliability estimates in previous studies. Occasionally, particularly outside the U.S., reliabilities drop. In any event, the relevant reliability statistics are from your own investigation. This is obviously important if you have changed the wording a tiny bit, but in fact it is equally important even if you have strictly used the standard wording. Since these are all multi-item instruments, the usual reliability measure is Cronbach's alpha, but others are possible. If a subscale's reliability is low, sometimes it can be improved by omitting one or two items.

It is a terrible mistake to combine all the subscales together to get a single reliability estimate or a single score for an entire battery of measures (e.g., frames). For some reason, this sometimes seems attractive to beginning researchers, but it makes no sense. The Taking Conflict Personally instrument, for example, contains six different subscales and they all measure a different thing. What could it mean to add together positive relational effects and negative relational effects? Think of the subscales as each being their own independent measuring instrument. Reliabilities should be reported for each subscale independently and scores should be calculated for each subscale independently.

Argument Frames

[UTILITY]
When I argue with someone it is to get what I want.
Arguing is a way to get what you want.
If I want someone else to do something, giving the other person a reason to do something is the best approach.

I use arguing as a way to get things done.
If someone is arguing with me, I assume that we're on our way to settling something.
Arguing is meant to resolve issues.
I only argue to achieve a specific outcome.
The most important reason for arguing is to get something you need.

[IDENTITY]
I use arguments to display my intellectual ability.
Other people often use arguments to display their intellectual ability.
Arguments are useful in showing what I believe.
Arguments are useful in showing how smart I am.
You can learn a lot about another person by watching what sorts of things he or she will say during an argument.
An argument can reveal as much about another person's character as friendly conversation.
I use arguments to gain respect.
You can see other people at their best or their worst when they argue with people.

[DOMINANCE]
Arguing successfully is a way of being dominant over the other person.
Losing an argument means that the other person is dominant over me, at least for the moment.
When I'm in an argument, winning is more important to me than being kind.
When I'm in an argument, winning is more important to me than being correct in what I say.
Regardless of what an argument is supposed to be about, it is very often really about who has power over whom.
When I'm in an argument, I feel like I always have to win.

[PLAY]
Arguing is fun.
Arguing is sometimes just a way of passing the time between two friends.
I like to challenge what other people say, just to say what else they'll say.
Sometimes I say something outrageous, just to have the entertainment of defending it.

[BLURTING]
When I interact with another person I just say what's on my mind.
During arguments, I don't have time to think about what I'm going to say.

After an argument, I often regret some of the things I said.
In an argument, if I think it, I will say it.
I argue without thinking before I speak.
I always say what's on my mind.
During a heated argument, my mouth is engaged, but my mind often isn't.
When I make a point in an argument, I'm usually not very concerned about how the other person is going to take it.
I sometimes offend other people during arguments.
Sometimes when I think of a really good point to make, I just can't stop myself from making it, even if I should.

[COOPERATION]
I think it's important in arguing to feel flexible.
A genuine agreement from the other person is more satisfying to me than a forced agreement.
The other person's needs are really an important consideration to me when I'm trying to settle a disagreement with him or her.
The basic idea in arguing is to come together on some issue, not to overwhelm the other person.
People who think that winning is the main idea in arguing are a little immature.
When you're arguing with another person, you have to keep in mind your long term relationship with him or her in mind all the time.
I try to be cooperative when I'm arguing.
I am often competitive when I'm arguing. **reverse code**

[CIVILITY]
Arguments involve loud and negative voices. **reverse code**
Arguments involve cooperation by parties.
Arguments involve positive relational outcomes after they are over.
Arguments involve closed-mindedness by the parties. **reverse code**
Arguments involve successful problem solving.
Arguments involve irrational emotional displays. **reverse code**
Negative relational outcomes occur after an argument is over. **reverse code**
Arguments involve hostility. **reverse code**
Arguments involve genuine exchange of views by both parties.
Arguments involve physical violence. **reverse code**

[PROFESSIONAL CONTRAST]
For the items that follow, indicate which one of the pairs of descriptive items best applies to arguments.

competition 1 2 3 4 5 6 7 8 9 10 cooperation
aggression 1 2 3 4 5 6 7 8 9 10 assertiveness
uncontrolled emotionality 1 2 3 4 5 6 7 8 9 10 reason giving
violence 1 2 3 4 5 6 7 8 9 10 pacifism
dominance 1 2 3 4 5 6 7 8 9 10 issue resolution
personally punishing 1 2 3 4 5 6 7 8 9 10 personally satisfying
relationally damaging 1 2 3 4 5 6 7 8 9 10 relationally developmental

Costs and Benefits of Arguing

Notice that these items are all phrased in terms of "my friend." You may want to change this to "my romantic partner," "the other person," or something that better fits your study.

[INTENTION TO ARGUE]
I would respond to my friend by expressing disagreement.
I would not respond to my friend at all. **reverse code**
I would try to say something that was relevant but that didn't express disagreement. **reverse code**
I would engage my friend in an argument on that topic.
I would answer my friend by just saying that he/she was wrong.
I would answer my friend by giving my reasons as to why he/she was wrong.
I would agree with my friend. **reverse code**
I would avoid arguing with my friend. **reverse code**
I would be willing to disagree with my friend about this.
I would intend to argue about this with my friend.
I would intend to confront my friend about this, but in a friendly way.
I would be willing to engage in a discussion with my friend about this.
I would intend to express reasons showing I was right.
I would intend to exchange reasons and evidence with my friend to express my disagreement.
I would intend to dodge a possible conflict with my friend about this. **reverse code**
I would welcome a chance to engage my friend in a disagreement on this topic.
I would be willing to concede that my friend was right about this. **reverse code**
I would be willing to say almost anything to my friend to avoid an argument about this. **reverse code**

[GENERAL COSTS OF ARGUING]

If we argued, it would take a long time to settle anything.
If we argued, I would have to go to a lot of effort.
If we argued, the argument would get very complex and bring in a lot of issues.
If we argued, the argument would expose some of my feelings that I'd rather keep to myself.
If we argued, the argument would expose some of my friend's feelings that he/she would rather keep to himself/herself.
If we argued, we would settle things easily.
If we argued, we would be able to keep our emotions out of it.
If we argued, we would just stay on that single topic.
If we argued, it would damage the relationship between my friend and me.
If we argued, it would eventually improve the relationship between my friend and me.

[GENERAL BENEFITS OF ARGUING]

I would be better off if we had this argument.
I would regret it if we had this argument. **reverse code**
Having this argument would clear the air.
Having this argument would ultimately be beneficial to me.
Having this argument would ultimately be beneficial to the relationship between my friend and me.
Having this argument would ultimately be beneficial to my friend.

[RESOLVABILITY]

I wouldn't think we would ever agree on the issue. **reverse code**
I wouldn't see much chance that it would be resolved. **reverse code**
I would think it would go on forever. **reverse code**
I would think that a productive solution could occur.
I would think that it was just going to get worse and worse and never get better. **reverse code**
I would believe that the argument would be resolved in the future.

[CIVILITY]

If we argued:
The argument would involve loud and negative voices. **reverse code**
The argument would involve cooperation by parties.
The argument would involve positive relational outcomes after episodes were over.
The argument would involve close-mindedness by the parties. **reverse code**
The argument would involve successful problem solving.

The argument would involve irrational emotional displays. **reverse code**
The argument would involve negative relational outcomes occur after episodes were over. **reverse code**
The argument would involve hostility. **reverse code**
The argument would involve genuine exchange of views by both parties.
The argument would involve physical violence. **reverse code**

[OTHER'S REASONABILITY]
My friend would be reasonable if we argued.
My friend would be stubborn if we argued. **reverse code**
My friend would be open-minded if we argued.
My friend would change his/her mind if I gave better reasons and evidence if we argued.
My friend would be too sensitive to change his/her mind if we argued. **reverse code**
My friend would be mature about it if we argued.

[LIKELIHOOD OF WINNING]
If we argued, I think my arguments would be better than my friend's.
If we argued, I think my friend would see that my position was better than his/hers.
If we argued, I think I would have to admit I was wrong. **reverse code**
If we argued, I think my friend would have to admit he/she was wrong.
If we argued, I think I would win.
If we argued, I think my friend would win. **reverse code**
If we argued, I think I would have excellent reasons for my position.
If we argued, I think I would have excellent evidence for my position.

[APPROPRIATENESS OF ARGUING]
It would be appropriate to argue about this topic—with this person, at this time, and in this place.
It would be inappropriate to argue about this topic with my friend. **reverse code**
It would be inappropriate to argue about this topic at that time. **reverse code**
It would be inappropriate to argue about this topic in that place. **reverse code**
People would disapprove of me for arguing about this topic—with this person, at this time, and in this place. **reverse code**
I was brought up not to argue about this sort of thing in circumstances like this. **reverse code**
I am trying to teach myself not to argue about this sort of thing in circumstances like this. **reverse code**

Taking Conflict Personally

The Taking Conflict Personally items are usually presented in the following standard order. It does not put all the subscale items together. Therefore after the instrument is presented, a set of scoring directions is provided. The simplest way to get scores is just to add up the scores for each item (after reverse coding), for each subscale.

I usually take criticisms personally.
Conflict can really help a relationship.
I really hate to argue with people I don't know very well.
I hate arguments.
Conflict is a very personal thing for me.
When people criticize something I say, I don't take it personally.
Sometimes you can discover admirable features in a person who is arguing strongly.
It really hurts my feelings to be criticized.
Conflict can really hurt a relationship.
In conflict discussions I often feel that other people are trying very hard to make sure that I lose.
A deep conflict can really bring people together after it's over.
I think that some of the people that I often have conflict discussions with really like to pick on me.
Conflict is an intensely enjoyable kind of interaction.
Conflict discussions can really strengthen working relationships with other people in the group.
Conflicts have a positive impact on a relationship.
I don't like to be in conflict situations.
Conflict situations leave me feeling victimized.
Conflict discussions can really jeopardize working relationships with other people in the group.
Conflict discussions can really strengthen friendships.
I really hate to argue with friends.
Sometimes when there are a lot of conflicts in a week, I feel like I'm getting an ulcer.
The honesty that often results from a conflict situation can lead to stronger relationships between people.
Conflicts are not stressful for me.
Stressful discussions make my stomach hurt.
Conflict discussions can really jeopardize friendships.

When the rest of the group rejects one of my suggestions, I take it very personally.
After a stressful meeting, my day is usually ruined.
To me, it's fun to argue.
If you make a bad suggestion, people think you are stupid.
Arguing is not very stressful to me.
Conflicts have a negative impact on a relationship.
It doesn't bother me to be criticized for my ideas.
A conflict can really wreck the climate in the workplace.
I often enjoy conflicts.
Conflict situations make me feel persecuted.
I have a strong emotional reaction to being criticized.
I think that people often attack me personally.

Scoring Directions

For items marked with **reverse code,** you need to reverse code your original response to these items.

DIRECT PERSONALIZATION
1. I usually take criticisms personally.
5. Conflict is a very personal thing for me.
6. When people criticize something I say, I don't take it personally. **reverse code**
8. It really hurts my feelings to be criticized.
26. When the rest of the group rejects one of my suggestions, I take it very personally.
32. It doesn't bother me to be criticized for my ideas **reverse code**
36. I have a strong emotional reaction to being criticized.

PERSECUTION FEELINGS
10. In conflict discussions I often feel that other people are trying very hard to make sure that I lose.
12. I think that some of the people that I often have conflict discussions with really like to pick on me.
17. Conflict situations leave me feeling victimized.
29. If you make a bad suggestion, people think you are stupid.
35. Conflict situations make me feel persecuted.
37. I think that people often attack me personally.

STRESS REACTION

21. Sometimes when there are a lot of conflicts in a week, I feel like I'm getting an ulcer.
23. Conflicts are not stressful for me. **reverse code**
24. Stressful discussions make my stomach hurt.
27. After a stressful meeting, my day is usually ruined.
30. Arguing is not very stressful to me. **reverse code**

POSITIVE RELATIONAL EFFECTS

2. Conflict can really help a relationship.
7. Sometimes you can discover admirable features in a person who is arguing strongly.
11. A deep conflict can really bring people together after its over.
14. Conflict discussions can really strengthen working relationships with other people in the group.
15. Conflicts have a positive impact on a relationship.
19. Conflict discussions can really strengthen friendships.
22. The honesty that often results from a conflict situation can lead to stronger relationships between people.

NEGATIVE RELATIONAL EFFECTS

9. Conflict can really hurt a relationship.
18. Conflict discussions can really jeopardize working relationships with other people in the group.
25. Conflict discussions can really jeopardize friendships.
31. Conflicts have a negative impact on a relationship.
33. A conflict can really wreck the climate in the workplace.

LIKE/DISLIKE VALENCE

3. I really hate to argue with people I don't know very well. **reverse code**
4. I hate arguments. **reverse code**
13. Conflict is an intensely enjoyable kind of interaction.
16. I don't like to be in conflict situations. **reverse code**
20. I really hate to argue with friends. **reverse code**
28. To me, its fun to argue.
34. I often enjoy conflicts.

Dialogue Types

Two versions of the items are given here. These illustrate different ways to phrase things, depending on the researcher's aims. In the first version, the items are phrased in the past tense and are immediately useful if the researcher is asking respondents to report on an exchange that was just completed. The verb tense can be changed for other applications. The second set of the same instruments is in present tense and is more suitable for studying how people generally feel about these possibilities.

Past Tense Wording

[PERSUASION DIALOGUE]
I explained my position to the other person.
I gave the other person reasons for my position.
I made a case for my position.
I convinced the other person to see things my way.
I talked the other person into thinking the way I do.
I made sure the other person and me were on the same page.

[NEGOTIATION DIALOGUE]
I reached a compromise with the other person.
I made a deal with the other person.
I came up with an agreement that both of us could live with.
I made concessions hoping the other person would make some concessions, too.
I made sure that what we both wanted was accomplished.
I settled things with the other person.

[INFORMATION SEEKING DIALOGUE]
I asked for more information from the other person.
I tried to get all the details from the other person.
I asked the other person for the whole story.
I made sure I knew everything the other person knew.

[INFORMATION GIVING DIALOGUE]
I let the other person know more information.
I gave the other person all the details.
I offered the other person the whole story.
I made sure the other person knew everything I knew.

[ERISTIC DIALOGUE]
I used words to attack the other person.
I vented.
I took the opposite position from the other person.
I let all my feelings out.
I blamed the other person.
I quarreled with the other person.

[DELIBERATION DIALOGUE]
I worked with the other person to solve the matter.
I decided with the other person how we should proceed.
I weighed the options with the other person.
I discussed with the other person how we should do things.
I talked to the other person about a possible course of action.
I analyzed with the other person the consequences of our ideas.

[INQUIRY DIALOGUE]
I tried to find the truth.
I examined the reasoning behind our claims.
I insisted that we draw logical conclusions.
I established the facts before concluding anything.
I analyzed how we were moving from facts to the conclusion(s).
I made sure we did not make any mistakes when reasoning.

Present Tense Wording

[PERSUASION DIALOGUE]
I try to explain my position to the other person.
I try to give the other person reasons for my position.
I try to make a case for my position.
I try to make sure the other person and I are on the same page.

[NEGOTIATION DIALOGUE]
I try to make a deal with the other person.
I try to come up with an agreement that we both of us can live with.
I try to make concessions hoping the other person would make some concessions, too.
I try to make sure that what we both want is accomplished.

[INFORMATION SEEKING DIALOGUE]
I try to ask for more information from the other person.
I try to get all the details from the other person.
I try to ask the other person for the whole story.
I try to make sure I know everything the other person knows.

[INFORMATION GIVING DIALOGUE]
I try to let the other person know more information.
I try to give the other person all the details.
I try to offer the other person the whole story.
I try to make sure the other person knows everything I know.

[ERISTIC DIALOGUE]
I try to use words to attack the other person.
I try to take the opposite position from the other person.
I try to blame the other person.
I try to quarrel with the other person.

[DELIBERATION DIALOGUE]
I try to work with the other person to solve the matter.
I try to decide with the other person how we should proceed.
I try to weigh the options with the other person.
I try to discuss with the other person how we should do things.
I try to talk to the other person about a possible course of action.
I try to analyze with the other person the consequences of our decision.

[INQUIRY DIALOGUE]
I try to find the truth.
I try to examine the reasoning behind our claims.
I try to insist that we draw logical conclusions.
I try to establish the facts before concluding anything.
I try to analyze how we move from facts to the conclusion(s).
I try to make sure we don't make any mistakes when reasoning.

Argument Stakes

[RELATIONSHIP]

Because of the argument, my relationship with the other person (CHOOSE ONE)
    Ended
    Continued unchanged
    Improved
    Changed in important ways for the better
    Changed in important ways for the worse

How did you feel about your relationship with the other person(s) just before the argument started?
    I was satisfied with the relationship
    The relationship was important to me
    I hoped the relationship would improve
    I hoped the other person would feel better about me
    This was an important relationship to me
    The relationship gave me everything I could want in this sort of relationship

How did you feel about your relationship with the other person(s) after the argument episode was finished?
    I was satisfied with the relationship
    The relationship was important to me
    I hoped the relationship would improve
    I hoped the other person would feel better about me
    This was an important relationship to me
    The relationship gave me everything I could want in this sort of relationship

[SELF]

Because of the argument,
    I felt better about myself
    I felt worse about myself
    I felt the same about myself

During the argument,
    I was angry
    I was uncertain

I was disappointed in myself
I was happy with the conversation
The conversation made me feel sad
I felt guilty during the interaction
I felt some surprise during the conversation
I was worried during the interaction
I was thankful that I had this conversation
I felt the conversation to be boring
I was concerned about giving a negative impression of myself
I was carefully editing what I was saying

After the argument,
    I was angry
    I was uncertain
    I was disappointed in myself
    I was happy with the conversation
    The conversation made me feel sad
    I felt guilty
    I felt some surprise about what happened
    I was worried about what happened
    I was thankful that I had this conversation
    I felt the conversation was boring
    I was concerned that I had given a negative impression of myself

How did you think the argument reflected on you?
    It made me look good to the other person(s)
    It made me look worse to the other person(s)
    It made me feel better about myself
    It made me feel worse about myself

[UTILITARIAN]

Because of the argument,
    I obtained an important benefit
    I failed to obtain an important benefit I felt I needed
    I was better off financially
    I was worse off financially
    I did not change financially
    I moved ahead in my personal aims
    I fell behind in my personal aims
    I did not change in my achievement of personal aims

Index

A

Action, 25–26
Analogies, 171–174
Argument$_1$ and Argument$_2$, 15
Argumentative Theory of Reasoning, 145–146
Argumentativeness and Verbal Aggressiveness, 196–197, 217
   National Differences, 220–222, 233–235, 242–243
   Opposites Theory, 233–242

B

Bilateral Argument, 280
Blurting Frame, 45–48

C

Cheater Detection, 28–30
Civility Frame, 49–51
Climates, 275–277; see Situations, Subjective Features
Cooperation Frame, 48–49
Cognitive Biases, 148–149
Commitment Stores, 181–183, 258–259
Confirmation Bias, 30, 142, 153
Convergent Arguments, 168–171
Conversational Structure, 15–19
Costs and Benefits of Arguing, see Deciding Whether to Argue
Critical Discussions, 19–21
Culture Defined, 212–216
   Internalized and Precipitate, 213–215, 247
Culture and Argument, 211–248
   National Correlations, 242–246
   National Means, 219–227
   Project Description, 216–219

D

Debiasing Arguments, 149–160
    Cognitive Interventions, 151–155
    Motivational Interventions, 155–157
    Design Interventions, 157–159
Deciding Whether to Argue, 81–90
    in Organizations, 88
Definition Arguing, 1
Design of Arguments, 19
Devil's Advocate, 152–153
Dialectic, 179
Dialectical Tier, 142
Dialogue, 180–181, 275–276; see Commitment Stores
    Arguer Status, 186
    Cionea's Theory of Dialogues in Relationships, 188–206
        Meta-Dialogues, 190, 207
        Empirical Results, 192–206
            Correlations Among Dialogue Types, 199–201
            Couples, 202–206
            Operationalizations, 192–194
    Goals, 183–184
    Hamblin on Dialogue Games, 181–182
    Walton's Theory of Dialogue Types, 181–188
        Six Types, 184–186
        Seventh Type, 192
Dominance Assertion Frame, 40–42

E

Enthymeme, 14–15
Eristic, 185–186, 194, 197, 198, 200, 203, 205; see Dialogue
Evolution, 26–31, 144–147

F

Fallacies, 8–11, 164–168
Formal Logic, 3–8
Frames, 35–67, 217–218
    Associations Among Frames, 58–61
    Dialogue Types, 198–199
    Men v Women, 56–58
    National Differences, 222–224, 243–245
    and Personality, 61–66
    Undergraduates and Older Adults, 54–56
France and India Comparison, 242–246

G

Goals, 24–25; see Situations; see Processes in Interpersonal Arguing
    and Argument Frames, 37–45
    Primary and Secondary, 24, 93, 98
Goals Plans Action Model, see Situation Goals Plans Action Model
Group Arguing, 143–144, 146–147, 148–149

H

Hofstede Values, 230–231, 237–240

I

Identities, 3
Identity Display Frame, 39–40
Illative Core, 141

M

Meaning Management, 2

P

Plans, 25, 261–264, 271–272, 278–279
Play Frame, 42–44
Pragma–dialectics, 19–21
Processes in Interpersonal Arguing, 253–283
    Individual, 255–256, 265–273
    Observable, 255, 257–265
    Shared, 256, 273–281
Professional Contrast Frame, 51–53

R

Rationality Engine, 141–175
    Defined, 143
    Empirical Results, 161–174

S

Schemes, Argument, 8–11
Serial Arguments, 103–136
    Consequences, 113–115, 130–134
    Definition, 104–105
    Frustration, 135
    Goals, 125–131
    Interpersonal Relationships, 118–120
    Intrapersonal Dynamics Model, 123
    Males and Females, 121–122
    Motivational Energy, 135
    Situations, 118–122
    Tactics, 128–131
    Trapp and Hoff Study, 105–110
    Topics, 110–113, 120–121
Sex Differences, 56–58, 121–122
    National Differences, 227–232
Situation Goals Plans Action Model, 21–26; see Processes in Interpersonal Arguing
Situations, 22–24, 71–100
    Demanding and Inviting, 87–88
    Interpersonal, 72–75
    Primary Goals, 93–94
    Reasonably Apparent Features, 91–92
    Secondary Goals, 98–99
    Serial Argument, 118–
    Subjective Features, 94–97
Social Loafing, 156–157
Structure of Argument, 3–21
Syllogisms, 3–8

T

Taking Conflict Personally, 218
    National Differences, 224–227, 245–246
Textual Approach to Arguing, 2
Three Turn Sequence, 15–19
Topics, 75–80
    and Deciding Whether to Argue, 84–87
    Other People's Personal Topics, 80
    Personal and Public, 76–80
    Serial Argument, 110–113
    Workplace, 80
Toulmin Model, 11–14

U

Utility Frame, 37–39

W

World Values Survey, 230–231, 240–241

www.ingramcontent.com/pod-product-compliance
Lightning Source LLC
LaVergne TN
LVHW011944060526
838201LV00061B/4206